Social Values, Objectives and Action

Social Values, Objectives and Action

Jimmy Algie

A HALSTED PRESS BOOK

John Wiley & Sons
New York   Toronto

Copyright © 1975 by Jimmy Algie

Published in the U.S.A. and Canada
by Halsted Press,
a Division of John Wiley & Sons, Inc.
New York

Library of Congress Cataloging in Publication Data

Algie, Jimmy.
  Social values.

  "A Halsted Press book."
  Bibliography: p.
  Includes indexes.
  1. Social service--Great Britain. I. Title.
HV248.A45 1975 362'.941 75-12902
ISBN 0-470-02250-7

Printed in Great Britain

Acknowledgements

The following people have contributed indispensable elements to this volume:

Al Adams, Ike Alcabes, Margaret Atkin, Peter Bailey, Fred Best, Robin Bourne, Gill Bradshaw, John Bromley, Jane Burton, Terry Butler, Tessa Byrne, Angus Cameron, Alex Campbell, Vida Carver, Audrey Catford, Moira Clarke, Liz Crowther, Judy Deeks, Bill Eicker, Bill Freeman, Brian Freeman, Carol Fries, Charles Garvin, David Gill, Stanley Green, Arnold Gurin, Ted Hare, Anthea Hey, John Hicks, David Hill, Frank Honigsbaum, Naomi Honigsbaum, Audry Horridge, Alan Jones, Brian Jones, David Jones, Wendy Jones, Frank Jordan, Madhukar Joshi, Maurice Kogan, Al Kromholz, Jim Kyle, Glenda Lambert, Susan Lane, Kitty Lee, Peter Leonard, Carlos Leung, Sheila McFerran, Neil McLellan, Coral MacDonald, George Mallen, Rosemary Marten, Michael Maugham, Clive Miller, Henry Miller, Sid Miller, Robert Morris, Roland Newnes, George Newton, Phil Osborne, Dick Parker, Ervine Parry-Jones, Curt Purvis, Brian Richards, Peter Righton, Anna Rodgers, Clare Scarlett, Tony Scott, Bee Serota, Duncan Smith, Derick Stevenson, Andrew Szmidla, Don Thackray, John Thompson, Betty Titcomb, Anne Vickery, Peter Walkington, Hilda Watson, Maureen Webley, Stuart Weir, John White, Ken Whitehouse, Bernie Wohl, Doreen Wohl, Jepson Wulff, Helen Zalen, Tony Hall.
Their assistance does not necessarily imply agreement with the views here expressed.

45659

Contents

Introduction   9

Part 1: Objectives of Social Services

1. The Primary Task   19
2. Banner Goals and Social Scenarios   21
    i Banner Goals
    ii Social Scenarios
3. Missions or Preamble Goals   48
4. Political Objectives   59
5. Strategic Objectives   65
    i Social Objectives
    ii Enumerating Strategic Objectives
6. Balance of Objectives   177
7. The Community Plan: A System of Objectives   213
8. Tactical Objectives   215

Part 2: Action towards Social Objectives

 9. Programme of Implementation   235
10. Agency Clientele   244
11. Agency Services   250
12. Agency Resources   256
13. Targets   265
14. Agency Functions   272
15. Agency Roles   277
16. Service Operations and Processes   284
17. Operational Effects   290
    i Overall Operational Effects
    ii Criteria of Effectiveness and Professional Standards
    iii Measurement
    iv Methods of Evaluating Outcomes

18. Priority Objectives and Strategies   335
     i Priority Objectives
     ii Strategies

Conclusion: Integrated Managing, Planning and Action Systems   350

Appendices

Appendix 1. Social Services Programme Structure   359
Appendix 2. A Client Problem Dictionary   385
Appendix 3. A Service Activity Inventory   403
Appendix 4. An Inventory of Social Services Operations   438
Appendix 5. Defining Positional Objectives   442
Appendix 6. A Network Analysis of Homelessness   447

Glossary   456
References   467
Bibliography   477
Subject Index   482
Name Index   489

Introduction

Values, Objectives and Action

He gazed profoundly at the world, feeling it was not now
eye's sweet mirage
Kazantzakis (The Odyssey: a modern sequel)

What are the significant social values and objectives of present-day communities? How do they interconnect? How are they to be realized in practical action? These large and significant questions are addressed in the work insofaras they concern the managing, planning and delivery of Social Services. Alternative Social Services objectives and their action implications are defined in an attempt to piece together a philosophy of practice.

A value is something prized by a person or a group, a norm by which excellence, significance or desirability is attributed to various situations. Values are expressed by the use of verbs such as cherishing, being motivated by, feeling favourably towards, and similar hurrah-words. Objectives are values which have been sufficiently embodied in behaviour to influence what people seek in action.

Social Values

Value — that unfortunate child of misery of our science
Weber

'Social values are fundamentally changing at all levels of society and in every field of human activity'. Though sweeping, such clichés are dramatically and continuously restated. They usually act as a kind of intellectual 'keep-off-the-grass' notice to cater for what people cannot clearly explain. The social concern is genuine. It leads to such diverse developments as social planning, conflict strategy, management by objectives, planned programmed budgeting systems, social action programmes, social audit, and even a whole 'science' of values called axiology (an amalgam of the philosophy, sociology and practice of how to realize values in action). However, social values remain vague. Practical attempts to implement such methods as management by objectives often flounder for lack of basic value definitions. The 'science' of axiology remains a neglected academic by-way. The question is posed: how then can we map and define social values such that they have some operational and implementable significance?

Social Objectives

Tourist: Which is the way to the next village?
Irishman: You can't get there from here.

Most human problems of living have come the way of Social Services workers. The behaviours and situations of individual clients are diverse and complex, as are service responses to these situations. How can we group and relate them into coherent themes without depersonalizing or over-simplifying? Unless this question can be answered, Social Services policies will have the status of elaborate fictions, social plans will be haphazard, and professional practice will be fragmentary.

This work defines alternative Social Services objectives in the form of an overall ends-means schema. This ranges from the most general, abstract social goals, to which few community members would object, through to examples of specific deadlines of front-line workers in their everyday social work. The alternatives derive from action research, consultancy and training in varied Social Services agencies. Some of the logical links connecting each level are reviewed in an attempt to bridge the gap between social policies and Social Services practices. To talk of front-line experience being reflected in social policies, or of social plans being genuinely implemented, is to court cynical derision. If policy-makers, managers, practitioners, indeed consumers, can begin to correlate policy and practice, to relate stated values with concrete service activities, then the cynic may be confounded. Is this not the primary task of Social Services managers?

The objectives-setting and implementation process exemplified is customarily viewed as fundamental to the development of management studies, policy sciences, social planning, and virtually every major profession: it is sometimes seen as the foundation for any rational thinking about work. Yet aside from some credos of industrial profit-making enterprises; few published examples of the process exist, even fewer in the public services field.

However, pressure mounts for Social Services, like other public organizations, to define their objectives more explicitly. They are increasingly required to provide evidence of social results and benefits produced in relation to costs and legislative sanctions. If they are to be responsive and adaptive, Social Services will reflect community values and demonstrate this by explicit value statements relevant to significant social issues. Objectives of effective Social Services arguably should embody and reflect social values implicit in daily life, and their essential working principles should arguably be those of the democratic state. The results of this objectives-defining process may therefore be relevant to some wider issues of social values in society at large.

Why define objectives? To explore and define objectives is to open ourselves to alternative possible futures, thus extending treacherously narrow conceptions of what is possible. By ·larifying objectives, decision-makers may support their bids for scarce resources and gain general sanction within which specific activities may be undertaken at their discretion. Stated objectives establish the expectations of sponsors and clientele, and provide a rationale for daily decisions. Lacking objectives, an agency has no basis for evaluating effectiveness of action. If relevant objectives can be agreed, some hope for improvement is established, some degree of optimism necessary for any committed action, and some limits are set to fatalism, pessimism or resignation. Where objectives are ignored, activities become motiveless and ultimately meaningless. This can be disastrous as Kubrick's film "Dr. Strangelove" illustrated in extreme form. Here people became so immersed in technical procedures of nuclear bombing that concern for broader issues of value and objective were displaced. Only by projecting a future and attempting to realize it, can effective action be generated.

Social Action
'I like work. It fascinates me. I can sit and look
at it for hours'.
Jerome K. Jerome

Despite Jerome's wish-fulfilment, work rarely entails idleness. There are activities to perform and tasks to complete if objectives are to be achieved. Objectives are not merely symbolic statements: they embody commitment of energy. Otherwise the phenomenon arises which Mexicans, from bitter experience, describe as *projectissimo*, whereby the production of a plan functions as an excuse for taking no further action. When first formulated, the objective may have no more reality than a port marked on a map. Once the image is set, effort can be directed towards it. Ships may eventually anchor at that port.

Pattern of the Book

Objectives of Social Services
Effective work seldom occurs at random. Except in the myth of Sisphus, there is usually some reason or motivation for work. To define objectives of work is therefore, has been argued, the primary planning

Chapter 1:
The Primary
Task

and managerial task — the intellectual aspect of management.

Given the motivations for defining social objectives mentioned earlier, the process of clarifying objectives is illustrated in the Social Services arena. Social Services objectives are to be defined for each stream of interest and activity at the different levels of generality: banner goals, missions, political, strategic and tactical objectives.

Banner goals are grand abstractions which satisfy the condition of being what everyone would want for everyone — to promote certain community developments, to fulfil various citizen rights, to meet multifarious social needs, to ameliorate diverse social problems, to maintain freedom from undesirable constraints and the like. When stated in more concrete form, they provide scenarios illustrating a more desirable future. Chapter 2: Banner Goals and Social Scenarios

Missions are sub-objectives of banner goals which pinpoint their area of application. They cover changes in the individual's psychological responses (which is the emphasis of psycho-therapeutically casework) or change of the individual's social environment (which is the emphasis of community work and social planning). This leads to the following formulation of the generic Social Services mission: to provide improved transactions between individuals and their community so that they match up better, thereby reducing the incidence and prevalence of social problems in the community. This entails the subsidiary mission of remedying the social malconsequences of other community services whether provided by central and local government, industrial companies, voluntary agencies or indigenous community resources. The implications of such a mission for service developments are analyzed in terms of progressive interim scenorios. These attempt to show how agencies are led from emergency services through successive development of intelligence and monitoring, advocacy, and community organization, to various forms of service experimentation and social action. Chapter 3: Missions or Preamble Goals

Missions are in turn accomplished via objectives which require fundamental political choices. These are of essentially three kinds: those aimed at meliorating harmful social conditions, those aimed at improving the quality of life, and those aiming to provide legislatively sanctioned services efficiently to eligible clientele. One of three corresponding grand strategies are implied: an emergency strategy, where severest social problems have priority; a preventive strategy, where conditions are promoted which might prevent social distress arising; a development strategy which builds incrementally on existing services. Chapter 4: Political Objectives

Specifying these approaches further, various strategic objectives of Social Services are envisaged. Each of these is defined in detail in both positive and negative terms, (i.e. as promoting certain social benefits and reducing certain social disbenefits) and exemplified by tactical, case Chapter 5: Strategic Objectives and positional objectives. Alternatives are thus specified at each level of objective.

Interrelations between objectives are analyzed in terms which might allow the overall balance of agency objectives to be decided. Chapter 6: Balance of Objectives

The resulting map of agency objectives can be viewed as a model of the total agency, and possibly (dependent on community participation) of the desired social situation of the community served by the agency. This overall balance of objectives is attained by examining causal sequences between social problems and resolving conflicts in objectives by defining appropriate thresholds of effort. Chapter 7: The Community Plan: A System of Objectives

Through this method, criteria of effectiveness can be derived. These allow decision-makers to specific strategic objectives in terms of tactical objectives, which in turn leads through to redesigning current action programmes. Tactical objectives are exemplified using specific cases and specific positional tasks. Chapter 8: Tactical Objectives

Action Towards Social Objectives

Come down to earth. Let's see what you are worth.
Thus to the soil he bent to sow his fancy's forms.
And when he'd finished planting, his mind felt relieved.
. . . *Kazantzakis*

Any one Social Services objective may be implemented by means of varying action programmes. A comprehensive programme structure for a Social Services agency is exemplified. Action programmes consist of groups of service activities in which certain resources are invested to enable their delivery to clients. Each programme is then specified by inventories of service activities, resources, operations and clientele. Chapter 9: Programme Implementation

Clients may be regarded either as indigeneous human resources of the agency interacting with employed professional workers to achieve certain communally-agreed social objectives, or as themselves the subjects of social-service intervention. The two views lead to action programmes structured respectively on a social objective basis or on a client-group basis. Chapter 10: Agency Clientele

Services differ in the effects they produce. If they are to be efficiently delivered, services themselves will generate various requirements which condition, to some degree, which agency objectives are attainable. Chapter 11: Agency Services

The resources mobilized, allocated and used in delivering social services, have also to be budgetted. Resources include money, manpower, equipment, materials, facilities, information, skills. Since resources are invariably scarce, a further set of choices have usually to be made at this stage of the planning process. Chapter 12: Agency Resources

Action programmes are not always maintained indefinitely. They may have target end-points to be attained over particular time periods. Chapter 13: Targets

Targets are defined in terms of specific services delivered by specified staff using specific resources to a specific clientele within a specific time span.

However, once operational on a regular basis, action programmes may give rise to ongoing agency functions. Functions refer to the provision of services in a manner and at a time deemed 'appropriate' or 'fitting' to certain circumstances in accordance with certain obligations to be discharged as laid down by specific pieces of legislation. As a result of this provision, only such action is taken as is 'proper' given the nature of the circumstances and the nature of the situation, so that the service comes to occupy a certain delimited place in the scheme of things. Chapter 14 Agency Functions

In regularly carrying out such functions, a Social Services agency places itself in a certain role in relation to the community and to other agencies. Policy-maker, worker and client will occupy varying roles vis-a-vis each other, depending on which of these agency roles is perceived appropriate to the particular situation. Chapter 15 Agency Roles

Service operations are chains of interconnected activities performed in delivering a service. They produce at some predefined end-point, a situation which is in some way changed from the situation at the defined starting point. Analysis may be made of service operations not only as reflections of pre-defined objectives, but also in terms of the nature of these processes themselves. Chapter 16 Service Operations and Process

The overall effects and consequences of such operational processess are analyzed. Whatever the evaluated result, desirable changes have then to be stabilized. Alternative methods of evaluating outcomes against objectives are reviewed. Chapter 17 Operational Effects

The essential point is that the total schema of agency objectives will be viewed differentially depending on one's standpoint. The whole schema may be rewritten in terms of a typology of available service resources, alternatively in terms of ongoing agency functions, and so on at every level of consideration. The preferred framework depends on the focus of interest. If organizational coherence is to be achieved, some basic value structure, equivalent to a policy alphabet, must be established as a means whereby one framework can be overlaid on another at different levels of analysis and operation. Chapter 18 Priority Objectives and Strategy

We are left with a map of the Social Services agency endeavouring to make varied impacts on the complex and richly interactive social situation of its community. There are various elements to be matched and decisions to be made at each level in the process of such matching. Decision-makers have to make priority choices between alternative possible agency objectives, programmes, services, clientele, targets, resource allocations, operations, functions, and roles. At each level, the nature of the choice varies. Choice of agency objectives both conditions and is conditioned by available agency resources, and vice versa. Hence classification systems at each level of concern are divergent. This explains the complexity of the work process and of daily decisions made by those operating agency services. In making such complex choices at each level, decision-makers will tend to opt for one of various strategies and to make their choices on the basis of some ranking of relevant factors. In order to take adequate account of these factors, actual results achieved in relation to the objectives set in the first instance are evaluated.

Interrelating Values, Objectives and Action

Even within the single area of meals-on-wheels services, there are a vast range of significant activities to which social values are relevant. Although British eating habits are not overlaid with the Gallic kind of emotional-social associations, the cultural-emotional framework wherein food is consumed, remains a vital element. The stomach may be filled while the person starves. Nourishment comprises more than calorie content. For this reason, many agencies prefer transporting clients to luncheon clubs rather than transporting meals to client homes. There is a difference between meals delivered like offal to cattle by delivery men scurrying around the district to earn their incentive bonus, sometimes leaving a package outside the door if the client answers the bell tardily, and a mini food pantry proffered by someone whose whole style and manner of food service acknowledges the significance of the interchange for those about to enjoy their lunch. The difference is analogous to "grub" shoved in front of corner cafe customers, versus the relish with which the expert chef delivers a feast to patrons of the haute cuisine restaurant, savouring the response as a personal reward.

The basic nature of the eating process — for many elderly persons, symbolic of eating itself — demands that meals-on-wheels services are not mechanically administered like postal services. As Savarin said in "Physiologie du Gout": 'Tell me what you eat and I will tell you who you are.' Meals-on-wheels services may be run in a manner which reinforces the individuality of those receiving meals, acknowledges expressed food preferences, and recognizes the emotional connotations of eating. These values are embodied in such general statements of Social Services objectives as promoting individualization and self-determination, and providing emotional outlets and fulfilment for emotionally deprived individuals.

Unless decision-makers can operate smoothly with such concepts, moving coherently and easily from one level to another, from specific services to general social values, the gap between policy and practice will grow ever larger.

If adequately evolved, a comprehensive map of objectives represents, to coin a phrase from linguistics, the 'deep structure' of agency work.

The overall approach embodies an attempt to derive a comprehensive, systematic and integrated managing, planning and action system (IMPACTS) based on goal-setting, goal oriented action and evaluation of outcomes. In using this framework in practice, it is important to recognize that in most work situations, there is a limit to how far decision-makers can afford to be comprehensive and systematic, given the requirements for practical and immediate action.

Part 1:
Objectives of Social Services

1| The Primary Task

Rapid changes in post-war society have had major effects on social life and on how people perceive and value it. There is increasing conflict among social values. There is confusion about how to describe and discuss value issues meaningfully, and what counts as social benefits. There is mounting confusion about how to articulate values in terms of concrete action. This state of affairs reflects itself in the difficulty which social services agencies have in formulating their objectives meaningfully in terms of the impact they seek to make through their services on problematic social situations in which clients and communities find themselves.

How therefore in this situation can social policy-makers, social planners and managers of social services agencies define meaningful social objectives in relation to social services and action? Without some coherent and practical answer to this question the effective management of social services agencies is unlikely to develop. For the question reaches to the heart of such relevant disciplines as social policy-making, social planning, social administration and professional social work, as well as being the starting point for such practice methods as planned programmed budgeting systems, management by objectives, operational research and even task-centred casework. A primary task of the social services may be seen as being to formulate, in participation with all those involved, a comprehensive network of social and service objectives, to integrate these into a coherent, logically interrelated system of ends, and to render these objectives operational by establishing clear links with service and action.

The 1970 Social Services Act,[1] the Seebohm Report,[2] central government policy guidelines, management consultants' reports on social services, corporate planning group edicts: none of these progress much further in this direction. Typically, they redefine boundaries and provide structural machinery without enunciating comprehensive social policies.

Results to be achieved by social services agencies lie *outside* the agency. They consist of agency impacts to be made on communities and their members. The task therefore becomes one of formulating a network of social objectives with and for the community itself as a basis for social service agency objectives.

A first attempt will be developed further in subsequent chapters. It was derived from analysis and comparison of statements of social and social services objectives by a diverse group of practitioners from several disciplines and from many parts of the United Kingdom.

2 | Banner Goals and Social Scenarios

Maximum Welfare, not maximum population is our human objective.
Toynbee.

I. BANNER GOALS

'Workers of the world unite.'
'Life, Liberty, the pursuit of Happiness.'
'Liberty, Equality, Fraternity.'

These historically famous banner goals were the impetus behind the international Communist movement and Lenin's creation of the Soviet State, the American Constitution and the French Revolution respectively. They are common in declarations of national and international purpose, in constitutions, charters, covenants and organizational creeds. Despite scepticism as to their practical relevance, banner goal statements are influential in organizational settings. Agencies use them to breathe new life into themselves, set themselves on a new course, boost sagging morale, stem despair of ever coping with the social problems confronted, or to halt the process of disintegration. As an example, the following statement of banner goals developed by board and staff at the instigation of the director B. Wohl, was instrumental in revitalizing the Columbus South Side Settlement.[1]

Philosophical Framework of South Side Settlement
At South Side Settlement we believe in the citizen's ability to shape his environment and the character of his community. We value the idea that people should be fully involved in mutual problems affecting their lives and in developing resolutions of those problems. Creating a democratic community demands active, thinking citizenry, unafraid of responsibility, actively experimenting with means to meet changing needs of its members.

Inherent in our approach is a value system encompassing the following concepts:
Our primary objective is improving quality of human life by creating a *community of culture and concern* rooted in economic and social justice. The struggle to build community is the struggle to replace narrow-self-interest with the broadening principles of mutual aid, sharing and social welfare. The social community we seek is characterized by: local government responsiveness to needs of citizenry; citizens organized for responsible participation in their government;

replacement of alienation with positive feelings of dignity, identity, self-worth; elimination of oppression in any form; celebration by citizens of their common humanity.

Alienation, the estrangement of persons from each other, affects all segments of our society. Meaningful involvement of people in processes of self-government while sharing the search for solutions to mutual problems reduces alienation.

An understanding of our culture is fruitfully developed in the presence of racial, class, religious, sex, age, belief and background differences. Participation in all Settlement programmes is open to all. Services focusing on specific cultural heritages and identities, for example, those concerning the struggles and values of black, Appalachian white and working class people, are central to our purpose. We welcome *richness of difference* as a source of cross-fertilization, presenting opportunities for new human achievement through interdependence. This implies mutual acceptance and trust, reciprocal respect but not necessarily consensus.

Freedom can be enlarged only by increasing acceptance of social responsibility. We oppose the tendency of many in our community to seek freedom without responsibility, to search for individual satisfaction divorced from social response. Only through social interaction can people protect their rights and enhance their potential.

Conflict, the state in which there exists opposing alternatives, is neither negative nor indicative of community breakdown. At South Side Settlement we consciously use conflict to create conditions for learning, movement, change. Our settlement is an arena where ideas are consciously introduced across lines of difference. They are then examined, rejected, refined and yet again examined in order to unleash the potential for meaningful social change and reduction of alienation.

An essential complement to resolving conflict is *celebration,* the act of sharing with family and friends the whole gamut of human emotion and experience. Celebration is the job of living that provides the physical and psychological energy to endure even in the face of what at times appear to be insurmountable odds.

South Side Settlement programmes reflect the *conscious testing of ideas*. We see ourselves as a laboratory for social change and understand that experimentation can result in failure as well as success. Effectiveness of South Side Settlement programmes is determined by the extent they measure up to our philosophy. A philosophy has to be tested and modified in practice. All facets of our programme are open to challenge and change.

Stirring words. They to some extent reflect the language of the J.F. Kennedy 'New Deal', L.B. Johnson 'Great Society', even the Richard Nixon 'Great Goals' programmes, which marked some degree of American consensus on social goals, a greater consensus than their British equivalents expressed in co-temporal Party manifestos. The Seebohm Report and derivative agency credos had similar status vis-à-vis social work professionals and policy-makers. 'To promote social environments positively conducive to individual growth and development' implies revision of the values and feelings about ways in which communities should help their members, moving beyond previous bureaucratic provisions. 'To serve wider social needs of individuals and communities' is an objective which similarly moves the social services in the direction of universalism and away from client-specific, means-tested, social casualty services.[2] Bureaucracies, like local authority social services departments, might similarly revitalize themselves through the process of formulating and reorienting themselves to similar banner goals. Attempts have been made in innumerable reports to committees throughout Britain at the initiation of the new social services departments.[3]

Given their potential influence, what is their nature? Banner goals are general but grand abstractions — evangelical ideas arousing people's minds to inspire mass movements, new social policies, and revolutionary approaches to what work is done. They are summing-up concepts embodied in the grand design which represents the agency's philosophy. Generality does not necessarily imply meaninglessness and banner goals should not be so obvious as to be trivial. What then is their relevance? Banner goals function as emotional rallying-points with which large numbers of different people can identify, thus inducing motivation and a basis for cooperation. This is important at times of widespread feelings of pointlessness, of an absence of living for great objectives — prevalent at a national level among liberals, the Press, the young, the universities, and the radical professions and at a corporate level among workers with varying backgrounds. They have general consensus value in that they mark the extent to which beliefs and values of persons within the same social culture or system have begun to converge. They are sufficiently divorced from all particular circumstances to be applied in different ways under differing conditions. They have taken over from religious and societal codes, being nowadays open to continuous reinterpretation. Although in this sense unattainable ideals, overall concepts embodied in banner goals can be approximated within any prescribed limit. They are open concepts shaped by many distinct factors signalled by lower-level objectives; place-markers awaiting concrete application. The precise compromise of these factors or sub-objectives in practice situations, governs their combination, hence the sum total of what is meant by 'welfare', 'social health', 'community wellbeing' etc. They are aide-mémoires of our goals: final points at which a continual stream of 'why?' questions terminate. We have developed no other, more specific language in which to discuss the overall directions of movement in large corporate institutions embracing highly diversified operations, like local authorities, or in complex social communities embracing variegated social processes. Any attempt at analyzying, planning for, integrating or simply talking about complex social systems cannot at present avoid such a language. Publicly recognized spokesmen for values — politicians, policy-makers, managers, sermonizers, evangelists, protesters, media men, practitioners — make frequent, explicit and overt appeals to them. They constitute points of reference, though being subject to change as a result of changes in community values. Reluctance to use such a language has forced social policy discussion into debates about isolated social problems, little effort being given to eliciting interactions between such problems as a whole in their socio-economic-political contexts.

Banner goals are sometimes regarded as little more than public relations sales talk by social services professionals on a level with such slogans as: 'Never knowingly undersold'. Alternatively, they may be seen as vital links between theory and practice, the central means by which practitioners keep themselves constantly aware of the value implications of current methods of provision and the hall-mark of any policy-making which is not based on a set of blindly manipulated socio-technical instruments. Reluctance to indulge in discussion and analysis at this level derives from the bureaucratic tradition in which social services originally developed, which may blind those involved to ideological issues embodied in social provisions.

What are banner goals based on? They should be clearly rooted in deeply held, deeply felt beliefs, values and interest of the community, and should occupy a commanding position, being generally acknowledge by the community and the agencies which serve it, and thus ultimately controlling other objectives. They should refer to a set of complex factors peculiar to the community and its agencies at a particular time, and to consequential aspects of roles and performances. Among these factors should be included whatever values and needs cause concern to the various interest groups or publics comprising the community and whatever may be ameliorated by available therapeutic techniques. If such criteria were met they would define those higher-order states of social affairs which satisfy the conditions of being what everyone would desire socially for everyone else, and what everyone would hope others would desire for everyone else, socially speaking. Disagreement with such values tends in varying degrees to seem absurd, unfeasible, perverse, or mistaken. In opposing them, we are involved in a conflict of inner attitude and incapacity for coherent, effective action. This is shown by the reactions encountered by anyone saying: 'I like being in the state of deep unhappiness' or 'I rejoice in bondage' or 'I attach a high value on people misinforming me'. Conflicts of inner attitude which result from opposing such basic social values produce the same kind of inner disquiet wrought by logical contradictions in those who try to countenance them conceptually. Some degree of self-evidence may be claimed for banner goals.

Is it possible to construct a sphere of social objectives and values which is more than the mere product of personal pontification by single arrogant individuals? Are there things which anyone would value over and above purely personal valuations? Are there social values which transcend local cultural determinants, political creeds, or religious schisms? We are talking about such dominant social values as traditional hedonic objectives of universal pleasure and happiness: everyone, no matter who he or she may be, should have whatever he likes or wants whatever it is, subject only to constraints of feasibility and clashes with others' likes or wants. Other dominant social objectives include maintaining community survival *to some degree* as the sort of community it is; developing community welfare including living standards, services and goods available to community members and some attainment of its non-materialistic, social ideals; achieving some reality-adjustment amongst community members; adjusting to things as they are rather than seeking false security in fantasy; maximizing opportunities, freedom from constraint, individual control of external circumstances, freedom of choice, self-fulfilment, physical and mental well-being; impartiality in respect of personal interests in treatment of others; lack of bias in analysis of factual evidence; and commitment to changing ineffective and debilitative practices. We seek to be impartial in seeking these values. We value both the attitudes associated with such seeking and such impartiality and certain cognitive, social and psychological attitudes having some affinity with these attitudes. All these social objectives fulfil (with due restrictions arising from conflict) certain conditions which admit them to the realm of basic social values, transcending (without overriding) specific personal interests and particular persons, and are thus worthy banner goals of social services agencies. Through recognition of such goals, the Welfare State has become more than an achieved situation for developed countries, and includes a consensual agreement on principle by parties of both right and left.

Typically, these values give rise to such statements of social services banner goals as the following:

1. To Promote Welfare and Morale

To promote the welfare and morale of people over and above earned incomes. To promote and distribute wealth as the stock of useful and exchangeable assets which directly or indirectly lead to social satisfactions and fulfilment of wants. Workers aim to promote welfare in the sense of social gains accruing to groups of consumers, including allocation of service resources. Welfare relates to the well-being of every member of the community undr discussion. Morale may be defined by favourable attitudes on the part of group members towards that group, in particular towards its objectives and leadership. Welfare is pervasive. Everyone contributes to it through taxes and rates, and are recipients of welfare at one time or another since everyone is at various times dependent on social supports.

2. To Promote Social Health

To promote the social health of the community and its members.

To free the individual from objective disturbances of social functioning or their effects. This refers to the social services role of providing a cordon sanitaire around communities.

3. To Meet Social Needs

To detect the potential and actual social needs of individuals, groups and communities, and where necessary to fulfil, satisfy and provide services to meet these needs in partnership with those seeking help. A need is defined as whatever is required for a person's health or well-being: anything someone consistently wants over a period of time if treated as a structural feature of his personality. People have needs because they are able to think. Unfulfilled needs lead to internal disturbances which set off specific drives, sometimes manifesting themselves in demands. Needs are requirements of which a person becomes aware when he acquires values, which demand he should strive for an objective in a given fashion in a given situation. They denote lack of something considered 'valuable'. Problems may be resolved or ameliorated (e.g. homeless youngsters may be lodged in guest houses at local authority expense) without the basic needs which caused them being met (e.g. insufficient housing or employment). Or needs (e.g. for income) may not translate themselves into demands until problems become too severe to ignore (e.g. many are reluctant to claim entitlements unless desperate).

4. To Resolve Social Problems

To resolve community social problems and distress arising from them, thereby reducing the pool of such problems. Frequently the point of departure in setting objectives is the social problem, even generalized goal-statements being redundant. Planning frequently begins with open situations like those raised by such questions as: what can be done about the social disorganization at the core of many cities? Or what should be done about high rates of mental retardation?

Returning afresh to problems in this way may gain a temporary respite from the usual grooves of thinking in a way that increases opportunities for innovation. More often, earlier investigation, experience, or decision-makers' policies are used to add some statement of an objective to facts about the problem, such as: 'let us develop community work'; or 'avoidable retardation owing to genetic defects must be decreased'.

5. To Articulate and Meet Social Interests

To help people articulate, meet and secure their own social interest by undertaking activities relevant to these. An interest is a claim worthy of consideration, a right to a share of something, to particpation in an activity, a right to be heard by those who decide. It is whatever is valuable or useful to the individual (or group), whatever helps to get what he (or it) wants satisfactorily. To have an interest is to have a claim on others in respect of something. This need not be valid and may be ill-founded, but it must be plausible. Interest involves subjectively structuring the immediate social environment in terms of one's own individual interests. Satisfying interests offers the possibility of reducing tensions.

6. To Articulate and Meet Social Preferences

To help people articulate, meet and secure their social preferences. The chief problem is how to devise social mechanisms through which these preferences might be expressed. The dilemma is familiar to community workers seeking to evince and elucidate the preferences of diverse community members, often by community audits or surveys of various kinds. Systematic methods used to generate group preferences may include delphi[4], paired comparisons[5] priority scaling[6], personal construct methods[7], or formalized trade-off procedures.[8]

7. To Respond to Social Demands

To respond or get others to respond to concrete claims or demands on services, perhaps stimulating people to express their needs, problems, interest, and preferences in the form of demands.

8. To Secure Social Rights

To help people claim, procure and secure their individual rights or claims on community resources and services to which they are entitled by law, precedent and evident need, at the required level of quality. These may be based on some system of rules prescribing correlative duties, such as payment of grants to a mother for her children's upkeep. They may be regarded as intrinsic to the nature of man qua man, as with the universal right of people to shelter, leading to demands that any homeless person be given accommodation.

9. To Improve Levels of Living

To enable individuals to use and develop resources which affect their living conditions, to enhance these or to alleviate undesirable conditions, regardless of vicissitudes beyond the individual's control. 'Level of living' is a Scandinavian concept adopted by the United Nations Research Institute for Social Development.[9] It refers to the extent to which a given population's needs are satisfied. Resources are further defined as means for acquiring goods and services. Needs in this context are defined as what people have, and how they behave. Community workers work on the assumption that characteristic social problems arise at different levels of living. Thus the middle-class housing estate although lacking financial or housing stress, often as desperately requires community organization to deal with problems of isolation and boredom as other estates require help in coping with the results of economic hardship. Aspirations diverge, though most aspire to higher levels of living than those currently experienced. Though those who have least, often have fewest wants. Situational improvements cause aspirations to escalate. Experiences of U.S. Headstart programmes are familiar:[10] once existing provisions begin to meet basic needs, they are soon outstripped by rising aspirations.

10. To Administer Shared Benefits

To reallocate benefits, services and money from those psychologically, economically and socially rewarded for productive services, to those not so rewarded. The basic conception of the welfare function here is to supersede market mechanisms in some areas by extracting certain goods and services from it, or so to modify market conditions as to produce social outcomes which the market would not otherwise have produced itself. Agencies may serve only part of their potential target clientele. One area office may be overflowing, while another catering for a similar market or need is virtually deserted. Or a centre 'draws' well in one sector of its territory while failing to attract the population from another sector. This is in line with general tendencies of unequal distribution of social services, the middle class making good use of what is offered, the very poor failing to get a proportionate share or to benefit through significant redistribution measures. Thus, in the field of family counselling, critics charge that professional, bureaucratic, and funding constraints of local authorities led to the systematic disengagement of agencies from adequate service to the poor. Social planning cannot be done unless means are found to make choices with reference to these critical aspects of social policy.

11. To Reduce Poverty and its Effects

Poverty, like welfare and mental health, is a portmanteau word embracing varied states. People are socially poor when they fall below a certain level of social benefit compared with others. People are poor in a psychological sense just by feeling poor — like businessmen retiring from their £8000 jobs to their £2000 pensions. Poverty of appreciation is the inability to use available resources to attain one's own contentment. People are also poor if they are so deprived of customary social resources that they cannot share in affluent society customs. The objective is not simply to combat absolute poverty — absence of food, shelter, clothing and warmth so that ill-health and premature death are avoided — but also to reduce comparative poverty i.e. to narrow the gaps between the 'haves' and 'have-nots'.

12. To Promote Community Development
To promote a supportive social environment which is positively conducive to each individual's growth and development. To achieve a better arrangement of social materials than at present. To render the community more responsive to its own members by opening out opportunities and providing supportive mechanisms.

13. To Develop Community Participation
To prepare people for participation in community life by providing them with information, guidance and insight, and by extending personal choice.

14. To Develop Human Potential
To develop human capacities and realize each individual's potential. Social services stop short at helping individuals to attain their full potential. Family workers terminate relations with clients once family members get along fairly amicably together.

15. To Maintain Freedom from Undesirable Constraints
To promote and retain maximum freedom from constraints — of the body from lack of food and shelter, of the individual from excessive rigidity of behaviour, of the mind from excessive prejudice. To increase the numbers and variety of social alternatives open to clients in their existing situations.

16. To Reduce Social Tension
To pinpoint key causal variables of personal and social tension, and thence to alleviate this.

To summarize, social banner goals may be broadly stated as follows: *To make social services available on non-market criteria to assure a basic level of social health, to enhance community well-being and individual functioning, to facilitate access to services and institutions generally, and to help those in difficulty and need.*

II. SOCIAL SCENARIOS

A central problem for social and community workers is how to perceive, understand and interpret the social situations of their clients and communities, and how to define more desirable situations. How do workers take account of the varying views of extant and requisite social situations, including their own, when the meanings participants attach to situations are unobservable? A failure to make conflicting social objectives explicit forces us into passively accepting given definitions of problems as presented by major institutions. Yet few current pictures of social reality are any longer taken for granted by any group. All are challenged. Can citizens render definitions of their social world and their expectations of it more explicit? Are we forced to use metaphysical language of grand abstractions to compare, contrast, agree, and work together towards some more requisite social situation?

One approach to developing such a language for comparison is to set up social scenarios which outline qualitative characteristics of alternative possible futures or models of community. They are detailed, concrete images of how the social world would appear were all social banner goals realized.

Community Social Scenario

Working with practitioners at several levels and from several regions, a desirable community future was mapped out in the following scenario.

It is open, communitarian and altruistic, being composed of self-reliant individuals, who assess situations by their own personal judgement. The community is planned holistically, organically integrating work, domestic life and play. Community members give expression to their membership in uninhibited and authentic ways. Resources are allocated to public benefits. Workers have a say in management, deriving fulfilment from their work. Vocation is sought out and cultivated, community energies are fully harnessed, and social groups are laboratories for resolving their own problems experimentally. At block, neighbourhood and regional levels variety is encouraged. Democracy begins with daily decisions, people only seeking power if they have positive programmes with supporting arguments and evidence. Unusual and unpopular opinion is given full rein; innovations are tested. Friendship is easy, social classes and races are factually equal. Results of social science are accessible for all to use in daily living. Each community forms an active society in charge of itself, rather than being chaotically unstructured or restructured to suit the logic of existing administration. Principle leads to corresponding action. Maturation is easy; there are plenty of activities for a child to observe, participate in, learn, contest and improve, and their contributions are used. Each citizen finds his community's way of life relates deeply to his own motivations, beliefs and endeavours. He experiences his whole society as a community. Freedom from constraint and pursuit of happiness are maximized.

The procedure could be taken further by utilizing Helmer's 1968 simulation game,[11] first conducted in Pittsburgh, in which various social groups — teenagers, women, older people, unskilled workers, the poor, the cultural élite, the middle class — chose which of several alternative social situations they would prefer if alive in A.D. 2000.

Agency Scenario

An equivalent scenario for requisite social services operations was developed, the overall model for which may be stated as follows.

Social services agencies intervene to improve (or to prevent deterioration in) transactions between individuals and their social environments so that they match up better, thereby seeking to reduce the incidence, prevalence and severity of community problems. This normally entails that they cope with, make good and remedy the social malconsequences resulting from inadequacies of other community services provided by different agencies or through indigenous community resources.

This overall model is analyzed by the agency into a series of multiple functional agency objectives covering diverse areas of social concern. For example, one such objective might be to achieve interrelations among residents of Old People's Homes which better meet their emotional-psychological needs for social integration and reduce their isolation through the use of groupwork methods. Another might be to supplement the nutritional deficiencies of those semi-mobile clients whose health would otherwise be impaired, by delivering varied, interesting and edible meals to their homes at the necessary temperature and regularity.

Client and Community Social Problems

Functional agency objectives are primarily addressed to a range of social problems (e.g. social isolation) experienced by individuals (e.g. elderly living alone) and communities (e.g. Old People's Homes) at varying levels or degrees of social pathology, and comprehensively defined in a *social problems dictionary*[12]. One problem may be social isolation; another, inadequate nutrition.

COMMUNITY SOCIAL CONDITIONS

The prevalence and incidence of social problems thus defined are monitored by *community audits,* using various social indicators. This provides a social report on the changing conditions of the community.

The following groups are of interest to the agency, the total numbers of each being monitored in the community audit:

    (i) persons with a problem in the community;

(ii) persons whose essential problem is unresolved;

(iii) persons returning to the agency prior to a successful resolution of the target problem;

(iv) persons whose incidental problems are unresolved;

(v) persons experiencing some consequential problem after the successful treatment of an initial target problem;

(vi) persons whose essential problems are unresolved by the agency or service;

(vii) persons experiencing a problem as a consequence of the side-effects of service activities;

(viii) persons experiencing a problem after leaving service;

(ix) persons with a problem whilst experiencing service.

CLIENT BOMBARDMENT

The numbers of clients with varying social problems who are actually contacting the agency are monitored by *intake audits*. These provide an account of how many latent social problems of the community actually translate themselves into articulated demands on service in some form, i.e. how much of each community social condition is manifested to the agency.

UNEXPRESSED COMMUNITY NEEDS

There is a difference between needs (prevalence and incidence of problems) as revealed by community audits, and demands (client bombardment of agency services) as revealed by intake audits. This difference represents the amount of unexpressed community need in the form of social problems not articulated in terms of specific client demands on service and the total potential market of need to which outreach services might address themselves. This difference may be called an *intake gap analysis*. A frequent example is provided by the isolated elderly person, or by those entitled to benefits they do not claim.

Agency Service Activities and Development

EXTANT AGENCY SERVICES

The degree and range of agency services currently being rendered in response to the problems handled are monitored by *workload audit*. Each service has a certain degree of actual impact or effectiveness on each social problem. A range of social treatments, service activities or provisions are developed to help in varying degrees ameliorate or resolve these problems, and are comprehensively defined in a *service activity inventory*. For example, sponsored luncheon clubs in day centres with supporting transport; meals-on-wheels providing nutritional supplements for the non-mobile poor; or friendly visiting services for the non-mobile lonely. Services are delivered to clientele experiencing the defined problems.

There are various states of service which are of interest to the agency and these are monitored in the workload audit according to the total number of problems that the service:

   (i) handles;
  (ii) resolves;
 (iii) ameliorates;
 (iv) alleviates;
  (v) soothes;
 (vi) leaves untouched;
(vii) exacerbates;
(viii) might potentially handle;
      and
 (ix) total number of problems other services could handle.

POTENTIAL AGENCY SERVICES

Potential service activities and treatments which an agency might render in response to varying community social conditions constitute its options for service development and delivery. They are derived from an analysis of which services have proved effective in handling social problems. This is called a *service repertoire audit*. Each potential service has a certain degree of probable impact or effectiveness on each social problem. For many agencies, these might include behavioural modification services and treatments, psycho-physical therapy in occupational workshops, neighbourhood helps, and so on.

SERVICE DEVELOPMENT DECISIONS

The difference between existing agency services (of a defined degree and range) as revealed by workload audit and the potential agency services which might be delivered as revealed by service repertoire audit, constitutes the options for decisions on service development. They include the option of heavier investment in existing services as well as investment in new services. This difference is determined by a *service provision gap analysis*. Thus many agencies are seeking to divert their investments from residential to community care provisions.

PROBABILITY OF PROBLEM RESOLUTION ETC.

Degrees of probability of problem resolution, amelioration, alleviation, soothing, or ineffectuality as a result of social treatment or service delivery, are assigned on the basis of monitored results from the past. Thus, weekly youth clubs have been shown to be less likely to relieve the burden of children on slum parents than adventure playgrounds. This probability is determined by *evaluation audit*.

PROBABILITY OF PROBLEM IMPINGEMENT

Community problems which are currently unexpressed in the form of demands or unmet by any agency services, may surface in the future. In response to these existing agency services may be extended to cope with them, or new agency services may be developed. The degrees of probability that hitherto unmet or (formally) unrecognized problems will impinge on the agency at various future times can be assigned. They would be assigned according to various criteria such as pressure from interest groups (e.g. Central Government, councillors, ratepayers, community groups, clients, neighbouring professions, staff and so on). This probability is determined by *social trend analysis.*

PROBABILITY OF SERVICE DEVELOPMENT

The probability of future service development and investment is determined by two things: the probability of existing services resolving a problem and the probability of hitherto unrecognized or unmet problems impinging on the agency. This probability is determined by analyzing the gap between problems and services *(problem-service gap analysis).* Many agencies, for example, found their services were not geared to providing for the needs of the physically handicapped as sanctioned by Alfred Morris's Act.[13]

Organizational Service Units

The following functions are allocated amongst various organizational units.

A *diagnostic* or *needs analysis unit* principally focuses on community problems, and performs the following functions:

   (i) Adopting, updating and revising the social problems dictionary in conjunction with operational groups;

  (ii) performing periodic community audits of social conditions and consumer studies with periodic social reports on changes in the prevalence and incidence of problems, hence some report of the impact on community and client problems by the agency;

 (iii) searching out unmet needs, unclaimed rights and untouched problems in the community;

 (iv) stimulating the articulation of these needs and rights in the form of demands on service or the claiming of rights;

  (v) performing periodic intake audits of client bombardment;

 (vi) undertaking the intake gap analysis by which unexpressed community needs are defined;

(vii) performing the social trend analysis by which the agency determines the probability of problems impinging on the agency in future;

(viii) securing agreement with all decision-makers across the agency

on priorities among social problems by means of priority
scaling;

(ix) performing the problem priority scaling with relevant agency
decision-makers to achieve an agreed ranking of problems;

(x) performing the intake and closure criteria analysis in terms of
problems to ensure that the agency is not so overloaded with
multifarious problems at any one time that service resources
are far outstripped;

(xi) analyzing the agency budget in terms of problems;

(xii) consulting with advisory and training operational agency
groups on the nature and dynamics of various problems
handled in order to help improve diagnosis.

A second organizational unit — the *service planning unit* — primarily
focuses on service activities. It performs the following functions:

(i) Adapting, updating and reviewing the service activity
inventory in conjunction with operational groups;

(ii) performing periodic workload audits of extant agency services;

(iii) performing service repertoire audits which define potential
agency services;

(iv) undertaking a service provision gap analysis on the basis of
which service development decisions are made to ensure
existing services are adequately developed to cope with
problems taken on by the agency;

(v) performing evaluation audits on the degree of effectiveness of
agency services on problems;

(vi) securing agreement with all decision-makers across the agency
on priorities among services by means of priority scaling;

(vii) performing the service priority scaling with relevant agency
decision-makers to achieve an agreed ranking of services;

(viii) performing the intake and closure analysis in terms of services
to ensure relevant agency services are not so underdeveloped
at any one time that priority problems cannot be handled;

(ix) monitoring the flow of clients through the agency by
transaction audits;

(x) locating inadvertent client 'drop-outs';

(xi) coordinating policies, plans and operations with neighbouring
services available to the agency or to which clients may be
referred;

(xii) performing a skills analysis which matches the social problems
dictionary and the service activity inventory on the basis of
which work can be rationally allocated;

(xiii) analyzing the agency budget in terms of service activities;

(xiv) consulting with, advising and training operational agency
groups on treatment and service methods, and how to improve
their delivery, efficiency and effect.

Operational service units focus on running service programmes — actually delivering services to agency clientele according to agreed agency priorities, in an effort to reduce the prevalence, incidence and severity of community problems. They perform the following functions:

(i) Receiving client demands and claims;
(ii) diagnosing client problems;
(iii) ordering client problems according to agreed priority criteria;
(iv) allocating services to client problems according to agreed priority criteria;
(v) developing a coordinated treatment plan and targets for each client and community problem;
(vi) acquiring adequate information to take service decisions effectively;
(vii) treating client problems, using available services;
(viii) assessing the degree to which targets are met and services are effective;
(ix) closing cases or completing service activities, hence discharging clients;
(x) feeding back information relevant to and required for planning, including the nature, degree and quantity of problems handled and the assessed effects of specific service activities on problems;
(xi) implementing (or feeding back information designed to correct) agency policies and priorities;
(xii) performing problem-service gap analysis as a result of which agency plans are corrected by revising problem or service priorities and consequential resources allocated;
(xiii) developing personal skills thus improving problem diagnosis and service delivery;
(xiv) monitoring and reporting on the total social situation of the local community concerned.

The formal organizational structure may either (on a polyarchic model) [14] be adapted to the organizational units outlined herewith, or the tasks may be allocated within the existing formal structure using whatever roles are appropriate. No prescriptions of organization structure are necessarily implied. The particular organizational framework necessary would be determined by organizational analysis.

Agency Transactions

As a result of extant services being bombarded with clients, the agency undertakes certain transactions with its clientele. A transaction might simply be a social worker visiting a client for eight weeks on a short-term casework basis seeking to resolve the client's debt problems, or it may be a specialist home help visiting a family weekly until some sense of domestic management is established.

Each such transaction is monitored in terms of the types of problem and service activity involved, the relative agency priority assigned, current budgetary allocations used, and the probabilities of service initiation and completion at each point in time. Agency transactions are determined by certain variables:

Structural variables or those relating to the basic capacity. Certain services (e.g. groupwork) are available at a certain level (e.g. three groups each meeting once per week) as determined by available resources (e.g. a groupworker) given by the annual operating budget (e.g. £8000 per annum for groupwork). These services are developed by various means like inter-referral structures by which caseworkers refer clients for groupwork treatment.

Condition-reporting variables, meaning those relating to the ongoing agency capacity as a result of demands on and use of services. Certain client problems (e.g. isolation) consume available service (e.g. groupwork) time and resources (e.g. £8000 per annum) to some degree as determined by the number of clients with their varying problems (e.g. isolated elderly) receiving varying services.

Priority variables, meaning those relating to the relative agency significance (i.e. amounts of time and other resources) allocated as between various client problems confronting agency services. They determine the probability of a client being accepted for service, and regulate the queue of clients having varying problems for services with varying capacity. One variable is the comparative degree of weight given to preventive work vis-à-vis social casualty work, or to community vis-à-vis residential care.

(i) PROBLEM PRIORITIES

On the basis of the above analyses, degrees of priority are allocated to social problems across the board. Thus, children's problems at level D of social pathology (as defined in the social problems dictionary) may be agreed as having greater priority than problems of the physically handicapped at level A of social pathology (again defined in the social problems dictionary).[15] It may be agreed that individual problems having ramifying social effects on a whole housing estate should have greater priority than individual problems whose central interest in (in view of other more severe problems) is the social worker's skill-development. These and similar decisions made across the full range of agency social problems allow the agency to rank problems by priority, allocate resources accordingly, and order queues and waiting lists for services. The decisions are made by problem priority scaling.[16]

(ii) SERVICE PRIORITIES

Broadly, the same principles apply to determining priorities among agency services. Thus the provision of occupational workshop activities for aiding the return to employment for those who are poor, may be agreed as having greater priority than occupational workshop activities for providing diversions for those who are bored. The decisions are made by service priority scaling.[17]

(iii) INTAKE AND CLOSURE CRITERIA

On the basis of the above analyses, intake and closure criteria are determined in respect of all social problems for which the agency provides services. Thus, the residential intake groups are able to assign an order amongst those awaiting places in a residential home on the basis of diagnosed condition and agreed ranking of problems in relation to residential services. The fieldwork intake group are able to assign amounts of time to be spent on various cases according to agreed ranking of problems in relation to casework services. These criteria are established by intake and closure criteria analysis. The criteria may well change over a period of time as community problems and needs vary, and policies are adjusted accordingly and new services are developed.

These agency transactions are monitored by *transaction audits* in which the current agency capacity available at any one point in time is monitored, together with any new additions to or predicted demands upon basic agency capacity.

EFFECTS OF TRANSACTIONS

Transactions between agency and clientele result in certain effects associated with the passage of time and the efficacy or otherwise of service.

Inter-service Referral Some inter-service referral may occur. The client may be re-referred back to the agency from outside (e.g. from the G.P.) having completed service once before (e.g. having received home help whilst mother was in hospital); he may be referred between services within the agency (e.g. from caseworker to day centre) or to other agencies (e.g. to Housing); may himself contact another service, either internal (e.g. a therapy group after receiving casework support) or external (e.g. Claimants Union) to the agency; or he may leave the system (e.g. by discharging himself).

Service Effectiveness The service has a certain impact or effectiveness on the client problem resulting in a certain degree of probability that the client will (or will not) return to the service within a defined time period. The problem may be resolved (e.g. the homeless family is housed securely and adequately), ameliorated (e.g. the homeless family is housed securely though inadequately), alleviated (e.g. the morale of an unemployed worker is somewhat restored through work in an occupational workshop), soothed (e.g. the bored and handicapped old person is helped by diversional day centre activities), or untouched (e.g. the homeless youth still sleeps on the streets at night). These degrees of effect represent changes in degrees of problem severity or social pathology as defined in the social problems dictionary.

Service Side-effects Services delivered may have certain side-effects or concomitants which are not directly intended or related to the prime objective of providing the service. They may prevent any additional client problem occurring (e.g. though the homeless family remains unhoused, family break-up is avoided by casework and other support services). They may alleviate a concurrent client problem (e.g. though still in debt, the marital relationship between the couple is improved so that the debt problem no longer threatens to break up the marriage). They may induce another concurrent client problem (e.g. domestic and decision-making dependency induced through home help and casework support). They may lead to deterioration in another concurrent client problem (e.g. marital discord exacerbated through wife's participation in tenants' group). They may have no side-effects or concomitants, be they positive or negative, on any concurrent client problems (e.g. marital disharmony is untouched by securing adequate housing for the formerly homeless family).

Termination Side-effects Service termination may have effects on the problem situation. It may alleviate a concurrent client problem (e.g. husband's jealousy of caseworker's influence on family decision-making); or prevent a concurrent client problem emerging (e.g. the threat of domestic dependency if the home help's services were to continue past the point where they were needed to render the problem family's home liveable in again). It may induce a new client problem (e.g. hostility of housing agencies to the client through the latter's participation in a successful Squatters' group action); or cause deterioration in a concurrent client problem (e.g. resentment at the groupworker's closure of a therapy group being projected onto all State services with a consequent deterioration in relations with Social Security).

Problem-to-Problem Translator Matrix The resolution (or non-resolution) of one client problem through services delivered may generate a further client problem. Symptom-substitution may result in one problem replacing another (e.g. the child no longer throws temper tantrums, but becomes incontinent). Non-resolution of a problem by a service may generate a further client problem (e.g. the child's delinquency is not resolved by his admission to a children's home and approved school, but increases in the variety of offences committed through contact with other delinquents and in severity through the need to survive when he absconds). Or non-resolution of a problem may not generate any further problem (e.g. though still in care, the child does not manifest any additional psychological problems).

These effects are monitored through *evaluation audits.* However, the effects may manifest themselves through (and at the time of) initial service contact, as the client awaits service, during service delivery, as service is temporarily suspended, or after service is completed. Each must therefore be related to one of these points through information provided as clients pass through the system.

Information System

A *social decision simulator* summarizes the current position of the agency in respect of all these situations and conditions to provide a comprehensive map of its current performance and operation. This evidently requires that information is collected which is relevant to each situation, and that this is related to the flow of clients through agency services. The information may be gleaned from four sources:

(i) factual information recorded (e.g. numbers of clients contacting the agency);

(ii) assessments made by workers (e.g. the degree to which a client's problem is resolved, ameliorated, alleviated, soothed or untouched by services delivered);

(iii) results of empirical research (e.g. probability of a service resolving a client's problem given a certain level of input);

(iv) periodic assessments by external auditors (e.g. those conducting consumer studies).

This information may be monitored in several alternative ways:

(i) by one-off audits (e.g. community audits to determine the assessed extent of various needs);

(ii) by extrapolating from national research and surveys (e.g. the Amelia Harris survey on the elderly) [18];

(iii) by means of an ongoing information system (e.g. ICCIS) [19]

It may be necessary to gather information in whatever way is feasible to build on the initial impression of the total picture. This total picture is tested against reality by prediction, an evaluation of erroneous prediction and the subsequent adjustment of the model to tune it with reality. As a result of such 'tuning', further information is gathered or existing information is checked to achieve a greater degree of accuracy.

In order to monitor current service effectiveness at this level of sophistication, a computer-based information system monitors the flow of clients through agency services and their current status in terms of problem type and severity, and the amounts and types of service received at any one time. The information system is thus used to provide information needed to run the decision simulator, and take the necessary decisions on agency development.

CLIENT STATUS

The information system records information on client status. Clients may have a problem but have not contacted a service (e.g. the elderly person not claiming her benefits because pride causes her to disdain 'charity'). Their contact with a service does not result in receipt of service (e.g. there is no follow-up interview). They are initiated in a service (e.g. meals-on-wheels are delivered); continuing in service (e.g. the meals-on-wheels continue to be delivered); service is suspended (e.g. meals are prepared by a home help); or service is terminated (e.g. worker and client agree that further visits are unnecessary). This may be because service was completed (e.g. the problem of child-parent antagonism is resolved after eight caseworker visits); or the service was ineffective and no substitute was found (e.g. the additional grants from Social Security were spent on alcohol instead of food); because the client voluntarily withdrew (e.g. felt the caseworker to be intruding on his privacy and asked her not to come again); or because of the non-appearance of the client (e.g. the homeless family moves to another area). It may be due to the client's death or, finally, because service resources were exhausted in respect of that client (e.g. the caseworker is making no impact on the client's problem and has no more time to experiment).

PROBLEM STATUS

The information system records the current problem status — whether the problem is resolved (service being about to be discontinued), ameliorated (service being re-requested if deterioration sets in again), alleviated (realistic appraisal made of what any additional service might further achieve), soothed (additional services being sequenced into the treatment plan), untouched (experimentation on new service activities taking place), or continuing unsupported (decisions being made to discontinue services through lack of success, lack of problem priority or insufficient service resources).

SERVICE STATUS

Current service status is recorded in the information system. From this it is possible to determine which clients are currently in the queue for service, are receiving, have completed, or are not receiving service. Also immediately available is information on the types of service available for each problem, the probability of service effectiveness per problem, the availability of service (when and how much) and priorities of service allocation per problem.

WORKER STATUS

The information system records the status of each worker's workload: which clients are allocated to which workers (and the time taken in view of skills used); what appointments are scheduled, planned, requested, predicted or accepted for the future so far as each worker is concerned; changes in client assignments and appointments; messages between workers; each worker's authorizations to certain pieces of agency and client information. This ensures that information is available and used at the time it is needed for action by the information-recipient, rather than being transmitted at a time convenient to the information-transmitter, thus saving onerous delays in communicating information between agency personnel.

AGENCY STATUS

Overall agency status in terms of cumulated summaries of information of each type, is available for overall planning purposes. It is thus possible to determine how much of which services is being deployed for which problems in which areas with what effect over a period of time, thus giving exhaustive information on all key aspects of agency functioning.

Summaries of the total agency situation vis-à-vis all such transactions and their effects, is regularly cumulated in terms of contacts (numbers of persons contacting services), caseload profile (numbers of persons receiving services), and outputs (numbers of persons leaving services with or without problem resolution). A constant social account is retained of the numbers of clients with problems of varying kinds being handled by the agency, as compared with estimated numbers of those community members requiring help with each problem as yet unknown to (or ineffectively treated by) the agency. This provides a basis for service expansion and development.

USE OF SYSTEM

Workers and managers use the system to get any information to which they are entitled directly and immediately, being connected to the central data-bank through typewriter terminals.

Social Simulation Models

Thus agency situations are constantly monitored. Computer-based social decision simulation models and community-client information systems may be used for this purpose

Two alternative types of simulation models of the social situation of the community have been developed: *Dynamo* [20] and *Homunculus* [21]. Both allow us to simulate changing community social structures, together with consequential social needs and problems.

Once a generic model of the community structure is adduced, decision-makers feed through the model specific information on the community such as numbers and types of social problem, the degree of associated pathology, numbers of social needs of different types which are not articulated in the form of any demand on services, geographical clustering of problems, ramifying effects of problems, representation of diversified community interests, channels for communication of community needs and interests, influence structures within the community, and so on.

Decision-makers use this model to predict what is likely to happen if the community continues to function according to the operational principles on which the simulation was built. If each variable comes out as forecast, the simulation is judged to represent the operation of community structures adequately. Decision-makers can then test out in advance with the agency model, the probable consequences of community action: of increasing certain communication channels between service agencies and community groups, of distributing new information to the community groups in different ways, of creating more consumer participation by various methods, of forming new groups of various kinds around certain community concerns, etc.

Three alternative types of simulation models of the agency's operations in pursuit of certain social objectives have been developed: *Simpol*,[22] *Hawsim*[23] and *Sodesim*.[24] Both allow decision-makers to simulate the totality of changing agency service operations.

Once a generic pattern of services and service activities is adduced, decision-makers feed through the model specific information on such aspects of their particular agency's work as numbers and types of presenting social problem, degrees of associated social pathology, numbers of clients with manifold characteristics, take-up of services and their differential impacts, service benefits and disbenefits, numbers of workers with varied skills. This results in a balance sheet of agency performance covering all variables relevant to daily decisions.

Managers use this model to predict what is likely to happen if the agency continues to function by the operational principles on which the simulation was built. If each variable comes out as forecast, the simulation is judged to represent agency operations adequately. When predictions turn out to be wrong, the model is further adjusted to the real-life situation so that better predictions can be made in the next round.

Once the simulation is sufficiently accurate to win decision-makers' confidence, experimentation begins. Instead of painfully — often disastrously — experimenting with real life situations as obliged to at present, decision-makers experiment on the model instead. They test out in advance probable consequences of decisions: of changing resource allocations between services, of changing service delivery patterns, of changing the mix of staff skills through training programmes, of changing priorities amongst client groups, and so on. What happens in the model will probably occur in real life if the decision is implemented. We begin to predict precise effects of alternative actions, and make decisions accordingly.

Simulation models form a cornerstone of systems design. Critical functions and decisions of social services agencies and their communities are mapped, together with all feasible variations. The simplest form of mapping is a network diagram, familiar from network analysis [25]. In more complex form, the map is translated into a mathematical picture of reality, mathematical equations symbolizing every agency operation and its interrelationships with all other operations. A dynamic representation of the totality of changing servie operations is produced. As the urban planner's model maps traffic flows through towns, so the social planner's model simulates flows of clients through agencies and outcomes of service.

By the use of such client and community information systems, agency decision-makers have access to information which potentially increases their capability in several areas. They are able to monitor day-to-day, week-to-week, and month-to-month operations so that operational problems may be quickly and responsively detected and corrected; and can audit both previous costs and the assessed effectiveness of services so as to evaluate alternative policy changes. The under-utilization of resources (especially scarce professional manpower resources) can be assessed; and the allocation of staff to client service on a daily basis. Clients can be tracked through the social services system, which is especially useful in preventing unplanned-for client drop-outs from the system as a result of referral to other agencies or services, or delivery of the service over a long period.

Managers can cumulate and review evidences as to various, actual, potential and predictable social problems of community members, clustering and correlating these with key social indicators, and reviewing evidence as to the degree to which these are or are not being (or being perceived to be) met. Any worker having legitimate access can retrieve an automatic summary of any of his or her client case histories. Comparative problem situations (e.g. mobility) and treatments (e.g. kinesiological therapy [26]) of which the agency – or some other agency – has had experience can be reviewed. They can quickly identify the range of appropriate currently available services and resources for each client and client problem (e.g. the amounts of residential care available); and can reliably and speedily transfer client information from section to section within the agency (or to any other agency sharing the system). Finally, confidentiality in respect of any piece of information about any client can be better secured by nominating and enforcing rules of access.

The Social Systems Approach

Social systems technology essentially comprises an approach to managing and redesigning the totality of the social situation as a dynamic whole (e.g. the total social services department serving a defined community) whose configuration is given by the interaction of interdependent components.

Social communities are treated as complex interconnected social entities rather than as social interest groups, their social problems as interlocking clusters rather than as isolated symptoms, their services as part of an integrated social treatment strategy for the community rather than as uncoordinated fragments, and associated action research programmes as an integrated attack on the full range of professional, managerial and organizational problems of agencies which synthesize the methods of each within the systems framework, rather than as partialistic research of isolated elements. It is thus one of the very few approaches which offers some practical responses and potential ways of resolving those current problems such as defining objectives and desired outcomes of services, measuring service effectiveness, and detecting and analyzing need, which occur in the managing of large, complex operations having many variables. The transmission of information, reporting of transactions, flow of people, delivery of services, and the expenditures of monies in all the separate systems for social support and across their boundaries at the neighbourhood, municipal, regional and national levels are all of such complexity that their evaluation requires the application of social systems technology.

Uses of Scenarios

The revival of frankly utopian thinking is not far removed from timetables of ordinary management: a gathering of energy in the present by imaginative declarations of what is in one sense a future, in another an experience already known and felt. Earlier utopias had dates and places. New utopias are active, immediate choices: ways of defining and sustaining a struggle. Increasingly, planners recognize the need to identify qualitative aspects of objectives before setting specific performance targets. Differences between success and failure in implementing such plans depend on the degrees of commitment made by workers throughout the agency (and perhaps citizens through the community) to objectives planned for or envisaged. The problem is not so much one of seeing the eventual shape of an effective community, but of bringing this into effective relation with the whole of our experience.

Since scenarios are models of community and of agency functions, they provide frameworks within which theories and hypotheses about social services are testable. The test does not lie in their truth or falsity; rather in whether they are fruitful sources for setting specific social service objectives.

Having sketched such scenarios and banner goals, we now have to move from this generalized level towards more specific targets, policies, statutes, programmes, divisions of responsibility, administrative structuring, manpower decisions, funding decisions and evaluation and monitoring methods.

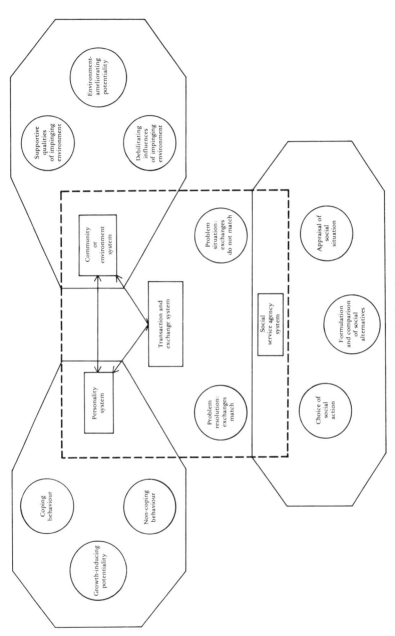

Figure 1. General Model of Social Services System

47

3 | Missions or Preamble Goals

Jago also believes College progress depends on him. He is a weak man with a mission.
C.P. Snow, The Masters

If unsupported by specific lower-level objectives banner goals become empty and meaningless shells, shoddy facades to disguise tyranny, prejudice, exploitation, stagnation and intellectual bankruptcy. The language of crusades and causes becomes illusory when deliberately used by politicians and managers to foster false illusions. As it stands, the language of 'welfare', 'mental health', and 'socialization' gives a pseudo-scientific veneer to moral judgements and to paridigms of human nature presupposed by culture. Thus formulating banner goals is futile without more detailed specification in terms of missions.

What are Missions?

Missions are sub-objectives of banner goals, pinpointing their area of application. They are attempts to envisage the desired state of affairs as a whole: in principle attainable, but not within the period planned for operationally. By relating to agency effects on its community they are concerned with basic problems and fundamental needs.

Missions should be valid in terms of the underlying assumptions of the agency and its culture. They concern human behaviour, needs, values and decisions. Like first premises in logical arguments, they provide planning premises for decisions made and the context within which to formulate specific objectives. Ultimately they must remain unproved and unmeasured, because there is nothing to prove or measure them against. If we try to prove or disprove them we are involved in an infinite regress. They are simply agreed. They are meta-goals (i.e. supra-objectives which shape some sense of direction) providing foundations for specific agency objectives. Time and effort can be wasted trying to specify targets which contradict such underlying agency assumptions. Once formulated and agreed, missions provide decision-makers with agreed guidelines and planning becomes easier.

When stated specifically, we find few goals shared by a sufficient majority. Hence missions, like banner goals, are expressed in a generalized form. They must not be continuously subject to change, some minimum goal-stability being essential for plans to be practically useful. Continuously changing missions simply indicate inadequate initial definitions or unstable organizations.

Missions should therefore embody sufficiently fundamental values to preclude their sudden change or abandonment, though opinions about their relative importance shift rapidly. They constitute relatively stable centres around which the resolution of agency conflicts pivot. From them we predict probable changes in subordinate objectives. Generalized and hopeful, they represent value allocations, carrying expectations of and a rationale for action, though not prescriptions for carrying this out.

Types of Mission

Defining social services missions entails choosing the locus of agency intervention in community affairs. This may be determined by:

1. Institutional Change

We wish to change the relevant social institutions, for example, by strongly advocating a change in the industrial norms of retirement at 65. Workers may call on management and organizational theory to support such an attempt at institutional change.

2. Sociological Change

Where the major causes of individual problems are community deficiencies, we may seek to engineer changes in the social system: for example, in urban renewal programmes which relocate citizens inconveniently. Workers typically call on sociological theory to support efforts in this direction.

3. Psychological Change

Where the major causes of need are defined by the individual's emotional responses to conditions of his life, we may seek to change individual behaviour by counselling. We seek to help clients understand situations more objectively, supplying them with the means to live with and adjust to their problem situations through increased flexibility in behaviour. Psychological theory is used.

Contexts of Missions

Social services locate themselves on the area of overlap between several systems. Within the overall context of local affairs, we can map the network of services in which these missions involve social service agencies:

1. Social welfare administered through social services systems, in which efforts to support and enhance individual, family and community role performances are central.

2. Fiscal welfare administered through income-maintenance systems. This is characterized by transfer-payment devices to ensure socially defined minimum income levels, the primary responsibility for this lying with the Department of Health and Social Security in the U.K.; and the Bureau of Income Maintenance, Federal Department of Health, Education and Welfare in the U.S.A.

3. Occupational welfare administered through an employment system. This concerns elucidating and enhancing talent, job counselling, and placement. In the UK the Department of Employment has primary responsibility; and in the USA the Federal Department of Employment (the US Employment service at State level).

4. Physical welfare administered through a medical system responsible for maintaining and improving physical health. Regional hospital boards are primarily responsible in the UK; the Health division of the Federal Department of NEW (with equivalent State departments) in the USA.

5. Educational systems which include responsibilities for socialization and job preparation. The UK Ministry of Education and the US Office of Education with local authority and State counterparts are the relevant organizations.

6. Recreation systems characterized by a concern with pleasure and self-enhancement. Responsibilities are spread between institutions like the Arts Council; Baths, Parks and Recreation departments; Department of the Environment, etc. in the UK; while in the USA the responsibility is split between the Federal Department of the Interior, NEW and municipal authorities.

7. Correctional systems characterized by powers to deprive people of liberty. Primary responsibility lies with Police, Probation and Prison services in the UK; with corrections services administered by the Federal Department of Justice in the USA.

8. Physical planning systems whose services are designed to revitalize socio-economic, cultural and communal life in run-down areas, including developing community facilities and urban amenities, and providing housing on non-market criteria. Town Planning, Housing and Architects departments are primarily responsible in the UK; the Department of Housing and Urban Development in the USA.

In each service the following four aspects are critical: living conditions, redistribution of wealth and rights, the participative process and the individual's status.

Mission Fulfilment

The missions outlined above are fulfilled through two primary fields of social services activity which may be considered from the two perspectives of social planning and case therapy:

The Social Planning Perspective
In so far as social services agencies are concerned with developing social environments, they have vital contributions to make in planning the social aspects of other public services. The objective is *to relieve environmental pressures which customarily arouse individual social problems by manipulating the social environment; to ensure that the basic necessities of living delivered by other services are provided without undue stress for individuals; to help people use the opportunities open to them through market-provided or community-sponsored services.*

Social services departments might achieve this objective if they act as sources of negative feedback to other community institutions (e.g. Town Planning, DHSS), using evidence of failure to achieve the most feasible provisions. The centrally relevant discipline is sociology.

The Case Therapy Perspective
The social planning role, previously the prime concern of town planners, is new to the traditions of the British social services which were, until recently, rooted in the casework tradition which emphasized the need to improve the individual's ability to cope.

This role embraces the objective *of providing the individual with a series of specific techniques which help him manage himself and his affairs within the setting of his social culture.* Sub-objectives include extending individual freedom from personal constraints and extending personal resources: *to help individuals remove those major constraining factors which radically inhibit or reduce their abilities to fulfil specific social needs and negotiate their particular circumstances more effectively.*

These needs might comprise basic physiological or biological needs for food, shelter, clothing, warmth and health; economic and safety needs for security and order; social or interactional needs for social and emotional affection, personal esteem, self-respect and independence; group esteem needs for being a willing participant in a cohesive group; or self-realization needs for some form of personal fulfilment.[1]

When pushed to the ultimate, both social planners' and caseworkers' views of the agency role could lead to the view that they are able to change everything including larger social forces. This is open to the practical objection that we lack the capability for effective large-scale social engineering, though social systems technology offers some possibilities.

The assumption underlying casework-based views may be caricatured by saying that the healthy person is able to cope with everything. This is open to attack on the grounds that many social forces impinge too comprehensively and powerfully for normal individuals to master. Radicals argue that even if individuals did have more power, rebellion would be more appropriate and rational than adaptation to destructive forces.

Either way, both individual and social environment are constantly changing as a result of the other. There is a limit as to how much we can change by some kind of intervention. These two perspectives risk bifurcating the social services profession so that work with personal factors affecting individual and family functioning is viewed separately from attempts to alter social systems, structures, conditions and environments which constrain individual fulfilment. Evidence drawn from economics, sociology, psychology and cybernetics increasingly generates concern with the specific interplay to be found between objective community situations and the way people assess these subjectively.

On the basis of this argument, the central objective of the social services agency should be *to improve the match or the interaction between the individual client and his social environment.* Any behavioural or social change produces a rearrangement of the transactions between an individual and his social environments. If these transactions go awry, we talk of 'problem behaviour' or 'social anomalies' and say that only in these circumstances is intervention called for. This effectively delimits the field of intervention to the transactional system which is formed from the client-community interactions. Social services objectives thus become manageable, being focused on relieving troubles in person-to-community and community-to-person encounters.

Primary Mission

These considerations lead us to a formulation of the primary overall mission of social services agencies as: *to promote improved transactions between individuals and their social environment (or community) so that they match up better, thereby reducing the incidence and prevalence of social problems in the community.*

We might further define 'improvement' as promoting individual-community transactions as free from constraint as possible. Scarcely anybody wants individuals so fenced in by community demands that they cease to function as individuals, nor communities lacking any life-style of their own as a unity apart from the sum of separate individual pursuits. A conflict may occur between external social environment and subjective inner care of self. The task for the individual — and for the social worker in helping the individual — is to develop strategies for coping with such a conflict, often through some combination of more effective internalized procedures, a greater understanding of social expectations and a greater assertion and expression of self. Attitudes and beliefs are consequently formed which bridge the gap between the individual's psychological states and objects of orientation in the social environment.

The term *community or social environment* may be used to cover one or several of the following elements: immediate client family or intimate friends; client work colleagues; immediate client neighbours at block level; other relevant client reference groups; impinging institutions (e.g. Housing); wider networks of client relations and influences in the neighbourhood, or in relevant non-place communities; or some reference to habitat, cultural area or natural region.

A neighbourhood may be defined as a small inhabited area: as relations holding between inhabitants; or as qualities of their geographical and psychological propinquity to each other — a unit small enough to encourage 'neighbourhood spirit' while large enough to be relatively self-contained.

A community is the smallest group of people in a geographical terrain united by common bonds — of culture, of consciousness of territorial propinquity, and of face-to-face relations — so that its members have common interests of place. It is an aspect of the way people interact with each other beyond what is coerced, necessary, or functional. Beginning with the child's family experiences it extends outward to include peer groups, neighbourhood, congregations and nation, in some senses even the human race. For practical purposes such common bonds unite at least three neighbouring families (the lower limit formed by the Reindeer Chuckchee and other isolated communities) to perhaps 10,000 (the upper limit defined by some urban geographers).

There are implications for practice. Concerned as it is with interfaces between client and social environment, the primary focus of professional intervention becomes the *process* by which decisions are made and fruitful social relations established. Workers aim to create an accepting and facilitating social climate and to develop procedural means through which individuals are encouraged to think through their problems, taking viable decisions using their own skills and resources. Intervention is directed towards decisions themselves, rather than to specific, pre-conceived problem-resolutions, or to specific forms of relationship. This is implied in talk of 'non-directive therapy', of 'enabling', or of 'catalystic' functions. From this viewpoint, the social services are seen as main line services — the normal means by which individuals and communities fulfill their social needs.

The situation is reversed if workers take as their targets either specific client problems or specific community problems, rather than their interrelationship.

Consequential Mission

The overall mission then leads on to a consequential or subsidiary mission which may be stated thus: *To cope with, make good and remedy the social malconsequences of the malperformance of other community services* as provided by central and local government, industrial companies, voluntary agencies and indigenous community resources.

Where economic institutions fail to provide sufficiently varied and numerous jobs with sufficiently adequate and continuous income, social services provide work-relief, sheltered employment, secure income transfers, job retraining and rehabilitation. If family, neighbourhood and associational social institutions fail to provide material, mental, emotional, social and cultural supports, social services provide domiciliary, day and residential care of various kinds, fostering, adoption, and groupwork. If the child cannot benefit from educational services through parental illness or lack of clothing, social services supply home helps, visiting nurses, or arrange for adequate clothing. If a person cannot receive hospital treatment because their dependents would be unattended, temporary fostering or a neighbourhood mother may be provided by social services. If someone cannot participate in religious institutions, lacking money for appropriate burial, social services may arrange the burial.

In such ways social services not only remedy the failures and deficiencies of other services and institutions caused either through the ineffectiveness of the service or institution or the individual being unable to take advantage of what it offers, but they help the individual at those points where it would levy too great a personal or social cost for him to help himself. The recognized professions have developed too slowly on the social side. Suppose medicine were fully socialized. Would not medical men, institutes and organizations look after certain interests that the social worker must care for just because medical practice now falls short? Thus viewed, social work is an endeavour to supplement certain existing professions pending their completed development.

This objective implies the need for related services to be developed within social services departments. These take the form of:

Emergency Services
A set of immediate, first-aid, caretaker or emergency services are provided which people call on when other services break down. These

are exemplified by homeless family units as originally conceived, that is as temporary long-stops which are used when the housing provisions of the public or private sector fails to meet the housing needs of individuals or families. Such services account for the immediacy, urgency and pressure felt by many social services agencies in many of their cases. If the nature and effectiveness of emergency first-aid services are not to be lost — if for example, homeless family units are not to become simply sub-standard permanent housing — social services agencies must provide other services leading to the restitution of problematic client situations to more tolerable, adequate, and desirable levels. These will inevitably be more 'positive', 'aggressive', 'attacking' and 'preventive' in design, rather than simply acting as long-stops or fail-safe devices.

Intelligence Services

The second set of services may be called intelligence services. They consist of collating information on the current problem situations handled for presentation to other community agencies in order to articulate points at which these are failing. Their long-stop position enables social services agencies to gain insight into and to reveal accurate information at this level. Many clients arrive on the doorstep of the social services department because other community organizational resources have broken down. Social services cases may therefore be used as a barometer of other services' failures — a primary source for monitoring the effectiveness of these, and for local intelligence about all social resources of the community whether contained inside or outside the local authority.

This function consists of using intelligence gathered on problems and their dynamics to comment on the social consequences of plans formulated by other agencies — for example the social consequences of new motorways, urban redevelopment, new schemes for providing income transfers and for refuse collection, of new housing estates and new towns, etc. Such contributions typically take place through the Local Authority Chief Executive's Corporate Planning group, regional inter-organizational working parties, through evidence submitted to Government Commissions, and through inter-agency exchange procedures. Such contributions are based on an intimate knowledge of the casualties created by the existing policies, plans and methods used in other services.

Intelligence and monitoring services are themselves insufficient to fulfil this objective. There is nothing more stultifying than one group passing a continuous series of critical judgements on another. Were social services departments to have no other role than to communicate a continuous, well-evidenced, negative commentary on the non-beneficial consequences of other services like Muggeridge-style public service Cassandras, others would soon react negatively. This could result in other agencies creating and expending energy in elaborate defensive mechanisms vis-à-vis the social services. At its worst, this could include continual guerrilla action aimed at undermining the basis and reliability of evidence presented by social services agencies, excluding these departments from access to even the minimum amount of relevant information needed to carry out their basic emergency functions, or discrediting any agency efforts or successes which have made an impact on community social problems. An example of resistance to the use of social services intelligence was the refusal of some Housing Authorities to take seriously propositions by the social services on the cost-benefits of treating certain portions of housing services as genuinely *social* rather than as profit-making construction services. Another is the refusal of some medical authorities to transfer mental health cases or records to social services departments after Seebohmization.

Advocacy Services

Social services agencies have therefore to analyse and interpret accumulated intelligence in a manner leading to positive proposals and plans which are related to social problems. Intelligence services, no matter how well-based, may be inadequate to engender an effective impact on those community problems which hit social services agencies with the full cumulative emotional force which each enraged and embittered client brings forth.

Efforts must therefore be made to activate social planning proposals; to support these proposals with reasoned argument, evidence and sophisticated political vigour; to overcome such resistances from other agencies as are rooted in ignorance, inadequate information, stereotyped responses or inertia; and to generate changes in other agencies which reduce overall ineffectiveness. This is normally referred to as the 'advocacy' role.

Characteristically, advocacy services may result in temporary victories, in pious statements of missions by target agencies or even in statutes, as with Morris's Disabled Persons' Act,[2] without leading to any concrete change in the situation. Advocacy therefore needs to be carried further until the advocated and agreed changes are implemented.

Community Organization Services

Hence a fourth set of responses are required from social services which may be termed 'community organization or social planning'.

Social services agencies have a set of objectives which cannot be achieved given their available (or foreseeable) resources. To be effective, they have therefore to develop extensive inter-organizational relations with other agencies – Health, Probation, Supplementary Benefits,

Department of Employment, Housing services etc. — in order to realize these objectives.

Social Experimentation Services

No matter how well social services agencies develop inter-organizational exchange mechanisms, their influence on others is necessarily limited. Target agencies inevitably assign greater priority to objectives related to their own primary functions than to secondary objectives associated with their function as instruments for the fulfilment of social service objectives. Advocacy and exchange agreements with target agencies must be supplemented by social services taking more positive action of their own. This kind of social experimentation consists broadly of initiating, experimenting with and demonstrating methods, services and treatments which provide new, more effective responses to social problems which intelligence services have revealed as ineffectively provided for at present. If any of these social experiments prove fruitful, other agencies ought eventually to take them over.

In the British context, where service agencies are based on professional specialisms and statutory limitations, this kind of experimentation is difficult to mount. Its value has been well illustrated in the American situation where some voluntary agencies have demonstrated the benefits derived, for example, from hiring medical practitioners to pinpoint medical bases of social problems encountered. Currently, the field of homelessness provides a critical area for such experiments, though many social services agencies fight shy of such methods, fearing that the worst social problems of housing might fall forever into their lap.

Social Action Services

Even where effective, new responses occur in one problem area, the service provided may generate an unintentional geographical shift of the problem to other areas. Apparently effective community care programmes for the mentally ill in some areas may result in clients migrating to institutions in adjoining areas. Conversely, as one local authority opens new facilities for the homeless, it may find itself swamped with families from other areas where no such provisions exist. As the pool of problems grows too large for its new resources, so it begins to limit any further development of its services so that queues form. In this way, society's responses to problems may be reduced to mechanisms for shifting them on from locality to locality so that they are kept at arm's length and never fundamentally resolved. Political or social action which has not only local but also national ramifications may be required of social services agencies.

Interim Scenarios

Missions thus have implications for service development which we have briefly sketched above. These service developments constitute progressive, time-phased interim scenarios which illustrate how the overall requisite scenario at the level of banner goals might, stage by stage, be brought to fruition. Even if the logical and inevitable progress from emergency services, through the successive development of intelligence and monitoring, advocacy, community organization, and social experimentation services to social and political action is rejected, alternative service development plans are required.

4 Political Objectives

Is politics something more than the science of exigencies?
R. Churchill

Political Objectives

Banner goals and missions are in turn accomplished by certain political objectives.

Political objectives are intermediate abstractions.* They embrace decisions to change agency orientations by refocusing operations; are postulates or principles of sufficient generality to provide guidance on shaping, formulating and sharing objectives; and embody legitimate expectations of service. To define the aim is to welcome the idea. They are focal points for policy debates – the language used in agency controversies and planning negotiations. Their time-span for change often lasts the length of tenure of the agency's political leadership.

At one time, most public services had a five-year planning horizon corresponding to elections. Since governments, councils and boards now take decisions which commit organizations for longer time periods

---

* To the extent that all values and objectives chosen constitute political choices in the widest sense, it is difficult to define any one level of objectives as involving a specifically political choice. Conversely, politicians may campaign on behalf of virtually any level of objective, from the most general level of reasserting fundamental values such as increased freedom to highly specific levels as in community politics. However, there is evidently a level of abstraction beyond which general philosophical aims lie more or less beyond competing political views (e.g. 'life, liberty and happiness') and prior to which political choices of individual workers are more or less marginal, given the content of operation (e.g. how the social worker spends his time). For this purpose, it may be convenient at this level to talk of 'political objectives' when major choices must be made as between radical change ('reformist objectives'), social integration (c.f. 'one nation' and 'moderation' speeches of politicians) and greater administrative efficiency. This is not intended to imply any specific point at which politicians enter the debate over objectives, but rather to indicate major alternative directions in which political choices may move our emphasis or under-emphasis of objectives.

(albeit within the constraints of a pre-existing, inherited scenario), there are no longer adequate indicators of the time-span of a political objective. No one can say exactly what the state of affairs will look like if and when a political objective becomes reality.

The agency has to make a major choice between three main political objectives: change objectives aiming to meliorate harmful social conditions, integration objectives which aim to improve the morale and quality of community life, and service objectives which provide specific services to 'eligible' clientele.

Change or Reformist Objectives

Change objectives are specific, limited, circumscribed, concrete and action-oriented. They entail completing concrete tasks and resolving particularized problems of community functioning. The objective may be to change some aspect of social structure detrimental to the community (e.g. curbing discriminatory employment practices); to strengthen and rationalize existing services (e.g. coordination of community care provisions); or to establish new services (e.g. subsidizing community action). They embrace feeding the hungry, sheltering the homeless, treating the physically or mentally sick, changing noxious community practices or relationship patterns. Framed on the basis of predetermined, often largely unquestioned, values, they tend to produce statements of objective expressed in terms of 'meliorating certain harmful social conditions' or 'helping certain underprivileged groups in the community to organize themselves'. Typically, they characterize the role of advocacy agencies.

Integration Objectives

Integration objectives entail explorations to locate common values among relevant community groups which serve as a foundation for united action. Consequential activities have as much value in serving expressive needs as in achieving concrete results, as with many forms of consumer participation. They include creating a self-sustaining and self-propelling community planning system; stimulating interest and involvement in community affairs; fostering collaborative working relationships among community groups; generating widespread identification with the community and its values; locating and developing indigenous leaders; and reducing personal and community conflict. The emphasis is on the participants' experience in interacting with each other. The outcome is communal learning, current solutions and achievements of specific community problems being less important. Such objectives tend to be expressed in terms of 'improving the quality of life in a specific way' or 'bringing together a variety of heterogeneous and haphazard welfare schemes'. Typically, they define the role of the community settlement worker.

Change and Integration Objectives

The more change objectives are emphasized, the greater is the stress within the agency on consensus, legitimacy, the fusion of ends and means, and the avoidance of controversy – all that is understood by cooperative rationality. The more integration objectives are emphasized, the greater will be the stress within the agency on conflict, legitimacy for each specialized interest, autonomy for each sub-structure and the avoidance of choice – all that is understood by individual rationality.

A paradox thus arises. The more effectively the agency fosters social change, the more internal consensus on common, shared objectives is required from its staff. Conversely, when the agency pursues social integration, staff representing a wide diversity of community interests and values tend to be recruited, the agency being seen as a microcosm of the community it serves, and internal conflict inevitably ensues. To accomplish major changes successfully, all agency forces are directed to one common end. The less this is our aim, the greater the internal diversity tolerated. Arguments about whether the social services are 'acting as agents for social change' or 'propping up a mouldy society' are introduced at this point.

Change-oriented agencies often seek to achieve their objectives regardless of whether the people involved are consciously or vociferously demanding the particular changes at this point in time. They may view their primary task as being to stimulate need so that it gets embodied and articulated in the form of overt client demands. The degree to which agencies achieve their change objectives in the face of resistance becomes the barometer of how far community development is proceeding despite pressures from established interests in maintaining the status quo.

Meanwhile, integration-oriented agencies do not proceed with any course of action without first gaining positive client agreement and support, preferably acting only from explicit client initiatives. Their initial task is viewed as removing prior professional or ratepayer prejudices as to what shall be defined as need. 'Needs' are seen as the sum total of client demands. The degree to which agencies achieve consensus on objectives becomes the symbol of the integrated community values desired.

When agencies seek to achieve change, they may mount programmes to educate, indoctrinate, confront or mobilize actions against other institutions. Conversely, integration-oriented agencies explore the possibilities and limits of inter-organizational cooperation, compromising as necessary to achieve this.

Achievement values embodied in 'change' objectives and egalitarian values embodied in 'integration' objectives potentially conflict. In practice, most agencies do not pursue one political objective at the expense of the other, but work with complex operational objectives which include elements of both. Thus a community settlement may adopt Alinsky-style methods[1] in pursuing specific social changes, or a pressure group having a specific mission may broaden its base of appeal by recruiting advocates of causes only tenuously linked with its central endeavour, slowing down its action programme to secure agreement among hostile or indifferent community groups.

Service-Oriented Objectives

These contrast with objectives of those service-orientated agencies which are predetermined by eligibility requirements based on administrative precedent or statute. There are usually degrees of latitude in interpreting administrative precedents or statutory clauses in respect of individual cases, and there are always exceptions. Many agencies emphasizing eligibility, in practice come to operate more like agencies seeking to respond to client demands.

Each sub-unit of the service-oriented agency has virtually autonomous, parochial objectives which are rarely subsumed to any more general end. Objectives are incorrigibly plural and heterogeneous. The agency views its primary task as one of finding attractive schemes (or methods of advertisement) to bring to the agency door 'unmotivated' people who could use the service. Less ambitiously, it may attempt so to arrange things that agency efficiency is nowhere impaired, specifically reaching out to a highly selective clientele, selection taking place on a clientele, problem, geographical or socio-economic class basis.

Grand Strategies

These alternative political objectives imply one of three corresponding grand strategies which may be used to guide service development and delivery: an emergency strategy where severest social conditions have priority, a more attacking preventive strategy where conditions are promoted which might prevent social distress arising in the first place, and a development strategy which builds incrementally on existing services.

Emergency Strategy

The commonest strategy of agencies is to ensure the maintenance of basic subsistence: thus the material needs of those unable to maintain themselves (the socially disadvantaged, dependent, underprivileged) are met by providing selective concentrated services. This emergency strategy reflects the 'negative' or 'defensive' approach, manifesting itself in crisis intervention.

Objectives underlying the emergency strategy can be further specified, firstly at the level of the individual or family. Workers aim to help individuals or families with various problems to overcome or lessen these, particularly those in the last or final stages of dependence, disintegration or despair. At the community-wide level, agencies issue statements about encouraging development of community identity and ensuring more active and widespread community involvement in provisions for need and in mutual aid. Workers seek to intervene in personal, family, group or neighbourhood crises in such a way as to lessen and minimize suffering and distress, establish a new equilibrium as a basis for improvement, and restore those concerned to the point where they can again arrange their own affairs to their own satisfaction.

Developing this theme further, four objectives related to professional standards of performance were clearly stated in Seebohm:[2]

(i) To assess the extent of the problems and to lessen individual and family stress by assisting them to overcome a specific need, disability or misfortune, and to offer a supporting relationship when it is required to give people confidence to surmount difficulties.

(ii) To mobilize community resources, interests and activities, to meet need and to attain the maximum participation of individuals or groups in the community in planning, organization and provision of services.

(iii) To secure coordination and joint planning between statutory and voluntary organizations catering for any particular need, and to establish mutual critical interaction between local authority and voluntary agencies.

(iv) To provide technical and professional help, stimulation and grant aid to organizations able to assist in community work – i.e. to provide a community-based social service.

The Preventive Strategy

A second strategy is to help, to a specified extent, prevent social distress arising. It is a strategy reflecting the 'positive' or 'attacking' approach to social welfare and manifests itself in an early intervention in the chains of circumstances leading to deprivation and handicap.

Preventive strategies can be developed at individual levels: 'to give early and effective help to vulnerable individuals or families', and at community levels: 'to help promote conditions which lessen overall risks of social distress'.

Using the Seebohm conception[3] to spell out these objectives in terms of professional performance standards, we derive the following:

(i) To meet those needs at present neglected and to locate families who should normally be a special concern of the agency though they may not use our services at present.

(ii) To bring about necessary environmental changes and collaborate with other local authority departments in socially planning the community environment.

(iii) To ensure services are more accessible and comprehensive to those who need to use them and that everyone has ready access to sources of information about available services.

(iv) To develop services in ways relevant to changing patterns of community needs and conditions and to unite the efforts of people in particular neighbourhood communities with those of the authorities.

If social services are to remain viable as a profession, they must address themselves to the rapid social and economic changes which are overtaking us. This means either responding to these changes as they become manifest, or anticipating them and revamping operations accordingly. Neither approach is entirely without risk: responsiveness may come too late, when change is characterized by its rapidity and professional methods have become obsolescent. Anticipation may come too early and trends misinterpreted may lead to professional behaviour that is impractical, ineffective or inconsistent with actual needs as they unfold.

The Development Strategy

The development strategy is based on the assumption that in affluent communities at least, subsistence needs preoccupy people (even the 'disadvantaged') less than aspirational (non-material, psychological, cultural and interpersonal) needs.

This opens the possibility of revamped social services assisting enhanced social functioning and individual fulfilment throughout the total population − of spending more money and time helping people acquire additional skills and competencies to achieve an improved quality of life. The developmental strategy implies a systematic approach to expanding and reallocating services in response to changes in community needs.

We can take a firmer hold of this strategy in terms of the following objectives:

(i) To educate the community in the work of the agency and the social problems it is trying to handle;

(ii) To help cater for the aspirational needs of community members;

(iii) To cooperate with research and intelligence units in collecting information about services, communities and needs.

Each objective can be further delineated in respect of the five elements: standards of professional performance; level of service provision and financial performance; resource acquisition, development and utilization; control of overheads; and innovation.

5 Strategic Objectives

I. SOCIAL OBJECTIVES

If political objectives, as outlined in the previous chapter, are to have any operational meaning and import, we must further define what phenomena social service agencies handle – what is meant by 'social needs'. What are these needs, what sort of impact do we wish to make on them and what are working agency objectives in relation to them? Answers to such questions are embodied in strategic social objectives which are the effectiveness areas defined within the social system. They do not require any fundamental redefinition of the system itself. Effectiveness areas are those areas of operation or activity in which the agency might make the optimal, feasible impact on its community in terms of needs and demands met. Within each effectiveness area, we may define specific time-bounded targets or results which signal whether such an impact has been made.

Strategic objectives are varied and complex intentions which have been identified, examined and adopted as a result of analytic planning processes. They commonly take the form of conditions of intervention, constituting the organizational link between values and action, between plans and their implementation, thus enabling practitioners to take a purposeful stand on problems and changes once regarded as adventitious.

Working principles of the social services are essentially those of the democratic state. Therefore, strategic objectives of social services departments when broadly stated cover the whole of a local authority's operational activities. Moreover, treatment and intervention methods rely on the existence of natural recuperative social processes – those of the individual, the family and the community – in the same way as medical treatment relies on the body's recuperative powers. Thus, an overriding objective of treatment must be to stimulate, quicken and augment processes which naturally characterize problem change. Objectives of social treatments, provisions, programmes and services will be identical to those of the fulfilled individual living happily in an effective social community. For these reasons, few professions serve objects with such breadth and temporal length. The problem is to operationalize them in respect of services that agencies might provide.

Social services increasingly assume supportive roles previously carried by such social institutions as kinship systems, the family, neighbourhood, friendship systems, and social community, given the continuing demise of these. This is seen most clearly in residential institutions which constitute a home as well as a work locale for clients and workers alike. However, similar considerations hold for fieldworkers, domiciliary and day care workers, where though the client's physical dwelling may not be run by the agency, the client requires agency help in fulfilling certain of his crucial functions within it, from rent-paying to social contacts. For many social services workers, formalized executive relations are inappropriate since their clientele regard them as substitute family or friends, and the agency as a substitute community. Work relations in such agencies may come to seem more like friendship and the family linkages of private life and leisure than executive business-style relations. In such conditions, the objectives of social services agencies must relate not only to the efficiency of service delivery but to social life itself.

Previous Social Objectives Schemes

Countless attempts have been made in many areas of research and theory to derive schemata of social objectives, most being remarkably similar and also lacking operational specifications. Some examples of such schemata are outlined below.

Experimental studies in human needs are one source, the 1940s studies of the Harvard Psychological Clinic constituting a standard reference.[1] Social planners like R. Mayer,[2] D. Gill,[3] and R. Warren[4] have analyzed social objectives in terms of basic functions of social systems; provision for physiological needs, nurture, care of the sick and dependent, production-distribution-consumption of services, protection or social control, socialization, social participation and mutual support. Management consultants and operations researchers in the social services field have sometimes endeavoured to define service output objectives, one of the most neglected but fruitful attempts being that developed under the Pittsburg Values Study of the Health and Welfare Council.[5] Here the main objectives were defined as assurance of minimum necessities for daily living, maintenance of physical and mental health, improvement of social relations and responsibility, enrichment of life and enjoyment of leisure. Most British consultants to the social services like McKinsey, P.A. and Booz Allen have focused on tactical service objectives.

Axiologists or value cartographers such as Hartmann,[6] Brentano,[7] Meinong[8] and Findlay[9] take a somewhat different starting point, endeavouring to educe social objectives from a consideration of basic human values which seem to repeat themselves through all communities. However, the end result correlates highly with earlier examples derived from other fields, the objectives being defined as: freedom from constraint, control of external circumstances, impartiality in the treatment of others, lack of bias, self-actualization, happiness, autonomy, commitment, consciousness, independence, equality, justice, individualism, rationality, satisfaction, self-determination, valuation, strength and selfhood.

Many historians of philosophy, ethics and political science, have produced similar inventories of social objectives when summarizing the work of various schools of social philosophy. Thus, from a study of social ethics, Downie[10] explored such values as equality, freedom from constraint, fraternity, respect for persons, respect for rights, responsibility, objectivity, and consequential roles deriving from adherence to such values. These schemata are very similar to those of policy scientists like Lasswell,[11] Brecht[12] and Friedman.[13]

Other schemata derive from casework theory and practice, a notable recent example being that developed by Reid and Epstein[14] where the key targets were interpersonal conflict, dissatisfaction in social relations, relations with formal organizations, role performance, social transition, reactive emotional distress and inadequate resources. Whilst this schema is helpful for many purposes, each classification potentially embraces too many disparate elements for detailed analysis and targeting. Thus interpersonal conflict may result in emotional, mental or physical distress, or may be caused by deviance from group norms, regression, value conflicts, social incompetence, etc.

Anthropologists studying comparative cultural values as revealed in myth and ritual — like Von Mering,[15] Spencer[16] and Kluckhohn[17] — similarly provide a fertile source for recurring human values. Inter-Nordic[18] comparative studies of living conditions and social needs provide a further range of objectives from a community development standpoint.

A further source of social objectives are cyberneticians' simulation models of human personality like those of Blum,[19] Hunt and Hovland,[20] Rosenblatt,[21] Uhr and Vossler,[22] the Gullaborns,[23] Colby, Watt and Gilbert.[24] Of particular interest is the Loehlin model[25] in that it was built on the Harvard Psychological Clinic experiments.[26]

Some attempts have been made, for example by Rescher at the Rand Corporation,[27] to derive a register of social objectives on the basis of social survey questionnaires to citizens linked to consideration of societal values of the future. This work is closely akin to that of value-impact forecasters like Hazard[28] and Baier[29]. A further variant of the social survey method has been the development of value tests like that of Allport-Vernon-Lindsey,[30] from whose social value scales many of the value impact forecasters derived definitions of values.

Lastly, we may mention the analogous schemata of values derived by H. Hyman[31] in his study of value systems of different classes, S.M. Lipset[32] in his study of democratic values, and E. Spranger[33] in his assessment of values deriving from basic human motives.

Social Objectives Enumerated in this Volume

Derivation of Objectives

While heavily value-oriented and quite explicit about the values in their ethics of practice, social workers have rarely in the past stated what they want for people beyond such things as improving morale, satisfying needs and the fulfilment of rights. The objectives outlined on pp.79–176 are based on central values and beliefs which appear to be held by social services personnel and their theorists and which influence or condition their work. They were derived from the analysis and comparison of statements of the departmental, divisional, sectional and case targets of diverse practitioners from many parts of the U.K.

A remarkable uniformity in values was evident. In one form or another, similar objectives are alluded to again and again by practitioners and trainers in justification of various social work activities. They appear to be central to social service accounts of the individual, the community and their interrelationship.

They require further substantiation, elucidation (or alternatively, disproof) through research. They are also of interest in that they permeate writings of sociologists, psychologists and policy-analysts, and the conceptual framework within which social services personnel operate. They may not even be capable of reformulation in a form which admits of scientific evaluation. If this is so, then their usefulness lies in marking out some of those values which have an influence on practical action which it would be inappropriate to endeavour to prove or disprove. Thus, though this schema is the outcome of extensive investigation, it can only be regarded as a rough preliminary plan to guide the perception, interpretation and development of action programmes.

Abstraction and Specificity

However abstract these classifications may be, they are at a level of generality which is constantly referred to in discussing action and practice. Latent in conceptual systems and policies of all known political, economic, sociological or psychologically oriented institutions are categories of equal or greater abstraction. If social plans are to be formulated, it must be possible to operate smoothly with such conceptualizations. It is equally important to connect general categories of reference both to the policy process and to actual practice by systematic principles of procedure.

In starting to question these strategic social objectives, by asking, for example, why pursue one rather than another, we find we can only debate their justification or otherwise in terms of the higher-order language of political, social and ethical philosophy. For weights to be attached, various values must be reviewed as well as their precise meaning and implication. Higher-level objectives are so generally accepted, that from an action standpoint few ethical issues are raised.

Although probably unavoidable even for practitioners, the debate is likely to prove too abstract to be of practical relevance for many oriented to action. But once questions arise as to how we might practically implement strategic objectives, the debate moves down to the lower-order language of practical action and is conducted in terms of available resources. These more specific strategic objectives, taken separately, give rise to some of the major ethical dilemmas facing practitioners.

The central task of corporate management and social planning is perhaps to find some coherent, consistent and agreed match between these two levels of thought and action. When people attempt to describe how values and action, social policy and practice, objectives and operations interact, they come under attack from two quarters simultaneously: from social policy-makers, theoreticians, philosophers and politicians on the grounds that we need more sophisticated concepts; and from practitioners protesting that the objectives as stated are too conceptual to be operationally tested.

Problems of Classifying Objectives

Some theorists would counsel practitioners not to expect too much from the everyday terms used to indicate certain states of affairs. They have evolved from circumstances which emphasize typical cases and have often not been tested under conditions which demand precise definition.

Even comparatively well-marked states of affairs like frustration, cannot be reduced to a single class of responses or attributed to a single set of activities. They take as many different forms as there are differences in circumstances. Take isolation, for example. The newly widowed may be profoundly isolated through the death of husbands. The isolation of amiable extroverts finding themselves among strangers for the first time is of a different quality, while the rejected child's isolation is different again.

Practitioners working with these problems realize only too well that within any one objective is to be found a vast heterogeneous population, a diverse range of different clients and symptoms, different service and treatment methods being appropriate for each. For example, under the objective of promotion of growth, development and social learning would be included the mentally retarded child, the wife whose marital problems emerge as the result of unresolved early childhood problems in relating to her father, and depressed city enclaves subject to urban renewal programmes. One-to-one educational therapy and remediation programmes, community development programmes, and a reflective consideration of developmental factors in the casework situation are set side by side. Yet regression may underlie and manifest itself in a wide range of differing problem situations. Techniques developed to cope with more pathological forms of regression may be transferred in modified form to less severe situations. A lesser, narrower behavioural fragment may be a trait indicator for a wider piece of behaviour.

The same final state may be reached from different initial conditions and in different ways. There is a wide and varied number of alternative combinations of habits, of mind, feelings, of lines of behaviour and action which can be put together to achieve the desired outcomes. Several different inputs or operations may be functionally equivalent to the extent that resultant outcomes are equivalent. The same considerations apply to traditional classifications of objective by clientele. The 'physically handicapped' for example, may comprise a vast range of diverse disabilities entailing widely different problems. Among these, those with sensory handicaps may be recognizable as a medically diagnosed group. Yet two partially hearing people of the same age with identical audiograms and I.Q.s. may be at quite different levels of language development, responding quite differently to the same treatment. Individual case targets can only be set by more intensive assessment, by diagnosticians willing to view each client as unique, avoiding stereotypes of thought and being prepared to find things which differ radically from the expected.

Though these objectives overlap, no two are exactly alike. Each contains something uniquely different from the others. For example, reducing some of the ill-effects of physical incapacity might eliminate some economic wants where the person concerned is unable to support himself because of these effects. Yet even if all social disbenefits of physical ill-health disappeared, economic want would not disappear entirely in consequence.

Previous Classifications

Mention may be made of the affinity of the classifications in this volume with the work of axiologists (Hartmann,[34] Findlay,[35] von Mering),[36] social survey researchers (Rescher,[37] Powelson),[38] value impact forecasters (Hazard,[39] Baier[40]), social casework theorists (Reid and Epstein,[41] Stein,[42] Perlman,[43] Specht and Gilbert)[44], policy scientists (Lasswell,[45] Friedman[46]), educational theorists (Goldstein),[47] political scientists (Brecht).[48]

Professional Objectives

In setting policies by which professional action is guided, the same process of professional theory development applies. Unless social services objectives align (at some level of generality) with the classifications used in professional psycho-social studies they will form administrative superstructures overlaid on professional work, unrelated to the substantial content of daily activities.

Complexity of Objectives

The social services endeavour to make some impact on personality, community and their interaction. Since personality and community are outcomes of numerous interacting forces — now one and now another assuming primary significance — it is impossible and unrealistic to denominate any one of these factors as forming the basis for a unified, single objective for the work of social services agencies.

Workers handle mixed and complex states of affairs such as often characterize multiple-problem families, or may deal with subtle states of affairs which tend to characterize the problems of highly educated clients. Practitioners cannot afford to think in terms of a single aetiology or explanation when most problem situations comprise multiple factors. In most cases, therefore, a mix of strategic objectives operates and to fulfil an objective in one area, practitioners will often have first (or simultaneously) to achieve an objective in another. For example, a wife may ask for help with a financial problem; the practitioner asks what her husband feels about the matter only to find she dare not tell him, and the issue of marital relations thus arises.

The same operations may help to achieve two or more strategic objectives simultaneously. Thus psychodynamic-based caseworkers have argued that improvements achieved in client relationships are likely to achieve all the objectives listed, and many community workers attribute multiple results to effective community development.

Policy-making

There is probably no known life problem which has not been brought to social services workers: problems of how to survive physically and emotionally and of wanting to die, of wanting children and wanting to get rid of children, of loving and of being unloved, of being afraid, and so on. In controlling agency operations as a whole, in allocating resources for coming years, in assessing whether to develop in other directions, managers cannot exhaustively take account of all variables considered by field or residential workers in their daily dealings with each client. Policy-making is a matter of putting together what belongs together, though in applications to each specific case, workers must necessarily apply more specific considerations being cognizant of more variables than any policy schema ever comprehends in detail.

Policy-making, planning and management must have at least as much variety as the many and varied situations decision-makers seek to control, but if an attempt is made to work with each problem situation in turn at the policy level the task proves hopelessly big. Even if this were feasible, policy-makers should need to consider all situations simultaneously — and this is impossible, since human brains only retain five (at most seven) 'bits' of information at any one time.[49] Grouping client problems and agency activities in response to them is thus the basis of policy-making.

It should be emphasized that the system of grouping together as one category, the many different forms in which states of affairs manifest themselves (e.g. 'dependency') and describing a host of behavioural changes under one classification is a misleading over-simplification if wrongly used. It would be a misleading procedure if the professional fieldworkers were to deal exclusively in these gross, large terms in handling individual client situations for lack of any further refinement or sophistication of concept. The dangers thus lie in using over-simplified assumptions for treatment, not in the activity of classifying itself.

The professional basis of justification for this approach is that specific and unique *outcomes* of psychological processes which vary from individual to individual, seem to co-exist with a generality in the character of these processes. Having averaged out common results over groups of cases and filling in the blanks with informed judgements, we can then pinpoint the truly exceptional, precedent-setting cases. If we are unable to do this, agency policy would be impossible to formulate in any meaningful way. Each case would have to be decided on its own merits by top agency management: each would constitute policy.

Strategic objectives must remain the focus to which resources and operations are directed, otherwise success on individual case targets, which constitutes only partial success in the total context, may be over-valued. Failure to achieve sub-objectives may be met by re-defining action programmes with higher-level ends in view.

Dynamic Nature of Objectives

Even as investigations begin to generate insight into the total system, the overall situation surreptitiously (sometimes dramatically) changes. For no person can achieve complete individualization, emotional fulfilment, awareness, rational behaviour, etc. and as life processes do not reach static conditions there is no finality in the conditions leading to the objective. Individuals and social environments constantly change. Moreover, no list of social objectives can be formulated for all times and places. For example, medieval man was (according to Burckhardt)[50] and modern Chinese man is (according to Croft)[51] unable to experience the need to be or be regarded as an individual, so the objective of individualization or self-realization would not apply.

These objectives represent interactions, as is common to all events relevant to social processes. Thus for the client to attain awareness of his situation or himself the worker may have to supply him with knowledge of the social, psychological and natural context and his understanding of this knowledge, and for the client to function more effectively physically, the worker may have to assist, or get others to assist him in attaining physical health, comforts, safety, etc. and gain client acceptance of this assistance.

Content of Objectives
Firstly each objective is based on a psycho-social variable on which the social services agencies seek to make some impact, the variable itself denoting a syndrome into which a great number of behavioural patterns can be placed. Secondly, all the objectives refer both to a social state workers seek in some way to promote or to its converse which they wish by some means to limit, as well as to the malaise or benefit which results from such a state. Finally, each refers to the processes through which some sort of social change is accomplished and the resultant states of that process in the social system.

These resultant states are described in all social services fields, being used at various levels of analysis and attached to various phenomena. Sometimes they refer to the individual's subjective conscious feelings; sometimes to their objective manifestations in behavioural patterns, consistencies and broad response predispositions; sometimes to necessary elements of the social structure; and sometimes to values which might desirably be realized in action. Each has a structural base in the objective conditions as well as psychic consequences in terms of the individual's awareness.

The concepts they embody are not simple: they have often defied specific definition, are two-edged and can disintegrate as well as unify.

Levels of Application: Individual, Group and Community
Each objective can refer to changes in individual behaviour, thus having psychological implications, or to changes in collective group behaviour, having sociological implications. By collective behaviour we refer to the process of inter-stimulation in groups whereby common impulses and moods are aroused, spread, organized and mobilized on specific objects of action which tie the group together. Each individual member of the group is influenced by as well as influencing such collective moods.

Moreover, each objective is stated in such a form that it may be applied in such different contexts as intra-psychic, person-to-person relations, person-to-group relations, group-to-group relations and community-wide interconnections as expressed in terms of social factors. For example, there can be no clear distinction between individual and social adjustment. Facets of personality and individual need are related to societal sectors or levels of need.

Strategic objectives may be described as universal in that they characterize both macro (community) and micro (individual) levels. Even social interaction is often used by social scientists to denote the self as socially interacting with itself. 'A single individual in a room working at a problem, talking to himself, thinking out loud, is technically regarded as engaged in interaction. In so far as the interaction is with the self — a social object — the actor is engaging in social interaction.' (R. Bales).[52]

That these objectives apply at both individual and community levels of intervention is justified by the continuity of biological and social bonds. This is shown for instance in the way the child's initial specific dependence on the mother gives way to dependence on his extending social environment as he matures.

Ends and Means

Within this schema of strategic objectives, it remains an open question as to whether some (e.g. awareness) are simple means to attaining others (e.g. social integration), rather than ends-in-themselves.

Many therapists set limits on the objective of promoting client awareness. Awareness has been shown not to be an essential pre-condition for personality or behaviour modification. Awareness of the circumstances producing and accompanying symptoms does not automatically achieve their removal. Moreover, awareness achieved by clients varies according to the therapist's theoretical orientation as demonstrated by Marmor.[53] By this evidence, awareness should be a subsidiary objective, contributive to behavioural changes in directions suggested by other objectives, but not always indispensable to it. Awareness does seem to be an essential precondition for engineering changes in overt, public policies which shape our social environment. Citizens unaware of public policies and their effects cannot question them. This view would place awareness as a sub-objective of environmental modification. Many argue strongly that awareness is intrinsically desirable, whether or not it contributes to resolving problems. They would certainly not wish to place awareness as secondary to various attempts at behavioural modification. The factors are interrelated and cannot be distinguished as either cause or effect of one another, other than with reference to the specific situation. Similarly, self-determination is valuable not only in itself, but also as the necessary condition of other objectives — for without self-determined choice, there is no valuation.

.

Positive and Negative Poles

Objectives may each be defined in positive or negative terms, the negative state evidently being the converse of the positive.

Where negative forms of goal statement are preferred, social services agencies are seen as the community's fail-safe mechanism, mopping up problems which are fall-out from other areas of social initiative and endeavour, or delimiting the ill-effects of others' initiatives. We seek by means of social services to avoid or *reduce* various undesirable states of affairs, ill-effects, disvalues, side-effects, negative concomitants, decrements, penalties or disbenefits such as income insufficiency, child neglect and abuse, poor health and education, substandard housing, delinquency. Stated in negative form, an objective is designed to act as a negative or aversive reinforcer or stimulus so that staff shun the situation to be avoided, or direct efforts at preventing it from occurring. Negative objectives are essential to evaluation, for obtaining negative feedback, and taking corrective action.

Negative, ameliorative objectives primarily relate to treatment at the individual level. Workers may concentrate on using client interviews or the client's life situation to achieve counter-conditioning effects: the equivalent of what behaviourists call systematic desensitization or extinction.

Where objectives are expressed affirmatively in terms of *promoting* a certain quality or realization of a certain value, we think of social planning agencies as taking positive initiatives to help create what are conceived of as desirable communities. The positive aspect consists of a comprehensive system of social objectives and policies, which through their combined effects, shape the overall quality of community life, the living conditions of members, human relations to one another and to the community as a whole. Positive objectives refer to a desired result, outcome, output or state of affairs which is sought; some value workers aim to realize or embody; some benefit to be achieved or need to be met. Stated in positive form, the objective is designed to act as a positive reinforcer or stimulus, attracting staff efforts towards it. Positive objectives are essential to staff and consumer motivation — they switch on the optimist's green light.

Promotional objectives chiefly concern preventive action at community level. Workers may strengthen specific behaviour, perhaps through equivalents of what behaviourists call operant conditioning or by conscious selection of more appropriate responses which clients are prompted to perform in real life.

The very conflict between these approaches may provide the key to defining social service objectives. Workers wish to promote certain desirable future situations in respect of individuals, groups and communities. How far this is done is limited by the potentially conflicting objective of promoting and maintaining client self-determination. Workers wish to reduce constraints under which individuals, groups and communities operate so as to enlarge their freedom to pursue diversified and varied pursuits. The process is an enabling one — one feature within the community is usually only promoted by limiting and reducing constraints and obstacles which hinder the realization of other features. Social services are established as a result of disparities in the degrees to which individuals, groups and communities enjoy these social values.

The promotion of desired conditions should be included in any treatment plan along with a reduction of problematic conditions. This prevents one problem being replaced by others, as well as mitigating any adverse emotional reactions to the behavioural or structural change. As behaviourists have demonstrated, the use of positive reinforcers is usually more effective than the exclusive use of negative reinforcers.

Let us look, for example, at the dependency-independency scale. It is a scale with degrees: we are all both dependent on and independent of each other. All are dependent during major significant periods — childhood, schooling, illness, old age, pregnancy, childbirth and rearing. It would be pointless therefore to dichotomize givers and receivers, those taking more from the economy than they put in and those who pay the difference, those wealthy enough to contribute more than they receive and the 'improvident poor'.

Relativity of Objectives

Strategic objectives embody loose concepts, well understood and applied in practice over a wide area of human behaviour, but neither uniform nor well-bounded. For example, in some circumstances it is difficult to see the distinction between alienation, depersonalization, anomie, and mental or physical instability, since all five states tend to merge; or a client may have an assured income whilst feeling financially insecure, or feel secure about his physical needs though continuously on social security, and so on. Most behaviour could ultimately become anti-social or disfunctional just as most could also be beneficial, depending on the frames of reference.

The concept of 'normal' in relation to each state also varies with our degree of knowledge, changing community standards, statistical distribution of various factors over a given community population, or changing capacities to make some impact on the social state concerned. Eczema and dermatitis, once not regarded as illnesses, are now given hospital treatment; tuberculosis was once a 'norm' in certain working-class communities — bronchitis still is.

Positive sociological terms cause grave problems if used normatively. Social integration is classified as pathological for those compulsively submissive to external demands, or as a more ideal state in the context of effective therapy groups. We need some basis in practice situations for distinguishing ups and downs, better from poorer human conditions.

No objectives, however formulated, can mark any absolute values from which to judge social processes, nor are they necessarily peculiar to any particular person or group. Potentially, an analysis of objectives can be conducted openly. Value-commitments of the group under study can be built on while disregarding particularist, parochial, tribalistic limits within which the group expresses them. No absolute definition of justice is needed. The common societal concept of justice may be induced from assumptions underlying the definition used by various communities and groups, from Powellite segregationists through WASP liberals to Black Power activists, stripping the concept of any peculiar limitation to whites, to Anglo-Saxons or middle classes. Universalizing the values held by the subjects of study provides a starting point for a critical social science.

Local Application

Associated with each objective is both a time baseline from which the socio-psychological process alluded to by the objective begins, and some existing community situation. In each individual case, it is desirable to define the specific threshold of the state referred to in the objective (e.g. dependency) beyond which its promotion, and below which its reduction, become non-productive. These thresholds define the upper and lower limits of viable intervention. Thus against each objective as stated in general form, the clause may be appended 'to the extent that this is functionally beneficial to the individual and his community'.

Each objective, therefore, applies differentially to specific local community situations with reference to specific agency service developments. Local application requires that one group or one individual be taken as the point of reference (e.g. in uni-directional community action this would be the group with power; in one-to-one casework, one member of the family).

II. ENUMERATING STRATEGIC OBJECTIVES

The objectives in the following inventory are stated in both positive and negative form. They are envisaged in terms of helping (a) to reduce individuals' (or families') incapacities to cope with their social environment (or promote capacities to cope); (b) to reduce growth-inhibiting elements in the individual's social environment (or improve growth-inducing elements); (c) to reduce the mismatch between individuals and their social environment (or promote a better match); and (d) to reduce obstacles to the fulfilment of agency objectives through appropriate interventions.

Under the first group are included such incapacitating behaviour as physical malfunctioning, mental instability and breakdown, emotional stress, depersonalization, insentience, anomie, dependency, inarticulateness and regression. The second group comprises such growth-inhibiting elements as insecurity, economic poverty, effects of breakdown, debilitative social environment, inequality, stigmatization and socio-cultural deprivation. Social phenomena like social malfunctioning, occupational ineffectuality, alienation, deviance and ennui comprise the third group. Whilst in group four, obstacles to the melioration of these social problems such as overall client-community ineffectiveness, the application of market criteria, agency and staff stagnation and agency ineffectiveness are dealt with.

Relation to clientele

Each objective relates to the needs and problems of some or all of the following clientele: infants, juniors, young people, parents (including unsupported parents); the elderly (and widows); the physically ill and handicapped (including the blind, deaf and dumb); the mentally ill and handicapped; the homeless; the unemployed; addicts and legal offenders.

Levels

They may be applied at the following levels: individual (such as client, claimant, patient, probationer, or resident); primary reference groups (such as client family or residential sub-group); secondary reference groups (such as friends and acquaintances; and block, neighbourhood, institutional, national and wider non-place community networks).

The number of possible sets of intra-societal relationships involved fall within the following reciprocal types: individual − individual; individual − group; individual − community; group − group; group − community. By 'group' we refer to those social aggregates below a total community level such as families, local firms, voluntary associations, neighbourhoods, unions or political parties.

Locations

The objectives relate to social work performed in all its various locations, that is private, individual home settings, social services offices, residential homes settings, day centres and clubs, hospitals, schools, child guidance and child welfare clinics, and industrial welfare settings.

Opposing objectives

Some social services practitioners quite baldly advocate opposing objectives to these. Some examples follow: Let us:

    (i) Recognize that certain conditions are irredeemable and that since we have no effective remedy for them, forego hopeless attempts to handle them through social services.

    (ii) Standardize provisions and levels of service across client groups and across areas.

(iii) Recognize different socio-cultural standards among people and thence the separation which follows from this.

(iv) Foster responsibilities of those in positions of power and authority to provide and plan for the less fortunate.

(v) Simply provide statutorily mandated services to those who ask for them without seeking to estimate the social effects which will inevitably be difficult if not impossible to pin down.

(vi) Reduce indulgent ego-centred self-expression leading to egocentricity.

(vii) Promote people's acceptance of their own limitations and reduce the illusion of continual growth which if propagated, may lead to frustration.

(viii) Help people to become more adaptive to their situations.

(ix) Rely where possible on market mechanisms with minimum interference in these.

(x) Recognize that there are certain unacceptable forms of gratification whose mere presence is an offence to many community members.

(xi) Evaluate effectiveness of services by how far they increase productive contributions of individuals to the community.

A. To promote individuals' (or families') capacities to cope with their social environment
To reduce individuals' (or families') incapacities to cope with their social environment

Practitioners work directly with the individual person (or family) towards fuller participation in his social world via some form of personality adjustment or modification of problem behaviour, which will better help him cope with personal stress, thus eliminating maladaptive, disfunctional responses.

Many social service activities focus on relieving the personal distress of individual or family, variables within the social environment being assumed to be constant in respect of the specific intervention. The focus is on the autonomous individual as the locus of behavioural uniformities and discontinuities, and on clients as a group with vested interests. The pre-eminent objective of the individual is to satisfy his drives, needs, instincts and impulses.

This range of objectives may be stated in these general forms:

1. To promote each individual's well-being.
2. To meet the human and social needs of individual citizens.
3. To improve and maintain the individual's coping behaviours, variously referred to as life styles, adaptive mechanisms or adjustive patterns.

4. To help clients neogitate reality more efficiently and effectively; to improve the individual's behaviour in so far as it is consciously directed to his environment; to increase the individual's broad repertoire of behaviour and resources.
5. To remedy disfunctions and behavioural irregularities of individual members (and perhaps their families) which cause disfunctions in the community system to which they belong.
6. To define, preserve or develop behaviour which oppressive community forces have distorted, tabooed or arrested.
7. To return the individual to full status in society and his community.
8. To develop and maintain the family or appropriate family substitutes as the centre of emotional release, understanding, mutual support of members: an emotional depot from which individual members sally forth to cope with the external environment. (Families sometimes stick together at too destructive a cost to one or more members, and they take varied forms.)

To some degree in all situations clients improve by changing themselves rather than being changed by agency interventions. This factor modifies the interpretations of each objective.

These objectives tend to centre on the ethic of gratification, the claiming of individual rights and spontaneity. The social sentiments which cement communities are thought to be love and fraternity.

1. Promote Physical Well-Being and Fulfilment of Physical Needs Reduce Effects of Physical Malfunctioning or Breakdown

'If anything is sacred the human body is sacred'
Whitman

POSITIVE AND NEGATIVE POLES
Workers aim to maintain and improve individuals' physical well-being, not merely the absence of disease or infirmity. Well-being embraces some sort of internal bodily equipoise, physical maintenance, body utilization, physically visible manifestations of personality, and some kind of adaptation to environment. The objective relates to the physical virtues of strength, dexterity, endurance, cleanliness, even presentable appearance, looks, dress, and to materialistic values of comforts, amenities and conveniences. *They seek to promote those conveniences and amenities of living which release people from drudgery.*

Workers aim to reduce and make good inconveniences and social disbenefits of physical impairment, deficiency, and disturbances of function by reducing incapacity for physical self-care, physical pain and discomfort, and associated subjective feelings. Indirectly, they help to reduce morbidity, the incidence of illness and disability in the community.

CLIENTELE

Workers are concerned with problems of social functioning as a result of physically disabling conditions. These cover temporary conditions (demarcating the 'ill' from the healthy), the constitutionally delicate, and those involving more permanent defects (demarcating the 'disabled' from the 'fit'). They include states of gross physical defectiveness present since birth, and more minimal departures from average function. They range from partial sight and mild heart conditions through hemiplegia to progressive, terminal illnesses resulting in chronic incapacity demanding maximum physical care. They include perceptual and motor impairments, neurological deficits, sensory defects, metabolic disfunctions, speech disorders, limb deficiency, poliomyelitis, muscular, orthopaedic, auditory and visual deficiency, spina bifida, hydrocephalus and multiple handicaps.

INDIVIDUAL SERVICES

Services directly contributing to this objective include aids to daily living and home adaptations; supportive care arranged around physical health treatment programmes; support and guidance for clients and relatives in cases of terminal or traumatic illness; client referral and advocacy with medical specialists to safeguard access to treatment; nutritional and genetic counselling; meals-on-wheels to maintain nutritional levels; specialized workshops and residential care provisions; sentinel systems to avoid physical catastrophe as in hypothermia cases; and helping clients to use physical conveniences, amenities, household gadgets and appliances.

In casework, workers seek to influence clients to take medical treatment they need but resist. Preventively, they may forward this objective by detecting pathological changes present in the body before discomfort or functional disturbances prompt consultation with doctors. Workers' scope in this area is evidenced by the amount of untreated defects — squints, respiratory infections, epilepsy, deafness, etc. — common among school entrants in poor neighbourhoods which often remain untreated even after diagnosis at school medicals.

In the residential situation, this objective is being fulfilled if residents have regular medical check-ups. Hygiene standards are high. A rapid response is made to acute and obvious symptoms (e.g. strokes, vomiting, diarrhoea, depression). Continuous surveillance is maintained in respect of chronic or long-standing illness. Though residents have a choice of doctor, one G.P. is assigned to the Residential Home on a permanent contract so that there is continuity of medical advice.

COMMUNITY SERVICES

At wider levels, this objective embraces programmes which render technological advances available to the poor and disadvantaged. This may take many forms, from the application to welfare operations of systems technology developed under space programmes to the provision of television sets for those deprived of any recreational enjoyment. The tramp outside the Salvation Army hostel shaving with a battery-operated electric shaver, or the use of the coil by a mother who would otherwise bear a family of ten, are poignant examples. Services are required which increase the spread of benefits derived from technology to individuals throughout the community where before they were predominantly beneficial to collectivities (e.g. companies) or the already prosperous.

With 70 per cent of the nation's work force involved in producing amenities to make life pleasant rather than producing necessities to make life liveable, amenity resources are highly developed. This is important in that amenities of living are potentially more useful to the disadvantaged than to the competent. If people are taught to use them properly, supermarkets and refrigerators revolutionize the lives of inadequate families, for since they can bulk-buy food on pay day and store it, apportionment of income on nourishment is guaranteed throughout the week. In contrast, more sophisticated families, even if deprived of these resources and in straightened financial circumstances, so budget as to ensure well-appointed nourishment through the week.

SPECIFIC TARGETS

Specimen case targets falling under this objective include:

   (i) To improve access to medical care facilities for clients.
  (ii) To refer through for medical diagnosis all appropriate cases.
 (iii) To ensure nutritional needs are met through a varied diet.
  (iv) To provide clients with the physical amenities and conveniences they need.
   (v) To foster each client's capacity to cope with his specific physical handicap.
  (vi) To develop client's physical mobility to its fullest capacity.
 (vii) To ensure adequate continuity of medical care.
(viii) To help clients take full advantage of technological advances, including aids to daily living.
  (ix) To alleviate fears of forthcoming medical treatment.
   (x) To reduce limitations of physical deficiencies by increasing the range of activities undertaken to the fullest feasible extent and arranging appropriate compensations.

2. Promote Rational Behaviour and Mental Stability
Reduce Mental Instability and Breakdown

'I've mental joys and mental health,
Mental friends and mental wealth'
Blake

The role of social services agencies in relation to these objectives is sometimes direct, for example in casework with the mentally ill. It is sometimes indirect, as when the duty mental health officer signs a fit person order for a mentally ill client to be received into hospital.

POSITIVE POLE
Workers aim to promote mental stability. By this we refer to the organized totality of the individual's emergent sensations, beliefs, perceptions and activities. Workers help to balance the individual's responses as a whole to internal or external stimulation in relation to past experiences and future expectations. *They seek to promote behaviour which is rational.*

From among those alternatives available within the limits imposed by external circumstances, workers *help clients to make choices logically appropriate to their situations,* being based on sound reasoning, intelligent insight, and having internal consistency or coherence. Much time is spent in developing individuals' calculative, deliberative or intellectual abilities — intelligence, know-how, realism, practicality, versatility, and so on.

Rational behaviour might be further defined as action which an individual would choose if he had relevant knowledge of the consequences of his action and equal freedom of choice as between all action alternatives. Choices are consistent to the extent that the person would make the same choice in any replicated situation where no additional knowledge or extra discretion is available.

Through rational thinking, individuals organize and comprehend their experience and infer the existence of their own needs or motives. They develop the capacity to restructure situations or resolve problems by grasping interrelationships. This covers more specialized mental factors — verbal, reasoning, memory, number, spatial factors and receptive-expressive functions.

Workers seek to replace behavioural distortions (extreme avoidance responses warding off stressful events, escape responses, extreme aggressive responses) with more adaptive or competent responses (thinking, planning, reasoning). We may work to resolve entanglements in existing activity, restore continuity and redirect habits. A successful conclusion of such efforts may be the client's choice of more appropriate courses of action.

NEGATIVE POLE
Thence workers may deduce correlative objectives of *reducing the kind of irrationality, neurosis, prejudice and mental aberration in which choice is exclusively dominated by aberrant emotions, drives, instincts and impulses. Workers seek to reduce the effects of intellectual impairment and disturbed mental functioning.* Education, knowledge

and skills are prized over superstition and ignorance.

Intelligence and rational behaviour is a collection of overlapping capacities rather than a single identifiable faculty. Workers include here states of mental defectiveness present since birth and more minimal departures from average functioning such as some changes accompanying ageing. In extreme forms, there is a preponderance of irrational determinants of behaviour. Consequently, maladjustment to physical and social reality increases, often in the form of delusional behaviour. In the more extreme forms of mental instability, damage and breakdown — psychogenic disorders, minimal brain damage, cerebral palsy, established behaviour or personality disorders — workers can hope only to reduce some social ill-effects.

SERVICES

Services include safeguarding access to treatment by detection and referral through to psychiatrists. In the casework situation, workers may attempt negatively to reinforce thoughtless and over-impulsive behaviour, either through the client's life situation or through the interview situation. Logical incompatibilities are made apparent; cognitive skills are developed. Thus the promiscuous husband comes to see that he can only expect his extra-marital affairs to incur either his wife's jealousy, or a demand for a similar extension of extra-marital permissiveness by her. Parents learn to adopt objective and pragmatic attitudes when faced with difficult family situations, to relax inhibited reactions and to redirect damagingly aggressive tendencies.

Workers themselves use cognitive processes of insight learning to develop the client's understanding of the unanticipated consequences of his action to himself and others. Approaching problems and alternatives thoughtfully, logically and systematically, the worker provides a model for rational, problem-solving behaviour which the client may employ for himself in future times of stress.

Since we are here concerned with reducing the debilitative effects of mental instability in its various forms, workers may seek to help clients avoid situations in which humiliation and lowering of self-regard are probable, or to develop counteractions through which clients efface humiliations by resuming action using new styles of behaviour to overcome difficulties: infavoidance and counteraction strategies.

SPECIFIC TARGETS

Specimen case targets falling under this objective might include:

    (i) To promote more rational decision-making processes in respect of given problem situations.

    (ii) To enlarge client knowledge, know-how and information in respect of certain situations.

    (iii) To help clients develop calculative and deliberative capacities by analyzing the alternative courses of action available.

(iv) To help clients define problems more specifically.

(v) To help clients compensate for the social ill-effects of specific mental deficiencies.

(vi) To explore with clients problems and issues in their life situations.

(vii) To provide clients with relevant information about their rights and about community resources potentially available to them.

(viii) To analyze, interpret and respond to clients' relevant perceptions and attitudes about their own situations.

(ix) To help clients to mentally comprehend the significance of specific handicaps and problems.

3. Promote Emotional Stability and Fulfilment
Reduce Emotional Stress

'Stress breaks the bow'
Syrus

POSITIVE POLE

Social services agencies seek to endorse in various ways the whole area of human satisfaction associated with emotional stability and fulfilment. *Workers promote satisfaction of felt needs and drives* by the discharge of tensions as they arise, promoting pleasure which accords with the individual's impulses or goal-achievement to some extent irrespective of consequences of pleasure-directed behaviour and the gratification accompanying them. In addition to working with the client's rational behaviour, workers help to balance various dimensions of feeling, for example extroceptive (those determined by observable, tangible, physical conditions) and introceptive feelings (those diffuse, intangible inclinations prompted by fantasy, mood, subjective speculations and imaginings).

Emotions may be generally defined as states of strength or weakness of responses occasioned by any one of a group of activities or circumstantial contingencies. They concern basic human needs for affection such as solidarity, sympathy, cohesion, a sense of love and the enjoyment of sensations. Particularly important among our emotional predisposition is favouring, being sympathetic to, empathetic with, affectionate towards or loving others. This may take the form of an emotional striving to attach oneself to another *(eros)*; the extreme form of selflessness *(agape)*; or simply of increasing favourable or reinforcing behaviour towards others. Gouldner[54] has shown how social services inherited a Nonconformist tradition of philanthropy which sometimes negates this hedonic objective.

NEGATIVE POLE

Workers endeavour *to reduce debilitative emotional pressures, tensions, strains, stress and suffering whether caused by external pressures ('stressors') or internal conflicting motivation, attitudes, needs or values.* This is particularly relevant when two or more incompatible pressures hit the client simultaneously, as when choices must be made between equally undesirable alternatives.

Part of this aim is *to reduce frustration* caused by the temporary or permanent obstruction and thwarting of felt needs and drives by the interruption of goal-setting behaviour, or by the non-receipt of accustomed reinforcement. This may occur through a lack of emotional, sexual, psychological, social or intellectual opportunities and outlets owing to chance, ignorance, incapacity, age or other factors. Frustration may result in the transference of emotions from an unavailable object to another available object only superficially connected with it (i.e. displacement).

Long lapses between the instances of gratification from the preferred source create frustration for the individual. Repeated gratification through frequent rewards eliminates frustration.

CLIENTELE

Disturbed affective states, like anxiety or depression, may accompany all the other problem situations outlined above, and indeed take over as the client's major concern or problem rather than the situation which precipitated the distress. The focus of treatment is reducing the distress.

If grossly lacking in normal emotional fulfilment, an individual's desires find devious outlets in more or less disguised ways which may give rise to neurotic suffering or to behaviour censured as criminal or depraved. This equally concerns the more extreme forms of emotional tension — hysterical symptoms manifesting themselves in cramp, paralysis, deafness, anaesthesia and fits; reactive depressions which stultify all activity; hysteric disorders such as aphonia; those only able to perceive reality through their own emotional prison; acting-out behaviour where destruction, violence and anti-social action become defensive responses to quiet anxiety. Phobias, such as agrophobia, claustrophobia, excessive fear of certain animals or objects, escapism, school phobias and so on, are other extreme examples. Prolonged emotional strain can lead to somatic disorders such as colitis, asthma, urticaria and other skin reactions, premenstrual syndromes, perforated ulcers, ischemic heart disease and hypertension.

INDIVIDUAL SERVICES

The target in many cases is to develop integrated emotional responses more favourable to the efficient organization of ego-functions and to facilitate clients' resolution of constricting emotional conflicts. Clients come to find it less essential to protect themselves defensively against the recognition of those emotional tensions surrounding problems or associated with their inability to resolve problems. This reinforces client problem-solving capacities.

Combined with other forms of help, a purposeful release of feelings is itself used therapeutically within the casework relationship. Not only may this act as a beneficial cathartic experience and a means of psychological support; it may prevent damaging repressions and tensions. A release of pent-up feelings may free clients to perceive their problems objectively, thence to move constructively towards a solution. Clients may relieve their tensions by relaying them through (and perhaps off-loading them to some degree onto) workers. ('She listened to everything, and out it goes — like pouring out sorrows to old pals.')

By building up clients' resilience to stress and frustration, workers help them to find new ways to restabilize themselves. With help, clients resist panic at the onset of tension. The individual client is helped to develop viable responses to cope with those unwelcome impulses, drives, emotions, ideas and elements in his situation which constitute negative reinforcers and produce aversive stimulation, thus threatening emotional stability. The aim is to achieve normal functioning by reducing anxiety and inner tension to tolerable levels.

Workers counterpose client tension and anxiety with respect for confidences and optimism about problem solutions. They may evoke pleasant emotional responses — friendliness, approval, reassurance or affection — in client life situations, or employ a series of graded tasks incompatible with (therefore counter-conditioning) maladaptive anxiety, guilt or depression. Clients find their predicaments more tolerable when feeling buoyed up by workers' sustaining procedures. ('Without her, I don't think I could have come through at the time.')

Two events are here simultaneously involved — emotional behaviour itself and the manipulable conditions in which it functions. To remedy emotional behaviour which is dislocated, workers often attack the external circumstances which cause it. For example, they do not work to hold a family together at too destructive an emotional cost to one or more of its members.

Tension and stress in any one area of functioning affects all others, making for temporary emotional instability. Relieving emotional tension in one aspect of the client's life lightens pressures in other areas. Although unable directly to measure whether a certain need has been fulfilled, indirect evaluation is feasible by reviewing associated tension levels. For whenever a need exists in an individual or group, a tension is created which is only released when that need is satisfied.

COMMUNITY SERVICES
At the community-wide level workers may assist others in combating

the effects of mass alarms and hysteria — an objective brought into sharp focus by social work during Ulster riots. Emotional stress and instability of a similar kind may characterize whole communities in less violent settings, and is an appropriate object for community-work intervention.

SPECIFIC TARGETS
This objective may be further specified in these terms:

A. *Marital Relations*
  (i) To promote relationships supportive to each partner's individual needs.
  (ii) To help partners complement their family roles in ways most suited to their respective personalities.
  (iii) To define personal needs and self-images of each partner, aiding mutual fulfilment of these needs.
  (iv) To define perceptions and expectations of the marital relationship derived from childhood, helping mutual realignment.
  (v) To define conceptions and expectations about self-control brought to marriage, aiding appropriate realignment.
  (vi) To define tensions and degrees of satisfaction provided by sexual relationship, exploring methods of reducing tensions and increasing satisfactions.
  (vii) To define family communication methods, helping improve them accordingly.
  (viii) To define the family roles each partner performs, and the degrees to which these are consonant with self-images and expectations, working through role-realignments as appropriate.
  (ix) To define the impact each partner's behaviour makes on the self-image of the other, helping the process of behavioural adjustment accordingly.
  (x) To define how the performance of each as parent, housekeeper or breadwinner affects the relationship, helping improve performance or mutual adjustment to the level of performance.
  (xi) To define family decisions taken (e.g. whether shared or hidden), helping improve decision-making processes accordingly.
  (xii) To define which partner deals with social stress and its associated emotions, exploring ways of reducing stress.
  (xiii) To define each partner's capacity to acknowledge and examine problems, including their own roles.
  (xiv) To define the nature of defences and emotional reactions.

    (xv) To define each partner's motivation to improve the relationship, helping this to be used constructively.

    (xvi) To define what marriage offers each, increasing appreciation and sense of value as and where appropriate.

    (xvii) To define the destructive or constructive impact of the relationship on each partner, helping them make appropriate mutual adjustments.

    (xviii) To define the influences of relatives, friends, neighbours and others on the sexual nature of each partner, helping these to be used constructively.

    (xix) To define emotions about children born outside marriage, working through any behavioural dislocations engendered by these emotions.

B. *Family Planning*

    (i) To assist family-planning decisions.

    (ii) To define whether parents seek to limit the family, and help them take appropriate steps accordingly.

    (iii) To define what having children means to each partner and work through the consequences.

    (iv) To define the emotions of each about birth control (fears about religion, impact on the relationship or on themselves individually), and helping them take appropriate steps consequentially.

    (v) To define parental capacities to cope with accessions to the family (e.g. mothering, physical care of children, material provision), aiding decisions made as a result.

    (vi) To define the probable impact on the mother's physical health of further pregnancies, aiding decisions to be made as a result.

    (vii) To define parental capacities to use differing forms of family planning, aiding consequential decisions.

    (viii) To define parental fears of clinics, working through these fears as appropriate.

    (ix) To define relations between mother and health visitor (and/or G.P.), helping the client to utilize the help provided more effectively.

Separation Issues

    (i) To assist partners to take appropriate decisions on the maintenance or disbanding of their marriage.

    (ii) To define partner's motivation to preserve or conclude the marriage, working through the consequences accordingly.

    (iii) To define how destructive the relationship is to parents and/or children, exploring whether damage can be reduced.

    (iv) To define what impact separation has on each parent and/or children, helping partners to take appropriate steps consequentially.

(v) To define the probable family consequences of postponing decisions.

(vi) To enable such decisions to be taken less destructively.

Children

(i) To promote children's emotional security in the home.

(ii) To preserve mother-child relations wherever possible.

(iii) To define parents' emotional contributions to their children, fostering these as necessary.

(iv) To define children's degrees of reassurance that they are loved, fostering this as necessary.

(v) To define the degrees of parental absorption in their own needs and emotions, working through consequences accordingly.

(vi) To define the degrees to which child control mechanisms relate to the needs of the child and/or situation, rather than exclusively to parental feelings, helping in appropriate behavioural modifications.

(vii) To define the degree of unhealthy parental conflict in front of their children, exploring consequences.

(viii) To define the degrees of parental competence in physical care, helping to improve the effectiveness of physical care as necessary.

(ix) To define the level of responsibility the child is expected to carry in relation to age and maturity, working through consequences.

(x) To define the degrees to which the child is confused as to his role in the family, helping increase clarity accordingly.

(xi) To eliminate (as appropriate) parental threats to leave their children or place them in care.

(xii) To reduce the lack of contact or communication with the child in so far as this is debilitative.

(xiii) To define the extent to which the child shows signs of problem behaviour (e.g. uncontrolled provocative behaviour, withdrawal, fear of visitors), helping to eliminate the causes of this or in the process of behavioural modification where appropriate.

(xiv) To define the child's relations to each parent and siblings, helping to develop these relations as appropriate.

(xv) To define the child's ability to play imaginatively, helping him to develop capacities accordingly and remove blocks to constructive play.

(xvi) To define the child's level of attainment in relation to his age.

(xvii) To define the child's play opportunities in the home and in the street, working through consequential decisions to be made.

(xviii) To define the nature of joint family activities, fostering potentialities for these as appropriate.

(xix) To analyze alternative methods for resolving these problems.

(xx) To agree on decisions and action by parents and children accordingly.

(xxi) To evaluate the effectiveness of action taken.

Single People

(i) To define the degrees to which primary reference groups constitute a supportive framework for emotional fulfilment, helping improve the situation as appropriate.

(ii) To define the range and depth of contacts with other reference groups, helping improve these as appropriate.

(iii) To define clients' opportunities for increased contact and emotional fulfilment, helping the realization of these opportunities as appropriate.

(iv) To define alternative methods for resolving these problems or using these opportunities.

(v) To assist the client in making decisions and taking action which provides emotional fulfilment.

(vi) To secure psychiatric help for the client's increasingly severe emotional disturbances.

Residential Situations

To identify points at which residents need relief from pressures of people and situations.

Overall

(i) To provide clients with opportunities for emotional relief by unburdening themselves.

(ii) To provide clients with opportunities to relay, project and to some extent offload their worries onto the worker.

(iii) To release the emotional tensions of clients by providing opportunities to discuss their worries freely.

4. Promote Individualization
Reduce Depersonalization

'So to be unique — none quite like us — that's the idea, isn't it? — and for that substantial uniqueness, as well, to be solid, so we can pinch it, pat it, poke it — that is, there you have — aren't I right? — the bottom of our desire'.
Wyndham Lewis, Childermass.

POSITIVE POLE
Workers seek to promote and maintain individuality; unique personal identity, integrity, continuity and authenticity of self; self-sentiment; self-regard; self-actualization; achievement of full individualization, differentiation, intrinsicness, and integration of the total personality in all aspects.
Humans seem to need a clear, intact conception of selfhood which accords with others' perceptions and responses: a positive feeling of the acceptance of one's self without complaint, including the acceptance of any shortcomings of which one is less proud relative to one's recognized strengths. The existentialist concept of authenticity, with its more exigent view of individuality, influences many younger workers in pursuing this value.

NEGATIVE POLE
Workers seek to reduce depersonalization, collectivism, groupism, bureaucratization, institutionalization, self-devaluation, self-diffusion, self-deprecation, loss of identity by individuals, groups or communities.
Workers oppose the concept that 'all you are' is what you organizationally represent; they seek to reduce individuals' uncertainties in answering the question: 'who am I?'; and combat authoritarianism intruding on individual lives to render them by turns obsequious, sychophantic, irrelative or so many units.
The prevalence of depersonalizing situations in slums is well attested by evidence. In one Liverpool survey children had to complete a sentence in an attitude test beginning 'When I look at other kids, and then at myself, I feel . . .', 82 per cent of slum children judged themselves unfavourably ('I feel sad', etc.), compared with 30 per cent of non-slum children.

CLIENTELE
Practitioners may be concerned here with inconsistent self-images, self-derogatory views or distorted self-conceptions; with adolescents' identity crises as they relinquish family and school for new adult statuses in wider social environments; with personality disorders; with those exhibiting a stereotyped zombie-like conformity of behaviour, manners and styles of living. The developing processes of self-conception and self-actualization may be disturbed to produce sociopathy, delinquency, criminality or mental-emotional breakdowns. They are also concerned with clients who find their dealings with organizations troublesome because they are bureaucratically or summarily served.
Workers fortify individuals' sense of their personality as derived from social statuses and anchorages in various groups. They strengthen clients' own particular interests, aversions, predelictions, successes and

failures in so far as these aid self-identification and evaluation, reinforce the individual's coherent though varied system of responses or modes of action as manifested in diverse social contingencies; give every encouragement to people in developing their private selves even when unattractive modes of expression are chosen.

Implicitly workers promote the belief that the individual is an end-in-himself, never a means — a continuous being distinguishable from others. As such, he ought to realize and fulfil his own autonomous judgement, notwithstanding the weight of persuasively conformist social pressures. It is not simply a matter of ego development — of fortifying the clients' beliefs about self so that he feels himself a fully-fledged, normal human being, conscious of his uniqueness and worth irrespective of his usefulness to others — but it is also hoped he will increasingly recognize the unique qualities of those close to him. An overall aim is *to restore individuals to full status in their communities.*

In terms of social planning, we have regard to social differentiation by which individual roles become specialized, and the sense of localized individual identity and culture among whole groups of people, their characteristic needs being characteristically expressed.

Agencies define problems not only in terms of specific needs and the demands of individuals, but also those of the particular group or local community circumstances. Specific cultural patterns, configurations and practices shared by group members are well heeded in work with local groups. For example, fostering is recognized among West African immigrants as a cultural substitute for a widespread traditional cultural pattern: in Lagos households 25 per cent care for relatives' children; 20 per cent of children live away from home. This cultural trait is buttressed by the traditions of working wives, extensive family sacrifices for child education, wide discrepancies in wealth and occupational status within families, and continuous familial dependencies deriving from kinship loyalties. It is hardly surprising, therefore, that most of the 5000 Commonwealth children in British foster homes are West African.

Clients often need help to free themselves from the strangleholds of bureaucratic cultural patterns which lock them into client roles when they are ready to become ex-clients. Conflicts arise between the individual's personal identity and his prescribed social role in institutional frameworks. As Baldwin noted in *Nobody Knows My Name:* 'There wasn't, no matter where we turned, any acceptable image of oneself, no proof of one's existence. One had the choice, either of "acting just like a nigger" or of *not* acting just like a nigger. Only those who've tried it know just how impossible it is to tell the difference.' Rapid socio-technological change renders the identity problem, which blacks have always had, more universal for many citizens of contemporary communities. 'The negro wants to lose his identity because he does not know his own identity' . . . Elijah Mohammed.

At the political end of the spectrum, workers may help to protect the freedom of every citizen to dissent from local and central policy and from majority views. This includes safeguarding, sometimes creating opportunities to influence local and central government policy, in the aggregate to influence it decisively, and perhaps to circumscribe regulatory bureaucratic powers. Social services managers endeavour to make human service units smaller to avoid creating masses which population growth encourages – mass social work (i.e. community work?), mass teaching (i.e. comprehensives?), mass medicine (i.e. hospitals?), mass psychotherapy (i.e. public relations?), mass politics (i.e. party politics?).

INDIVIDUAL SERVICES

Individualization is the foundation value of social casework. In theory at least, differential treatment precisely meets the clients' needs when considered against his particular background and history.

Where caseworkers cannot individualize the services provided they can at least differentiate the manner or style of service delivery. ('She was more interested in me than filling in the welfare forms.') Only when he begins to feel recognized and understood as a particular individual, does the client participate in relationships in which he may obtain help. The degree to which workers actually take action (e.g. contacting others on the client's behalf) is usually perceived by clients as indicative of genuine worker interest. ('Out they go and do things for you instead of just sitting always yapping about it.')

Workers reinforce the individual's differentiated ego. Counterposed with the client's self-devaluation is the worker's concern for his problems and the hopefulness of their resolution, which engenders in the client a more positive self-regard. Workers help clients to correct distorted and under-valued self-images by examining the external reality in detail, or demonstrating the nature of the erroneous self-conceptions, their origins and their functions. Discrepancies between the client's reasonable appearance and behaviour and his deep-seated feelings of unlovability may be demonstrated as originating from inaccurate perceptions of the hostility of others. (Worker: 'I'm surprised you feel you do badly when so many others reckon you manage pretty well'.) Thus the child is taken through his school records to pinpoint personal strengths he had undervalued by comparison with classmates. Even within a context of negatively reinforcing problem behaviour, clients may be restored to some confidence in themselves and their capabilities.

COMMUNITY SERVICES

Treating the individual as an individual does not confine agencies to one-to-one intervention methods exclusively. Programmes for improving residential services illustrate the kind of service delivery fulfilling this objective. Residents are encouraged to keep personal furniture and possessions. Block toiletting, regimented meals and outings, institutionalized arrangements for clothing and impersonal interior and exterior decor are superseded by more personalized and spontaneous outlooks. Individual tastes and interests are fostered. Rigid rules are relaxed so that residents may breakfast in bed, stay out late, smoke in their own rooms, or generally 'do their own thing'. Being residentialized should not be confused with being ill. To the extent that the client accepts his residential situation, dissatisfaction with his sick state is lessened, and therefore his chances of recovery are compromised.

At a wider level, expert support in questioning official decisions provides a further service related to this objective, often buttressed by programmes to help clients feel at ease in claiming their rights. To this end, Claimants' Unions and Child Poverty Action Groups aid applicants at appeal tribunals and train relevant professional groups in consumer rights. Services designed to minimize bureaucratic intrusion into individuals' lives (e.g. Social Security applications of the cohabitation rule) and to help in dealings with formal organizations, are included here.

SPECIFIC TARGETS

We may further specify this objective in these kinds of terms:

  (i) To help clients preserve some awareness of, contact with and orientation to their roots.
 (ii) To foster clients' sense of their own physical and emotional space.
(iii) To reduce the degree to which individuals are valued solely in terms of what they represent to a network of organizations, rather than in their own right.
 (iv) To accept and recognize the risks entailed in unsupervised activities in residential homes and day centres.
  (v) To ensure all clients in residential institutions and day centres have regular face-to-face contact with at least one staff member.
 (vi) To develop the sensitivity of staff responses to individual differences.
(vii) To promote the client's sense of his or her own unique personal identity, self-interest and egocentricity.
(viii) To safeguard client's freedom from excessive family, group, institutional or community pressures.

5. Promote Awareness
Reduce Insentience

'Before all things, a means must be devized for improving our awareness from the outset'
Spinoza

POSITIVE POLE

Workers endeavour *to promote and restore to clients' lives awareness, sensitivity, sentience, meaning, understanding, relevant knowledge and the ability to face up to problems.* We are here referring to cognitive awareness as well as accompanying emotional changes. Workers aim to provide individuals with some perspective on the network of self-other relations. They promote reflective mental attitudes enabling individuals to become more clearly aware of themselves and their environments. Awareness includes individuals' consciousness of mental and bodily functions, of objects and situations in the external world, and of the perception of self as an individual and group member.

Awareness is an end-in-itself as well as one of the technical means of producing behavioural changes. This objective often demands the direct mental confrontation of threatening or unwelcome emotions, ideas and stimuli, with a view to understanding them. This approach often renders disfunctional ego-defence mechanisms unnecessary, the unwelcome stimulus being excluded from consciousness (repression), assigned to another person (projection) or object (displacement), or rationally justified (rationalization). Workers seek to promote in clients a recognition of the limitations in their own situations, reducing delusions, wishful thinking and fantasies in so far as these are debilitating. In extremis, this objective covers those cognitive processes unconstrained by reality as seen in the autistic individual.

NEGATIVE POLE

At the same time workers aim *to reduce insentience, insensitivity, lack of information, ignorance and the avoidance of problems.* This refers particularly to an awareness of shared community expectations, utilizing role-taking skills in structuring and interpreting relationships meaningfully, and some element of appreciation fused with knowledge. It may, for example, cover the medical social worker's correcting of cognitive misconceptions about physical illness which significantly contribute to disturbed reactions.

COMMUNITY SERVICES

To achieve this objective workers aim at a community level to disseminate relevant information more widely, for example that on citizen rights. The labyrinth of rules, forms and offices governing the distribution of state benefits, results in an estimated four out of five people being discouraged from applying for service reimbursements to which they are entitled. With more knowledge and information, potential consumers have a securer base for demands on service which might better fit their needs. Without such consumer knowledge, there can be no proper consent for reforms are only legitimated when based on information rather than an ideological bias.

It is particularly important to help clients know and understand policies underlying bureaucratic decisions. Where rules are secret or vague, decisions are unpredictable so we cannot plan our lives with confidence and security and workers can help by instructing clients on how to use statutory provisions or by rendering them more accessible.

Increased self-awareness increases consciousness of one's social environment. A developed community awareness leads to people knowing more about each other's behaviour, which forms a basis for shared expectations about the community as a whole and its resources. Community awareness takes varied forms. Group-workers develop awareness of others and group relationships; community workers develop political awareness of community power structures, of the locus of political leverage, of benefits distribution, and of ways and means by which power redistributions are accomplished. Communities which are equally poor in assets, but which differ in political consciousness, will have a different capacity for social action.

INDIVIDUAL SERVICES

Personal casework services take into account clients' engagement in the study, diagnosis and treatment of their own problems. As clients present facts, they are helped to understand possible explanations, for the incipient schizophrenic is as unaware of his problem as the incipient diabetic.

Worker supplies client with another viewpoint, a new perspective, sometimes in the form of direct advice and guidance on how he might extricate himself from his present mess. Effective workers not only enter the client's situation empathetically, but also evolve objective perspectives of the total situation. Treatment does not begin without the client explicitly acknowledging his problems. ('I began to see what I was all about and it was good her getting me to own up to it.')

Awareness of objective reality may be positively reinforced by approval; subjective fantasies negatively reinforced by disapproval. Therapists may seek to reduce delusional talk by looking away, telephoning or opening the mail; rational talk is stimulated by leaning forward, listening or nodding. Irrational, unconscious, vague and inarticulate processes which condition individual behaviour are raised for conscious inspection. ('I learnt new things about myself.')

Under this objective falls the process of insight learning. This involves helping clients to perceive relations between problem situations and alternative courses of action, and depends upon systematic approaches to problem-solving. Workers restructure and reorganize the whole problem situation (symbolically or directly), with the result that clients begin to bring earlier experiences to bear on the problem more easily, perceiving it in new ways which lead to resolution. Workers provide additional knowledge — about the universality of certain problems, common reactions to situations — which clients use in resolving their problems. New information is presented about the clients' present situation and their reactions to it, which helps them correct distorted perceptions and logical deductions which do not hold good. Thus the wife may be taught that her husband is not necessarily an active or incipient homosexual merely because he associates with homosexuals. Alternative responses to problems are tried out symbolically and overtly implemented if effective in rehearsals. ('We played it through a bit — pretending. Then afterwards I was doing it like we'd played it out, though not just the same.') So practitioners use interpretation, clarification, confrontation and reflection in the interview situation to increase the client's awareness of others, of his situation, of the dynamics of his own behaviour and interactions with others. Clients thus emerge with a greater degree of enlightenment — clearer, fuller, more adequate perceptions of their own troubled situations, often as a result of workers' stimulation of reflective processes. ('You still don't know your own mind after an hour's lonely brooding — you do after the welfare've questioned you a bit.')

A significant, perhaps undervalued role of social workers is that of purveyors, articulators and communicators to a wider public of social science research results and their relevance to such subjects as child-rearing practices, health care, human relationships, efficient home management, domestic budgeting, or personnel relations in work situations. More emphasis has, however, been given to social worker roles vis-à-vis the educationally deprived and as purveyors of socio-cultural changes in communities and their significance — for instance in the areas of increasing legal and social toleration of homosexuality, the changing (declining) status of nuclear family, pair-bonding as only one of many permissible arenas for sexual intercourse, the increasing acceptance of contraceptives and abortion, the slowly decreasing stigma attached to welfare claims.

SPECIFIC TARGETS

One or two more specific case targets may provide examples:

 (i) To improve the present situation in which the client shows insensitivity to others' needs and an inability to plan, by helping him to recognize his own problem or get help and to develop his attitudes and understanding of some aspects of his situation in some area of living (i.e. increased ability to plan, increased understanding of self and others, attitudes more favourable to social adaptation, unhelpful delusions eliminated).

(ii) To provide residents with the maximum amount of relevant information about their home and its environment.

(iii) To reshape clients' impressions about how others live.

(iv) To sort out with clients the pros and cons of each alternative course of action open to them.

(v) To provide clients with more information about their rights and relevant community resources available to them.

(vi) To encourage clients to study, diagnose and treat their own problems.

(vii) To reinforce negatively (but gently) problem-generating subjective fantasies about reality.

(viii) To reinforce clients' awareness of objective facts about their reality situation.

6. Promote Sense of Valuation
Reduce Anomie

'Nothing to look forward to with pride or look back on with hope'
R. Frost

POSITIVE POLE
In some sense, workers aim *to promote a sense of valuation, a system of orientation.* By this is meant some coordinated conception of the comparative relevance and desirability of various things in relation to human attitudes, needs and desires; some feel for standards by which things can be compared, evaluated and judged; some devotion to principles; some intimation of commitment and social responsibility; some consciousness of blameworthy behaviour; and some reverence for life. Conscientiousness, probity and trustworthiness are associated virtues for moral philosophers. Typically, we are referring also to the problems of the person who cannot sit down to think out what he wants and who pursues what would not satisfy him even if he had it.

Workers seek to promote in clients renewed expectations and hope on the basis of clients' potential in using their own resources more effectively. The individual is helped to adjust to prospective future experiences. He is prepared to make certain types of response to foreseen or anticipated situations. Some expectations are relatively stable in that they are based on comparatively constant norms, while others are unstable or baseless.

In so far as others have internalized comparable values, so that conformity is personally satisfying and necessary to evoke favourable reactions from others, value patterns are institutionalized. Other expectations constitute aspiration levels unique to the individual — standards he sets for himself. These standards refer to human capacities for acquiring motives which mobilize activity and are in some way selective or directive in relation to the social environment. We are involved with outlets, modification and blocking of instinctual energy as shaped by the ego and libidinal instincts. This may apply to persons and their behaviour, to events and their interrelationship, to property and its ownership, to services and goods, and the satisfaction these give. The external world must feel significant for inner dreams to be touched. Due credit, status and recognition for good points scored in the game of life are important here. Value and disvalue are recognized to the extent that they are attributed to oneself and confirmed through social interchange. The concept therefore includes self-worth, self-respect and self-esteem, as well as respect for others as humans rather than as fillers of particular roles.

Thus much social services time is spent helping individuals and groups to define a system of orientation comprising various attitudes, perceptions, knowledge, values and norms through which they respond and orient themselves to diverse situations. ('I knew where I was going again once we'd talked.')

However, there is an additional feature. Neutrality is impossible amidst the varied forces striving for one value or another. Any intervention implies some value propagation. It becomes impossible to retain antiseptic neutrality towards other's values. Thus delinquent gangs and criminal sub-cultures may consciously recruit members from among the unsuccessful; community workers may consciously recruit adherents for social action programmes from the same groups, thereby opposing the sub-cultural value orientation with alternatives. Value neutrality may in practice implicitly condone injustice, deprivation and exploitation.

Value conformity is sometimes left to the marketplace (where the *Clockwork Orange*-style delinquent and criminal sub-cultures may sometimes make the running), sometimes enjoined by subtle coercions (social workers functioning as latter-day Calvinistic 'vigilantes' or Savanorolan 'ragamuffins'), sometimes purchased (through services with strings attached, mixing insults with favours), but often propagated through persuasion.

NEGATIVE POLE

The obverse side of this objective is *to reduce anomie, apathy, social irresponsibility, negativism and nihilism within a given milieu.* Anomie refers to personal disorientation and desocialization i.e. a retreat by the individual into his own ego. It arises through social situations in which norms and social structures are themselves either lacking or conflicting.

It covers the impairment of the individual's capacity to make any valuation or judgement on any situation whatever.

We are particularly concerned here with those socially or emotionally displaced persons who have lost the compass of their lives, no longer having any social or emotional roots, but only disconnected urges and no sense of community, continuity, obligation or responsibility, so that their activities lack self-regulation. Anomie is the predominant factor in suicidal clients who have lost any basis for existence. In extreme nihilistic forms this means not only despair and negation, but also the desire to despair and negate: an attitude of total rejection of current norms and complete negativism.

A further sub-objective is to reduce normative ambivalence — the coexistence of opposing emotional or intellectual attitudes (or drives) towards a person, situation or idea. Several schools of psychotherapy give special attention to the lack of meaningful values or the lack of coherence between conflicting values in the individual's life as the cause of mental upsets which may be as serious as traditional neuroses.

CLIENTELE
Here we are concerned less with clients who fail to gain certain benefits they seek than with those unable to enjoy benefits because they are unappreciative of their value: for example, the elderly widow who depreciates the benefits of her independence by comparison with Arcadian fantasies of the residential home.

INDIVIDUAL SERVICES
In casework situations, this objective is associated particularly with abreactive, cathartic and ventilating techniques. Workers pursue this objective when increasing ego-involvement, identification and invest-ment of energy in various values and their articulation. Thus they may indicate to the wife qualities in a husband she had previously perceived as entirely 'bad', or seek to improve the feedback processes by which individuals understand more clearly the effects of their own action. ('I wondered what I could have been thinking of all this time. It knocked me out to see what came after and what I'd really done.')

Workers' advice to clients is only accepted if it directly connects with existing client cultural and value systems, and these client values can only be changed at the periphery of their value system. Workers have to 'talk into' the clients' own fundamental beliefs, though clients begin to value themselves and aspects of their own situations differently after talking with effective workers. ('She was concerned about little *me* — about all of us — about everything happening. I saw things round the other way after I'd come out.') They help clients know and decide what they want and think on issues and to value their own opinions. The objective includes almost any service wherein steps are taken in delivering it to protect the sensibilities of those served, ensuring that they do not feel belittled. Dependence on the community's treasury should not imply any enforcement of the community's prescription for their way of life.

Workers may increase clients' awareness of accepted socio-cultural norms (e.g. in respect of home maintenance or child-rearing); help them to envisage the difficult consequences and problems arising from norm-rejection (e.g. loss of shelter, punitive neighbours or institutions); help them to incorporate these norms into their behaviour given their agreement (e.g. training in home maintenance and child-rearing practices); or alternatively, assist viable living despite norm-rejection (e.g. locating and using broad-minded landlords, neighbours or institutions), and find alternative modes of social approbation (e.g. through affinal social groupwork). Many of these procedures constitute the approach to treatment which has come to be called logotherapy.

COMMUNITY SERVICES

This objective embraces the development of some sense of personal responsibility on the part of individual citizens for the social situations they help to create. As such, it forms part of any genuine public relations programme of social services agencies. It embraces agency responsibility for developing social accounting services for their communities. This involves establishing social information systems for gathering regular trend series of social indicators and special mechanisms for data falling outside these series; feeding information back with appropriate speed, in an appropriate form to the appropriate agency; and evaluating changing social situations accordingly. Social indicators research, value impact forecasting, and social simulation models developed by systems technologists, point the way forward here. More controversially, the objective also comprises services which implicitly or explicitly entail some element of value propagation, or at least agencies may be viewed as having some responsibility to reawaken sufficient interest in social values for a debate to be mounted on these involving all community members.

On a different though related level, the community worker notes what is possible, projecting this into the future so as to enable people to glimpse what an intrinsically better future would look like, and to seek its realization because it appears attainable in practice.

People presuppose alien values are held by others, thus concerted social action is thwarted. Value divergence in many cases results from a lack of genuine opportunity to realize the values concerned, or through compulsion associated with them. This is an arena for community work action.

SPECIFIC TARGETS

A few more specific targets may help to exemplify the objective:

 (i) To reawaken the client's appreciation of certain positive elements in his social environment.
 (ii) To restore some sense of goal-seeking activity in client's lives.
 (iii) To grasp the implicit values inherent in the client's sub-culture.
 (iv) To connect with the client's belief-systems about reality so as to modify them in a manner appropriate for improved social functioning.
 (v) To enable clients to value themselves differently in relation to others.
 (vi) To explore and develop the client's relevant valuations of others, including dependents for whom he cares.
 (vii) To promote a dialogue with relevant external critics of social work.
 (viii) To help clients receive and use negative feedback.

7. Promote Self-Determination
Reduce Dependency

'Where does your white love leave me? It won't leave me the power to make myself a communist. It takes away my free choice to be a queer. It robs me of the will to be a junkie. It does all for me: nothing left over for me to do ever.'
Jules Feiffer, *Harry, the Rat with Women*

POSITIVE POLE

'To promote self-determination, self-help, self-care, self-direction, assertiveness, self-sufficiency, autonomy and purposeful behaviour.'
Under this heading we allude to qualities like a sense of personal commitment and involvement, and responsibility in relation to goals, as well as to independence, volition, deliberate decision, will and its application. It relates to the striving aspects of experience; the virtues of the will such as industriousness, fortitude, perseverance, endurance and initiative; and the freedom to make choices.

This objective forms part of the gospel of rugged individualism beloved of the protestant ethic — the right to endeavour to shape one's own life, to work out major facets of one's own destiny, or to go one's own way. As it becomes harder for individuals to go their own way under conditions of central planning and complex interdependencies of civilization, traditional values of personal independence are increasingly threatened.

The hope is that individuals in the community are able to say with conviction 'I can do so, but I could do otherwise. It depends on me.' They become self-sustaining, self-maintaining, self-governing individuals. To this end, recognition must be given not only to the individual's need and right to freedom from interference and undue constraint in making his own choices and decisions (the Utilitarian's concept of negative freedom); but also his need actually to exercise that freedom in practice by purposeful, willed behaviour in the direction of his own choosing (Leibniz's[55] concept of positive freedom). Individuals should have control over their own external economic and social affairs, being free to influence (to some degree) the behaviour of others in ways that accord with their own beliefs and needs.

Among others, Aptekar[56] emphasized this objective in casework practice at the individual level. 'Pick one conception without which modern casework simply could not exist — the idea clients must determine how their own lives shall be.' Workers help clients to increase their mastery over their situations and over themselves in and through the social work process itself. Individuals and groups should not be bartered from command to command. Every intervention should be made with the consent of, as well as in the interests and for the benefit of, the individual concerned.

NEGATIVE POLE

We may state the objective negatively thus: *to reduce dependency with the possible concomitants of reducing coercion, deference, fear of hostility, the giver-power of service providers, the powerless inferior position of service-recipients, and the gift as a tool of manipulation.* Dependency is manifested in a passive submission to external forces wherein the individual readily admits inferiority or defeat with resignation, helplessness or despair.

Public dependency is a rising social problem. Everyone is dependent during major significant portions of their lives, and many arguments on behalf of universalist services are based on this principle. Dependency is a normal nurturance-need or coping mechanism up to the point where it becomes the individual's dominant technique in striving for a desired objective. Thereafter it may result in passivity, irresponsibility, neurotic or psychotic helplessness.

The child's dependency on the parent can become so obviously abnormal that the parent unwittingly uses transference to induct the child into a pathological role attuned to his own securities and defences. The boss can manipulate the worker's dependency to stabilize productive output. Interpreting Morel Commission evidence, Miller[57] showed the same tendencies in social service provision, concluding: 'Welfare assistance in its present form tends to encourage dependency, indifference, and ennui.' Studies by Timms and Mayer;[58] Strupp, Fox and Lessler;[59] Lipkin;[60] Briar;[61] and Roberts, Wiltse and Griswold[62] all show the common client detestation of dependence on welfare and disdain of being patronized.

COMMUNITY SERVICES

Self-determination relates not simply to individuals' choices and pursuits of their own goals, but equally to that of groups and communities. Autonomy, purposiveness and social sovereignty of deprived, disadvantaged or weak groups, communities and neighbourhoods ought not to be subjugated to or dominated by strong groups. The aim of much community work may be construed therefore as promoting wider ranges of choice within communities, as well as fostering the mutual support function (or substitutes) mentioned elsewhere.

Part of the objective entails increasing the citizen's influence on the nature and development of each local community. Consumers should participate in and influence the planning of all services. Community action groups are encouraged and sponsored in asserting their rights. Resident responsibilities are increased in all aspects of running local authority homes. Community work is seen as an educational process aiming at personal growth towards self-direction and responsibility, as fostering self-determination for the community in establishing its social utilities.

Social action is one significant medium by which whole groups of individual citizens and clients develop their autonomy. Social activists develop and harness the power necessary to make community interests felt in social decisions. In group and community work, the aim is often to mature the protesting attitude into an objective one. Concrete proposals and the concrete implementation of these proposals are evolved from protest. Community organizations are created 'so that so-called "little man" gathers into his hands all the power he needs to shape his life' (Saul Alinsky).[63]

INDIVIDUAL SERVICES

Through casework, workers seek to develop the extent and variety of individuals' personal resources, helping clients mobilize their capacities to cope with problems.

With this objective in mind, workers may endeavour to reduce a child's overdependent behaviour by systematically modifying unconscious parental reinforcement practices. Various modified versions of operant conditioning may be used: the therapist approves client statements indicating independent behaviour (which thereupon increases), or disapproves client statements indicating dependence (which thereupon decreases). Or dependency is decreased by the worker engineering the presentation of negative reinforcers, withholding positive reinforcers or reducing inconsistent and intermittent reinforcement conditions in therapy situations.

The under-assertive child is paired with a more assertive child in the play situation so that each modifies the other's behaviour. The client is helped to see he is over-generalizing responses of dependence learnt as a child in relation to his parents, that is, that over-dependence on others is inappropriate in mature adults responsible for families. Aggressiveness is reinvested in activities the individual has decided to undertake so it no longer erupts in violent or escapist forms.

The worker develops his own and others' attitudes so that clients are viewed as active, participating decision-makers, not passive, dependent objects to be moulded by institutions. At first, worker and client may determine outcomes mutually. Treatment does not begin until the client explicitly expresses a willingness to attempt to resolve his problems. The client is then helped to exercise effective choice in fulfilling mutually agreed objectives. The presentation of even one genuine alternative may be of inestimable benefit to his morale, even if the choice is nothing more than a bus ride or a walk to the service locale. Understanding his own problems, the client begins to take self-steering, corrective action. He may begin to play a larger part in shaping the relevant situation, system or institution preparatory to assuming more responsible and adequate roles outside the helping system. At all times, workers safeguard the client's right to refuse treatment, to give or withhold consent on specific decisions within it, and to participate in the treatment process itself by jointly working through problems.

Therapeutic procedures under clients' control allow them to maintain or modify certain aspects of their own behaviour by symbolic rewards or punishments, which are relatively independent of the contingencies operating in their current environments. This is especially valuable when appropriate environmental consequences are lacking, delayed or beyond workers' control. It is likely to be an important means of achieving the generalization and persistence of therapeutic changes. Such changes are facilitated when perceived by clients as self-engendered rather than worker-induced.

Workers ensure that clients (particularly those seeking material aid) do not feel emotionally blackmailed into doing things which are unnatural or out of tune with normal behaviour patterns in order to appear 'deserving'. ('I didn't have to lower myself in any way at all.') Similarly, workers do not intrude into the sphere of client self-regarding activity without invitations to do so, confirmation that involvement should continue, and immediate responsiveness to veiled demands that they should withdraw to safer terrain ('You don't keep on at people about what they feel about everything even if you are the welfare.') There is a sense in which it is felt that the individual consumer of social services should increase his scope for the exercise of choice, thus restraining authoritarian and paternalistic elements which Dahrendorf believes always characterizes welfare situations.

Practical aids are provided like patient operator selector mechanisms

(POSUM) enabling many physically handicapped to direct their own lives fully and autonomously. Daily minders and nurseries are used to relieve mothers who are unsupported or in other ways have lost their independence of action in being tied to family care. Resident participation in homes exemplifies this objective. When meetings first start there is often general agreement about the boredom of the long evenings. Initially residents protest against staff negligence, but soon decisions emerge on the need to organize discussions, lectures, mêlées, games and diversions. Thus normative rules begin to correspond to the residents' needs since they result from opposition to their own situation.

Methods of service provision are as important here as specific services provided. Agencies should only provide services (e.g. sheltered housing) if by so doing clients are freed to become more independent in respect of another service (e.g., custodial care). The methods whereby welfare recipients give a certain amount of community service to repay 'welfare loans', exemplifies the importance of such principles.[64]

SPECIFIC TARGETS
Specific targets under this heading may be exemplified as follows:
  (i) To define the degrees of client dependency and its causes.
  (ii) To define alternative methods by which client self-determination may be stimulated.
  (iii) To increase individual clients' range of choices in relation to treatments, treatment times, treatment practitioners, social contacts, planning of activities, personal expenditure, self-management, and use of facilities.
  (iv) To provide residents of Homes with maximum freedom of action within constraints which are unavoidable if the Home is to function effectively.
  (v) To increase client freedom from unnecessary constraints of institutional processes.
  (vi) To minimize the numbers of calls on external help the client finds necessary.

8. Promote Self-Expression
Reduce Inarticulateness

'We wish to plead our own causes. Too long have others spoken for us'
Freedom Journal, 1827

POSITIVE POLE
Promoting self-expression, verbalization and articulation, particularly of emotions, feelings and thoughts is implicit in many field operations of personal social services. Adequate expression of emotion is essential for

the individual's effective functioning, and workers help clients gain adequate outlets for the libido's drives, instincts and energies. This does not necessarily take verbalized forms of communication. States of feeling may be expressed by phatic communications wherein no precise meaning is articulated. Also involved are the needs of individuals and communities to be seen and heard, and to make some impression on others through affirmation and self-exhibition. This embraces the objective of *assisting individuals and groups to formulate their needs*, translating these into demands articulated in ways that lead to their being met. Here we refer to values stressed by axiologists — forthrightness, openness, frankness and genuiness.

NEGATIVE POLE
Conversely, workers release blocked impulses for overt expression. They bring thoughts, wishes and feelings to consciousness or verbalized expression by reducing the hold of neurotic inhibitions, guilt and repressions in some of their clients and client groups. We seek to reduce the effects of impaired specific linguistic expressive functioning, mutism, and organic speech defects.

If strangulated, emotions may be redirected to substitute objects or persons by displacement. Inhibited emotional expression through a fear of the consequences may raise the level of emotional excitement to intolerable levels occasioning neurotic, unrealistic outlets, amnesic episodes, language and speech disorders, motor disfunctions, and longer-term functional disorders of the kind associated with psychosomatic illness. Within the same syndrome falls defensive inhibition — the fundamental mechanism of all traumatic neuroses. Traumatic inhibition may produce frigidity and impotence in the sexual sphere, concentration difficulties in the mental sphere, fear of forming or expressing opinions or making contacts in the social sphere. It can also function in a very indiscriminate way, for example an individual's legs may be paralysed because he was running at a time of trauma.

Within this sphere of activity, workers concern themselves with repressions of thoughts, wishes, feelings from consciousness, neurotic inhibitions in the form of hyper-sensitive responses to undiscriminated stimuli, unauthentic expression of self, expressive-receptive disorders, expression of grossly immature impulses, and at an altogether different level, language disorders. Inhibition can also have positive effects, some defensive mechanisms serving as efficient protective devices in the face of acute dangers.

At an individual level, the main concern is to reduce the disabling sense of guilt (often accompanied by remorse, self-reproach, shame, anxiety or embarrassment). The guilt-ridden individual is dominated by the knowledge or unconscious thought that he has contravened some individual, social, ethical, cultural or legal norm. This particularly relates to such contraventions where minor self-imposed penalties are harshly applied by individual conscience, the community and state institutions.

Workers aim *to reduce excessive self-punitive reactions for minor social transgressions or failures.* Impaired self-regard comes with inferiority feelings associated with such guilt. When consciously felt though of unconscious origin, these feelings may take the form of neurotic anxieties and the felt need for reparation. They range from self-reproach (e.g. of the melancholic) or accident-proneness, to masochism or suicide.

INDIVIDUAL SERVICES

One casework target may be to achieve more developed verbalized attitudes and understanding. Clients are encouraged to express their feelings, thoughts and attitudes freely, especially hostility — 'to get problems off their chest'. Training may be given in communicating with others effectively. With more severe problems, workers help the client to find outlets for aggression other than violence. A central task is to help elaborate the restricted speech codes of culturally deprived and educationally backward families.

The degree of expression is often taken as a barometer of the depth of the relationship. Self-expression may help relieve pressures and tensions, align client perceptions with those of others, lessen the burden of problems by helping clients to share them. It may be used to render the casework relation a model through which clients test out and experiment with other kinds of relationship. Clients receive considerable relief through unburdening themselves to workers, and such ventilation may itself improve the situation. ('I didn't stop talking once in all the time I was there. I told them things I couldn't have told anyone else. Marvellous. I came out a different person.')

Workers promote assertive responses, including the overt expression of negative feelings of hostility and anger, and of positive feelings of affection and friendship. This may counter-condition inappropriate anxiety aroused in interpersonal relations. Practitioners may endeavour to increase verbal responsiveness in psychotic clients by exposing them to talkative and expressive people as models.

Workers may use verbal labels when reviewing relevant past experiences of problem behaviour so as to increase the client's discrimination between tendencies and exceptions to them. This helps the client describe his situation to others who may also be able to help. Clients may be able to open up the problem situation in discussion with family and friends after the experience of doing this with the worker. Verbal labels themselves may function as cues for guiding behaviour.

Clients' feelings of guilt are counterposed with workers' warm and sympathetic treatment which produces client reactions of optimism and confidence. Workers may desist from reinforcing certain responses so that they are extinguished. The client thinks and talks about problems creating guilt or anxiety in himself (e.g. sexual behaviour). Workers desist from criticism which reinforces guilt or anxiety (e.g. by being a permissive, attentive audience in therapeutic sessions).

COMMUNITY SERVICES

No community is fully responsive to its members. We seek, on behalf of our community, a full expression of citizen values, interests and concerns. The social ideal is an uninhibited, authentic, educated expression by community members of their membership.

Freedom of expression can be restricted by local authority officials or by community intolerance. How much tolerance of dissent is there in institutions such as schools, factories and offices?

SPECIFIC TARGETS

We may begin to specify this objective further along the following lines:

   (i) To define and work through situations in which clients are unable to express themselves — with the worker, in social contacts, in other agency contacts.
  (ii) To define under what conditions the client is able to express himself, building on these experiences.
 (iii) To define which client emotions block self-expression.
  (iv) To define alternative modes of possible client communication with (and evoke appropriate responses from) significant others in their social environment.
   (v) To enable clients to discuss problem situations openly with family and friends.
  (vi) To work through the inauthentic expression of thoughts and feelings.
 (vii) To reduce the repression of interests and values of dissident community sub-groups.
(viii) To help culturally and educationally deprived clients elaborate their restricted speech codes.
  (ix) To expose inarticulate clients to expressive people as role analogues.

9. Promote Growth, Development and Social Learning
Reduce Stultification, Regression, Retardation and Decline

POSITIVE POLE

Workers seek to strengthen individual growth and social learning; to maximize the individual's powers and potentialities; to facilitate the individual's cohesive and harmonious development through successive stages; and to ease the individual's social transition from one state of affairs to another.

During these stages, the individual's ego integrates the timetable of his organic needs with the rhythms implicit in his social environment. As characterized by Erikson[65] for example, these are stages of trust, autonomy, initiative, industriousness, identity, intimacy, generativity and ego integrity. (Gesell,[66] Ilg,[67] Piaget[68] and Sullivan[69] have alternative schemata.)

NEGATIVE POLE

Similarly, *workers seek to remove stultifying and retarding influences; to arrest declining individual capacities; to minimize regression to earlier patterns of behaviour or stages of ego-development which result from anxiety avoidance, or one-sided unbalanced development.* For example, attempts may be made to reduce the effects of specific perceptual-receptive learning impairment.

CLIENTELE

Typically, this objective concerns regressive tendencies where responses from the past are dredged up to replace more adult responses. For example, the child reverting to infantile toilet behaviour under stress; the young person's fear of his punitive father being displaced onto his probation officer as an equivalent authority figure; the wife seeking solace with her parents after matrimonial rows.

In advanced forms regression results in pathological behaviour. Most mental disorders handled by social services involve varying degrees of regressive behaviour — for example, the schizophrenic's egocentric, animistic or self-transparent feelings about himself. Problems of mental retardation, learning and behavioural disabilities fall within this area. Frostig programmes[70] of educational therapy and remediation are relevant, together with their extensions to stultified mental and behavioural growth of a less severe kind.

This objective also has applications with clients who experience abrupt social transitions from one situation to another, resulting in changes in the individual's social field, for example migration to new locales, a job change, becoming a spouse or parent, etc. The problems may centre around any stage/s of the transition process: uncertainties about making the transition, upsets about impending transition or post-transition disorientation.

In one sense, the objective is to help the individual realize the other strategic objectives discussed herewith, according to an adequate and viable developmental progression. Faced with clients unable to cope in significant areas of living, the worker initially protects and supports them ('to fulfil safety needs'), helping them achieve a stronger sense of individual identity, self-valuation and self-interest. It may later become important, as they gather strength and independence, to help clients participate in the community system ('to promote social participation'), changing the rules, policies, procedures and structures which lock them into dependent, passive client roles. Were workers to help a client achieve greater social participation before he is able to assert his own individual identity and needs, however, the outcome could be deleterious to both the client and the groups in which he participates, for the client's disability initially impairs effective participation.

We are concerned with responses and behavioural changes which emerge with a definite order and regularity in relation to the direction of the total growth trend, or in relation to the patterns characteristically generated by social transitions in the individual's life.

SERVICES

The objective of growth and development includes the sub-objective of *prognosticating the pattern of potential client improvement (his 'development dynamic')* and sequencing intervention accordingly so that gains in functioning will be sustained.

Another service objective within this context is *to define, preserve or develop behavioural qualities which oppressive social forces have distorted, tabooed or arrested in many community members.* Workers reinforce or strengthen those of the individual's responses to situations and other persons which hopefully he finds more adequate than those used previously. The individual is assisted in developing attitudes which form a better bridge between personal psychological states and external situations.

INDIVIDUAL SERVICES

Learning is a reorganization of the cognitive field which generates or changes activity. The individual who learns, then reacts to an encountered situation in new ways which cannot be explained on the basis of native response tendencies or temporary states.

Workers may encourage the client to reflect on influential factors in his developmental pattern (including consideration of early life experiences) in order to help him understand how his past influences his present. Renewed social learning may follow. Thus a wife unjustly complains of her husband's neglect; the worker induces her to envisage her contemporary and childhood situations in just such a position; she sees that she is carrying over to the husband childhood feelings about her father.

Workers teach the client to use his experience in one situation to inform his responses and behaviour in subsequent analogous situations, taking full account of new, contemporary influences. The client learns to understand the principles by which an immediate problem is resolved and perhaps the principles of problem-solving in general. The client's new insights are transferred to new situations. Gradually workers eliminate in respect of the problem behaviour, the processes of retroactive inhibition, by which later items tend to interfere with the recall of previous items, and pro-active inhibition where the first item is learnt more easily than the second, and the second more easily than the third, and so on. Practitioners help the client to develop attitudes as the means by which understanding is carried over from situation to situation. For example, parents are induced to relinquish inhibited reactions and control aggressive tendencies in favour of more objective, pragmatic attitudes when faced with difficult child-control problems.

Workers may give specific guidance and recommendations to clients which directly influence their behaviour. This may include information as diverse as where to look for a job, whether to stay with a husband or not, or how to retain the spouse's affection. This may also involve sorting out the pros and cons of situations on which conflicting advice has been given. ('She said to me, "do this and that will happen. Do the other thing, and that other thing'll happen". I did. It did. It worked out O.K.')

By various forms of environmental manipulation, workers may rearrange elements in the client's life situation so that they decondition (or at least do not serve to reinforce) the client's regressive or infantile reactions and reinforce more 'adaptive', 'mature' or 'functional' responses. For example, the wife's childish needs and reactions distort her attitudes towards men; these are deconditioned by helping the husband to focus his own previously uncontrolled anger onto those specific problems which cause it, to eliminate his own retaliatory behaviour which confirms his wife's distorted perceptions, and to express sympathy and approval at opportune moments.

With the more severe problems of retardation, social services collaborate with education and other services to change family hostility to prolonged schooling of their mentally retarded children; involve families as well as children in remedial educational programmes; extend and enrich informal learning opportunities in the home or in community centres; discover symptoms of retardation at an early stage; screen 'at-risk' child populations; and provide more small group hostels, day care, temporary residential care and domiciliary support.

COMMUNITY SERVICES
This concept may be extended to include promoting the growth and development of groups or communities, that is *to develop a social environment which can do better justice to potentialities of human nature.*

Whole groups of people undergoing stress — typically those in socially deprived twilight zones — may revert to infantile modes of adjustment. Outsiders are unwelcome; people submit to the authoritarian leadership of local demagogues (witness Paisley, Craig and the I.R.A. in Belfast); community amenities (e.g. street furniture) are vandalized.

Workers promote the social growth, development, reconstruction and upgrading of whole communities and social groupings (particularly the depressed enclaves). Schemes are mounted to raise the aggregate level of living; the income level of inhabitants is raised; job opportunities are developed within the community; rents are supplemented; resources are so concentrated in the area that it becomes more attractive to skilled professionals recruited to improve services and provide leadership; the quality of homes is improved. Alinsky-like[71] advocates build on the strength of concentrated numbers of people, using their own social power to promote their own interests. Migrants from the area are lured back into it. Parallel considerations apply in social services contributions to new town developments, as at Milton Keynes, Thamesmead and Peterborough.

Practitioners are seeking to develop the process of socio-cultural growth or accumulation whereby new cultural elements or traits are progressively and cumulatively added to those already present (by inventions, discovery and cross-cultural borrowing).

The *community or locality development* movement is central to this programme as is evidenced by such statements of objectives as *'to accelerate the pace of the deprived community's social and cultural development'*; *'to help increase resources, amenities and skills of community to match rising national levels of social expectations'*; *'to promote better living of the community particularly through active participation of its own members'*.

Community development is seen as an educational process aiming at personal, group and community growth, U.S. community workers in this area being aptly named 'field educators'. Field educators make people in culturally deprived areas aware of the delimiting constraints on them. They focus their energies on a particular developmental need affecting the entire deprived community, and collaborate with community members in specific action programmes which constitute focal growth points.

Three different types of community development fall under this objective. First, field educators may get a new social or technological technique embodied into a community. Thus they were instrumental in getting the Ministry of Agriculture to introduce a hybrid corn into a seed strain which was weakening after long, continuous propagation in a depressed farming community. Second, they may help communities adjust to the social consequences of technological and other changes. For example, accompanying industrialist teams introducing new industries into communities advise people on how to use increased earnings to take advantage of modern technology, build better houses, develop better social amenities, or to work through new social patterns established by the advent of new industry. Finally, they may help communities to engage their own resources and to work cooperatively in identifying and resolving their own developmental problems. Thus representative community councils have been developed which jointly appraise with local administrators the realistic community situation, communicate their findings to the community at large, and jointly formulate comprehensive social development plans.

In all these activities, development comes as community members see the need for it and learn how to make desired changes. To institute a particular project is often less important than initiating the process by which community members learn to establish significant projects of their own. Community development activities are undertaken not simply to resolve a particularized problem or meet a specialized need but also to augment growth and maturity in civic affairs. This applies when individuals are taught skills necessary in contributing to collective thinking or in eliciting effective contributions from all members. Through such means, agencies develop an atmosphere in which individuals and groups begin to contribute effectively to their own social change and improvement.

SPECIFIC TARGETS
A random sample of case targets defined under this objective included:

(i) To define and develop available, unused client skills and opportunities and obstacles to their use.

(ii) To eliminate bed-wetting in a 12-year-old suffering from enuresis.

(iii) To define the causal chain of regressive behaviour in the family situation.

(iv) To define the sequence of intervention and problem treatment which will most probably lead to sustained growth and development in an individual's or family's multi-problem situation.

(v) To reduce infantile reactions to stress in the husband's work situation.

(vi) To help the father react to his children in a manner which will cease to infantilize them.

(vii) To help the wife recognize how she is transferring her feelings towards her father into the form of unjust complaints of her husband's neglect in the present situation.

(viii) To help the philandering husband to carry over behaviour which evokes positive responses from his girl-friend into his relationship with his wife.

(ix) To help the husband focus his own previously uncontrolled anger into those specific, delimited marital problems which give rise to it, to eliminate his own retaliatory behaviour which is confirming his wife's distorted perceptions, and to express sympathy and approval when appropriate as part of a programme by which the wife's distorted attitude towards men is deconditioned.

(x) To interest educationally deprived children and clients in reading by encouraging mothers to borrow books to read to their children at home.

(xi) To teach the client family the skills of contributing to group thinking and the rewards of exercising them in civic group situations.

(xii) To help clients learn from each other by encouraging cross-class, cross-problem and cross-age interactions among clients.

(xiii) To help clients make the transition from one social state to another with minimal adjustment problems.

B. To Promote Growth-Inducing Elements in the Individual's Social Environment
To Reduce Growth-Inhibiting Elements in the Individual's Social Environment

This objective contains various elements:

1. To arrange conditions in the client's social milieu so that growth-inducing elements are positively reinforced, and growth-inhibiting elements negatively reinforced.

2. To help the individual to counteract the debilitating influences of the community system (including the family and work sub-systems).

Thus, a worker's main concern may be to reduce environmental stress rather than to modify client reactions to it. This may take the form of providing money, accommodation, clothing, or of influencing others in the client's social surround to modify their attitudes towards him.

3. To limit the extent to which the community system submerges and exploits individual members.

The objective of the work system is to efficiently produce objects and services for profits and benefits for the community or for defined community groups. Only in recent years have companies begun to recognize or pay lip-service to their social welfare functions.

4. To serve community needs — the larger super-system in which the individual or family system is embedded.

This is the objective of community protection. Social service agencies are established by the community for its own protection, as well as to help clients individually. Poverty is not only undesirable for any individual but economically and politically dangerous, and individuals have some obligation to contribute to community well-being as well as to their own.

5. To reduce disfunctions of the community system which cause disfunctions among individual members, that is to reduce anxiety-evoking elements in the environment.

   Individuals change by the social system changing its rules, procedure, policies and structure.

6. To help engineer a community system which is functional in the context of the individual client's disfunctional behaviour.

   For example, the worker may arrange that problem behaviour which normally elicits attention is ignored by the client's family and friends.

7. To improve the qualities of impinging social environments with which individuals are actually and actively in contact.

   The quality of community patterns, institutions and practices contributes to the emotional and psychological needs of individuals. In the later stages of the client's treatment, as he gathers strength, independence and facility, it may become important for the client's social system to change responsively.

8. To open up new possibilities for clients to reform the social situation and system in which they find themselves.

   To some degree and in some situations, clients improve not by changing themselves in some kind of fixed environmental social situation, but by changing the social environment itself.

9. To influence the community and its major institutions which impinge on the helping system.

   The emphasis is on situational and cultural bases of individual functioning or discontinuity. The focus here shifts from the first set of objectives to the significance of individual behaviour as this derives from the role individuals play in advancing adaptation within and mastery of the social environment and behaviour traits acquired in the course of socialization. Social work practice (particularly community work) concentrates on particular segments of the social environment encountered by people. An attack is made on the causes of social disorganization.

10. Promote Fulfilment of Safety Needs
Reduce Insecurity

Many theorists regard the individual's need for 'safety' as a 'care need'. Its obverse, neurotic anxiety, is a 'care disorder', since other neurotic and psychotic symptoms may be interpreted as defences against it.

POSITIVE POLE
Workers aim *to help the individual fulfil his basic minimum needs and*

necessities for daily living: safety, security and comfort. Thus the social services provide some assurance of the basic physiological needs of food, shelter, clothing and the treatment of illness; emotional needs for belongingness and reward gratification; mental needs for intellectual vitamins and nourishment; social needs such as assurance of income, work, mobility and freedom from violence or interference. The concept of succour summarizes much that is contained here.

The city family must have an adequate dwelling as the centre of its life activities and adequate nourishment to render any activity feasible. Included here are safeguards against exploitation or corruption by others, particularly in the case of those who are vulnerable because young, weak in body or mind, inexperienced or in a state of physical, official or economic dependence.

In respect of this objective, the problem is not so much one of ensuring that basic needs are provided for each family and individual, but more a matter of ensuring that individuals feel secure and safe in the knowledge that these will be provided on a continuing basis. The individual projecting a future for himself where everything is uncertain except for the eventual realization of his fears, is likely to behave in ways which increase his insecurity and hopelessness. His off-job situation may make it increasingly difficult to hold down a job or to budget his household expenditure. Threats to survival are usually partly internal and partly external to the individual.

NEGATIVE POLE

The objective may be stated in terms of disvalues to be avoided. Workers seek *to eliminate, reduce, circumscribe or extend the immunity of individuals and groups from apprehensions, anxieties and insecurities (ranging from uneasiness to complete panic) in reaction to real or symbolic, actual or potential dangers, hazards, risks, nuisance and threats.* These may be physical, mental or emotional. They may include material want, dietary deficiency, social hazards and contingencies, distorted personal perceptions or disproportionate reactions. Resulting emotional and mental states may include feelings of rejection, feelings of isolation, attitudes of alarm towards life, feelings of suspicion, jealousy and hatred, guilt, lack of self-esteem or feelings of unworthiness.

Free-floating anxiety is a specific feeling of fear detached by a strong repression from its object. It may continue to operate from the unconscious mind as an irrational or generalized fear. Insecurity is an emotional state which, if chronic, determines pathological reactions such as incapacitating fears, obsessions and phobias. We include here compulsive reactions associated with certain objects such as school, hospital, or with certain situations such as separation from parents, darkness, open spaces (agrophobia), closed spaces (claustrophobia), etc.

They include more extreme forms of anxiety which, for example, characterize dysthnic disorders. Individuals respond to continuously increasing stress first by lag in response, then by over-compensatory response and finally by catastrophic collapse.

A group dimension exists as when each person becomes so concerned for his own safety in situations of panic that he cannot cope with group demands. In so far as the incidence, focus and intensity of anxiety between different groups can be compared, it is equally possible to talk about community-wide intervention to lower the level of group anxiety. Insecurity sometimes determines the structure of the social group. Problems of mass insecurity, anxiety levels and mental inbalance arise in the sociological context of political and economic psychology. Whole communities may be subject to insecurity — witness the fears of mugging.

COMMUNITY SERVICES

Community work and social planning are relevant at this community-wide or institutional level of social service intervention. Encouraging industries of certain kinds to move into an area of high unemployment may make an impact on wider manifestations of the problem. Career programmes may involve placing the sub-employed in jobs where employers are financially assisted to open up reasonably well-paid opportunities, assisting employees in their new jobs, and employers in learning how to handle them. Assisting people in taking up entitlements from bodies like the Supplementary Benefits Commission helps protect individuals from drastic material want.

Workers seek to provide freedom from want. This involves a minimum income level, access to such services as housing, medical care, education, recreation and other qualitative aspects of living embodied in the other objectives stated herewith.

Perhaps the most effective single way of achieving this objective is to reverse the deliberate disengagement by which the discarded, the ignored, the vulnerable, the 'hopeless' and the chronic are not accepted for service. We must seek ways of increasing the relevance of agency services to these groups, rather than screening them out on the grounds that they do not fit ('have unrealistic expectations of') our services, or that improvement and change is unlikely. This entails adapting services to people's felt need. A range of studies including Timms and Mayer,[72] Ballard and Mudd[73] in England, to Pomeroy, Yahr and Podell,[74] and Silverman[75] in America, and the Danish Social Reform investigation,[76] all demonstrate how large this gap is in Western societies.

INDIVIDUAL SERVICES

Falling within the objective are programmes for protecting individuals from neglect, illness or danger as a result of their presence in particular social environments. Thus individuals are helped to avoid pain, physical injury and illness by developing their ability to take precautionary measures and are concerned with preventing people from discomforting or endangering others. Children are entitled to protection from neglect or ill treatment by parents, and even in less problematic family situations, mother-child relations are recognized as of paramount importance in satisfying individuals' basic needs for social security, and many interventions are based on this premise. Psycho-analytically based casework is likely to make some impact where emotional insecurity results from early client experiences of parent-child relations.

In many situations covering the range of insecurity problems, therapeutic counter-conditioning is used. Workers establish a set of responses which are antagonistic to the anxiety-provoking behaviour so that it is eliminated. Antagonistic responses include deep muscle relaxation, avoidance responses using shock therapy and respiratory changes. For example, the client is taught deep muscle relaxation in the presence of feared objects or situations either in simulated or real-life situations, or through systematic desensitization processes. Anxiety-extinction might be achieved by the permissiveness of the therapist.

Within the interview situation, workers are careful to avoid the anxiety which would normally arise if the person attempted to do, feel or think of certain things in another's presence. Equivalent techniques are employed in permissive group therapy sessions or in the use of permissive audiences in psycho-drama.

SPECIFIC TARGETS
We may further specify this objective in these terms:

  (i) To promote clients' security in relation to the outside world.
 (ii) To define and work through the client's perceptions of threatening elements in his external social environment.
(iii) To define and work through the client's anxious responses to threatening elements in his external social environment (e.g. avoidance of contact).
 (iv) To explore with the client alternative ways of reducing insecurities, uncertainties or sense of threat in relation to his external social environment.
  (v) To build on the client's capacities to cope with threatening elements of his external social environment.
 (vi) To receive into care children who are deprived, whether through lacking parents, being abandoned, or being in need of protection through neglect.
(vii) To maintain protective care for residents in care.
(viii) To provide a safe place for dependent clients while the family responsible are at work and play.

(ix) To care for clients' basic needs for rest, nutrition and safety.

11. Promote Economic Security
Reduce Economic Poverty

'Whatever you may do, wherever you aspire,
First feed the face, and then talk right and wrong.
For even the saintliest folk may act like sinners
Unless they've had their customary dinners.'
Bertholt Brecht, The Threepenny Opera

POSITIVE POLE

Workers aim *to promote economic security.* This objective implies that people have a right to assistance when they sink down in misery, and that this state should be prevented by establishing the individual's economic security. Workers recognize and abet not simply the individual's right to a basic minimum income to purchase the necessities of life, but also his right not to be so lacking in customary resources as to be unable to share in community customs. Poverty is not merely absence of money, it is a reinforcing cycle of handicaps which reduce choice and opportunity, rendering the poor man's son a poor man in his turn.

NEGATIVE POLE

Workers aim *to reduce economic poverty, income deprivation, insufficiency, dislocation and diseconomy.*

The intention is *to reduce poverty* whether defined in: absolute physiological terms as absence of food, health, shelter, warmth and clothing; sociological or comparative terms as a defined standard below which none should fall; or psychological or disutility terms as what poor people feel as hurtful about poverty.

This entails the objective of seeking *to prevent, detect and alleviate income deprivation* where family income falls down to subsistence levels; *to prevent people suffering housing deprivation* because of relative obsolescence in physical structures of dwellings, inadaptability to special but indispensable occupant needs, inaccessibility of basic amenities, overcrowding or exorbitant rents. Further objectives are *to reduce social deprivation* in the hope that families will be prevented from falling below a level generally regarded as causing hardship by comparison with current community living standards; and *to help clients manage their income* so that economic difficulties are not engendered by faulty budgeting procedures.

CLIENTELE

Poverty continues to be a stark, unsolved problem though its structure is changing in that it is no longer shared by persons from many walks of life, the poor having become a group with special characteristics.

Distressingly, those suffering most from these deprivations are familiar groups — those whose income is low, unstable or inadequately used; single-handed mothers who are widows, deserted, separated or unmarried; the aged living alone; families without a male earner; victims of prejudice; those lacking education or training; children from dislocated social structures; families where potential bread-winners are sick or intermittently employed; large families in privately-rented uncontrolled furnished accommodation; coloured immigrants; caravan dwellers and travellers; the handicapped and disabled; the unemployed. The client lacks certain tangible financial resources — money, food, shelter, employment, transportation, etc. Economic subsistence is taken for granted by those outside the poverty segment, but economic security is not just a question of each having as of right sufficient cash to pay for necessities. Each person has some rights to a sufficient income to support those basic human passions which are regarded as normal within high-income societies, for comfort, frivolity, the relief of monotony, even irresponsibility. Income maintenance programmes or assured annual incomes may deal with the economics of the situation but scarcely suffice to satisfy the aspirations of poor people to reduce their alienation.

COMMUNITY SERVICES

At the community level, the aim is to provide a certain floor to possible economic disaster. This involves programmes for redistributing the share of the lowest income groups in the economic pie relative to the rest of the community. Provision of regular income is the key variable from whatever source it derives, whether employment, social security, private income, capital or insurance, income transfers or indirectly through service provision. Services include financial assistance or economic concessions to clients; assistance in handling over-harsh creditors; meals-on-wheels or luncheon vouchers for those who would otherwise fall below tolerable nutritional levels — in fact all services whose delivery might make some impact on economic instability.

A primary instrument in achieving this objective is fiscal welfare policy. Fiscal welfare changes the pattern of current and future claims by taking less in tax and rates (and thus increasing net disposable income) when a citizen's child is born, when education is prolonged, when ex-wives are to be maintained, when citizens reach a specified age, and so on.

Anti-poverty measures include national fiscal welfare policies administered through such mechanisms as the social security system, non-profit subsidies, partial rate remissions, welfare foods and milk, school meals services, financial assistance to children with special grants (e.g. for school uniform, expenses, clothing, milk, etc.), education maintenance allowances, free state services, services with remission systems such as recuperative holidays, support in residential care, day nurseries, domestic help, contraceptives and medical care services.

The great problem in these fields is the labyrinth of rules, forms and offices which govern the distribution of these benefits in which poor, inarticulate or ill-informed families get lost. An estimated four in five of those who could be reimbursed for services do not apply, whether because of ignorance or discouragement. If all potential benefits were taken up by those entitled to them, they would make an appreciable impact on income deprivation. Thus major tasks for social workers are getting such benefits taken up, and contributing informed information and judgement which might help the distribution of State services so as to make some impact on poverty. Another is to change the official definition of poverty used by other State services (for example from the current 68 per cent to 78 per cent of the average manual worker's disposable income).

INDIVIDUAL SERVICES

Workers are often instrumental in helping clients to combat threats to continuity of income through chronological age, retirement, prolonged unemployment or disability, by referring them through to — sometimes negotiating with — local social security offices. Facilitating objectives might include encouraging selected income-increases by various methods, or encouraging ownership and management of property in the broadest sense. On occasion, people are helped to achieve an economic toehold through negotiated loans, typically for house purchase.

This objective was undervalued by many psycho-dynamically oriented caseworkers in the 1960s. ('The gas bill was not the real problem — it was simply a projection of infantile urges towards dependency.') Many were severely criticized for providing services which were irrelevant to the needs of major portions of agency clientele. If clients are to be satisfied, material needs must be given early attention. ('She got down to the money side straight after I told her.')

SPECIFIC TARGETS

We may further specify this objective as follows:

(i) To estimate income needed for client survival, and ensure its provision.

(ii) To define client's problems in meeting essential commitments (e.g. spending patterns), enabling him to meet them given the interrelation of these and other problems.

(iii) To define the attitudes of creditors and the severity of imposable sanctions where this is relevant.

(iv) To define with the client appropriate attitudes to essential commitments and methods of meeting them through income.

(v) To define and organize commitments outside direct client control.

(vi) To define clients' rights and entitlements to benefits or contributions from service agencies, working through their feelings about claiming these.

(vii) To build on the earning potential of family members.

(viii) To help the client use his own resources optimally.

(ix) To help the client family share responsibility for its financial self-management.

(x) To develop the client's willingness to share his knowledge of the financial position with other members of the family where this is appropriate.

(xi) To secure indirect financial supplements through direct service provisions.

12. Promote Capacity to cope with Crisis
Reduce Effects of Breakdown

'Everything is going down the drain!'
Client of H. Parad and G. Caplan

POSITIVE AND NEGATIVE POLES

Workers aim to *promote individual and community capacity to cope with personal or social emergencies, crises or disasters.* In negative form this means *to reduce the total range of effects of individual or community breakdown on both individuals and communities. To prevent problems degenerating into complete disaster* also forms part of this objective.

Crisis means that major changes are proceeding at a rapid (perhaps exponential) rate, producing sharp conflict, tensions and heightened costs to the individual or the community. The following may be distinguished: the crisis phases of heightened tension, attempts to use habitual coping mechanisms, calling into play emergency problem-solving mechanisms, and finally reorientation to post-crisis situations. The situations of those undergoing crisis change significantly from the starting conditions. The change is either temporary pending restoration to the previous condition, or a permanent, basic metamorphosis.

Certain hazardous life events influence everyone's personal experience in one way or another — pregnancy, birth, death, cataclysmic role transitions, incapacitating illnesses, etc. Such events affect not only those individuals immediately concerned, but also the family and other groups within the social network. Or a whole community system may undergo crisis, the system itself needing extensive specialist forms of social care, as in embattled Ulster in the

1970s.

Workers seek to resolve predicaments and minimize the emotional-mental-physical effects arising from acute (often prolonged) disturbance to the individual's expectations of himself and his relations with others. These may occur as a result of sudden alterations in the field of social forces acting upon the individual. Such disturbances include the loss or threatened loss of a significant relationship, the introduction of one or more significant others into the social orbit, and a transition in social status and role relations as a consequence of such factors. The emotionally hazardous event overpowers the individual's equilibrium in that his habitual problem-solving activities are inadequate to cope. The event often calls for new methods of solution in relation to the person's life experience if long-range ill-effects are to be avoided.

COMMUNITY SERVICES

This objective contains a political aspect in that it may also involve *reducing the ill-effects of debilitative, non-productive community tensions* and mitigating controversies where the net effect is liable to worsen the problem situation which gave rise to them.

Crisis-mobilization on a community-wide basis, as when perilous 'natural disasters' like floods, fires, life-endangering strikes or riots occur, involves mobilizing for collective use those assets which mostly remain dormant, typically conscripting citizens' private time for public service. Usually only a small fraction of additional community assets (such as currently unused manpower and money) need be mobilized in such cases, for a small, sharp increase in communal action exponentially increases the relative use of available energies. For example, only an extra 4 per cent of Nigeria's population was mobilized to handle, relatively successfully, the food crisis when civil war ended.

A related type of programme is the priority approach to areas of critical social deprivation where community services are breaking down. This is exemplified in urban aid programmes, educational priority areas, and by the programme of community development projects. Such initiatives parallel the U.S. Anti-Poverty and Model Cities programmes targeted on the urban crisis in American communities.

INDIVIDUAL SERVICES

This objective has often nurtured programmes of positive discrimination favouring the most troubled, disadvantaged individuals in communities.

It may involve reinforcing survival techniques among the disadvantaged so they can better cope with crisis situations. People may have reacted to crisis or failure in work, domestic or community life through participation in a criminal or a seasonal economy. Workers may seek to help clients develop more adaptive, efficient or socially accepted survival strategies. Clients and their attitudes may be prepared in advance of possible future crises, by injecting maximal supports to influence client resilience at the time of the crisis itself, or by crisis mobilization. Crisis is often a catalyst for major change. With some families, temporary eviction or temporary family break-up proves to be the catalyst for beneficial change in the longer-term.

Workers may encourage key influences in the client's environment (friends, relations, caretaking agents) who strengthen his tenacity. They may depress devitalizing, disabling or destructive influences so that the balance is tipped towards a new equilibrium which is reanimating rather than debilitative. This equilibrium may be established or revived through brief, time-delimited work with predicaments so that the client can face future threats with some sense of personal competence: the essence of crisis therapy. Workers may use the Redl type[77] of life-space interview to exploit behavioural episodes which have in the past represented disturbances in ego-functioning, thus utilizing crisis as grist for therapy.

Workers cannot foresee all future client circumstances. They must therefore build a repertoire of responses on which the client may call in adjusting to new circumstances as they arise. Many therapeutic systems encompass this preventive aim of reducing susceptibility to future breakdown in addition to ameliorating current problems.

SPECIFIC TARGETS
Some examples of these are:
  (i)   To develop client and client family capacities to anticipate, cope with and prevent crises.
  (ii) To develop client and client family capacities to cope with alarming outbursts of verbal or physical violence, episodes of acute withdrawal or sudden switches of affection.
  (iii) To endeavour to achieve the peaceful resolution of crises rather than all-round exhaustion and resentment.
  (iv) To reduce the total range of debilitative effects on individuals of temporary (or more permanent) family breakdown.
  (v)   To utilize client crises as catalysts for further development, adjustment and self-fulfilment.
  (vi) To prepare clients for potential future crises.

13. Promote a Supportive Social Environment
   ## Reduce Debilitative Elements in the Social Environment

POSITIVE POLE
Workers endeavour *to promote a social environment which is supportive and growth-inducing in respect of physical, social and cultural elements and their interrelation, and can therefore be*

understood as a community. This objective refers to all that is understood by 'community spirit'. Workers hope *to improve the restorative structures within the environment,* to ensure that sympathy, support, comfort and sustainment are available to the weak, disabled, inexperienced, infirm, defeated, humiliated, lonely, dejected, sick or mentally confused. A supportive environment refers to all those social functions which individuals cannot carry out alone or through existing institutions. By social environment we mean that system of spatial and temporal regularities of human structure which influences the biological and behavioural activities of the population as a whole and of individuals. Social environments which are supportive in terms of providing physical needs (food, shelter, clothing, warmth), psychological needs (love, affection, belongingness, orientation), and social needs (opportunities for forming relations, achieving social status, education, recreation).

The significance of this objective is clear. Slum-dwellers disproportionately suffer from social problems while lacking internal community structures for dealing with them. People with problems cluster in — perhaps gravitate to — depressed areas; personal and social pathologies are 'contagious', thus problems become self-perpetuating and the area more run down than ever. Moreover, fewer experienced professional workers of all kinds work in slums so that they frequently have to depend on externally imported services.

A supportive community is one planned as a whole with an organic integration of work, living and play to facilitate a coherent, painless life in a responsive environment. Its inhabitants grow increasingly sensitive to and considerate of each other. In such environments, we can justifiably make predictable expectations which provide a stable frame for daily activities. In some deep sense, it fosters positive mental health, being an appropriate object for human adjustment.

Such a communitarian environment depends on common forms of experience developing among individuals. The contrast is with the kind of hostile environment which is not only alienated and atomistic, but also manifests high levels of aggression and violence. One critical element is the degree of community stability or mobility in terms of local population shifts, for a population constantly on the move normally lacks the continuity necessary for the spontaneous, 'informal' support of its members. Another element is the degree of aggression or violence among its members.

In some spheres, everyone understands the interdependence which necessarily characterizes complex, modern urban communities. Thus water, gas, electricity, sewage, roads, postal and telephone services are developed without concern that this increases citizen dependency on these services. At various times, citizens necessarily depend on community social support services in the same way.

NEGATIVE POLE

Workers seek *to reduce those debilitative elements in the individual's social environment inimical to his growth, development and stability.* Under this heading, one aim is to reduce aggression against individuals in the form of (often violent) encroachments on their self-regarding sphere of concerns and activities. The political element of this objective may involve *reducing the overall negative social effects of the administration of community services or lack of provisions on the lives of individuals and families.*

COMMUNITY SERVICES

Services meeting this objective range from the reception into care of those children deemed in need of protection, together with appropriate boarding-out and residential care provisions, to immigrant settlement schemes and liaison with societies representing minority groups. To develop a more supportive community, the shifting relations between treatment agencies and other helping institutions — central and local government, research groups, courts, professional associations, employment agencies, family and social action groups — must be altered. Acting in unison, voluntary agencies might begin to build the kind of supportive environmental nexus which Freemasonry and Rotarianism provides for certain more fortunate groups. This is perhaps the central social planning task of social services agencies.

INDIVIDUAL SERVICES

At the individual level, efforts to help people through the medium of their immediate social environment of family, friends and neighbourhood — what in community work is sometimes called environmental manipulation — fall under this objective. Modifying the effect of the social security system on the family system exemplifies the broker activities by which workers seek to promote a supportive social environment.

The objective covers many casework activities, from encouraging cooperative sexual behaviour in the impotent husband's spouse to helping a mother develop warm, affectionate, nurturant relations with her child. Workers may engineer situations in which positive reinforcement for disfunctional behaviour is withheld. They are concerned, for example, with the rewarding or punishing nature of client behaviour and its consequences, which may lead to interventions in the wider life situation of the client. As the client's drives begin to express themselves through increasingly functional behaviour, he may find himself in opposition to a social environment unfavourable to those drives which are thereupon externalized in the form of aggression. In some socially adverse environments, stresses on the individual warp him and may induce mental illness no matter how healthy he would have been given some happier environment.

This is often the cue for more intensive environmental manipulation and activities designed to foster a sense of caring among relevant client contacts. Contingencies of the problem situation may often have a greater effect than workers' treatment. The worker ensures that situational contingencies are used to the full to get beneficial results. Sometimes the need is to define which family and community resources the individual might use in improving his problematic situation. By discussing their predicaments, which they may be better able to do having as it were 'rehearsed' this process in the casework interview, clients may begin to open up therapeutic possibilities in their own networks of family and friends.

A major service comprises supplementing intrafamilial cooperation in various ways. Families are expected to provide material, mental, emotional, social and cultural support for their members. As a rule this no longer embraces extended family relations — uncles, brothers, grandparents — and family disintegration often undercuts intrafamilial support even from cohabitants or from adult children for their aged parents. The State, however, sticks closer than a son and Hegel's doctrine of its supremacy over the family as a support mechanism seems more than ever relevant. As devices for socialization, families are increasingly by-passed as over-conservative either by the State (witness the concentration on children of deprived families under Educationally Deprived Area programmes in the U.K. and Headstart in the U.S.), or by the children themselves. Ignoring these tendencies has sometimes resulted in workers vainly seeking to bolster disintegrating families as the basis for support. The objective must surely be to use intrafamilial support so far as this is still possible in individual cases, but where it is not to compensate by building and substituting other support networks wherever this is possible.

SPECIFIC TARGETS

This objective may be further specified as follows:

    (i) To define debilitative and disabling elements among client reference groups, neighbourhood or community systems causally contributive to actual (or potential) client problems.

   (ii) To define alternative methods for improving these disabling environmental features (e.g. bad housing), and implement the most effective.

  (iii) To develop a willingness to take decisions and action which will be helpful to, rather than debilitative for, clients within the relevant client system or wider community with due regard for non-intrusion of privacy.

  (iv) To increase the range and depth of community information and understanding of debilitative conditions causally contributive to client problems.

(v) To assist the client in seeking some improvement in physical environment, social relations and economic circumstances.

(vi) To open up to clients the therapeutic possibilities of their own networks.

(vii) To improve the environment for children by better standards of care at home, wider play opportunities, and by encouraging parental involvement in their activities.

(viii) To develop an interest in the neighbourhood's appearance by encouraging people to come together, and by helping them to identify sources of information, assess facts and invoke the aid of various authorities.

(ix) To associate organizational representatives in a concern for the overall wellbeing of neighbourhood personnel.

(x) To encourage both small and large groups to seek the active involvement of prestige figures and community leaders.

14. Promote Equality of Life-Chances
Reduce Inequality of Life-Chances

'Been down so long that it don't bother me'
Negro spiritual

There is a general egalitarian principle, embodying the right to equality of opportunity and underlying most major world religions, utilitarian enlightenment and socialistic philosophies which penetrates every aspect of social service delivery and practice. Every individual and social group is viewed under this principle as of equal intrinsic worth and, therefore, entitled to equal civil, political, social and economic rights and treatment, and of being subject to equal constraints.

POSITIVE AND NEGATIVE POLES
To promote a greater equalization and evening up of the life-chances of individuals, groups and communities, or stated negatively: *to reduce social underprivilege arising from the inequities and injustices of life-chances.* Life-chances comprise the individual's or group's supply of services, goods and external living conditions. The equality principle may be treated numerically (the egalitarian ideal) or proportionally (the meritocratic ideal).

This objective applies in many spheres. 'Equality' is used for making comparisons between different things in relation to some common quality. It refers to equalization of such things as power, wealth, income, health, status, consideration, opportunity, treatment or benefit for people of different races, religions, locales, colours, sexes, socio-economic classes, interests or reference groups. Equality before the law implies that every citizen has access to public services on an equal basis according to the law, thus the administrative apparatus should treat all citizens in the same way. Such notions are essential to the viability and integrity of democratic processes.

The objective can then be detailed in terms such as this: *to reduce the degrees to which some are given better opportunity, consideration or treatment than others in any respect, in advance of any rational and justifiable grounds being produced for unequal treatment on the basis of relevant differences of natural condition between them.* This saves us from excluding preferences warranted by differences in situation or desire between one person and another. All persons have an equal claim to the recognition of their interests. This also relates to the objective of social mobility — the opportunity *to better one's condition irrespective of geographical or cultural starting point.* The objective relates particularly to those receiving insufficient resources or status in relation to the rest of the community.

The following questions are relevant: How far do individuals have opportunities to achieve whatever their talents can bring? How far is the individual's socio-economic status relative to that of others in the community? Is it determined by his own abilities and efforts rather than by his social origins and circumstances of birth? How much equality of opportunity do we have? Is this increasing or decreasing?

One element of equality is desert or the fair deal — each individual gets what he merits or deserves. An extreme emphasis on individual talent and the aristocracy of ability would be intolerable for those condemned to failure because they lack the particular talents valued in our present community culture. The desire for greater equality of opportunity must be tempered by the demand that the successful and talented share their good fortune with the less well endowed. This prompts a consideration of how far community benefits are distributed.

SERVICES
At the broadest level of social policy, this objective implies controlling the yields of production — both goods and services — so as to achieve as equitable a distribution as possible among different population groups and areas. The radical community work approach to welfare services as a means of redistributing power, resources and influence, represents a drive in the same direction at a more direct level. When adopted, this approach colours every aspect of a social service agency's work.

If we wish to pursue this objective more intensively, key factors would have to be identified which determined past inequalities: inadequate housing, poor educational facilities, minimal employment opportunities, and so forth. This might be accomplished either by reducing natural differences in health and strength, as when additional resources are poured in to aid the mentally subnormal or the physically handicapped. Or artificial and cultural differences in power, status and privilege might be reduced, as when resources are allocated to improving the lot of gypsies or the elderly.

The significance of this objective can be shown as follows: 1 per cent of the population receive as much income as the bottom 30 per cent put together; 10 per cent of the population own 80 per cent of all private wealth. 'Social and economic development demands sacrifices' but who makes the sacrifices and can they be more equitably distributed?

The major beneficiaries of a high-cost service like education can arguably be said to be the middle classes (½ per cent of children from unskilled or semi-skilled manual worker parents reach university compared with 14 per cent of professional and managerial groups), while the major users of low-cost services such as child care have been the under-class of the poor and deprived.

From one point of view, the total operation of social services agencies may be interpreted as a mechanism designed for redistributing income or other benefits by indirect means from the privileged rate- and tax-payers, to the underprivileged clientele on which agencies lavish their meagre resources.

Also implicit in this objective is the concept of territorial justice — *to reduce the lag and unevenness in service availability between one area or region and another.*

INDIVIDUAL SERVICES
The pursuit of selective policies of collective and comprehensive investment in the disabled will reduce natural differences in health, strength and status, while selectively investing services in twilight zones will somewhat diminish artificial cultural differences in power and privilege. The provision of holidays for underprivileged families leads to a slightly more proportionate equality of opportunity in respect of recreation, and keeping area offices open to all-comers and other similar moves in the direction of a universalist service will help to achieve numerical equality in which everyone is given the same rights.

A specific contribution to the equalization of income can be made by giving direct financial aid or implementing economic concessions such as reduced transport fares, electric, gas and telephone charges. Inequalities of opportunity are reduced by supplying vocational guidance and job placement centres. When the hospital social worker argues against a patient's discharge on environmental grounds, she is evening-up chances of good health in relation to other patients whose home environment facilitates earlier discharge.

Workers equalize the power situation somewhat when sponsoring clients' claims to their rights at the social security office, ensuring adequate legal representation in the courts enforcing client entitlements to state rights (especially those rarely claimed) advocating changes in community planning on the basis of evidence supplied or forecast by social workers, using legal processes for a legal review of the way administrative processes work; sponsoring test cases on behalf of individuals to establish rights not obtained and publicizing the results of these; demonstrating the deprivation of rights and extending the range of individual rights by use of the tribunal and appeals system against the application of bureaucratic discretion to individuals; or in meetings of the Chief Executive's Corporate Planning Board when social services directors support and encourage a shift in emphasis which gets housing viewed as a social service. The key service is help in overcoming discriminatory social and structural barriers and the worker often takes up the client's side in a range of disputes with officialdom. ('I knew she was on my side once I'd heard her telling them off.') Workers reduce inequalities of power or capacity of a different kind when supplying the physically handicapped with aids and adaptations, or when by advice and counselling they supply clients with knowledge and understanding which will enable them to cope better. Educational instruction in things like domestic management and family care, together with consumer cooperatives and councils, fall into the latter category.

Clients often get a psychological lift from the processes of equalization, for example from the mere fact of a social class differential between themselves and the worker. ('It makes all the difference talking to someone who speaks so nicely — you come out on top of the world.') Involving recipients themselves in distributing and providing services may be vital in that equality and equalization become less possible if one person constantly takes the role of magnanimous donor, the other the role of perennial recipient.

COMMUNITY SERVICES
One central objective of community work is *to increase the power of the underprivileged* by speaking for them whilst educating them to speak for themselves. Egalitarian objectives demand sophisticated political skills in the struggle for redistribution of income, housing, employment, education and other claims and rights to community resources in favour of the underprivileged. Workers may be concerned with unmasking the more-or-less conscious deceptions and disguises of specific interest groups, and are involved in many activities and transactions having the effect of increasing the prestige of individuals with lower official status.

Movements and services promoting social equality must develop unique political action strategies derived from the egalitarian, humanistic base. To avoid self-contradiction, they cannot adopt manipulative and competitive models of political action inherited from and fitting non-egalitarian market philosophies wherein each interest group struggles to maximize its own non-egalitarian shares and no group struggles for social equality for all. The essence of any action strategy to promote social equality is absolute honesty in disseminating factual information about the links between non-egalitarian policies and existing social circumstances. Constructive political education must be directed at all community groups without attacking any one group or person; objectives, value premises and organizing principles having destructive consequences for all must be demonstrated; value changes must be induced through changes in the perceived self-interest. Real advantages accruing to all community groups from establishing egalitarian communities must be analyzed and explained.

Workers seek to organize the poor and underprivileged groups, to increase their self-confidence, to increase their action capacity, their command of utilitarian assets, and hence their power potential as based on these assets. Given the financial inequalities of the poor, their only source of power in relation to the rich is themselves. This entails creating effective community organizations.

CONSTRAINTS

Constraints customarily regarded as hindering the full achievement of this objective include a variety of institutionalized social arrangements:

    (i) the sanctity of private ownership of natural resources like land, means of production, many other services and goods;

    (ii) the right to accumulate, to will, and to inherit private property;

    (iii) the owner's rights to use property as he sees fit, subject only to limited social constraints, in free enterprise for the purposes of generating private profits without regard to indirect socio-environmental costs;

    (iv) the production and distribution of services and goods in accordance with the principles and dynamics of a free market economy;

    (v) a system of relatively stable social stratification as an organizing principle of position and role allocation;

    (vi) a system of unequal rewards and limitations for incumbents of differentially valued roles;

    (vii) narrow scope of universal entitlements by virtue of community membership;

    (viii) formal and informal systems of governance in which political power correlates with economic power;

    (ix) overt and covert controls of mass communication media by centres of concentrated economic power, resulting in the selective flow of information;

    (x) a system of unequal education perpetuating stratification and systematically indoctrinating the young into the dominant ideology of the extant social order.

SPECIFIC TARGETS
   (i) To maintain full citizen status for all clients.
  (ii) To develop and enlarge clients' ideas of their rights.
 (iii) To reduce discrimination of any one group of clients over others.
 (iv) To help improve the social life of all clients irrespective of their starting point.
  (v) To neutralize inequalities in staff treatment of clients.
 (vi) To increase the power of clients in deciding their own treatment and in the running of services.
 (vii) To sponsor representative client interest groups.
(viii) To educate clients in political skills necessary to attain rights and benefits.
 (ix) To advocate client interests in the face of opposition.
  (x) To safeguard the rights, needs and benefits of the underprivileged in community planning.

15. Promote Tolerance
Reduce Stigmatization

'Mutual forgiveness of each vice . . . opened the gates of paradise'
W. Blake

POSITIVE POLE
The positive side of the same coin may be expressed thus: *to extend the degree and extent of tolerance, permissiveness or acceptance of deviations from social norms, and hence to promote a greater variety and heterogeneity of social behaviour.* Toleration implies giving equal treatment to minority groups, which entails a limited acceptance that social benefits should be extended to those of whom we do not approve, out of a mixture of belief and humanity.

Associated with this are efforts to promote the openness of people's minds to other persons, groups or ideas so as to increase the likelihood of mutual understanding and the recognition of relationships being formed. It is necessary *to reduce tensions in the community separating young and old, poor and affluent, handicapped and non-handicapped, and those with ideological differences.* The toleration-stigmatization or acceptance-rejection continuum operates in terms of belief systems, personality and inter-personal relations.

NEGATIVE POLE
One major social services objective may be stated along these lines: *to reduce the stigma, discrimination, discredit, scapegoating and*

victimization attaching to a variety of individual deviations from norms and expectations. By stigmatization is meant unfavourable treatment, exclusion, rejection or attributions of inferiority to certain groups on arbitrary irrational grounds having little to do with the actual behaviour of those stigmatized.

Associated with this are efforts to reduce the way people close their minds to other persons, groups or ideas so as to decrease the likelihood of hostile reactions. An endeavour is made to reduce prejudice and bias which is loaded, distorted by predelictions and unquestioned assumptions, and to combat the belief systems which buttress prejudice assessments or statements, thence the adumbration of rigid ideologies for which proponents demand universal observance.

CLIENTELE

Stigma may cover physical deformities, character blemishes, class or family stigmata transmitted through lineages or associations with others rather than through any innate attributes of the individual. It may give rise to various more or less institutionalized or rationalized forms of discrimination. At the level of inter-personal relations, some are personally hostile to stigmatized persons or groups. At the level of community and interorganizational relations, some organizations or their employees may formally exclude certain groups from relevant and significant sources of information.

Those who have dealings with the stigmatized person do not accord him the respect and regard he expects to receive in virtue of the non-deviant aspects of his social identity. This objective therefore involves erasing the sharp lines drawn between the excluded and the included, facilitating the ease with which 'stigmatized' and 'normal' can intermingle in the same social situations to the point where the very concepts cease to apply meaningfully in the situation.

COMMUNITY SERVICES

At the community level, we are talking of minorities or sub-groups having distinct physical features, customs or cultural patterns who are excluded by dominant power groups from participating in cultural life. Minorities may be singled out from others in the community for differential or unequal treatment. They therefore regard themselves as objects of collective discrimination. For example, conceptual elimination of the mentally ill led to closing off this group in institutions located far from the centres of daily community life.

Examples of such community stigmatization abound. Thus the Richmond Fellowship was refused permission to convert a Liverpool house into a psychiatric after-care hostel after intense pressure from local residents' associations. The position of a local planning authority in such a case is a difficult one. It should provide enlightened leadership, but it also represents the rate-payers. If local residents do not want a hostel near at hand, it is not sensible to put it there. Another common example is landlord discrimination against unmarried mothers who have difficulty in finding rented accommodation. As one in fourteen babies are born outside wedlock and one in twelve in the first eight months of marriage, the unmarried mother is regarded as more deviant than she actually is. Public education is the only way to resolve some of these problems and social services aim to extend the boundaries of understanding and acceptance by increasing information, knowledge and understanding about various kinds of handicap. Leaflets, public talks and teach-ins by representatives of stigmatized groups, press releases, the recruitment of volunteers, workshops, local television and radio programmes which include representatives of stigmatized groups, community meetings and other information services, may all serve this end. In the area of race relations, legislative provisions support the objective of reducing a particular stigma. It is generally recognized that legislation alone cannot eliminate social prejudice, and this heavily depends on less tangible community work and education programmes.

Gaining circulation for softer social labels in referring to particular handicaps may contribute towards changes in public attitude. Thus the 'National Assistance' becomes 'Social Security', the 'unmarried mother' becomes the 'unsupported parent', and the derogatory status connoted by such nouns as 'pauper', 'lunatic', 'disadvantaged', and so on are eliminated.

The way agencies define a person affects his life chances and career alternatives. Social definitions are established which are used by both the person himself and by relevant others, a process of self-fulfilling prophecy being set in motion. Thus, trouble-makers are labelled as mentally ill in some institutional situations. Revising agency categorizations of clients may contribute much to this objective: for example, shifting from such labels based on medical or psychiatric symptoms as 'burnt-out schizophrenic', to social need or problem behaviour syndromes such as 'isolation' or 'alienation'. Similarly, agency eligibility standards used in determining who receives help have wide-ranging social repercussions, tending to segment service-recipients by type. Returning from humiliating means-test questions at 'the Welfare', black comedian Gregory found himself jubilant at the sight of firemen fighting the fire in his house without first questioning his financial and ethnic status.

Bateman[78] has shown that normally-sighted children educated in the same class as blind children, have more understanding attitudes towards blindness than those who have never encountered it. Mixed Rudolf Steiner-style day centres have successfully recruited from those clients having relevant skills and are based on analyses of client needs rather than on named client groups. This has led to client groups which previously stigmatized each other collaborating in joint activities. All of which has implications for the social service directors' contribution to overall community planning. It may considerably affect all aspects of social services work, for example, in recruiting volunteers or lessening feelings of helplessness experienced by the handicapped in some communities.

INDIVIDUAL SERVICES

At the individual level, problems of marital, parent-child or neighbourhood-family relations sometimes fall under this heading. They are directly linked to patterns of acceptance and rejection by both sides, as Erikson demonstrated.[79] Thus the intolerant teacher is helped to understand the child's problems and the landlord his tenants'. More specifically, in situations where neighbours petition against the presence of a particular problem family on a housing estate, workers might canvass potentially friendly neighbours, interpret family problems to petition ring-leaders, and exert organized counter-influence with relevant local groups and institutions. Fundamental worker acceptance of the individual client as an individual is maintained no matter how unacceptably he behaves.

Clients seeking material help often spend much effort in special pleading, both in the hope that by ingratiating themselves with workers their case will be counted as exceptional, thus qualifying for direct aid, and to free themselves from the felt stigmatization of financial dependency. In such situations workers aim to reduce the client's feelings of shame based on guilt at accepting 'charity', for example by tactfully raising the subject of financial problems and by so providing help that the client does not experience it as unpleasant ('It was done like it was a loan.')

The effective worker demonstrates trust in the client as having a genuine problem and presenting it honestly, without in any way imputing suspicions that the client is dishonest or cadging ('They seem to know you're telling the truth or you wouldn't be there less there was something going wrong somewhere.')

SPECIFIC TARGETS

Here we may mention briefly such targets as:
  (i) To promote acceptance of others' personal eccentricities with humour and tolerance wherever possible.
  (ii) To foster tolerance of deviant or diverse behaviour, or acting out.
  (iii) To foster tolerance of inner-directedness and emotional disturbances.
  (iv) To reduce stigma, discredit, discrimination, scapegoating and

victimization of the client by others or of others by the client.
(v) To extend the boundaries of clients' (or others') understanding by increasing information and knowledge of the background, causes and suffering of those stigmatized.

16. Promote a Heterogeneous Social Environment
Reduce Socio-Cultural Deprivation

'I'm depraved on account I'm deprived. So take me to a social worker.'
From Gee Officer Krupke! in West Side Story

POSITIVE POLE
Instead of a monolithic, homogeneous, monotonous community, democrats by and large seek a pluralistic community which maximizes the individual's opportunities for expressing and realizing diverse desires and interests. Workers seek *to assist the community, the group or the individual in developing a heterogeneous, richly varied and stimulating range of work and leisure activities, providing stimuli from which people may draw inspiration and motivation for thought and action.*

NEGATIVE POLE
Between any two groups, cultural norms may differ widely. Social perception of that difference, or differential treatment by others, may be great or small. Workers assist individuals and communities with problems and opportunities arising from social differentiation. By implication if not by overt and conscious design, workers promote variety, richness, experiment, spontaneity, novelty, originality and socio-cultural variation. Conversely, they aim *to reduce excessive homogeneity and uniformity among community members especially in respect of a consonant social, cultural or religious neighbourhood context, and to ameliorate socio-cultural deprivation.*

A homogeneously uniform community actualizes only a few narrowly related values. These values develop in a one-sided intensification instead of the total range of values unfolding in all fullness. For example, on many modern housing estates young people are not inducted into any social matrix in which they must learn to deal with others, and thus have no opportunity to expose self-images fixed within family and friends to social tests. Extreme homogeneity and stereotyped behaviour in a community, a group, an institution or an individual produces entropy, the system becoming more like itself and running down until it eventually dies.

Homogeneity characterizes the slum, that is the impoverished socio-cultural setting which has restricted opportunities for intellectual and psychological development, or is actively deleterious in compounding the inadventitious circumstances of its members. The clientele under this objective are typically those living in such zones — the culturally handicapped. They have few contacts with others outside their own neighbourhood locality or with beliefs and values other than those inherited through family socio-economic class, and there is little variation in daily activities.

The city tends to be a social leveller. People from varied socio-cultural backgrounds congregate there, exchanging parochial views for the more universal ones shared by other city-dwellers. The city is essentially a vast communications network, and a major environmental determinant is the cost in time or money of overcoming barriers to interactions, like visiting others who are geographically distant. The more communications improve, the greater the number of social options open to any one community member, and the more options open to the individual, the more the latent diversity of the urban population can be expressed. People with similar social interests and values who live near each other can maximize their interaction and share common facilities.

Instead of interactions being accepted for lack of other available alternatives increased mobility allows 'non-place' communities to develop based less on propinquity, occupation or social class than on mutual interests and consciously chosen life styles. This process brings diversity back to the city, rendering it a more interesting and stimulating environment, and increasing the range of choice open to people in the social relations they form. People participating in increasingly heterogeneous communities reverse *Brave New World* trends in which people become increasingly stereotyped and unable to break from those roles ascribed to them.

There is a basic human need for variability of social roles and norms to provide outlets for varied personalities. Hallmarks of stimulating environments are creative disorder, continuous change, expanding diversity, disruptive innovations and functional dislocation. Such environments are purposefully rich, complex, unzoned and decentralized, constituting a social forum where inhabitants encounter a mix of dissimilar people and events on common ground. Coping with such dissimilarities entails some recognition of conflict being important to human experience.

COMMUNITY SERVICES
Creating a heterogeneous community implies a policy of mixing clientele in terms of social, cultural and economic class; universalist rather than selective services; and a wider tolerance of social deviance. It implies an agency objective of encouraging heterogeneous clientele drawn from all classes, not just the poorest economically, from all races and from all locales, rather than developing services to intensively meet one specific type of need.

In his work with the mentally handicapped for the Wessex Regional Hospital Board, Kushlik[80] has demonstrated the ill-effects of artificiality and induced dependency from concentrating people with the same level of handicap in one residential institution. Urban planning programmes demonstrate the range of similar ghetto effects which arises in neighbourhoods rendered artificially homogeneous by forcing people with social problems (or even the same income levels) into a special area.

Many social planners regard as a primary task the demonstration and prevention of the ill-effects of social stratification created by housing policies. By mixing the types of housing, architecture and employment opportunities in the various sectors of a region, different groups of people are attracted. This is a first vital step to vary the population composition of an area.

Practically, this might suggest that area offices should be located on the borders between disadvantaged and prosperous areas, rather than in the geographical centre of the socially deprived area, as in this way clients come from all socio-economic classes. In residential settings, on similar principles, a mix of backgrounds and conditions should be drawn upon when selecting residents and staff, using the resulting conflicts therapeutically. Social planners seek to create a balanced community of heterogeneous composition in each neighbourhood giving individuals a viable function within it. This standpoint often informs many social service contributions to town development plans.

Workers reduce homogeneity in client environments, for example by providing holidays for those ensconced within the same neighbourhood without the relief of other environments. In social work practice at all levels, workers are encouraged to recognize the problems and conflicts arising from sociological variations, taking into account whether these derive from socio-economic class, or cultural and regional differences. No urban social worker would be worth his salt who confused the very different traditions of rural and urban West Indians, for example.

INDIVIDUAL SERVICES

At the individual casework level, this objective implies exploring alternatives and reducing fixated and obsessional behaviour whereby people persist in responding to problem situations and developing certain styles and attitudes they have learnt even though new responses or attitudes would prove more successful. We are concerned to reason out or symbolically rehearse in thought alternative possible solutions of client problems. Workers concerned often promote that behaviour in others towards their client which reinforces changes. Reinforcement may be arranged in terms of family encouragement and support, assistance from home help, meals-on-wheels and day care personnel.

SPECIFIC TARGETS

A few specific targets which ultimately derive from this concern provide some illustration:

    (i) To develop a more varied and interesting diet in residential homes and in the meals-on-wheels service.

    (ii) To provide a range of diversified and interesting means of outlets and stimuli for clients.

    (iii) To provide a wider range of varied, interesting and mentally stimulating activities in residential homes, day care centres and in the community.

    (iv) To foster staff capacity to tolerate and cope with value diversity and deviance amongst clients.

    (v) To promote a diversity of interests among clients.

    (vi) To encourage a mix of clientele in terms of socio-economic class, problem and geographical spread.

    (vii) To promote community centres with a diverse range of activities for diverse interests.

    (viii) To locate area offices on the borders between neighbourhoods of different socio-economic class composition.

    (ix) To promote free expression of a wide range of beliefs, attitudes, interests and desires within the neighbourhood.

    (x) To foster more varied client activities.

    (xi) To foster more varied client contacts.

    (xii) To expose clients to greater range and variety of values, beliefs, attitudes and interests.

C. To Promote a Better Match between Individuals and their Social Environment
To Reduce the Mismatch between Individuals and their Social Environment

This set of objectives relates to the consequences and effects of the individual's action on social arrangements, his structuring and patterning of situations and of the immediate social system around him, and the reverse of this influence in the course of the transaction:

1. To increase the types, amount and variety of exchanges between the individual person and his social environment, and to improve the match between them.

    Individuals must achieve certain kinds and amounts of exchanges with their social environment if they are to run their natural cycle of growth and development. Failing these exchanges, their growth and development is limited or distorted, resulting in disabling consequences.

2. To maximize the client's motivated interest in the social community around him.

3. To promote and preserve the individual's role and status in the social system of which he is a part.

   We are talking about balancing the twin objectives of community protection and client rehabilitation. The social environment and the individual's action have constantly to be evaluated according to how far they fulfil both the community (societal) and care (individual) needs.

4. To promote those transactions between individual and environment which induce natural growth and development of the individual and are simultaneously ameliorative to the social environment, rendering it more conducive to the growth and development of other community members.

   Many kinds of exchanges between the individual organism and his social environment are destructive to that environment. They threaten the survival of the offending individual as well as others who depend on the same social environment.

5. To see that environment-directed behaviour and environment-originating action are such that an appropriate exchange takes place with feedback to both the individual and his social environment.

   A change in the individual's disfunctioning behaviour is seldom effected or sustained without modification through the client's own efforts of the social environment within which he functions.

6. To match the individual's coping patterns with the qualities of the impinging social environment to produce growth-inducing and environment-ameliorating transactions.

   Intervention includes efforts to change either the individual's coping behaviour, or qualities of his impinging social environment or both, depending on the relative amenability to change involved.

7. To mediate the conflict or impasse between the individual's needs and those of the community.

   Encounters between individual organisms and communities may leave both changed. The functional autonomy of individuals implies the possibility of their survival apart from a specific community system, but also helps to maintain the community system.

8. To assist in reconciling and resolving conflicting demands and functions of the social environment on the one hand (including the work and family systems), with demands and functions of the individual on the other.

   Both the individual client system and the community system may have to change in order to effect an overall functional resolution which answers the positive needs of both individual clients and individual communities.

9. To give the helping system more scope to develop an organization which has a much more fluid boundary between itself and the community institutions.

The agency or helping system is anchored to both the individual organism and the social environment. The interaction between the individual and the social environment constitutes the transactional system, which in turn provides the agency's action field.

17. Promote Social Competence
Reduce Social Malfunctioning

'We must impart to the weak the technical, social and political skills which will enable them to get bread, dignity, freedom and strength by their own efforts'
Eric Hoffer

POSITIVE AND NEGATIVE POLES

Central to the social services task is *promoting social competence, adaptive efficiency to environmental changes, and behavioural equilibrium, assisting the acquisition of basic skills.* These manifest themselves in viable lines of conduct and patterns of behaviour. They are typically characterized in terms of a harmonious, equilibrial, wholesome and healthful adjustment of the individual, group or local community on the one hand, and the conditions, situations and persons constituting the wider surrounding environment, both social and physical, on the other.

The individual, group or community respond to a changing social environment by adaptively changing themselves to aid their own survival, functioning and achievement of purpose. Hopefully, the social services assist this coping behaviour, or at least *reduce maladjustment, incapacity for self-care, disabling habits, behavioural disturbances, disharmony, disequilibrium and instability,* all of which prevent this process from operating effectively. Workers seek to reduce faulty internalization which is attended by ineffective defence mechanisms or incomplete conflict resolution.

Workers aim *to enlarge the capacity and ability of individual, group or subculture to understand, master, orient themselves to and participate in prevailing customs, habits and behaviour of the community.* This includes social attainment in the areas of self-help, communication, social-relational ability and improved role performance. Clients are helped to make better use of resources available from job, school, home, family or wider community settings.

Social work provides education in those fields of living neglected, in respect of certain individuals, within conventional educational frameworks. Because adaptive efficiency can only be attained through the individual's own efforts and initiatives, workers help clients to develop their independent capacities to fulfil community expectations if they so choose. Increased client-effectiveness in key areas of daily living depends on learning a wider range of possible adaptive responses.

6 Balance of Objectives

What seems good to one seems bad to another. What well-ordered to one, confused to another. What is pleasing to one, displeases another.
Spinoza

Interrelations of Objectives

While naive consensualists tend to regard all social objectives as simple and ungraduated, naive pluralists regard all social objectives as graduated in a way that does not permit of any comparison or reconciliation of these graduations. More sophisticated approaches are concerned to develop intelligent insight into the interrelations of differentially graduated objectives lying along the same scale. These interrelations need to be viewed as a total system of objectives. This approach is more characteristic of the behaviour of the best statesmen, politicians, social and national planners. It has been characterized by Karl Mannheim[1] as 'substantive rationality' — a form of planning more appropriate to guide human affairs in the modern world.

Social objectives are not independent of but interact with each other, constituting a comprehensive system. Through its aggregate, avalanche, ricocheting effects, this entire system (rather than the effects of any specific social objective) shapes the common domain of all social objectives. All extant social objectives, policies and plans of a given community, operating together as a system, exert a decisive influence over the entire social services domain. Any specific social objective, policy or plan, or any specific cluster of social objectives, influences a specific segment within the broad domain of social objectives and policy. This proposition is supported by anthropologists' observations in all known communities which indicate that overall quality and circumstances of living and the nature of intra-community relations do not evolve randomly. They tend to follow coherent patterns developing over a period of time from a continuous interaction between natural, physical and biological forces, man-designed principles and courses of action, and chance events. It is the man-designed principles and courses of action which constitute the community's social objectives, policies and plans.

Social Values, Objectives and Action

Causal Sequences and Patterns

Since agency objectives and the social problems or states to which they
are addressed interact, the pattern of causal interconnection between
these objectives and social states may be mapped. To do so requires
that some proven correlations (or failing these some hypotheses about
relations) between agency objectives and social problems are developed.

For this purpose, it is relevant to draw on research into social
problems at the community-wide level, such as Liverpool Corporation's
famous study of social malaise[2] where a number of significant social
indicators were correlated, or research into social problems conducted
at the individual level of functiong such as Jehu's studies.[3] Thus from
the Liverpool study we see that malicious damage, fraud and theft
correlate with low socio-economic status and overcrowding; burglary
and assault correlate with unemployment, job instability and run-down
places of residence; childcare problems correlate highly with
overcrowding, large families, dilapidated dwellings and low socio-
economic status, as does unemployment, job instability and clothing
problems; mental subnormality correlates with theft, dilapidated and
overcrowded housing, and debt.

Similarly, research may help determine the relation between
supportive and heterogeneous environments. Rosenberg, Suchman and
Goldsen[4] in case studies on social situations of aged and religious
groups, have tried to demonstrate that a given minority group should
constitute about 40 per cent of the population within a particular
neighbourhood to ensure there are sufficient minority group members
at hand to provide an adequate base for a supportive system of social
relationships. For when a minority group member becomes too isolated
from other members of his immediate reference group, he has no choice
but to form relations with majority group members which may not
always be beneficial.

The problem is not simply the shortage of concrete empirical data,
but also the fact that such data as we do possess throw light on
one-to-one relations and links between two variables in isolation, rather
than the ramifying effects which occur when all the variables in the
social system concerned together with the agency responses designed to
meet them, are interrelated and changing simultaneously. Some
comprehensive set of hypotheses is required about causal sequences and
patterns connecting various social objectives and the problems which
can then be tested in the context of the total community system and
the agencies which serve it. The use of community simulation models
developed in social systems technology may provide a valuable
instrument for testing such hypotheses. Meanwhile, the sources for such
hypotheses lie in psychological and sociological theory, together with
informed judgements of social scientists and social services prac-

titioners. Such hypotheses as have been publicly formulated are of varying worth for this purpose. Few have undertaken the kind of analysis which led Rescher[5] to assert that the expansion of the welfare state has led to a devaluation of economic security as such, erosion of initiative, flight from responsibility, growing dependence on and resentment of authority, rising and probably unreal expectations, growing dependence on physical comfort whilst being reluctant to admit it, and reappraisal of public service.

Let us explore what some of the causal sequences connecting social problems (and the agency objectives in trying to meet them) might look like were such a programme undertaken. There are some fairly typical and familiar sequences or chains of events in the build-up of the client problems to the point where they are impossible for the client to control.

For example, the typical stimulus-response (S-R) sequences in the build-up of homosexual impulses: male person in public place (S); client glances towards person (R); person returns glance (S); client feels mild emotion and fantasy, giving an additional glance (R); visual contact between client and male established (S); client's emotions and fantasies intensify and additional glances are given (R); physical proximity established (S); heightened client desire (R); heightened desire of other male manifest (S); verbal contact (R); interpersonal communication established (S); initial physical contact (R); physical contact reciprocated (S); intense client emotions, memories, fantasies (R); reciprocated intense emotions, memories, fantasies of other male manifested (S); physical involvement (R); body contact (S); homosexual consummation (R). Similar sequences can be worked out for any area of behaviour which is problematic.

Progression
The working groups which contributed to the strategic objectives outlined on pp. 65–176 assumed a certain causal pattern or sequence amongst them which was revealed in the ordering and progression of the objectives listed.

The basic physiological-biological nurturing needs of health, food, shelter and clothing seemed most basic, giving rise to the objectives of *reducing effects of physical impairment, mental instability and emotional distress* and *reducing insecurity* arising from these and the *economic poverty* which causes them. Once such needs are secured, the identity maintenance objective *(individualization)* becomes paramount, and this entails *promoting awareness and valuation* (of self and others and of relevant situations). Given such awareness and valuation, *self-determination* becomes possible, and hence *growth.*

Turning from the individual's capacity to cope with his social environment to the objectives related to the improvement of the social situation to reduce its debilitative effects, we begin at the least ambitious level of promoting the individual's *capacity to cope with crises* and then move to engineering a more *supportive social environment.* The latter entails some degree of *equality* and hence *tolerance* which in turn makes possible a more *heterogeneous, stimulating and diversified social environment.*

These individual-oriented and community-oriented objectives give rise to others which concern efforts to improve transactions between individuals and their communities. Here we are concerned with improved *social competence* and *occupational effectiveness and status,* both of which are preconditions for effective *social participation.* Genuine *social integration* is not possible without full participation of community members, and *social gratification* at both an individual and community level is the desired outcome.

Hypotheses of Causal Sequences

However, the working groups subjected this assumed progression to some criticism. Let us look at the other social problem situations on which the strategic objectives of social services agencies listed above are focused, to draw forth hypotheses about their causal interconnections based on the experience and informed judgements of groups of experienced social services practitioners and social scientists. What hypotheses may hold promise of more fruitful development as a result of research?

SOCIAL INTEGRATION

How does *social integration* fit with other values in the social value domain sketched out above, for example with *self-determination?*

The individual exercises self-control of his own conduct within the framework of the normative order with which he identifies, that is with reference to the social norms he internalizes from community culture. The community culture (the 'generalized other' of Freudian psychology) is composed of those with whom the individual interacts. He is then able to establish relations with others sharing the same norms. This is the crucial relation between self-control and social control, between *self-determination* and *social interaction.* Healthy socialization implies the development of self-regulatory behaviour patterns, carrying with it some abiding sense of autonomy.

The concept of self-determination is sometimes used as a basis for justifying not merely individual independence but the perfect satisfaction of all human desires. Self-determination also implies an equivalent responsibility to the community. For example, the social worker would not wish to reinforce the complete self-determination of a father spending all his income on personal pleasure without providing for his family's needs. The father may control the wealth of the whole family, and have within his power resources which he is incapable of using appropriately but which his family needs; but the mere fact that resources vital to the whole family happen to be possessed by one individual does not entitle him to demand that his family surrender all control over these.

Other factors must also be considered, including those which affect his family's happiness. Is his family able to maintain itself alone in an economic sense? If not, the family suffers and social security may have to support the family financially. Should social security establish as a condition for his economic independence the ability of the individual to protect certain human rights in his family? Will he be disposed to respect the rights of his family or will he selfishly claim 'full economic self-determination' for himself, regardless of his family's needs? There should evidently be some assurance of the ability and willingness of the individual to meet his responsibilities as a member of the family.

Some conditions, needs and requirements must be met if the community system is to survive in dynamic equilibrium or maintain some form, pattern, configuration or design, irrespective of conscious human objectives, intentions or motivation. Other conditions, needs and requirements are determined exclusively by individual whim without any loss. Every individual is an autonomous, whole person and at the same time is a part system whenever he joins any human group or collectivity.

The potency and autonomy of the individual in his relation to the community system means he is not passive in the face of it. When community patterns of life fail to gratify him in the specific environment, he may and does modify them. He extricates himself from conventional beliefs and traditional skills, and constructs new sub-groups within whose confines he protects himself from the claims of the old community pattern and secures support for new patterns of behaviour. Individuals are sometimes socialized to have a measure of functional autonomy and are invested with far more of the community culture than they require for successful operation within this community. Seen from this perspective, the socialized person's autonomy serves to enhance the continuity of the community system precisely by loosening his dependence on the fate of his community system.

Social competence and *awareness* are two conditions of social integration. A person only identifies with his social role to the extent that he is able to attain the necessary skills to perform that role. An internalized *awareness* of others and of external social norms is a critical aspect of the socialization process, but those whose consciousness has expanded may well become less well integrated into their social communities, as Marcuse[6] sought to demonstrate. The less conscious the individual, the more he tends to be immersed in the broader community around him.

What then is the relation between *social integration* and *valuation* or its obverse, anomie? *Anomie* is the fulfilment of desocialization and *deviance*. It leads to rejection of social bonds and any sense of obligation or concern for others, a turning away from reality so that inner life assumes a dominant position. In the extreme form of autism, it produces a greater emphasis on private, incommunicable, organic processes at the expense of social reference.

Yet, commitment to certain culturally transmitted values may induce anomie, which entails renunciation of (or disbelief in) socially shared values. Workers seek to promote a sense of personal client valuation but not to the point where this becomes narcissism or egophilia with resulting self-absorption, extravagant demands for attention, praise, honour, aid or gratitude and asocial behaviour.

And what of *emotional stability* and its obverse, *frustration* in relation to social integration? The process of socialization (and social integration) is sometimes described as a series of frustrations. Excessive behavioural conformity — over-integration — often leads to accumulated resentments which increase emotional instability. Examples of the frustration-deviance sequences have been developed by Dollard, Miller, Doob, Mowrer and Sears.[7]

Are the values of *equality* and *social integration* self-reinforcing or self-checking? Though it is commonly averred that each individual should get what he merits or deserves, people also commonly believe that no one should be condemned to failure just because he may lack those skills valued in our community at this particular moment of its development. No one should be forced to become alienated from the community in which he lives. Those whose merits enable them to gain, should share some of their prosperity with those less opportunely endowed. Equal rights and duties with others in relation to certain fundamental interests and rights is the basic condition of all communal life. Greater equalization of wealth is thought to eliminate distinctions, creating a greater sense of social integration and fraternity.

SOCIAL PARTICIPATION

How might we conceptualize causal relations which might hold between *social participation* and other elements of the value domain?

Social participation would appear to be conditioned by *physical well-being, emotional stability,* some *sense of valuation* and its expression, and some degree of *tolerance.* Declining physical competence through age, illness or handicap constricts the degree of social participation. Inner emotional discords and conflicts may induce the social withdrawal of some individuals which in turn perpetuates the withdrawal of emotional interest in the external world, increasing inner emotional discord still further in a deviation-amplifying cycle. Modes of social interaction are conditioned by value patterns and interests. An individual is able to establish relations with others of the same group in so far as they govern their conduct according to essentially compatible social norms. Different value orientations will differently condition the character of social interaction, whilst shared meanings with others through reciprocal communication is an essential pre-condition of interacting and participating with others in the social process. In respect of the fourth conditioning factor − *tolerance* − we may note that a sub-group regarded as alien to the dominant group is often consciously or unconsciously excluded from full participation in community life. Tolerance is the reverse of ethnocentricity, being the willingness to confront and collaborate with those distant from oneself.

Social participation has been observed to be a conditioning factor in *awareness, mental stability* and *self-determination.* Awareness and consciousness originate in a social act of participation in some form. Isolation is often a predisposing or precipitating factor in mental illness, particularly schizophrenia. Alienation deprives the individual of opportunities to exercise substantive rational judgement. Presenting negative reinforcers during the treatment process may raise the motivation beyond the optimum level of social interaction involved, perhaps even leading to neurotic or psychosomatic illness. The isolate is an individual who receives no choices and makes no choices, fixed in a dependent and passive role. We seek to reduce isolation but not to the point where neurotic dependency on others is created. Possibly, the greater the individual's freedom from constraint and his ability to make his own self-determined decisions, the greater is the potential price to be paid in terms of isolation.

Social participation is thought to have two-way causal interactions with *social integration, individualization, occupational mobilization, economic security* and *safety needs* and also with the *efficiency and development of agency services.*

First, let us examine social participation and *social integration.* Some degree of social integration is an indispensable pre-condition of social participation. In the absence of any shared values, social participation between two individuals or groups would be irrelevant. Conversely, the state of being isolated or estranged, leads to feelings of alienation and disorientation. People may lack any sense of community, being alienated from their families, neighbourhoods and other social groups. A sense of community may do much to lessen alienation in some contexts. Alienation, however, may also result from conformity to social, institutional or cultural expectations and values which the conforming individual does not share. Furthermore, some degree of alienation may be a source for creative criticism and reform. If any social progress is to be accomplished, alienation must not become so pervasive that all sense of community is lost. When clients begin to oppose their own social situation effectively, normative rules begin to correspond more closely to the clients' needs. If people cannot fulfil their needs inside their communities, neither do they seem able to fulfil their needs in the course of complete exclusion from them.

Social participation interacts with *individualization,* for it entails, at some point, a degree of suspension of self, involving the acceptance of risk and the building of trust. It means putting one's suspended and undefended self temporarily into the power of the other — discovering who one can trust and how to build on trust. Yet again, unless the individual has a strong sense of his own identity and values in the first place, the value of his participation for the group as for himself, will be correspondingly limited.

Now let us look at social participation and *occupational mobilization* in conjunction. Occupational productiveness demands the specialization of function according to institutional principles of the division of labour. This in turn results in segmental roles in institutional settings and consequent alienation. Man's alienation from his work and its products, either through the system of economic production or the social structure, is a form of social unproductiveness which results from a deeper alienation from nature and from self.

What can be said of social participation when it is set beside the objective of promoting *economic security?* The exclusive pursuit of economic security may, as Marx so clearly saw, alienate the individual from his labour by the relations of economic production and the system of power relations. The separation of the individual's work activities from the products or other outputs of his work, results in his alienation from nature, from himself and from others. An improvement in material conditions may follow from changes in people and in their attitudes towards each other. This at least is the rationale for many community action programmes. Poverty seems to be experienced by isolated groups — old people, fatherless families, long-term sick and low wage earners.

Related to this are the causal relations with *security* and *safety needs.* Inner insecurity is created in the individual by participative social relations. Loss of security results in feelings of not belonging and of isolation.

Lastly, the interesting issues of social participation and *agency efficiency and development* may be mentioned. Efficiency (e.g. of service accessibility and delivery) cannot be justifiably purchased at the expense of consumers' silence on issues of service development. Conversely, service development cannot proceed effectively without some systematic analysis of the interactions and consequences which consumers may not have the time nor available capacity to analyze and understand. The results of analyzing service operations may indicate a certain direction of service development if consumer and community needs are to be satisfied, whilst consumers may nevertheless intuitively feel that a different direction of service development would be more in their interests. Systematic analysis may reveal causal connections which are counter-intuitive and therefore rejected when proposed through the mechanisms of consumer participation. Decision-makers have the task of communicating any reasoning − based on systematic analysis rather than mere intuition − to consumers participating in decisions about service development.

GROWTH

Let us take the social objective of *growth*, exploring the postulated relations it has with others.

Two conditions of individual growth are *equality* of opportunity, giving each person a chance to grow and develop to the maximum of his potential, and some *emotional stability*. Regressive behaviour is a common response to emotional instability. The means by which growth is achieved include the development of those *self-expressive* functions through which social culture is transmitted and a periodic breaking up (individualization) as a result of experience of the stereotyped responses. Maximizing human growth and potential includes maximizing capacities for socialization *(social integration)*. If cohesion into a social whole does not occur, growth is stunted.

Social growth and learning is defined by Durkheim[8] for example, as the means by which social integration is achieved by fixing in the child from the beginning, the essential similarities that collective life demands. The isolated youth's self-image is never tested, so that he emotionally fails to achieve growth. By contrast *anomie* involves the individual or the community differentiating back into his or its more elemental components − into smaller, primary or earlier groups or behaviour.

However, by promoting individual growth, particularly that of individuals living in depressed urban enclaves, individual mobility tends to be encouraged. The individual who develops his full potential will tend to move out of the depressed area in the wake of better job opportunities likely to be found elsewhere. As Schroeder[9] has shown, this has the effect of further concentrating the most disadvantaged who cannot improve their situation into a tighter, more *homogeneous* ghetto. The twilight zone serves as a recruitment centre for the most vulnerable as well as a port of entry into the main community system for those more able to make it.

According to these hypotheses, growth, equality, individualization, emotional stability, self-expression, social integration and social homogeneity would all seem self-reinforcing.

INDIVIDUALIZATION

What relations have been postulated between individualization and other social values?

When a person becomes, as in cases of severe *alienation,* oblivious of what he really feels, likes, believes or rejects he suppresses or eliminates essential parts of himself — he feels unreal to himself. Conversely, as the individual's *awareness* becomes more encompassing, he is more able to clarify his sense of self-identity. Development of self-identity implies development of the ego — the self which is valued — the source of ideals and *valuation.* From individualization and self-actualization is derived motivation and investment in living. ('The act of living out oneself is the only value of life' . . . Fromm).[10] This implies some ability to shape the external world so that it expresses in some small part one's own personal, individual identity. Awareness of *self-determination* and autonomy is the means by which the individual realizes himself as a self-sustaining, self-motivational, self-governing, individual entity — one complete centre of power. The opposite of self-determination is neurotic dependency which induces self-effacement.

Two conditions are necessary for the person to assert, develop and express his individuality in the external world. He needs a social environment which is sufficiently *heterogeneous* for him to seek out new situations in which he may express himself and formulate new motives for himself. Lacking such an environment, he would have no occasion to organize his dispositions selectively and responsively, which is a hallmark of the personality system. A second condition is some degree of *social competence* in handling his social environment. The clearer and more specific the individual's self-identity, the more guidance for his action this provides. The less the individual is able to call upon the localized behavioural system which is peculiar to him, the lower is his capacity to act competently and achieve changes.

Individualism is a creed profoundly opposed to all prescriptive privilege and the administrative protection of any rights not based on rules *equally* applicable to all. An extreme of individualization would deny to government the right to limit or reverse what the able or fortunate may achieve, for example by income transfers. By contrast, a major social objective is to fortify *stigmatized* individuals so that they feel themselves to be fully-fledged, normal human beings, protected by beliefs in their own identity, untouched by others' false expectations of them, and unrepentant about others' animosity. There is a sense then in which the essentially administrative value of applying service standards *equally* and impartially, based on some conception of territorial and class justice, must be balanced with the professional value of treating all clients as unique.

Furthermore, an extreme of individualism might also tend to negate *altruistic, other-regarding values* which supply a necessary condition for *tolerance.* Over-absorption in the uniqueness of one's own ego should operate in counterpoise with absorption in others' needs and welfare. One suggested approach to achieving this balance or counterpoise is the definition of individualization or self-actualization as the situation in which the individual fulfils his potentiality by becoming extended and actualized through entering into the perceived realities of others. Finally, the value of individualization relates to *emotional stability* in that if essential, individual parts of a person are suppressed, he becomes oblivious of what he really feels, likes, believes or rejects — in short, of who he really is. He becomes unreal to himself.

PROMOTING SECURITY
The value of *security* is clearly seen by many workers to interact with *social integration* and *competence* values and with the value of *self-determination*. Threats to survival often originate in problems of social organization, cohesion and integration. The individual's dispositions and modes of relating to others, which he shares with the bulk of the community's members as a result of early experiences they have in common, enable him to fulfil his security and safety needs within the existing social order.

Some degree of social competence is indispensable for maintenance of the individual and his family. Threats to safety produce anxiety. The anxious person becomes apprehensive and uncertain as to how to cope with the threat. His own behaviour is likely to increase his insecurity and diminish his social competence in handling the situation. This leads to the position, where for fear of jeopardizing other interests, the individual's resources for dealing with his problems are either absent, only partially exercised, or unused.

Physiological drives such as hunger and thirst lead the individual to acquire motives and forms of behaviour which result in the fulfilment of his safety needs. These acquired motives then begin to function independently of any further reinforcement of physiological conditions that brought them into being. The individual then begins to furnish and maintain his own drives autonomously. This process is recognised in treatment when anxiety responses are counter-conditioned by arousing assertive client responses — hostility and anger, affection and friendship. Safety needs may entail developing the individual's coping mechanisms, but not the kind which include (or induce) neurotic or psychotic dependency.

By promoting security and safety needs, workers may also indirectly contribute to the client's *physical and mental stability* and to *equality*. In safeguarding a family's safety needs by ensuring a mother is not nutritionally deficient during pregnancy, the possibility of organic or mental defects in children is reduced. Hence we contribute preventively to objectives of reducing the effects of physical or mental impairment.

Continuing with this example, the probability of the second generation producing children handicapped at birth is also lessened. This also applies to intergenerational inequalities entailed in poverty being transferred from one generation to the next.

Other Hypothesized Value Interrelations

It has been asserted that *tolerance* tends to decrease in the presence of *economic and psychological insecurity, lack of awareness,* unified *social value* systems and built-in *social inequalities.* Causes of *emotional instability* have been ascribed to frustration of the individual's freely directed impulses, physical and functional disorders, the coexistence of opposed values in the same person, strangulated forms of self-expression, and lack of material reinforcers such as food, clothing and shelter.

Awareness is often seen as a pre-condition of *self-determination* and *valuation.* Consciousness of self-determination is useful to man in his communal life because it induces a sense of responsibility. Whether based on illusion or truth, such consciousness has some value as an impetus for action. For awareness is a prerequisite for self-determination. Lacking awareness of self, one would be unable to determine one's action in accordance with that awareness. Expansion of a person's knowledge of himself, of his power and of the potency of resources and means available, expands his social options. The more aware an individual becomes of his identity, the greater becomes his sense of autonomous direction as more options are opened to him, and the less he is constrained by pressures from his social environment. A community that understands itself — or an individual person — is freed to act in accordance with and move towards a fuller realization of its own values. The community's or individual's self-identity is intimately linked to the values to which it or he is committed. We experience value when we discover meanings and congruity in our lives as individuals or as community members.

From some of the propositions enunciated by social workers during the course of analyzing agency values and objectives, we may list the following further hypotheses about the complex interrelationships which are assumed to hold between items in our value inventory:

SOCIAL COMPETENCE/SOCIAL INTEGRATION/
EQUALITY/ECONOMIC SECURITY
Social competence is developed to some degree by rewarding individuals according to their merits or deserts. Social integration implies that a social (and economic) minimum standard has been (or should be) established. Individual deserts are awarded above that minimum. The higher the social minimum, the less sharp are the conflicts over the equitable basis for rewarding individual merit and

desert. The lower the social minimum, the greater will be the conflict as to what constitutes an equitable basis.

SOCIAL INTEGRATION/SOCIAL PARTICIPATION/ INDIVIDUALITY/AWARENESS/GROWTH

Social integration involves the individual formulating some conception of the 'generalized other'. This conception involves abstracting a role from common elements of the attitudes of those whom the individual interacts with. The 'generalized other' amounts to the organization of social activity or expectations which the individual internalizes through cooperative participation in group life and collective endeavour. Through the role of the 'generalized other', the individual is able to develop consistency in his awareness of himself as a unique individual identity and develop unity of self. It enables him to broaden his perspective of the network of self-other relations and makes possible the growth of integrated personalities.

TOLERANCE/INTEGRATION/ALIENATION/EQUALITY

Less tolerance leads to more acts being defined as deviant. This leads to more discriminatory and unequal treatment of deviants and in turn to more alienation, leading to greater deviance still, thence to less tolerance of deviance by conforming groups. And so the cycle begins again.

SOCIAL INTEGRATION/GROWTH/INDIVIDUALISM/ SUPPORTIVE ENVIRONMENT

Some degree of social disorganization is needed for men to become adults. Promoting extreme individualism would result in the kind of free-range egotism and selfishness which would make a community a hostile and undesirable place, and one increasingly inimical to the flourishing of unique individuals.

EQUALITY/SOCIAL PARTICIPATION/AWARENESS/SELF-EXPRESSION

One handicap to achieving social justice is an inability to communicate. Not that the poor are inarticulate — it is more that they can rarely communicate *technically*. This is where the bureaucracy and planning machinery wins every time, the poor being unequal in terms of information and knowledge.

SUPPORTIVE ENVIRONMENT/PARTICIPATION/INDIVIDUALIZATION

Where certain customary reinforcers are lacking in a client's environment, this is likely to produce apathy and unresponsiveness and might be an important contributory factor to conditions of fatigue, depression and institutionalization.

ECONOMIC POVERTY/SECURITY/SUPPORTIVE ENVIRONMENT/
EMOTIONAL STABILITY

Swedish studies[11] have shown that low incomes and uncertain employment *(economic poverty)* create insecurity which is accentuated by obstacles in the physical environment *(debilitative environment)*. A quarter of those with low income were shown to suffer from severe depression and nervous tension *(emotional instability)*.

Status of Causal Hypotheses

The bold hypotheses and propositions which resulted from thus analyzing the causal interrelations between the social values assumed by practitioners, are rich in material for further empirical exploration. It would be vain to deny that many of the hypothesized relations lack any empirical confirmation at present and it may well be that some of them can never achieve any such confirmation as many appear somewhat arbitrary and logically unjustifiable. Yet some of the hypotheses may well have struck tinder. Since many form assumptions about values and their interrelations on which actual practice is based, they are worthy of further analysis and criticism, if only to bring them into line with the results of psychological and sociological research and to use such criticism as the vehicle through which relevant modern philosophical analysis can be transmitted to workers in a way which has bearing on social services practice. They form a first review of what might constitute a framework for considering the overall directions taken by social services agencies in response to a complex set of dynamic, interrelated social problems and a first step in moving towards a comprehensive picture of the dynamic systems with which we are concerned.

Whatever results from any further research into the causal interconnectivity of social values, we shall eventually have to aggregate the variables involved. Particularly problematic is the determination of the direction of causality among these variables or directions in the social services system, in that they are in dynamic equilibrium. The variables probably affect each other in opposite senses. Sometimes an increase in one variable or direction tends to lead to further increases in a related 'unstable' variable, whereas for the other stable variable there is a tendency of equal magnitude to counteract any changes. The magnitude of the product of the effects of the variables upon each other is as great as the product of the effects upon themselves. The direction of the causality often cannot be settled by reference to the direction of the lag between the fluctuation of the variables, since causality may operate in both directions. The relative magnitude of the effects of the variables upon each other is independent of the direction and amount of lag. Further detailed research would enable workers to give an interpretation to the size of the lag between the fluctuation of the variables in terms of signs of the effects of the variables upon each other and upon themselves. It would enable confirmation or disconfirmation of the hypotheses and informed judgements postulated by experts in the social services area. The precise method to be used is outlined by Simon and Ando in *Aggregation of Variables in Dynamic Systems.*[12]

Competing and Conflicting Objectives

A community or an organization are both systems composed of segments or parts interlocking to form a complex whole. Its operations and processes are multiple, many-faceted, and conflicting, and embody diverse values. Inconsistency among community social objectives can be expected as a result of continuous conflicts of interest among various community groups. For example, some ratepayers' associations want rate reductions, even if this means cuts in welfare programmes or contracting them out to private enterprise or voluntary agencies *vide* Braybrooke.[13] Some activist groups want a radicalization of the whole welfare system so that it becomes a major vehicle for redistributing wealth, and some pressure groups demand a better deal for the specific social need they represent, even at the expense of other needs.

Similarly, each agency section may have its own objectives. Field-workers aim to achieve maximum client benefits, or to take on as priorities those 'interesting' clients who 'respond best' to the treatments and services available, or to maintain the highest professional standards. The financial section aims to minimize the costs of helping clients, and therefore advocates high caseloads and priority being given to those clients it costs least to maintain. The administrative section meanwhile stresses the fulfilment of statutory obligations at all costs, completion of all data relevant to any client taken on, and ease of administration. Meanwhile, committees and managements often aim to achieve maximum coverage of all client demands, and to minimize trouble and complaints from the local electorate and client families.

Moreover this view is over-simplified, for if any participant in the system is asked what his or her objectives are the result will invariably contain implicit conflicts, whether we are talking of agency or of social objectives.

This inconsistency is right and proper. Valuations are often contradictory and unstable, even in the minds of individuals. Behaviour may typically be described as the result of compromises between valuations at different levels of generality.

Whether analyzing community or agency systems, it may be said that their parts interact. No objective exists in a vacuum or in isolation from other objectives. To a greater or lesser degree objectives partially conflict, and if each were pushed to its ultimate logical conclusion they would completely conflict. All achievement leads to unanticipated side-effects in other areas. Additionally, the means which used to attain any one objective are limited not only by resource availability, but also by those which are regarded as unacceptable. Acceptability of means in turn derives from other objectives independent of the objective being analyzed.

Facilitation-Inhibition Process

Thus in any organization, community or individual's personal life, it may be said that for every desideratum there is a counter-desideratum which conflicts with it. For every objective an individual wishes to pursue, there is usually another counter-objective which potentially or partially conflicts with it, which he also wishes to pursue.

The result is that one local objective in one part of the organization (or community) is partially thwarted by another conflicting objective in another part of the organization (or community). If a person tries to pursue one objective exclusively, achieving it as completely as possible, he soon meets opposition to his single-minded endeavours from inside (or perhaps from outside) the organization. The opposition, whoever leads it or whatever form it takes, is pursuing a counter-objective. In doing so, the opposition sets a definite limit on further achievement of the person's goal in the form of a counter-objective. A tendency or trait reaches its saturation point and reaction sets in. This constitutes the equivalent of the inhibition-facilitation mechanism as defined by psychologists in relation to personality systems, in which the presence of one stimulus renders another one ineffective to some degree.

On this basis it may be deduced that the objectives are capable of functional autonomy but are not structurally independent of one another. The presence of a competing factor weakens the strength of a response tendency. The competing element is an inhibitory factor. The strength of this inhibitory factor is a function of such conditions as the degree of non-reinforcement and the amount of habituation in working towards an objective.

A set of partially or potentially conflicting but compatible objectives with relative weights in relation one to another predominate in each section of the agency. The decision-maker is divided and sometimes inconsistent on the ultimate objectives he pursues. There is no ultimate long-run goal to explain the relative weights attached to each objective or resolve the conflict between the objectives. Life is a system of basic goal-sets. The more weight that is given to one objective or goal, not only will less weight be given to others, but also the more the other objectives of the set will need to be brought into focus. The sets of objectives constitute a complete explanation of the ups and downs of both individual objectives within the set in terms of their weighting and also of other sets of objectives. Only so much value can be allocated. What is allocated to one objective in terms of value, cannot be allocated to another. But once a certain proportion of the total valuation or available resources to one objective is allocated at the expense of another, continual pressure will be felt to reallocate so that the balance is redistributed.

Increase in relative power or emphasis in one direction results automatically in countervailing pressure in other directions so that the equilibrium of the system is preserved. Multiple balance or equilibrium is composed of a constellation of several independent agency drives or states, each of which have roughly equal strength or weight. It acts as a check on a distorted over-emphasis on one variable and thus helps to maintain the viability of the system as a whole. This applies as much in the balance of power between individuals within the organization as between diverse agency drives and potential directions.

Some conflicts are an inherent aspect of the system, while others are peripheral and produce non-productive tensions. The former should be recognized in structuring operations: the latter are minimized so far as possible. Continuous, violent and extreme disagreement on basic agency objectives and policies amongst different agency groups produces unstable, unworkable agency operations and structures. Conflict too has its threshold, and managers may have to generate the facilitation-inhibition process if it does not come into operation quickly enough.

The principle is as follows. Viable systems have to survive, and therefore no one particular objective, however desirable, can be pursued to its maximum value by a social services agency or any one of its sections, any more than it can in the personal life of a man. Maximize the service of one sub-unit's objective and the servicing of other needs is eroded. Similarly, at the societal level complete security, maximum affection, frequent and intense gratification, and so on are impractical aims. For if all the community's energy were invested in gratification, its social assets would be consumed but not replenished.

The operation of the facilitation-inhibition process then is critical to the survival of the organization (indeed, of the community). Several potentially, particularly or ultimately conflicting objectives have to be pursued simultaneously. We pursue each to a certain extent, achieving each objective to some degree and no further.

Conflict and Control Systems

Once the facilitation-inhibition process has been recognized, it can be used both as a method of controlling systems in terms of diversified objectives and as a practical principle of action. People can to some degree, have it both ways at once. The principle is similar to Godel's theorem: when we know something is a contradiction, this makes it not a contradiction. Looking back to Hegel, we may say that within any system there exists opposed, antithetical tendencies which work in contradictory directions, each aiming to dominate the whole field but each requiring also the presence of opponents as necessary to their significance if full account is to be taken of the total system, rather than merely some part of it.

This principle of inherent conflict as present in all objectives, values and their action manifestations does not mean that such conflict will impede their working in ordinary agency contexts. In the course of everyday operations, workers steer clear of conflict by refusing to recognize its existence in unwanted cases. Conflict will not arise so long as we remain resolutely oriented to a single course of action or sphere of value which we do not seek to connect nor see in relation to other courses of action, other objectives or value spheres. It arises only when the tiredness and ineffectuality of such single-action programmes or restricted one-level objectives is recognized, and an attempt is made to pass to something deeper: its point of emergence is not *within* smoothly functioning single-goal, single-value, single-action system components, so much as *between* competing objectives, values and actions which constitute the social and agency systems. Hence the conflict does not lead to a demoralizing paralysis. It provides a spur to deepening of people's grasp of multiple objectives, values and action programmes which is the essence of a sophisticated control system. Conflicts implicit in objectives and values are in fact only conflicts to those concerned to see the system as a whole from alternative angles.

Attainment Thresholds

But individuals have some social option to seek more as opposed to less. When policy-makers and managers in the social services talk about maximizing social interaction, they do not mean to say that nothing else matters. Nor do they mean there will not be occasions on which the opportunity for increasing social interaction will not be deliberately rejected in favour of some other desirable end. 'To manage' is to seek some means by which all desiderata are handled simultaneously, to balance and integrate potentially conflicting objectives. How?

These objectives will only begin to cancel out if we try to simultaneously pursue them to their ultimate, logical conclusion. Meanwhile, they can be pursued and realized up to a certain point without incompatibility. Objectives are susceptible to degrees of attainment or realization. Social life, for example, inevitably entails some degree of frustration and alienation so that this social disbenefit can never be entirely eliminated. Since it has many elements, an objective can be achieved in one respect and not in another. In fact, if effort is over-concentrated in any one of these spheres or on any one objective to the exclusion of others it tends to destroy any effective change and development of the agency. No effort can perfectly fulfil its objective. The achievement of one objective is paid for by yielding alternative opportunities in relation to another. Satisfaction of some needs reduces the individual's ability to gratify others because of limitations which scarcity imposes on individual capacities to satisfy needs and also because of the devaluing effect of very frequent rewards.

Taken to its extreme, self-determination would imply a kind of voluntarism which describes all social phenomena as directly dependent on the conscious, deliberate choices of individuals. On the other hand, social integration pushed to its logical conclusion implies a form of determinism in which no recognition is given to the fact that individuals are mobile to do other than they in fact do. A balance is sought between the impulse-restraining, appetite-constraining values like social integration with the impulse-gratifying, appetite-satisfying values like self-determination. Self-determination is promoted, but not to the point where it results in hysterical autonomy — isolated, fragmented behaviour out of keeping with the shared environmental context or the person's prior behaviour. The target is thus self-determination within a context of social integration.

Similarly, the value of social integration cannot be pushed too far without undermining the foundations of valuation. Deviance implies a falling away, a departure or a lack of something, usually the acceptance of certain moral norms. However, deviance may not always be caused by the lack of something, but may indeed derive from conformity with certain values and community forces which are disfunctional for the individual. A commitment to certain culturally transmitted values may, when these are unrealizable, induce anomie which involves ultimately a renunciation or disbelief in socially shared values. Past a certain threshold, there may be a rationality in deviance. When a man pursues goals he has been taught to prize and finds them unrealizable, it is rational for him to renounce these objectives. The community cannot be maintained as a socially viable place unless some are courageous enough to shirk the duty which respectable or powerful men around them define as theirs.

As a last example, let us define thresholds beyond which it would be disadvantageous to promote self-expression. Promoting self-expression may so unleash the undifferentiated, contradictory, a-logical impulses of the id as to reduce rational behaviour and controls, automatic and involuntary repression, or conscious, deliberate suppression of disturbing emotions, ideas or activities by discontinuing the thought or memory process. In doing so, the benefits of reasoning and planning may be lost.

Rational thinking is an essential condition of the individual's ability to share meanings with others. Through rational thinking the individual learns to interpret certain situations as calling for the expression of a certain kind and degree of action and perhaps emotion. It may equally undermine the individual's capacity for valuation, since individual impulses are characteristically instinctive, a-moral, and demand immediate gratification. Feelings of guilt which inhibit self-expression should be reduced, but not to the point where this destroys the possibility of valuation.

These attainment thresholds for various social values are largely based on propositions of social science theory or on practitioner hypotheses. Some well-evidenced research is relevant here. Thus, variation in the amount of frustration has been shown to be a function of three factors: the strength of instigation to the frustrated response, the degree of interference with the frustrated response, and the number of response sequences frustrated. Using these factors we are able to define the thresholds of frustration beyond which it is dispersed through overt aggression. The research aim here is to define thresholds with as much precision as in other sciences. For example, the critical survival threshold for the polar bear (now threatened with extinction) is 12,000 and there are between 10,000 and 15,000 polar bears at present in existence. This supplies us with a specific target-figure necessary to ensure polar bears do not become extinct.

However, even in those areas where data are lacking, it is possible to test out daily decisions which practitioners make intuitively about thresholds by analyzing daily operations appropriately. A case study in the application of integrated planning systems to an old persons' residential home[14] illustrates how the facilitation-inhibition process worked itself out in relation to the objectives of promoting social integration and participation on the one hand, and promoting privacy, self-determination and individualization on the other. Initial over-emphasis on social interaction among residents, though welcomed in principle, resulted in complaints about lack of privacy, insufficient time alone, some reduction in personal choice, and over-emphasis on group rather than individual requirements. The objectives of privacy, self-determination and individualization had unintentionally and unconsciously been inhibited in the course of over-attaining social participation and integration values.

This imbalance was rectified by establishing both potentially conflicting elements (increased interaction and increased privacy) as staff objectives within the same programme. Clearly more and better interaction among residents was desirable, but not beyond the point where their personal identity, interests and privacy ceased to be safeguarded. The two objectives held each other in check, and in the process allowed 'attainment thresholds' or criteria of effectiveness to be specified for each.

Criteria

Thus there is a limit as to how far individuals or agencies wish to achieve any one objective. Each objective is pursued and realized to the extent that it does not render pursuit and realization of another neighbouring objective implausible. The built-in conflict between these objectives defines the criteria of how far each can or should be pursued within the same agency programme of activity.

There is a limit as to how far any individual wants to reduce anxiety and insecurity. In trying to promote equality, workers help people to get treated more equally in various respects. Simultaneously, in trying to promote individualization workers hope to ensure for each person, individual consideration rather than treating them as units. Together, this results in a composite objective of reducing the degree to which any one person receives better treatment than others in any respect, in advance of any rational and justifiable grounds being produced for unequal treatment, probably on the basis of relevant differences of consideration between them.

Various thresholds may be defined for the intensity or fullness of realization of each objective — feasible points of realization which fall short of maximum optimal fulfilment. Once these fulfilment thresholds are passed and the objective begins to be 'over-achieved', certain pathological termini are reached and hubris sets in. Other related, conditioning variables and objectives are inhibited so that they pass certain repression thresholds. (This is the classical pattern described by curvilinear functions.) Over-fulfilment of social integration depresses and inhibits individual identity-maintenance, so that the whole situation becomes unviable and self-perperuating, or oscillating processes may be set up from which it becomes very difficult to escape. Thus, push the equality objective beyond a certain threshold and the result would be a Kurt Vonnegut society in which nimble dancers carry sandbags and specially pretty people wear masks.

The principle has received wide recognition through the concepts of 'over-kill' from atomic politics and 'over-sell' from marketing. This process is witnessed in the mismanagement of the British economy, and ecologists predict a similar loss of control environmentally ('the eco-catastrophe'). The threshold principle is the key to controlling the balance of objectives which will prevent a situation running away with its participants and the system taking over from the decision-makers.

Any growth which is exponential must level off at some point past a certain threshold or a point of absurdity would be reached. At some point necessarily, there is saturation. If we take the electrical industry as an example, from Franklin's experiments in lighting around 1750, the exponential increase in workers brings us to 200,000 employed in 1925, a million by 1955, and at that rate the entire working population would be employed in this one field by 1990. The problem is to define the saturated state and estimate its arrival date. The problem of growth — the approach to some ceiling — is a sigmoid or S-shaped curve in which the rate below and above its middle is often quite symmetrical. It therefore lends itself to easy prediction, since we assume that the rate above the mid-point will match that below, and then level off. These properties of the curve cause many statisticians to take it as a philosopher's stone for the charting of human behaviour.

A typical population grows slowly from an asymptotic minimum, multiplies quickly and then draws slowly to an ill-defined assymptotic maximum, the curve passing through a point of inflexion to become S-shaped. In this way we can indicate the limit above which the population is not likely to grow.

Ceiling conditions force the levelling off of the curve. S-curve analysis works only within some closed system based either on fixed resources, or on physical laws, or on some concept of an absolute. There is always a risk in using such curves for the purposes of prediction directly a closed system is transformed into a more open one. This is the basic principle of all control mechanisms.

The limit or threshold is not an absolute one as in the physical sphere, as in human environments and in social situations decisions may be postponed (as in the case of a family decision on whether to have another child). Substitutions are possible as in the case of bus or underground transport in place of private cars.

Exemplifying Facilitation-Inhibition Processes
Let us try to exemplify further the facilitation-inhibition process and its accompanying attainment threshold in terms of some of the social problems, needs and states of affairs which form the subject matter of the strategic objectives outlined on pp. 65–176 above.

Social integration and individualization clearly hold each other in check both in the lives of individuals and communities, so that each limits and is limited by the other in terms of how far an agency seeks to foster them.

LIMITS OF INDIVIDUALITY
The growth of individuality would not be possible if the self-negating elements in social integration were allowed full scope. The separation of the baby from the mother at birth — the first step towards individuality — is superseded in healthy situations by the mother-child relationship. The intimate mutual dedication of this relationship takes the place of earlier biological unity, reasserting the principle of cohesion and social integration. In Kleinian and Freudian theory, the individual strives through his life instinct to preserve and give expression to himself only to find himself up against a co-temporaneous death instinct (mortido or destrudo) which strives to negate and dissolve the individual, and

reassert the principle of cohesion by the immolation of the self.

LIMITS OF SOCIAL INTEGRATION

If the community's claims on the individual are such as to distort human potentialities, then to promote individual self-realization will imply transgression beyond established socio-cultural norms to new modes of individuality incompatible with prevailing ones. It might include assisting individuals to live dissident, non-adjusted lives. This may involve 'curing the patient to become a rebel or a martyr', as Marcuse[15] has described the programme of social action. Conformity without personal involvement takes the form of submission to necessity as represented by alien demands, and thence the stifling of individual personal needs. Adequate role performance may amount to alienated labour, perpetuating conditions of the individual's estranged existence.

INTERDEPENDENCE

The two objectives of individualization and social integration become compatible once the social solidarity myth is eliminated from the objective of social integration and the purified identity myth simultaneously eliminated from the objective of individualization. Viable social integration must include some common capacity to cope with variety and complexity. Individualization must include some element of influence from contingencies of the social environment. Self-organization and social organization are interdependent.

Individuals are always socialized to have a measure of functional autonomy and simultaneously are invested with far more of the community culture than they require for successful operation within this community. Seen from this perspective, the socialized person's autonomy serves to enhance the continuity of the community system precisely by loosening his dependence on the fate of his community system.

The prescriptions would seem to be as follows. To pursue integration to some degree — but not to the point of neurotic self-effacement or enforced conformity to external social standards which close viable lines of conduct which accord with individual belief and value. To pursue individualization to some degree — but not to the self-defeating point where the individual is so utterly distinct and hermetically sealed off from his social environment that there is no means by which this environment cannot reflect back to him who he is.

A similar process seems to operate as between the values of *social integration* and *self-determination*. It is important to raise social options, thereby increasing individual's capacities to transform social constraints, as opposed to continuous accommodation to whatever social pattern is encountered. Yet transformation of all social constraints and disruption of all social patterns would itself reduce the numbers of social options which any one individual confronts and hence limit his opportunity for self-determination. The two objectives of *self-determination* and *social integration* clearly hold each other in check. The client's right to choose his own options is recognized to the extent that he does not interfere with others' rights or harm himself. Thus, the individual may viably say: 'I do my own thing, knowing the points of conflict with established socio-cultural norms, but not transgressing them to the point where social disintegration develops among those around me.' On the other hand, too much cohesion in social groups sometimes restricts individual freedom to pursue one's own interests.

Deviance needs to be reduced, but not to the point where it results in compulsive acquiesence and a ritualistic conformity or submission to predetermined status and expectations which would be inimical to *self-determination.* Thus the head of a criminal syndicate and the civil rights agitator, the delinquent and the militant leader of a squatters' group, the mother who batters her baby and the paranoid schizophrenic who goes berserk should not be placed under the same conceptual umbrella. *Social integration* is an acceptable objective, but not to the point where it manifests itself in neurotic self-ingratiation – the reverse of *self-determination.* Value propagation in extremis results in cultural imperialism.

What of *deviance* and *rationality?* Past a certain threshold, there may be a *rationality* in *deviance.* When someone pursues goals they have been taught to prize only to find them unrealizable, it is rational to renounce these objectives. The community will rarely remain a viable place unless some are courageous enough to shirk the duty which respectable or powerful men around them define as theirs.

Social integration and *self-expression* facilitate and inhibit each other in the following ways. To the degree that the individual delays tension reduction and the expression of a specific impulse until the socio-cultural setting is appropriate, his behaviour accords with the reality principle. For example, the child learns to wait until dinner-time to gratify the hunger drive. To the degree that the individual discharges tensions and expresses impulses as they arise without regard for the consequences, his behaviour accords with the pleasure principle.

A person may be freed from many inhibitions and regressions with the intention of promoting greater self-expression. This may undermine the functions of the ego in bringing the individual into adjustment with his current situation. Excessive guilt feelings of individuals for minor social transgressions or failures may be reduced, but not to the point where the individual develops a paranoidal guiltlessness covering all wrong-doing and deviance. On the other hand, over-promotion of social integration may lead to an excess of inhibition, over-excitation resulting in reduced self-expression. Over-promotion of self-expression may lead to an excess of excitation over inhibition resulting in deviance and social malfunctioning.

Or take the objective of promoting a *socially heterogeneous community* vis-à-vis *social integration.* The more heterogeneous the community, the more complex become the links between personality and social environment which define social integration. Socio-cultural norms need to be defined precisely enough for the individual to know where he stands and to be able to predict the probable results of his actions, but not so precisely and inflexibly that they cannot take account of special factors. The product of the unifying functions of social integration and the forces for social differentiation as represented in the heterogeneity of the community or group, constitutes the social equilibrium relevant to any situation.

Thus social integration should not be taken to the point of homogeneity through submission, fear or sterile imitation, while in following the objective of heterogeneity the magnitude of behavioural variability should not be so great as to destroy any possibility of viable social integration.

The values of *social participation* and *individualization* also hold each other in check in ways which define attainment thresholds for each.

Social isolation is one of the dynamic variables in a failure to acquire personality. Personality represents the organization of tendencies to act which are developed by the individual in the course of his social interaction. The person becomes the individual as he comes to be shaped in the course of interacting with others.

Alienation deprives the total personality from opportunities to fulfil itself and thereby to exercise creative powers in influencing the conditions of its own existence. Alienation is conformity without involvement to alien, objective external demands rather than subjective, internal and personal needs. The process of social participation – for example in the form of community groups using their own power to change conditions – increases the individual's and group's sense of self-worth. The set of responses which an individual derives from his participation in organized social relations becomes generalized into a self which has a unity corresponding to the organization in social groups. Conversely, lack of self-esteem tends to produce withdrawal and non-involvement in tasks in the first place: 'You failed because you did not try, not because you were incompetent. If you had really cared, you could have succeeded.' (C. Silberman).[16]

Social relations which are formal, indirectly mediated, briefly face-to-face and specialized, often with clearly formulated rules governing the behaviour of members, create impersonality and depersonalization which isolate the individual from his fellows.

The prescriptions might be these. Social participation needs to be developed, but not to the formalized point where impersonality sets in, individualization is likewise a valued objective, but not to the point where social participation is forfeited, producing loneliness and alienation. It is probably undesirable so to reinforce those of the individual's attitudes in which he has strong ego-involvement when they are so contrary to the publicly-accepted view of objective reality as to render participation in social affairs unfeasible.

Let us contrast *anomie* and *security*. When a client or a community system have fruitlessly exhausted their routine responses to problem situations, then a certain randomness may be more useful than the treadmill and orderly plying of old methods and responses. This means growing anomie — an increasing anomic randomness. Anomic disorder, when it passes a certain threshold, may unbind wasted energies and sever fruitless commitments. It may make possible a ferment of innovation which can rescue the individuals or the community system concerned from destruction.

The relationship between *supportive* and *heterogeneous* social environments is interesting. Supportive environments tend towards homogeneity. Homogeneous communities are often those whose members are from a similar socio-economic class, enabling individuals to live with others who have like interests and similar social interaction patterns. They tend to be age-heterogeneous. Drawing on early sociological studies of the working class, we may say that they tend to be stable, enduring and based on a strong sense of community. The problem with this type of homogeneous community is that the pattern of services tends to be less adequate. Teachers tend not to want to teach in the down-at-heel end of the city, community leaders are less able, the quality of civic life is less rich, the social mix is narrower. Conflict and opposition provide the motive power and regulation of collective energy.

Heterogeneous environments increase the expectations of the more able disadvantaged by the mere fact of the social mix. They tend to distribute the best social services over a wider socio-economic field of action, and to make for a richer, more complex society, but also one in which the most chronically disadvantaged individuals can quickly lose hope. Individual mobility may be encouraged in the hope of dispersing the ghetto by integrating it with other socio-economic groupings in a heterogeneous community. Or existing facilities and structures may be retained in the area intact, building them up into more self-supportive communities and raising their aggregate level of living. To increase mobility and heterogeneity past a certain threshold would deprive the vulnerable and poor of a firm base for political power which must depend on numbers. To increase separatist development past a certain threshold, however, would be to repudiate the possibility of social integration among different socio-economic classes and the opportunities for individual development deriving from the juxtaposition of different life styles in one location.

The two objectives hold each other in check. One approach to the problem is to promote homogeneity at block level within a wider heterogeneous community at neighbourhood level. Efforts to develop and cope with a wider range of complexity and conflict need not escalate into a life-and-death struggle for survival.

Mapping the Social System

Having explored some possible interrelations among social values embodied in social service objectives, how can the total system of causality be brought together in considering the dynamics and functioning of the system, or at least one aspect of it?

For this purpose, it may be helpful to consider a specific type of problem syndrome — the familiar case where the two major problems in a family are marital relations and debt. From an analysis of several cases of this type, significant causal connections seem to hold for poorer socio-economic classes (classes 4 and 5 in consumer research terminology) between the following four variables — amount of debt; degree of insecurity and anxiety feelings; positive work motivations and performance; and income level (sometimes monitored in terms of the number of times income is interrupted by the client failing to hold down his job). In Figure 2, the arrows connecting the four circled variables represent causal relations.

Some causal relations are direct (symbolized by D). The sequence illustrated in Figure 5 illustrates four direct causal relations between four variables. A direct causal relation from one variable to another is one in which changes occur in the same direction. An increase in one causal variable (e.g. degree of debt) effects an increase in the connected variable (e.g. degree of insecurity and anxiety feelings). The causal flow between the two variables is 'increase — increase'. A decrease in one causal variable (e.g. increasingly unsatisfactory work relations) effects a decrease in the connected variable (e.g. increasing number of times income is interrupted). The causal flow between the two variables is 'decrease — decrease'.

Some causal relations are inverse (symbolized by 'I'). Figure 4 illustrates four inverse causal relations between four variables.

An inverse causal relationship is present when a change in the causal variable A in one direction causes a change in the connected, neighbouring variable B in the opposite direction. An increase in the causal variable (e.g. increasing debt) effects a decrease in the affected variable (e.g. reduced capacity to cope with the marital relationship). The causal flow between the two variables is 'increase — decrease'. Or a decrease in the causal variable (e.g. reduced capacity to cope with the

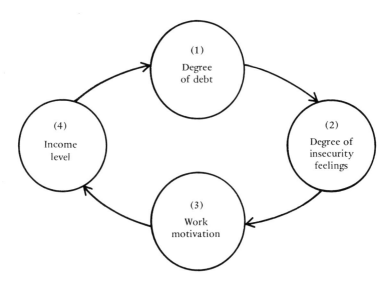

Figure 2.

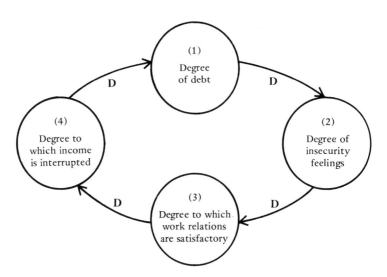

Figure 3.

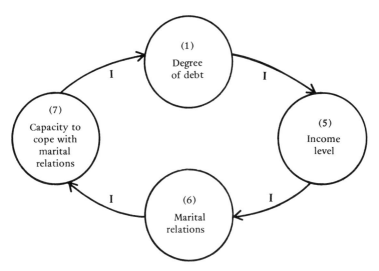

Figure 4

marital relationship) effects an increase in the affected variable (e.g. increasing marital discord). The causal flow between these two variables is 'decrease − increase'.

Any complex situation consists of several causal relations, some direct and some inverse. The pattern or cycle of relations which is set up determines the fate of the system or the outcome of the situation. To understand the situation or system, we must know what the causal relations are, whether they are direct or inverse, what the interactions are of the entire pattern of relations, and what the consequences of these interactions are likely to be.

Where the two situations exemplified come together as different aspects of a multiple problem within the same family, workers are handling not only the relations defined in each aspect separately but also the interaction between the two aspects. The resulting pattern of causal relation cycles may look something like that shown in Figure 5.

The several processes are connected either by direct or inverse causal arrows. For example, the *more* occasions on which income is interrupted (4), then the *more* the family's debts will tend to increase. This is a direct relation (symbolized by the arrow labelled 'D'). On the other hand, *decreasing* capacity to cope with the problematic marital relationship *increases* feelings of insecurity and anxiety. This therefore would be an inverse relation (symbolized by an arrow labelled 'I').

Some sets of processes in the network form four distinct cycles or

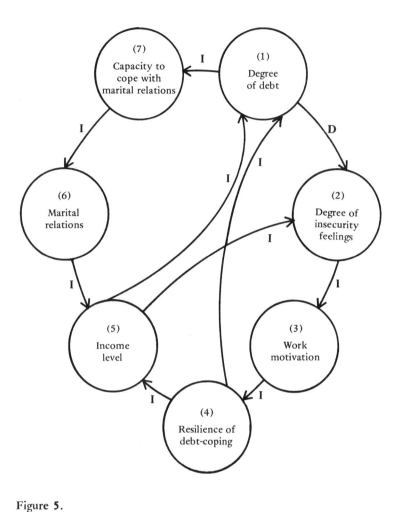

Figure 5.

Cycle of Interconnected Causal Relations in a Situation or System

Causal cycles:
(1)———→ (2)———→ (3)———→ (4)———→ (1)
(2)———→ (3)———→ (4)———→ (5)———→ (2)
(1)———→ (7)———→ (6)———→ (5)———→ (1)

closed loops, even though these loops overlap.

One is the cycle illustrated in Figure 2 which runs from (1) to (2) to (3) to (4) and back to (1). The greater the debt, the greater is the family's feelings of insecurity, which may directly prompt increasingly unstable work motivation and performance, and thence the greater becomes the degree of debt from short-term hire, dismissals, sackings, non-employment or inability to realize overtime opportunities.

The second cycle is illustrated in Figure 4 which runs from (1) to (7) to (6) to (5) and back to (1) again. With increasing debt (1), capacity to cope with marital relations is diminished (7), thence leaving the way clear for yet more marital discord (6), and lower income level either through compensatory domestic expenditure or breakdown of mutual income support, or loss of job through stress, and hence more debt (1).

The third consists of (2) − (3) − (4) − (5) − (2) (see Figure 5). Increasing feelings of insecurity (2), may directly prompt increasingly unstable work relations and performance (3), when these feelings have passed the point where they are readily controllable, possibly resulting directly in income interruption on an increasing number of occasions (4) through dismissals, sackings, resignations or short-time hire, which in turn decreases the capacity to cope with debt problems (5), thus generating still more intensive feelings of insecurity (2).

The final cycle consists of (6) − (4) − (1) − (6) (see Figure 5). With increasing marital discord (6), goes the tendency among poorer socio-economic classes of increasing the number of times income is interrupted (4), bringing with it more debts (1), so decreasing still further the capacity to cope with problematic marital relations (7), and thence leaving the way clear for yet more marital discord (6).

Every cycle or loop has a pattern of direct and/or inverse relations. For example while the second cycle illustrated has four inverse relations the third loop has two inverse and two direct relations. The best way to describe the loop is to count the number of inverse relationships. The most interesting feature of any loop is whether it has an even or an odd number of interrelations.

Now there is a startling and important property about any system or situation. [17] If a loop in the system has an odd number of inverse relations, it is self-regulating and self-correcting. It is able to counteract any deviations or aberrations which appear and, as it were, to put itself to rights of its own accord without needing any further intervention or management to correct it. Thus, if we leave the situation alone, it will tend to continue on its own sweet way, working through any inherent conflicts of elements within it, and so stabilizing itself that it will look very much the same in phase two in a year's time, as it does now in phase one. The only proviso is that no major new causal elements intervene meanwhile to set up a different situation and so change the nature of the system. On the other hand, if a loop in the system has an even number of inverse relations, it is deviation-amplifying. This is the reverse of self-correcting. Any deviations in it will be amplified unchecked. It will undergo more and more change and will probably become more and more chaotic and unstable until either it eventually destroys itself or some major intervention is made or some significant external circumstance occurs to check this process. The intervention or external circumstance cannot amount to anything less than either a new causal element being added to the situation or one of the existing elements being eliminated from it. Either way, the nature of the basic situation will be changed.

Let us illustrate this principle. The cycle increasing debt (1) — decreasing capacity to cope with marital relations (7) — increasing marital discord (6) — decreasing capacity to cope with debt (5) — increasing debt (1) has an even number of inverse relations, namely four. Therefore it should be deviation-amplifying. The situation is most likely to become increasingly chaotic and unstable, probably deteriorating to the point of catastrophe unless in some major way it is checked. If we trace the relationship, we will find this is in fact the case. Once even a small accumulation of debt has been taken on, debt will mount until the situation blows up in some catastrophe.

In relation to this family, we could just as easily start the cycle at any other point on the loop. For example, the increasing marital discord may provide the first manifestation of the problem rather than increasing debt. In the family under consideration, both the debt and the marital breakdown are symptoms of the underlying cause which may be explained either in fundamental terms of social, economic and cultural patterns in our society, or in terms of personal pathology, or the interrelation between the two. Thus, in this situation, where marital discord is the first presenting problem, this will tend to decrease the capacity to cope with debt which will itself help to engender further debts.

The reason for this fascinating phenomenon is that inverse relations are usually capable of reversing the effects of an earlier element, so that they become key points of control in the situation. However, two (or any other even number) of inverse relations cancel each other out. An even number of inverse relationships cancels out this capability of reversing the earlier effects within the cycle.

Clearly, since most major problems which social services handle have many interconnected causal variables, diagnosis of problems and treatments in terms of multiple interconnected causal chains are a more powerful instrument than the simplistic listing of primary and secondary variables which is the normal approach.

Treatment Sequences

Having analyzed the problem variable sequences, we can then work out

Workers aim *to promote client (or community) capabilities and skills,* whether at the physical or mental level.

In children's work this may cover promoting more effective child-rearing practices or coping with a specific problem like enuresis.

This 'social malfunctioning' objective applies to recognizable discrepancies between clients' desired and actual achievements. This may be expressed through pervasive and disabling anxiety; a demeaning, crippling self-image; unrewarding marital relations; conflicting child-parent relations; acute client dissatisfaction with self, his role performances or with interpersonal competences; or unsatisfactory peer-group performances. Clients may be unable to perform particular social roles — as spouse, parent, patient, student, employee, group member, and so on — to their own (or others') satisfactions. Acting out, compulsive behaviour, identity crises, over-compensation, day-dreaming or fantasy may occur when the primary task absorbing the individual's energy is constantly frustrated. Felt discrepancies, shortcomings and partialities resulting from comparisons of the actual with desired outcome are points of entry for intervention. Personality adjustment is defined by the difference between levels of aspiration and achievement.

'Social competence' refers to the ability to learn by experience, adaptively responding to new situations as contrasted with instinctual reflex responses maladapted to unusual conditions. Developing such adaptive efficiency is valuable in its own right and by no means implies the encouragement of client conformity to all extant community expectations or the acceptance of established values and customs. Social competence includes adjustments of the individual in trying to master his situation as well as his more passive adaptations to it.

INDIVIDUAL SERVICES

In the casework situation, workers explore what is available in the environmental surround, comparing this with what is actually used. They review the distinctive ways in which the client processes and uses potential resources, helping to overcome blockages to the use of these so as to provide him with a wider repertoire of responses. Workers may review with the client any relevant past experience of problem behaviour and situations, supplementing this with additional information, or symbolically reorganizing the circumstances so that alternative possible resolutions seem viable. Using themselves as role-analogues or models in therapeutic situations, workers may develop imitative learning in the client in relation to social competence.

In some situations, therapists may play parent roles by presenting appropriate models of interpersonal relations to children and young people, or by demonstrating viable behaviour towards children in the presence of parents. For example, they express affection, remain calm in the face of hostility, praise achievement and withhold any reinforcement of problem behaviour which natural or substitute parents may initiate. Knowledge of results contributes to efficient learning and performance. If client behaviour towards workers as substitute figures (e.g. substitute employer) can be modified, the modifications are likely to be generalized back so that less inappropriate client reactions develop.

Some degree of social competence is not invariably difficult to achieve, as it depends less on intelligence than on stability and perseverence which may be acquired through social education. Major elements in attaining this objective are training programmes which may be instructional, occupational or social and which are variously directive or non-directive, intensive or more relaxed.

Remedial instruction of all kinds; special-care units, junior and adult training centres, guidance and social counselling to families on home care and income management, half-way house hostels and sheltered workshops may between them provide a complete programme for rehabilitating residentialized clients to the point where they are sufficiently competent socially to step from the protected to the open community. Such services may be summarized under the heading 'investment in human capital'.

COMMUNITY SERVICES

At the community level, urban renewal schemes are often intended to increase the social competence of the poor, though many argue that they serve, counter-intuitively, to increase social malfunctioning through the experience of a great sense of personal failure which many engender. Milieu therapy of the kind developed by the Boston University North Point family project[81] represents one of the most fruitful attempts to raise the level of the social competence of whole communities.

SPECIFIC TARGETS

This objective may be further specified thus:

    (i) To improve the client situation from present ineffectiveness, unresponsiveness and non-use of external resources, to some defined degree of increased effectiveness in key areas and effort towards fulfilling responsibilities (e.g. job, home, personal relations, school, use of community resources).

    (ii) To promote and build on the client's capabilities to behave in ways acceptable to others in immediate or wider social environments (even though he may consciously choose other less accepted modes of behaviour).

    (iii) To promote the client's capacity to tolerate a certain level of frustration in relation to personal drives and appetites.

    (iv) To promote the client's capacity to control his own drives and impulses to the extent this is necessary for continued or renewed social functioning.

(v) To develop and build on the client's capacity to order necessary contacts sufficiently well to function at some defined level of effectiveness.

(vi) To provide clients with specific, meaningful guidance, or trained instruction and learning opportunities which directly increases their competence to cope with certain problem situations.

(vii) To develop and supplement capacities for family functioning including child-rearing, child care, care of elderly, or physically or mentally handicapped dependents and home maintenance.

(viii) To promote clients' self-organizing capacities in respect of day-to-day activities.

(ix) To mount relevant instructional, occupational and social education programmes.

18. Promote Socio-Occupational Welfare
Reduce Occupational Ineffectuality

'Shudder, you complacent ones'
Isaiah

POSITIVE POLE
Workers aim *to promote conditions conducive for mobilizing community members, to increase and diversify community social assets or those of particular underprivileged groups within it.* They seek to open up the latent energy of individuals and groups, to avoid its repression and to permit its investment in constructive behaviour. In doing so, the individual, group, and community social productiveness or efficiency are promoted and mutual aid encouraged. People in general wish to make their activities and organization efficient rather than wasteful, and the objective refers to basic human needs for achievement — accomplishment or mastery of occupational tasks to a standard which leads to the successful exercise of talents and capacities. The basis for this objective does not lie in the Protestant work ethic but in the development of the individual's sense of social effectiveness, usefulness and self-fulfilment which derives as much from satisfactory and enjoyable work as from the use of increased leisure. The phenomena of 'skylighting' — the performance of two or more jobs for pleasure rather than for bolstering inadequate income — exemplifies this issue of leisure-work. Workers are concerned to develop employment, whether as the principle source of income to provide for basic necessities or as the therapy for usefulness, the centre from which social contacts radiate, the badge of community status and belonging.

A person may doubt what he hears or sees but never what he does. Doing something, he becomes someone. Through action, we learn. Opportunities for experience must be created where action is not stifled, whether through the unmarried mother's domestic pressures where supporting her children ties her to the house, or a person's severe sense of inferiority inhibiting all action.

NEGATIVE POLE

Specifically, workers wish *to reduce apathy — the reluctance to act — and to combat under-employment, sub-employment and unemployment at source if at all possible, or failing that to provide useful occupational activities or substitute employments.* They wish to avoid creating a social underclass of people who feel themselves useless because their labour is rejected and the spectre of the unlived life. In one sense, this 'occupational' objective amounts to fulfilling safety needs and promoting economic security as of right. Workers seek to remedy those defects in an individual's performance or his immediate circumstances which stand in the way of his adequate participation in the economy. As the 1961 U.N. Civil Rights Commission concluded: 'a principal reason for continued poverty is lack of motivation to improve educational and occupational status'. Many attempts to open new occupations to underprivileged groups founder because so few come forward to apply. Many also fail because of socio-economic barriers, counteracting social conditioning, inadequate dissemination of information or uninspiring outreach programmes.

The individual produces certain social outputs, benefits or contributions or fulfils certain needs in relation to his own, his group's or his community's overall situation. These derive from his inputs into that situation in terms of efforts, skills, knowledge and other personal resources employed. Social productiveness may be defined as the ratio of social inputs, effort or resources to social outputs, benefits or results. Since work is an essentially human function, occupational fulfilment is included as an element of social productivity, as are economic contributions to self-sufficiency, wealth and power of the community. We want to achieve a closer balance between what people are ready to experience and what is actually experienced, between what is optimally desirable and what is feasibly attainable. From the individual's viewpoint, workers promote occupational fulfilment and reduce occupational frustration.

A local community's or sub-group's contributions may be similarly analyzed in terms of social productivity in relation to the wider environment. In community terms, workers seek to promote high standards of efficiency in relation to community social functioning.

Such questions have to be asked as how far can communities tolerate, even with the best of motives, the waste of their human resources? Do people have the right to work? If so, what effects does denial of that right have on the person and his community? It is difficult to argue with the general contention that people who want work should have work, and effective economic communities should provide enough jobs to go round without wastefully employing those in work.

Community needs are so large, real and urgent that for years ahead all national resources are in effect spoken for. There is the individual's right to work. Beyond this there is the community's right to use that work to improve its living standards. So long as people stay out of jobs, the development of the economy remains retarded and the workless breed new social problems for which economic resources again prove inadequate.

SERVICES

All those services which may be construed as investments in human capital, assist the attainment of social mobilization. These include enhancing labour-market skills by job guidance counselling pro-grammes, retraining groups for open and sheltered employment and all types of employment placement — sheltered employment, work centres, home employment, day centres, industrial out-work and contracted employers. Even more relevant are occupational workshops where employees can earn some kind of wage (even if minimal), or where bonus payments are made and where the workshop head actively endeavours to get new work and to run the workshop productively. Social planning schemes to generate employment and training opportunities to raise personal and family incomes in twilight zones would be included, even though social services agencies may only have advisory, advocacy or liaison roles in respect of these.

A work system can be effective in maximizing profits and services outputs, and disfunctional in destroying its human potential in the process. In the industrial field, promoting an increased responsiveness by the organizations to their members means reducing the need of corporate bodies to 'make' people comply with rigid prescriptions. To achieve this, industrial social workers need to foster company understanding and the use of the behavioural sciences in management. Motivation theory is an increasingly important adjunct to the central management task of getting the most out of the firm's human resources. This already happens to some degree in enterprising social services departments. Coventry, for example, use the social service departmental training officer to promote understanding of behavioural science aspects of management throughout the authority. Although often looked on as natural sources for this type of help, real work by social services agencies in this field has scarcely begun.

Meanwhile workers may concern themselves with such activities as changing the 'no work' ethic of a delinquent group by using clubs to selectively reinforce constructive work activities, and using the club settings for job placement. Or the reinforcement process of intensively helping a client with a poor work record to find a job as soon as possible after he decides to take one may be used. Workers may use client perceptions of them as experts or persons of authority having high status, prestige and (most significantly) competence to provoke imitative learning. Clients may be strongly motivated to improve their own situations, feeling they should repay the worker's efforts and interests. ('I did it to prove to her that I can, because she's done her bit for me.') Or workers may organize schemes for upgrading unqualified workers through on-job training schemes or by work reorganization procedures so that jobs fall within the client's competence. Managerial techniques of job training by breaking work down into component steps so as to simplify and reduce training periods together with techniques of job simplification, analysis and enrichment may be indispensable tools for social workers in this area. Kushlik[82] has demonstrated their value with the mentally handicapped.

Occupational welfare, provided by virtue of employment status, achievement and record, also takes the form of social security provisions in cash or in kind. Such provisions are alternatives to extensions in social welfare. Their cost falls largely on the whole population, their attainment by the individual often depends on the advocacy of social workers. Like social welfare and fiscal welfare, occupational welfare is a major redistributive mechanism.

SPECIFIC TARGETS
We may further specify this objective as follows:

(i) To work through the client's problems in relation to employment in terms of factors related to work motivation, performance and fulfilment.

(ii) To build on the client's work skills, reducing or limiting the effects of work disabilities.

(iii) To help the client order financial rewards and penalties from work (e.g. the differential between unemployment benefit and possible wage).

(iv) To help the client achieve additional work satisfactions.

(v) To work through the client's relationship problems in the work situation.

(vi) To help the client choose types of work in which he will be happiest.

(vii) To help the client work through the impact of the work situation on his domestic and social situation and relations.

(viii) To help the disabled client find some homebound employment or activity.

(ix) To help the client understand the organizational context in which he works.

19. Promote Social Participation
Reduce Social Alienation

'Suffer me not to be separated'
T.S. Eliot

POSITIVE POLE

Implicit in much of social work is the broad inclusive aim of *encouraging social participation, inclusion, reciprocation, mutualism, responsiveness and interaction, by which is meant reciprocal influencing among persons, groups and social forces in multi-lateral social relations.* Such interaction works through the medium of communication, which leads to some modification of behaviour.

Workers seek to help individuals participate authentically in the processes which shape their social behaviour, in group life and in collective endeavour, and to increase the investment of energy and ego-involvement in those activities, persons, events and situations which the individual finds significant.

Social participation may be defined in two ways. On the one hand, we refer to political processes by which citizens use their power to make their interests felt in social decisions and to make changes in prevailing social patterns, on the other, to the individual's affiliative needs to relate, draw nearer to, enjoyably cooperate and reciprocate with, and find gratification in productive association with allied others in the context of sociability or convivial gregariousness. This is referred to variously as the gregarious or herd instinct, the bio-social drive, the phylic force or fraternity. Social relations are developed which maximize the treatment of persons as ends rather than as means.

The specific target in many cases is to reduce the number of personal relations, usually devoid of emotion, in which the individual can be replaced or substituted by another without affecting the relationship. The more completely relations are mechanized, the more fractional contacts become and the less effective in generating emotions which are distinctly human.

Additionally, workers seek to promote social participation of community members in community structure and development so that it remains responsive and adaptive to members' needs. By this means, more people gain a share in their community, thereby reconditioning its structure. In the process, community members are themselves transformed. They advance along with the community which they themselves are changing. ('We are interested in this because we are a great family as well as wanting play space for our kids' — playgroup organizer). When this objective is pursued to its logical conclusion rigid distinctions between givers and receivers of services are eliminated.

NEGATIVE POLE

The negative side of this objective is *to reduce social alienation, distance, separation, withdrawal, isolation, anonymity and inaccessibility among community members. Workers reduce socio-relational inadequacy, be it caused through idiosyncratic, embarrassing, eccentric or antisocial behaviour.* This relates to the isolated individual's failure to establish or maintain communications or relations with those about him; to isolated groups whose accessibility to outsiders is in some way minimized; and to communities which withdraw from close connections with other neighbouring communities.

Barriers to wider contact may consist of physical or vicinal separation, as made manifest by unimaginatively-sited motorways, one-way schemes or the closing of key public transport services; social separation despite physical contact, as with blighted or depressed areas; political or economic isolation of one community from its neighbours; and mental separation where there is contact without genuine communication, as with schizophrenics.

We have all felt how alienation and purposelessness go together when we find outselves unable to make decisions because we do not really know what we want or what goals we seek. It is hoped that individuals who experience themselves as aliens, estranged either from the world or from themselves, divorced from significant aspects of their own experience and personality will be helped to reassert themselves as centres of their own worlds, as creators of their own acts, and able again to influence the conditions of their own existence. We have here to deal both with the objective state of separation and the malaise resulting from such a state.

Alienation occurs when the client's world is unresponsive to him. He feels himself subject to forces he neither understands nor guides, and loses interest in and commitment to life because it is not the real 'he' who is involved in living it. The state is graphically illustrated by Kafka's impotent, uncomprehending hero Joseph K whose very existence is in question. Alienation encompasses most if not all social relations, affecting the excluding people as well as the excluded, for the process of exclusion creates a distorted social world which cannot be eluded. Isolation is the failure of the individual through inability or preference to establish and maintain communications with those around him.

Workers seek to reduce estrangement between parts of the personality and significant aspects of experience. There may be actual estrangement leading to minimal contact with others, feelings of estrangement leading to disorientation, or a motivational state leading towards estrangement.

CLIENTELE

Target clientele includes anyone whose acts are his masters, from the person whose life has been so traumatically changed by a major accident that he is estranged from his own body, to the chronic depressive or schizophrenic who has lost interest in life. Clientele may also include the unclubbable delinquent, the hyper-introverted child, severely withdrawn or catatonic schizophrenics, autistics, and those suffering acute separation anxieties. People who are relocated through slum-clearance schemes intended to aid the poor may become more alienated through loss of familiar neighbours and places and the difficulties of adjusting to a new environment. In short, this objective embraces all clients who in their interactions with others feel they are overpassive or aggressive, resulting in isolation.

COMMUNITY SERVICES

The movement towards community participation is strongly oriented to the achievement of this objective. Community development projects at Southwark, Liverpool, Coventry and Glamorgan, typify the kind of service designed to stimulate social participation. It is not simply building a community organization of interested citizens around an issue, but the fact that this issue is won by citizens for themselves that is of significance. The stress is on the possibilities of voluntary association, mutual aid and cooperation. Such social participation increases the individual's sense of self-worth.

How can the individual citizen, especially if he lacks education, information, experience, influence, gall, resources, stamina and self-confidence get the services he expects as of right from large bureaucracies? If treated impersonally, kept waiting, treated unfairly, ignored or put off how can he redress the wrong and make a wider issue out of what bureaucracy may view as a matter of small moment?

Other methods might include: area offices as neighbourhood multi-service centres; an agency ombudsman; client advocates; improvements in the administrative law enlarging client and citizen protection; increased decentralization and delegation of decision-making; informal communication networks which feed client reactions back to staff; or provisions for practice fieldwork induction of newly qualified planners in twilight zones as teachers and social workers involved in community action, and as spokesmen for the poor. The last mentioned method is demonstrated by McConaghy's Liverpool 8 neighbourhood action plan[84] which directly resulted in the area being nominated a housing improvement zone under the 1969 Act.[85]

The specific intention of much community work is to mature the protesting attitudes into objective ones which express themselves in concrete proposals and implementation. Natural client protestors or insidious suggestions of staff, encourage clients to recognize services imperfections such as that particular apparatus is not functioning, meals are served lukewarm or too slowly, there are insufficient evening diversions, and so on. Soon the entire group participates in common protests. This leads to many clients, isolated in their indifference up to this time, emerging with beliefs and feelings of their own, and interrelationships are established. The main aim is to reduce any inconveniences of which all the people concerned are victims — the premises, the staff, the administration and the community in general bearing the brunt of such criticism. The group tends to organize itself, delegates being elected who are charged with transmitting protests to the relevant authorities.

INDIVIDUAL SERVICES
Participation by the community and client in service arrangements link services at community and individual levels. Effective social services use active client contributions to improve services. Workers seek to provide more scope for clients to change community systems, thereby increasing their opportunities to exercise initiative and autonomy within them.

At casework level, workers may use schoolteachers to selectively reinforce behaviour incompatible with social isolation among hyper-introverted children. Severely withdrawn, even catatonic schizophrenics have been treated by operant-conditioning regimes through tasks ranging from simple and complex motor responses, through imitative and spontaneous verbal responses, and finally to interpersonal communication and cooperation, each successively approximating to fuller participation. A selective reinforcement of participation has proved effective among hard-core delinquents in 'laboratory' clubs in high delinquency areas by rewarding first attendance with cigarettes, sweets and food. Additional reinforcement of further participation then follows through such activities as driving instruction, electronic equipment construction and talks with pop stars.

If the clients' opposition to their situations is not used therapeutically, it is expressed by rejecting treatment, by aggressiveness in the form of violence or escape. Residential situations used for active therapeutic treatment have resulted in the mutation of residents' energies through opposition, aggressiveness, activity, creation, contribution and self-regulation.

Services designed to promote this objective might include good neighbour schemes, recreational clubs, friendly and volunteer visiting, specialist social clubs, social contact bureaux, groupwork for client families, recruiting volunteers from among clients, and any services which help individuals or groups to improve relations with others.

Prominent amongst such services must be counted the casework and psycho-therapy in which clients are helped to value family and friendship relationships for themselves as a direct mutual sharing, by not possessing or imposing upon the other but helping the other to unfold on analogy with Buber's[83] postulated I-Thou relationships.

SPECIFIC TARGETS

A few specific targets deriving from this concern may be included:

    (i) To build on and develop the client's capacity to form fruitful relations with others.

   (ii) To define the nature of the client's relationships with friends, neighbours and external organizations.

  (iii) To define the client's attitudes to and expectations of the community and relevant contact groups.

  (iv) To define the client's ability to behave in ways acceptable to others (e.g. self-control, ability to tolerate frustration).

   (v) To encourage parents, relations and friends to participate in the client's social activities.

  (vi) To encourage community participation in public and social planning.

 (vii) To reduce the geographical isolation of clients by providing appropriate transport facilities.

(viii) To give clients some experience of what healthy group membership means.

  (ix) To resolve the client's feelings of fear and distress about the role he occupies.

   (x) To reduce the psychological isolation of clients by the development of, enrolment in and encouragement to attend relevant social clubs and gatherings.

20. Promote Social Integration
Reduce Deviance

'Only connect'
E.M. Forster

POSITIVE POLE

One significant objective of social services agencies may be *to assist the community in achieving amongst its diverse members some degree of integration, cohesion, consensus, inter-connectedness, recognition of law and concern for others so that members of different interest or reference groups, social classes, income brackets and races can live together harmoniously.* This may include the fostering of helpful family relations and intrafamilial cooperation.

In fact, the objective relates to many similar expressions of need such as companionship, affection, belonging, solidarity and intrafamilial harmony. The person has contacts with individuals and with groups he cares about, he is socially established, has roots, and is not in a social vacuum.

Social integration implies socialization, the process by which communities transmit prevailing knowledge, recognition and a minimal congruence of behaviour with those socio-cultural norms which constitute relatively consistent patterns of thought, action and behaviour, or with those social mores whose violation provokes sanctions against the violator. Norms emerge from social experiences and cultures of the community into which individuals are socialized by parents and their surrogates.

Workers seek to integrate individuals where they become involuntarily disengaged from primary or secondary reference groups. They hope thereby to fulfil individual needs for belongingness by knitting social lives together through face-to-face encounters, by plugging people into each other's lives without making everyone feel the same. We are all involved with each other. To live in a community is to live in one system, all of whose individual members and parts are interdependent.

In addition to maintaining consistent social arrangements, social integration entails fulfilling some necessary set of minimal conditions or norms which serve, enhance or maximize the chances of community survival in some (not necessarily its present) form. The individual internalizes the shared attitudes of others. Common elements in the individual's social environment are made up of the attitudes, expectations and activities of those with whom he interacts. The common elements taken together constitute for the individual a conception of the generalized other. His family is the generalized other in so far as it enters as an organized system into his individual experience. The individual imagines what 'people' would say or do 'if they knew' or 'when they know'. This implies identifying with one's social role by internalizing that role, adopting it as one's own, and striving to attain the necessary skills to conform with role norms. In psychological terms, this may involve strengthening the individual's super-ego whereby images are developed which inhibit or modify asocial behaviour.

This objective may be specified in two ways. In one dimension we are talking normatively of *assisting clients to understand, develop capabilities for adapting to, and where necessary to internalize socio-cultural-ethical norms or codes.* This is the social equivalent of biological adaptation. People's values must minimally form a sufficiently coherent unity if a community is to maintain itself as a going concern. Some degree of shared rational agreement is sought in thought and feeling deriving in part from a shared unity of sentiment, all of which tends to produce order where there was disorder, agreement where there was disagreement, clarity where there was confusion, consensus or productive conflict where there was unproductive tension.

In another dimension we are talking functionally of the interlocking system of reciprocal claims, expectations and overt acts which constitute our cultural environment, together with the client's acceptance of the reality of this situation. Unwritten, non-legal and unformalized social rules of the community are not only principles for determining disputes, but are also guides to the probable results of our actions. These must be articulated in sufficiently precise forms to be clear about them. Workers aim *to promote the social cohesiveness, harmony and efficiency of the community absorption of its members, reducing debilitative conflicts and assisting the community in achieving some degree of social coalition necessary for social functioning.* Devotion to family, friendship, cooperativeness and fellow-feeling are indicated, though reference to that set of virtues listed by moralists as group acceptance, avoidance of reproach and good repute cannot be completely ignored.

NEGATIVE POLE

These definitions of objective become clearer if stated in negative terms as being *to reduce dysfunctional deviance and social disorganization which leads to illegal action within a given milieu.* By this we mean decreasing behaviour which so intensively or persistently departs from socially, culturally or ethically accepted norms or expectations that it comprehensively or permanently so disturbs the social equilibrium of the community as to prevent viable interaction. Workers seek *to reduce transgressive behaviour and promote desirable responses such as altruistic acts and helping people in distress.* This objective refers to the control function whereby the community influences the behaviour of its members to prevent break-up by treating social aspects of legal offences.

Typically, juvenile delinquency is cited. Juvenile delinquencies include violations of laws, incorrigible and ungovernable behaviour, habitual truancy, desertion of home, engaging in illegal occupations, association with 'vicious' persons, frequenting unlawful places, and wilfully endangering the health or safety of self or others. Behaviour of psychopathic personalities is also cited since they are not mentally ill with a recognizable disorder but have 'deformed' personalities as judged by their behaviour in terms of a lack of conformity to community social requirements. Clinical, legal and emotional maladjustments are included.

A considerable debate arises as to what constitutes deviancy. Clearly, the concept is highly relative. What is 'normal' or accepted in one group can be deviant in another. The socially integrated individual struggles with the same needs and drives as the deviant, the difference lying in the manner they are dealt with.

At one end of the spectrum the concern is with those environments conducive to anti-social behaviour, with the development of criminal behaviour, or variable responses to social (e.g. parental) controls. At the other end the concern is with individuals who have completely rejected or failed to understand socio-cultural norms, resulting in an established pattern of anti-social or illegal behaviour. 'Deviant' ultimately means behaviour demarcated as unacceptable to the community.

Generally workers are trying to delimit behaviour which is socially harmful or productive of physical, mental or emotional injury to others of a sufficiently serious kind to merit intervention. An example is deviance manifested in psychopathic or sociopathic behaviour where the client lacks susceptibility to social motivations and reinforcement.

Since the word itself originally derives from statistics, indices for 'deviance' should in principle be easier than others to pinpoint. Deviant behaviour is simply that which diverges from the standard position. The extent of divergence in respect of any piece of behaviour may therefore be pinpointed in comparison with the equivalent behavioural mean for the particular socio-cultural or geographical group concerned.

COMMUNITY LEVEL

Workers may be concerned to limit and change maladjusted, self-destructive traits in whole communities. In so far as deviance is the product of wider social and economic influences, the focus of social services agencies will increasingly be on community-wide intervention. Social cohesion relates to the education process and the effectiveness of community mechanisms for mediating and resolving disputes without doing injustice to the positive, functional aspects of conflict as a source for innovation and reform.

Thus, the social integration objective comprises the sub-objective of acculturation. More or less continuous first-hand contact between two or more culturally distinct groups demands that one group takes over sufficient elements in the other's culture for them both to live together viably.

FAMILY LEVEL

At the family level, social integration relates to pair relationships. The need for social relations is evidenced by the close association of marital status and health. Married people have lower rates of death, suicide, alcoholism and mental illness than those who are unmarried or whose marriages are disrupted by death or divorce. More broadly, this objective concerns any disruptive conflict with specific individuals — within families between husband-wife, parent-child and sibling-sibling, outside families between teacher-pupil, doctor-patient, employer-employee and policeman-offender. One or both persons behave in a way the other finds unacceptable without either being able to withdraw from the relationship. Causes may include the nature of the interaction itself, divergent role expectations, the behaviour of each, or personality characteristics.

STRATEGIES

There are several broad alternative strategies for coping with deviance. The community worker may, along Laingian lines, treat the presenting client as the 'norm' and the environment as deviant, perhaps striving to increase the degree of community tolerance and non-stigmatization so that his behaviour is no longer labelled 'problematic'. This strategy is often used in an effort to integrate the mentally ill. The psycho-dynamically based caseworker may endeavour to strengthen the client's ego so that he may better control, organize and adjust to reality the impulses and fantasies generated in his unconscious, thereby eliminating problem behaviour. Workers may help the individual to achieve some degree of harmony with himself as well as his social environment by some process of acculturation.

A third strategy is to treat the interactional problem between client and community. This may require teaching the 'client' more sophisticated or discreet methods of fulfilling 'deviant' personal impulses, drives and needs: as when the overt homosexual in a homosexual-stigmatizing community is taught ways of satisfying his needs which will not cause personal or legal offence. Simultaneously, some modification of overtly stigmatizing and punitive community actions may be attempted, such as reducing pressures to close down the local gay club whilst not attempting the impossible task of changing community attitudes.

INDIVIDUAL SERVICES

Intensive casework with violent psychopaths, with young people who have extreme negative attitudes towards all authority figures, with the 'congenitally' homeless or unemployable, or those who are part of the unemployed or non rent-paying subcultures all relate to this objective.

One aspect of casework involves helping the individual to relinquish one set of social traits or behavioural responses which are problematic for him or self-destructive, and acquire a new set which are more adaptive and less problematic. A typical technique is to present negative reinforcers which may contribute to suppressing deviant responses, thence allowing more integrated client behaviour to be performed and reinforced. Of all the negative reinforcement techniques aversive therapy presents the greatest ethical problems. For it involves the use of noxins or aversive stimuli (physiologically-induced nausea, electric shocks, etc.) accompanying problem behaviour associated with previously pleasant subjective feelings (alcoholism, enuresis, fetishism, disruptive habits such as the child's compulsion to sleep with parents). The problem behaviour is thereupon discontinued so as to avoid unpleasant accompaniments.

Workers may use verbal labelling to generate anxiety in relation to maladaptive deviant behaviour. The disruptive hyperactive child's classmates may be enrolled in treatment by awarding points for non-disruptive behaviour, afterwards exchanged for pennies. Client attitudes, impressions and images about how others live may be reshaped as many clients are relieved to hear that others have similar problems ('It took a load off my mind just to hear about others in the same boat – meeting them seemed all I needed.') Another aspect is simply helping clients to understand their wider social environment, thus increasing sensitivity to their effects on others. Half-way houses, reception centres, short-term residential care and sheltered environments are all used from time to time as channels through which deviant clients are helped to orient to socio-cultural norms.

COMMUNITY SERVICES

There is a tendency for many communities to keep anyone not fitting the norm in some kind of social 'siding'. For example, many people donate to charity in the belief that they are helping to keep problems 'behind social bars', but what most of our minorities need is a chance to be properly integrated into the community.

By more rational social planning, the aim is to protect individuals and groups from certain detrimental kinds of bureaucratic behaviour. In doing so, social services planners may seek to make other services more directly sensitive to client needs and possibly to revise client views of government agencies as alien forces which must be manipulated into yielding benefits. ('Mum asks whenever I come back: "did they give?".')

SPECIFIC TARGETS

We may further specify this objective as follows:

   (i) To help clients cope with or satisfy to some degree reasonable (or irresistible) demands of family, neighbourhood, reference groups and institutional contacts in so far as these affect client requirements of these groups.

  (ii) To define those aspects of the client's behaviour which are creating problems for others in the immediate social environment, or reactions by others which the client finds threatening, stressful or otherwise disabling.

 (iii) To help clients identify patterns of behaviour which create problems for or are harmful to those in the immediate or wider social environment.

(iv) To help clients understand the link between problem behaviour and others' responses, so that they better identify and anticipate the consequences of their own actions.

(v) To help clients carry through decisions by modifying problem behaviour so that dislocating elements in relations with others are removed.

(vi) To afford protection for those in the relevant area of the client's social environment from dangerous, disabling or debilitating elements of the client's problem behaviour by modifying treatment.

(vii) To achieve some degree of consistency from the child's viewpoint between home and school environments.

(viii) To assist the social adjustments of working adults by achieving some degree of consistency from the individual's viewpoint between home and work environments.

(ix) To promote other-directedness and other-regard necessary for living in the community.

(x) To reduce or limit the distress the client causes to others.

21. Promote Social Gratification
Reduce Social Ennui

Though most recreational and cultural opportunities fall within the province of the market place, the State continues to expand direct public operation and complete or partial subsidy in these areas, as with recreational day centres for the elderly or cultural programmes socializing 'outcast' groups. Objectives of enhancing pleasure, fostering creativity and enriching community life with no ulterior ends in view provide as legitimate a base for some social services as any other, despite a certain puritanical backlash. The process of casting off the work ethos in favour of the leisure ethos is likely to disrupt many communities and requires radically different social structures, programmes and services. While potentially more leisure time is available owing to technological improvements, free time and leisure are not necessarily identical and free time may not lead to leisure. Increasingly available free time is also likely to create major social problems.

Although this objective is primarily sanctioned as the concern of such departments as recreation and parks or of bodies like the Arts Council, social services agencies are also involved. In France, leisure activities are accounted directly against welfare budgets, being recognized as an absolute need of human personality and a major determinant of the quality of life. Riesman (in *The Lonely Crowd*)[86] and Dumazedier (in *Toward a Society of Leisure*)[87] characterize the prerequisites of this objective, repeating syndicalist demands that leisure should form an integral part of welfare programmes.

Individual and family counselling will increasingly have to address itself to problems of leisure. New or expanded adult educational and recreational resources may be needed, enabling people to utilize their increased free time in ways which are personally fulfilling and socially productive, so that a sense of meaningfulness is linked to the use of free time as it is currently linked with work. During the next decade communities will probably face problems arising from more free time, and social work can contribute to developing a community awareness of shifting the emphasis from work to leisure.

POSITIVE AND NEGATIVE POLES

The social services seek *to enrich the individual's life and his enjoyment of his leisure through recreational and cultural pursuits. Workers promote opportunities for pleasurable activities, and the optimal use of leisure, providing outlets for individual and group interests and gratification. They are concerned not merely to fulfil existing interests but to cultivate and extend the range of people's interests. They reduce debilitative ennui, boredom, vegetation and restlessness in relation to leisure and at various times, endeavouring to safeguard the individual's right to repose and do nothing.* Although ennui is contrasted to gratification, another relevant antonym may be depression and over-seriousness.

Leisure activities are those amusements undertaken freely which fall outside the obligations of work, family and community. They function as relaxation providing recuperation from fatigue, as entertainment providing deliverance from boredom, as modes of personality development, and as determinants of community mental health. Taken in the broadest sense, recreational fulfilment must include the provision of outlets for aggression other than violence. Lack of recreational opportunity fulfilment is often characterized as one form of poverty.

The playful attitude may also characterize an individual's working life as when he finds enjoyment and pleasure from his work activities. It underlies the attempts by industrial social workers to foster job enrichment. Play tends to manifest itself in enjoyable, stressless, random, whimsical (sometimes fantasy-driven) behaviour which releases internal tension but achieves no external effects in that it is undirected, being undertaken without further purpose. Enjoyment cannot in one sense be a goal, but is rather a feeling which accompanies important ongoing activity. As Freud noted, it is always dependent on function. All major recreational fulfilment must essentially be generated within the group itself in some significantly spontaneous way.

SERVICES
This objective includes the provision of services helping people to achieve enjoyment, personal satisfaction and wider interests in a wholesome environment during their leisure. It includes some provision for excitement and a break in monotonous routines. Such provisions cover, for example, various kinds of socio-cultural promotion in new housing developments; the provision of suitable recreational opportunities and activities in day centres and clubs; developing adventure playgrounds; encouraging multifarious commercial entertainments in drabber areas; making constructive use of desolated areas, such as sports activities under motorways. As important as any of these may be simply the process of importing some sense of fun, bonhomie and joie de vivre into client relationships to replace the over-earnest, dour, saturnine, humourless, self-righteous prudery and decorum which, as Alvin Gouldner[88] comments, characterizes so many professional practices. Even the worker's encouragement of a disordered family to improve the appearance of their drab home may promote this objective, since aesthetic values constitute a significant element of social gratification.

Workers seek to create more opportunities for recreationally deprived individuals to discharge tensions and instinctual energies, and fulfil impulses as they arise, and thus to attain pleasure irrespective of the consequences of such pleasure-directed behaviour. The Freudian pleasure principle provides one theoretical base for our stress on this objective in the personal social services.

D. To Foster Agency Objectives through Direct or Indirect Interventions
To Reduce Obstacles to Fulfilment of Agency Objectives through Appropriate Interventions

The work system is too instrumental to help the individual in all respects. The boss cannot repair serious disability or malfunctioning, for his objective is to make profits or to deliver services, using the individual's resources instrumentally towards this end.

Likewise the family system fulfils too expressive a function to help the individual in all respects. The parent (or friend) has his own needs and either consciously or unconsciously may manipulate family members in order to keep the family (or friendship) intact. Since neither boss nor parent can sustain the role of remoulding impaired individuals, this has to be undertaken by the social service or helping system.

Social services function midway between the instrumental attributes of the work system and the expressive attributes of the family system. It functions like the work system in so far as workers help the client to cope with his problems in the real world, and increase his sense of reality and skill in coping with community institutions. The social services system also uses expressive media similar to those used by the family in building relationships, nurturing and giving support.

The helping system aims at *discontinuing those existing relations wherein transference (embodied in both work and family systems) is exploited by vested interests of other-related people.* The objective of the helping system is to do away with its original structure so that client and therapist evolve a new relationship. Therapists and clients undergo successive stages of role evolution: from client dependency on the therapist to the point where the client becomes maximally independent and able to fend for himself without therapeutic support.

The method used to engage a client in helping him find his own way is significant in that social health is a process, not merely the end result of the helping process. The agency has both to serve a function in the community and to serve its clients. The two functions are often not complementary but conflicting, and the agency has constantly to evaluate the functioning of its own system in fulfilling both sets of objectives. Social services personnel engage their clients to get things done jointly.

22. Promote Overall Client-Community Effectiveness
Reduce Overall Client-Community Ineffectiveness

INDIVIDUAL LEVEL

Workers seek *to help clients achieve personality integration* by which in a particular situation, single courses of action emerge from the various predispositions competing for expression in the individual, or by which some consistency of choice emerges in consecutive situations over a period of time. The individual must be considered — as a whole — a living human system of mutually adapted parts functioning together to maintain a unitary whole. Behavioural traits composing this unity of personality gain significance through their utility to the individual's overall life. Parts serve each other as instruments for attaining a common goal. They collectively constitute thereby a composite living structure in which parts are organs, mutually instrumental to each other and collectively instrumental to the life purposes of the whole person.

Individuals respond to varied environmental stimuli to which they are sensitive. These responses are adaptive if they effect the individual's continuing survival. Personality consists of the dynamic organization within the individual of those psycho-physical systems (referred to as habits, attitudes, emotions and dispositions) which determine his unique adjustments to social environments. Personality involves the organization or state of interrelatedness among predispositions which limit, facilitate or activate each other at all times. The predispositions themselves are organized into systems, the form of organization distinguishing uniqueness of personality.

Elementary units of personality are functionally dependent on each other, competing for expression at any particular time. These units must be sorted out. Priorities are assigned to the expression of each in given situations. A personality is integrated to the extent that such internal sorting and assignment processes are possible.

The intrinsic nature of the individual's behaviour as a whole has a shape of its own, forming a detailed entity which determines the specific part-processes and individual behavioural elements to which the previously stated social objectives refer. The stronger the individual, the more each part of the personality system depends on every other, and the more this interdependence affects every aspect of every part. All personality traits are structurally interdependent though functionally autonomous. One or other of the objectives outlined above are to a greater or lesser extent at varying times out of reach of all of us. A balanced life is often characterized by the achievement of all these objectives at some level of attainment.

The client may be helped to balance extroceptive feelings and introceptive feelings (see p. 85). Egocentricity of perception and conception may be balanced with impartial objectivity. Exocathection, by which is meant practical, concrete, physical or social action having tangible results which are highly adapted to the world as it stands, may be balanced with endocathection, by which is meant fantasy, reflection, imaginative and abstract thoughts.

Workers aim *to help clients harmonize their personal drives and the external demands made on them, especially where these conflict unproductively.* They do this by providing a frame of reference, a context, an orientation having some consistency and wholeness, which helps the client make meaningful observations, appropriate responses, or take significant action. Clients are thus helped to achieve some degree of order, organization and balance in their lives. Behaviour in a particular role may be quite consistent, but the same person playing another role may behave very differently. A state of continuous conflict demands control and inhibition of responses. This leaves the individual in a persistent state of tension which impairs his capacity to adjust himself effectively to conditions of daily living. Alternatively or additionally, the worker may act as a go-between among combatants in conflict situations, reporting information from one to the other and interpreting real motivations for action. ('He was tense all the time about this other thing and it had to come out somewhere in the end — so why not with me?') Combatants tend to cut each other off from hearing the very information which might heal their differences.

Given some degree of personality integration, choices made from alternative behavioural responses show considerable consistency from situation to situation. The individual is to some degree master in his own house, determining which disposition will be enacted, when and how it will become overt. Choices made in the past guide those made in the present. There is a discernable consistency of choice from one time to another which marks out individuality.

Allied to personality integration is the development of the individual's ego ideal and external expectations. Workers aim *to promote or maintain clients' hopes and endurance,* as well as some firm foundation for these in terms of the other contributory objectives listed. Some degree of optimism or faith in the ability of clients and communities to resolve their own social problems may be prerequisites for actually resolving them, as well as the availability of some client resources relevant to the problem on hand.

Values which cannot be realized sometimes warp a person or a community. Similarly, all things a person can and must do to realize his aims or values successfully can also warp him. Simultaneously, workers aim *to help clients achieve a clearer recognition of reality and some degree of objectivity* which implies clients distancing themselves from their own situations.

No individual, group or community utilizes more than a small sector of available goals, resources and incentives at any one time. Etzioni[89] demonstrated how dormant community resources are mobilized at times of crisis (as in Biafra and Bangla Desh), and Caplan[90] demonstrated similar phenomena at the individual level. A sub-objective may therefore be *to recapture faith in the capability and utilizability of existing resources and services to resolve some of our social problems, or our capability of generating new resources and services to resolve new social problems.*

The agency aims *to establish clearly the extent and nature of its interventions in the problem situation,* including relevant limitations on resources available for use. Workers explicitly establish at an early point with the client the degree to which he or the agency has the capacity or resources to help him in the manner expected. Failing this, the client may treat all worker efforts or interests as indicators that expected resources or help will be forthcoming shortly. ('They couldn't help me and she said so straight out. But it was a bit of help, just pouring it all out.')

Lastly, workers may *help clients in providing help for themselves and self-treatment,* so that they are able to handle problems on their own in future.

COMMUNITY LEVEL

At the community level, workers may under this objective be *synchronizing diversified agency programmes to deliver a better service to a designated population group or joining agencies in an inter-organizational structure to increase communication and foster cohesion.* They seek *to increase the community's capacity for change and innovation.*

Taking the perspective implied in this objective, we all become gestalt psychologists at the individual level of intervention and social systems planners at the community level of intervention.

SOCIAL ACTION

One aspect of this objective is *to promote concrete social action and reduce social inaction and passivity among communities and individuals.* Nothing leads more to ineffectiveness than prolonged discussion of the kind which serves only to postpone and stultify all action. On occasion, any action however ill-planned, ill-considered and chaotic is preferable to orderly, over-academic inaction. (Gypsy representative about a well-intentioned social work champion of his rights: 'Where does all their yapping get us? Nowhere.') Taking the plunge into the arena of action from the safe refuge of analysis involves handling problems of conflict and social dynamics rather than problems of explanation and social statistics. At the casework level, this may entail helping clients to plan their lives and actually take some action. The client's active orientation is increased. ('Now when I come out after seeing those welfare people, I really *do* some things. Before, I just loafed.') At the community level, this may entail what Alinsky[91] has described, when speaking of setting up a community organization, as 'going ahead and doing it together despite the uncertainty and controversy, and seeing what comes out of our interactions with each other.' The task is to open people to opportunities to experience new situations previously regarded as unattainable, and then see the response.

Inability to attain for oneself the key goods of life causes most people shame and hurt which count as social costs, not simply to the individual but also to his community. Social services provide social benefits by which these social costs are met.

23. To Promote Altruism
To Reduce Application of Market Criteria

It is the State's responsibility, sometimes acting through processes we have called social policy, to reduce, eliminate or control the forces of market coercions which place men in situations in which they have less freedom to make moral choices and to behave altruistically if they so will . . . Ways in which we structure and manage social service institutions can encourage or discourage the altruistic in man — can foster integration or alientation — can allow the theme of the gift to spread among and between social groups and generations . . . If it is accepted that man has a social and biological need to help, then to deny him opportunities to express this need is to deny him the freedom to enter into gift relationships.

Such quotations from Titmuss's *The Gift Relationship,*[92] aptly express the theme of this objective. Workers seek to develop the sense of the gift among communities: the right and opportunity of people, if they choose, to give in non-material as well as material ways. This refers to free gifts to unnamed strangers with no contract of custom, legal bond, constraint or compulsion, shame, guilt, gratitude, imperative, pentience, or payment, signifying a belief in the willingness of unknown strangers in the future to act altruistically. Such gift relations signify the notions of service to others, devotion to their well-being, generosity, open-handedness, fellowship and some feeling of inclusion in society. These are rights and claims which humans may make of each other in their social relationships, the institutionally based versions of which constitute the welfare system.

The gift relation is exemplified par excellence in volunteers who try to employ a moral vocabulary to express their reasons for entering gift relationships with unnamed strangers. Titmuss[93] for example, classified 80 per cent of the responses of voluntary blood donors as falling within the categories altruism, reciprocity, duty, each of which suggests a sense of social responsibility to others' needs. There seems to be a universal human valuation of compassion towards the needy, even if this value premise may often be put away or concealed while actual action moves in a contrary direction. Welfare decisions, it is generally thought, should be intrinsically altruistic, drawing upon ethical values.

However, the objective has wide ramifications for service planning and provision. Chosen instruments of social policy and management carry with them ramifying or ricocheting consequences throughout social life. Titmuss showed how the role of social policy and planning instruments (like the development of a private market in blood) may encourage or discourage the spread of ethical practices or exploitation, sustaining or reducing personal freedom in social life and in non-market institutions.

At the community-wide social planning level, it may be a crucial part of the social planning function of social services departments to reassert welfare values constantly. If so, one practical manifestation of this would be for social services personnel, in their collaboration with physical planners, to ensure that social variables are given full weight in the community structure and agency intervention models which are increasingly defined in mathematical terms. It may be that in the course of their welfare operations, social services agencies have a function in promoting certain valuational standards, for example of treating individuals as ends-in-themselves whatever the mode of service delivery.

A shared valuation is developing that welfare schemes, far from being costly for a community or society may actually lay a prophylactic basis for a more steady and rapid growth, saving the individual and the community from future costs and thus indirectly increasing productivity. At the same time, the administration of such schemes should be based on non-market criteria if they are to be effective. The market value of an individual cannot be the measure of his right to welfare and the acceptance of this has begun to release social services planning from the inhibitions laid on it by central government restrictions enunciated on economic criteria which ignore the welfare function. This leads to the requirement that certain services are taken out of the market, or so modified in their operation as to produce social benefits not available through the market.

Methods chosen for agency intervention in and treatment of specific social problems should be built on assumptions which can be justified on a Kantian categorical imperative. If built on other assumptions — such as a means-justified-by-ends basis, these methods may well become the vehicle whereby such assumptions are spread to other areas of social life. Means as well as ends, methods as well as objectives raise value issues. A plan which is evaluated as likely to meet social need better in the long term might be rejected on the grounds that it would fail to meet the present problems of clients in the short term.

This implies a benefit-allocation mechanism which functions outside of the market place. Unless social objectives are specified, the benefits will remain unquantified and open-ended.

24. Promote Agency and Staff Development
Reduce Agency and Staff Stagnation

Workers seek *to intensify and diversify the development of specific agency functions in pursuance of the strategic objectives outlined above, as well as to develop staff capacities.*

To the extent that a service is aimed at promoting various aspects of social health it is covered by the previous objectives. But there is also a concern about *how* services are run to achieve these objectives — about the implications of social services departments and institutions for the future of the community. Agencies are to be valued not only by what they do, but also by the terms, bases and methods by which they deliver services.

However effectively community social health is achieved, a negative verdict would be returned on departments which failed to respect staff (or client) rights in so doing, which did not provide congenial group affiliations, allow democratic participation, ensure the orderly development of the agency as an entity and its staff members as individuals, and recognize certain constraints on the means used. Even suppose for one moment it could be effective, the use of threats of violence or physical force is justly prohibited as a method of social work intervention.

Another major issue is the role of consumers in agency development. There are two sub-objectives within the agency system. One, to initiate and give directions as the super-ordinate authority in the system so that things can get done at least to the take-off point where the client can take over. Second, to provide maximum client participation every step of the way.

In achieving more satisfactory results for clients, workers might exercise too much repressive or directive power over clients' lives. But although too much can be done for clients so that they are no longer masters of their own personal development, we can also become so obsessed by client autonomy that very little gets done. Achievement objectives and egalitarian objectives may conflict.

This objective may be stated in terms of balancing client participation and the use of social work status and skills in achieving the objectives cited earlier. Workers aim *to help the client become a protagonist within his community and social situation in confronting outsiders with his new perspective in the use of facilities, resources and personnel to reshape the character of the helping system itself.*

Clients must be involved in the change process by joining workers in overhauling systems which have been created and from which they have initially been excluded because of their impairment. Helping systems are reorganized to take advantage of the great potential influence which clients can exercise on each other in channelling themselves in the more constructive direction. The level of agency responsiveness to community needs is determined by how far agency decision-makers respond appropriately to the information and messages they receive from community members. This process is equally dependent on consumer participation in service planning and delivery.

There is often much community resistance to any intervention or change sought by social services departments, either on grounds of cost to the rate- and tax-payer or on the grounds of interests vested against such changes. Agency objectives of fostering social changes and commitment to social interventions must be articulated and justified. This may entail using the social sciences as a rhetoric by means of which social changes are supported. This relates to the social service department's public relations role, concretely demonstrated by the number of invitations social services personnel receive to talk to all manner of local groups on many diverse topics.

In an effective agency, we may postulate that the following situation pertains: specific objectives have been defined in the tangible form of social states or benefits to be achieved, social decrements to be avoided or social problems to be resolved. Appropriate services and programmes are then designed, resource allocations allowing a sufficient level of quality and quantity of service to enable the achievement of these desired social states or benefits. The services so designed are operated efficiently; the take-up of services by those who require them is increased or optimized; professional staff and clients are increasingly included in the decision-making process; and daily decisions and operations are evaluated and controlled in terms of the degree to which the objectives have been, or have not been, achieved.

This entails the development and application of more systematic social planning, social management and social administration approaches, including the application of such approaches as Planning, Programming, Budgeting Systems[94] (PPBS), priority scaling, Management by Objectives[95] (MBO), organizational analysis, social cost benefit analysis, and cybernetic and operational research methods. It also implies the increasing and better use of mass media, direct consumer contact methods, mechanisms for effective staff and consumer participation and a general opening up of bureaucratic processes so that consumers feel more at ease in claiming their rights.

A further issue presents itself at this point. Social services agencies must reduce the level of risk-taking in welfare provision so that no essential community or client need falls through the net. Yet at the same time, it must encourage experimentation in new ways of resolving those major social problems agencies have hitherto been unable to handle.

Lastly, social service agencies have responsibility for mobilizing (e.g. by presenting an adequate case for) increased resources for appropriate expansions, particularly in the course of the universal budgetary battle for resources in competition with other public services or in fund-raising endeavours. Galbraith[96] has pointed out discrepancies between the increase in the personal ownership of consumer goods and the limited increments of such public resources and services as schools, hospitals, recreational facilities and welfare services.

25. Promote Agency Effectiveness
   Reduce Agency Ineffectiveness

Different agencies attach a different priority to each of these strategic objectives. How they respond to each objective determines what kind of department they will become.

One major objective is *to develop and improve the agency's capability of pursuing and fulfilling these objectives effectively.* This involves setting operational objectives, allocating resource priorities, controlling interrelated activities to achieve the results sought, structuring the organization so that it facilitates the work to be done, taking decisions which provide an optimal feasible match between objectives-resources-operations, and adopting the style of management behaviour which most effectively matches situational problems confronting us. Seebohm[97] joins the chorus of government committee reports on the values of management efficiency. These values relate to economic viability in local authorities, coordination of services, unitary management through the chief executive and policy committee, efficiency systems through which to evaluate performance by the achievement of objectives, the minimization of service cost, reducing fluctuations in service levels, deciding optimal planning intervals, and improving the forecasting of client needs.

The first stage in achieving this objective is to render services accessible to those demanding them. This entails area offices being as close to the neighbourhood served as possible. The North West Polytechnic study for Islington Social Services[98] demonstrated how urban analysis helps achieve this. The second stage is to decide on the basis of systematic and explicit rationing policies rather than inadvertence, which client problems shall receive service. The worker has then to diagnose the problems so that the priorities policy can be applied in allocating services. Once allocated, the service has to be efficiently delivered.

Part of this process consists of absorbing new professional knowledge and technology. As one example, the use of allocation models for anything from allocating airline seats to scheduling tankers raises the question of whether such models might help solve analogous problems of maintaining current and visible inventories of institutional space available in residential homes and, at the same time, rationalize the criteria used and make them visible. A computer-based information system might provide the technological base for case recording, preventing cases getting 'lost' between and among agencies and agency sections and allowing the immediate retrieval of all client and community data relevant to decisions being made by workers.

One might cite similar illustrations from such diverse fields as the application of television and programmed learning to the new methods of teaching basic human relations skills; methods derived from work study and ergonomics as applied to house-cleaning technology for home helps; kinesiology as applied to casework diagnosis and treatment covering particularly the areas of non-verbal communication; and the use of queuing models to reduce waiting lists for service or care, and so on.

The agency or helping system stands between the community and the impaired individual, and the community has its own needs to shape the agency. These needs are often far from optimally helpful in the reparation of individuals and the objective is *to ensure that the total outcome or product of the interrelationship between the individual community and agency systems exerts a constructive rather than a repressive or negative effect.* This objective concerns not only the results of the whole agency effort in fulfilling community needs, but also the impact of the agency on the individual clients and the methods by which these objectives are achieved. Although obvious, this value requires to be stated in that (as Gouldner[99] has observed) social service agencies may secretly value failure. If repeated often enough, it demonstrates the need to expand social service agencies further. Analogously Edgar Hoover argued for more C.I.A. funds on the basis of their continued failure to check the internal expansion of Communism.

The worker uses his developing understanding of the model of the concrete social situation with which he is working to test out insights, hypotheses, diagnoses and dimly felt formulations; to refine his understanding and to guide his earliest interventionary efforts. In a tentative way he has to start actively employing his knowledge and skill to find common ground and active engagement with the problems of the client, the group, or the institution immediately he contacts them, if he is not to be merely fencing, manoeuvring for position or dissembling. The method and style by which social work is undertaken therefore becomes centrally important.

The agency has to expose those social problems with which it must deal and search out those who are suffering from them, to give people suffering from those problems free and easy access to the services it provides to cope with these problems, encourage relevant people to use this access by actually claiming their rights to the service, to deliver services efficiently to them, to monitor and evaluate the impact of such services in actually resolving these social problems and to adjust the services accordingly. These are controversial programmes, as perhaps all significant programmes must be, and require considerable expertise in public relations on the part of social service managers.

Non-use of services by those in need reduces their effectiveness in combating social deprivation. Increased knowledge can be communicated through the mass media, by use of letters, leaflets, TV, radio and advertisements. But such means have limits, and the information-giving role of social workers, doctors, health visitors, teachers and others in personal contact with the public is essential. Training courses need to place more emphasis on a knowledge of practical details, and several social work agencies have recently appointed a full-time worker to keep social workers abreast of client rights. When in 1966-67 the Department of Health and Social Security allowed the elderly to receive supplementary pensions from the same book as retirement pensions, the rate of applications for supplementary pensions rose markedly. Take-up will only be maximized if applicants feel at ease in claiming their rights. Those in need will only make full use of services if the attitudes of officials, social workers, doctors and lawyers make them feel accepted, respected, and free of embarrassment. Larger numbers of handicapped come forward when services are developed which have sufficient promise of success to make them attractive. Intake from a wider stratum would do something to reduce the communication barriers that exist between the social professions and many of the working class. Social workers must combine with all others concerned with the social services to ensure that they are more fully used by the many in great need.

A significant sub-objective is to supply services spontaneously, continuously (so long as they are needed), without comment, perhaps on the model of Mormon welfare, without the formalism, delays, constant prying and ceaseless cajoling which has characterized State welfare since the 1930s.

The social services department becomes the centralized planning, development and funding agent of numerous socio-technological resources to facilitate planned and deliberate change in certain social conditions. It becomes the central catalyst in the application of social science policy and the main vehicle for social policy. In undertaking this social planning task, the department has to find the balance between intervention and non-intervention in client or community problems, between allowing the order-maintaining mechanisms to work spontaneously to restore equilibrium or deliberately and rationally planning the resolution of problems.

It is important to recognize the full consequences of agency intervention. For example, the client may use the agency (through its local worker) as a means of achieving his or her own ends. ('If you stop trying, I said to him, I'll go straight to the welfare.'). This may on occasion have the effect of merely transferring the problem from one part of the client system to another, and the effective agency will be concerned to analyze the total impact of all its interventions on the total client system.

In seeking to be effective, the agency has moreover to avoid a tendency towards the kind of welfare colonialism graphically expounded by R.M. Hilliard,[100] Director of the Chicago Public Aid Department: 'Society stands in the same relation to them [i.e. welfare recipients] as that of parent to child . . . Just as the child is expected to attend classes, so the child-adult must be expected to meet his responsibility to the community. In short, social uplifting — even if begun on the adult level — cannot expect to meet with success unless it is combined with a certain amount of social disciplining — just as it is on the pre-adult level.'

In the context of seeking to reduce poverty, programmes have been proposed for absorbing and upgrading into the social services the marketable skills of large numbers of untrained 'poor' people. New questions are opened up for investigation and planning, with prior need to determine whether the emphasis is job-creation or optimized service delivery. While these are not necessarily incompatible goals, and may even happily prove to be mutually reinforcing, the task of discovering the facts and developing their implications is important.

SPECIFIC TARGETS
We may further specify this objective as follows;

(i) By the most efficient means possible to continuously re-define and re-direct need by constantly searching for and pinpointing key causal factors which prevent the adequate attainment of the strategic objectives given above.

(ii) To define client (and community) demands for and expectations of agency intervention.

(iii) To define problem areas in which the agency may be able to intervene effectively.

(iv) To define which, if any, of the problem areas listed above are the key problems which will constitute target areas of intervention.

(v) To define alternative methods which the agency may use to intervene effectively in the community.

(vi) To explore and analyze alternative methods of resolving these problems.

(vii) To assist clients in taking appropriate decisions in the full understanding of probable consequences.

(viii) To define the perceptions, emotions and conceptions which each worker (or group of workers) brings to the problem situation.

(ix) To define the knowledge, skills and attitudes which each worker (or group of workers) brings to the problem situation.

(x) To build on and improve agency resources (including staff skills) which will help the agency to make a more effective impact on community problems.

(xi) To monitor and evaluate the results and effects of action in accordance with these decisions.

(xii) To refer clients through to other agencies where this is most appropriate.

(xiii) To define present gaps and deficiencies in provision.

(xiv) To sanction programmes with reference to statutory and legal provision, or rational guidance from D.H.S.S. on its application, or where this is lacking, to place requests with central government for its development.

(xv) To develop more integrated services by which integrated treatment strategies are evolved which embrace all available methods of intervention.

(xvi) To develop adequate information systems which cover known and expected demand, service access and service delivery in terms of manpower and techniques, and compatible and relevant departmental statistics.

(xvii) To develop methods of identifying new targets and gaps in service, for example through action research and development.

(xviii) To improve the agency's organization structure so that it is continuously adaptive to changing community demands and professional technology.

(xix) To disseminate information on new developments and effective service practice which will facilitate the migration of ideas and practice methods from one sub-field to another.

(xx) To reduce barriers between the agency and its community.

Embracing all these objectives at once, it may be said that the appropriate aim is to find the optimum, feasible balance between the pursuit and realization of each of these objectives in respect of the community served. This balance will now be explored.

the equivalent requisite treatment pattern by pinpointing the optimal intervention point and method to break the problem sequence or impulse chain. Take the case of the homosexual who wishes to foresake his homosexual practices. Workers can treat the client by educating him in attending closely to his own behaviour at key points so as to recognize the onset of such sequences, and by teaching him to interrupt them by switching to other thoughts or activities at this early stage before the impulse chain reaches an uncontrollable level. Alternatively, where the client wishes to maintain homosexual relations but wishes to eliminate those of a kind which have damaged his life in the past, he may be taught to select and interrupt the onset of such sequences when the other male is a certain kind of person (e.g. a minor or 'trade') or in certain locales (e.g. in public lavatories or on street corners) but not when other types of people are involved (e.g. friends of friends) or in other locales (e.g. friends' parties). Behaviour therapists have had considerable success in using such therapies based on problem sequence analysis in conjunction with other methods over a short intensive period of time without relapse during the two-year follow-up.

In multiple problem situations, more complex issues arise as to in which order its problem variables can be most effectively treated. Problem variables may be defined in terms of: the fundamental causal problem variable; the key or critical problem variable; the most directly treatable problem variable; the most controllable or completely treatable problem variable; the problem variable treatable with greatest certainty of success; and the most urgent or pressing problem variable.

Using these terms, workers can define various treatment sequences used in a number of different cases, decide which were effective and which ineffective, and then look at the individual situational variables to establish correlations between patterns of problem variables and patterns of effective treatment sequence.

It is clear that simplistic principles as to treatment sequence cannot be established. For example, it is not helpful to generalize from one or even several cases by saying that where marital relation problems are causative of debt problems, they should be treated first because the fundamental causal problem variable of marital relations may have to be changed if any progress is to be made on the debt variable. Nor is it possible to generalize the opposite principle that debt problems being the most pressing and urgent should be treated first before progress can be made on more fundamental, longer-term marital matters. But it may be possible to develop general principles of treatment sequence by exploring a more detailed pattern of interrelations between problem variables, analyzing them in terms of more specific variables such as the extent and duration of debt and marital dislocation, the numbers of individuals and institutions affected to various degrees, the numbers of additional problems generated, and sequences of the initial manifestation of the problem. It is the mark of the effective, experienced social worker or psychologist that he intuitively makes successful decisions on treatment sequence by weighing up these problem variables in his mind and recalling his past experiences of success or failure which bear on the decision. By developing treatment sequencing models, conscious comparisons can be made between the pattern of problem variables and the pattern of effective treatment sequence. They will not hold in all cases, but will probably tend to do so in the majority of these. Provided such treatment guide-lines are used not as rules of thumb but with discretion and are reinforced by personal judgement on each individual case, they can be extremely valuable for planning, training and daily treatment decisions.

Moreover, some conclusions about treatment sequence can probably be tentatively drawn. For example, in treatment workers will tend to concentrate first on fundamental causal problem variables in longer-term preventive work where client morale in other spheres is generally high; on the problem variable which is most urgent or pressing in climatic situations of maximum crisis or emergency; on problem variables which are most controllable or completely treatable where many other methods have been tried and failed, and on the problem variables which can be treated with greatest certainty of success where overall client morale is very low. Generally, psychodynamic-based treatment focuses on fundamental or critical problem variables, whereas behavioural therapists tend to focus on the most directly treatable, controllable problem variables or those which have the greatest certainty of positive pay-off.

In a selection of multiple-problem family cases from several different departments where financial and personal problems were entwined, we found that the sequence of treatment had been identical in those cases deemed by some workers to have been successfully treated and divergent in the cases deemed to have been unsuccessfully treated. In almost all of these cases the problems included physical or mental handicap in at least one member of the family, deep-rooted adjustment problems in one or several of the children, considerable debt and serious work or unemployment problems for the father, bad housing and general poverty in the family situation, and strong environment stresses on the family in some form which had usually been the immediate cause of referral in relation to the immediate crisis or problem episode.

The successful treatment sequence was invariably patterned as follows:

  (i) Remove immediate risks to the child (where these occur).
 (ii) Relieve immediate debt pressures by negotiation with relevant companies or courts and establish appropriate social security support.

(iii) Preliminary income management advice to family.

(iv) Establish father's work situation.

(v) Educate or otherwise treat longer-term child problems, and simultaneously treat adults' capacities to cope with emotional and social problems.

(vi) Improve adults' abilities to relate to other agencies.

(vii) Educate family in domestic management.

In cases involving both marital relations and debt, it is often a vital necessity to decide which of these problems to take first. Such a decision may be necessary where it is unviable for the social worker to even raise one of the problems before having made some positive impact on the other, more immediately pressing difficulty, or where treatment of one problem may be a waste of time without first treating the other. Even in cases where some simultaneous treatment is possible, it will probably be necessary to phase in the treatment process over a period of time.

In some cases, it may be more effective to treat the debt problem first — either within individual interview or over a succession of visits — perhaps on the grounds that once this basic material problem affecting biological needs has been treated at some possibly simple, symptomatic level (such as negotiation with landlords, hire purchase and utility companies) it may then be possible to tackle the more complex, deep-rooted problem of marital disharmony which may be causative of present difficulties. In other cases, the reverse decision may be better, as where it is evident that no further significant impact can be made on the debt situation until the underlying marital problem finds some level of resolution.

It could well be that once a certain threshold is passed in terms of extent, duration and consequential effects of debt, nothing further can be done until the resultant state of economic deprivation and insecurity is in some way altered. Alternatively, if that threshold has not yet been reached, it may be vital to start immediately with intensive work on this problem, leaving the more fundamental problem of marital disharmony until later, since the client would be unable to cope with or benefit from intervention in respect of this issue. The same may hold in the reverse if the marital disharmony has attained catastrophic proportions.

Diagnosis thus becomes a problem of defining the thresholds of intensity or severity for key variables such as debt and marital dislocation along several scales. Treatment becomes a problem of defining points at which intervention may significantly alter the interaction between these variables so that they cease to be not only immediately destructive but also self-perpetuating in the manner of the vicious circle. It is a question of delineating the right point and method of breaking into the cycle in which increasing debt problems reduce the family's capacity to cope with their marital relationships, resulting in increased marital discord which in turn reduces the likelihood of the family's capacity to resolve debt problems, which are thereupon intensified still further.

7 | The Community Plan: A System of Objectives

COMMUNITY PLAN

The sum total or system of interrelated strategic objectives constitutes the agency's community plan. Such a plan is a set of defined objectives and costed programmes associated with them which are developed in terms of impacts on the community made by services, psycho-social benefits to be achieved, needs to be met or problems to be resolved as an outcome of service delivery. This contrasts with an administrative plan in which the objectives are defined in terms of services rendered, without directly incorporating an evaluation of the *effects* of these services. Evidently, to generate a community plan is a complex process, the details of which we shall now explore.

Multiple Objectives

The break-up of the old dogmas has not led to an absence of objectives, but rather a plethora, and community plans now inevitably embody multiple objectives. We have entered an age of value pluralism and there is no ideology except that which the individual brings with him.

Pluralism involves the acceptance of multiple diverse objectives in that diverse and heterogeneous social ways of life are valued for their own sake and conformity or homogeneity is devalued *per se*. Pluralism may simply be used as a means by which decision-makers and participants refuse to choose or make qualitative decisions — an argument used by Marcuse[1] and his disciple Woolfe.[2] Or it may be a veiled means of allowing the operation of the free market in which each interest group is balanced by another and the welfare economy is viewed as a self-rectifying system. In both situations, organized interests are seen as always defeating unorganized majorities or unorganized, highly informed minorities. Alternatively, pluralism may be the means whereby policy-makers and practitioners come to grips with the complexity of individuals and communities in order to derive plans and policies sophisticated enough to cope with this complexity. A debate still rages between those seeking some consensual value basis and those pluralists who regard such a basis as impossible, if not undesirable.

The time consumed in attaining one objective will limit the time available for the pursuit of another. It is therefore necessary to weigh up the respective advantages of the different objectives to decide how much effort and time should be devoted to each. Decision-makers in large organizations are unable to embrace the full range of considerations in their minds. Objectives therefore need to be classified and categorized into classes that are useful for the decision-makers.

Controlling the Total System: Simulation Models

Once such systems analyses in terms of the interaction between social problems, values, objectives and their treatments have been completed, it is possible to use them as a basis for planning and operational decisions.

At this point simulation models (as discussed on pp. 42—45) are relevant, providing powerful analytic and research tools to cast light on the interaction of those variables explored earlier.

8 | Tactical Objectives

Tactical objectives are scheduled, short-range intermediate goals attainable within the period planned for. They are formulated so that workers are able to define how they shall achieve successive approximations to the desired social states outlined in the strategic objectives and form milestones on the way to achieving these. This definition is tied up with the percentage of new resources we plough into one area of activity or service rather than another.

Without specifying tactical objectives, strategic objectives begin to sound like clichés spawned by the fashionable concern for social problems, such as 'morale', or 'the quality of life'. To utter such ready-made phrases is to be absolved from action, the specific operational elements being lost in cascades of rhetoric.

Tactical objectives carry prescriptions, their mandate lying in higher-level aims and missions. They limit exaggerated expectations since they are founded on present competence and capability; imply implementation, specific commitments of resources and a way of doing things; express what is operationally feasible. For instance, malaria was once accepted as a norm and all related medical objectives were palliative rather than remedial. With the advent of quinine, however, the prevention of malaria becomes a valid tactical objective in medicine.

In one sense, tactical objectives are trajectory goals. They represent a succession of interim attainments through which the agency will progress en route to its realization of the requisite state of affairs, and which (together with developing methods) will in time alter the view of what this desired state is.

People tend to avoid defining tactical objectives, for they are specific enough for opponents to attack. Choices between two (or more) equally good objectives arise, as opposed to choices between what is considered good and what bad. They often represent a choice of what is thought to be slightly more good or beneficial, and a rejection (even though temporary) of what is thought to be slightly less good or less beneficial.

The achievement of each objective to some degree may resolve some of the problems which gave rise to it. For example, effective learning increases the individual's adaptive efficiency and social competence. Yet such learning of the individual or community invariably seems to create new problems of survival at a higher level which in turn demand new adaptive responses. Medical services provide us with the classic example. New medical knowledge means lengthened survival for all. This potentially increases the population density, which in turn threatens survival and thus some point of intervention is needed to break such a self-perpetuating loop or vicious circle.

The conclusion of one recent case where a worker intervened, apparently successfully, in what started as a crisis situation with the father in a mental institution, suggests the way in which some of the strategic objectives were fulfilled in respect of this particular client. He now pays the rent regularly and has moved from furnished to unfurnished accommodation (fulfilment of safety needs), holds down his new job (occupational productiveness), takes the children out (recreational fulfilment for the children), begins to enjoy doing these things himself (emotional stability and sense of valuation), attends the court and begins to pay his debts (less deviance), begins to see his friends again (social participation), improves his marital relationship with his wife (emotional fulfilment), begins to understand himself more (awareness), handles the children better so that they cease truancy (social competence), and begins to join local community groups which put pressure on the community and societal conditions which contributed to his problems initially.

The achievement of each of these targets in relation to this particular client contributes only minimally to each of the implicit strategic objectives for the community at large. What difference, it may be asked, does the regular payment of rent in his case make to the fulfilment of the 'safety' needs of the community as a whole? It may simply ensure that he has shelter at the expense of those homeless families in the community who are queuing up for his room in the absence of sufficient overall accommodation. However, the cumulation of records which show the current state of our provision (or lack of provision) for the shelter needs for all community members, initiatives to achieve minimal shelter for all members at rents they can afford, and corresponding efforts to achieve the allocation of a certain percentage of income by all community members to the shelter thus provided, together represent a programme for achieving the interim tactical objective of minimally adequate shelter for all community members. This is one milestone which contributes towards the achievement of the overall strategic objective of the adequate fulfilment of all safety needs of all community members. By formulating such interim states and their contribution to overall strategic objectives, we can begin to relate the specific work which any one worker undertakes on any one case with the ideals and motivations which lured him into the social services in the first place.

Tactical objectives represent statements of what an agency seeks to attain by its methods of managing and developing specific service programmes. To help us define ongoing tactical agency objectives, they are exemplified below in terms of (1) merger objectives, (2) field objectives related to a specific case, (3) community work objectives, and (4) a specific piece of practical social administration. The following generalized statements in respect of the British social services merger on Seebohm lines, may help us in defining ongoing tactical agency objectives.

1. Tactical Merger Objectives

Service Objectives

1. To extend the range and depth of penetration into community needs by developing community-based services more fully.
   Example: Workers hope to serve people in their own neighbourhoods as far as possible, and to extend preventive work by making an impact on hitherto unmet needs.
2. To cover a multiplicity of client needs, not merely narrow segments of them, by developing family-based services more fully.
   Example: The department endeavours to coordinate social policy with other agencies so as to treat the social aspects of the family as a whole and deliver services to family units in a more integrated way. A coordinated policy with hospitals should prevent unnecessary removal of patients from their homes for long, socially distressing periods.
3. To master a particular professional technology — to integrate a whole chain of professional knowledge which is wider than that held individually by child care, welfare or mental health officer or by domiciliary, day care, residential, case, group or community worker.
   Example: Intensive personal counselling and boarding-out services developed in the children's field are being reapplied in new forms to the care of the elderly and physically handicapped.
4. To capitalize on distinct areas of specialist knowledge.
   Example: Groupwork, community work, behavioural therapy, conjoint family therapy and similar services are becoming more widely available.
5. To develop new services which keep pace with rapidly changing community needs.
   Example: Domiciliary and day care services are being more intensively developed so as to decrease the need to place people in

institutions.
6. To maintain essential current services during new service developments.
   Example: One department established a small headquarters project team to cover those clients for whom essential continuing support is in danger of being interrupted by the transition.

Agency Intervention Objectives

To decide the most feasible method of intervention we can use to lead the given social processes to a favourable outcome.
1. Motivational: awaken person's desire to continue.
2. Containment: prevent deterioration.
3. Maintenance and amelioration: maintain person's status quo whilst ameliorating his present condition.
4. Rehabilitative: help people who might improve.

Economic Objectives

1. To accumulate sufficient resources to deliver service more effectively.
   Example: Many directors have used the increased economic power which attaches to size to put in strong bids for new resources before their honeymoon period is over. Some have already begun to use their greater capacity to plan, to undertake research, to innovate, and to compete for manpower.
2. To make economies of scale and reduce some overhead costs entailed by separate specialized divisions by combining common functions, coordinating service distribution, and making common use of existing services.
   Example: Some departments are pooling diagnostic effort in assessment and screening units. Many have pooled the transport facilities of the former separate departments by using integrated transportation models for the allocation of transport resources.
3. To increase client benefits per unit cost of worker time.
   Example: New approaches to evaluating service effectiveness are being developed and applied, for example, priority scaling.

Professional Objective

To increase the status of the social services profession so as to articulate and meet community social needs more effectively.
Example: The Seebohmization of social services agencies represents the assignment of administrative accountability for the social condition of the nation to one particular profession.

2. Field Objectives

At the field level, workers must consider objectives related to the individual case. Some interesting research has been accomplished in this area by Reid and Shyne,[1] Reid and Epstein,[2] Jehu,[3] Goldberg[4] and others. We will illustrate an approach to setting case objectives within the context of overall agency objectives, taking one case as an example.

The Case of Family X

The area office covers the central section of a town whose population is 70,000. The town is split west and east by a canal. The eastern sector consists of cheap lodging houses, and its population is shifting. The western sector consists of privately-owned, semi-detached houses and some new local authority housing estates whose tenants derive largely from areas to the far north and south of the city.

The main urban occupations are light industry and only five per cent of the working population is unemployed. Twenty per cent of primary school children have free school meals.

Most of the social services agencies are located in the eastern sector. Here there is to be found the area office of the social services department, the area offices of health, housing, employment and productivity, and social security, a general hospital with a psychiatric unit, a day centre for the mentally ill, a homeless family unit, a maternity and child welfare clinic, an adult training centre, and some voluntary agencies like NSPCC and the Family Service Unit. In the western sector are two family group homes and three homes for the elderly.

There are few community action groups or services organized on a voluntary basis apart from small-scale, isolated church activities. Youth services provide conventional clubs attracting six per cent of the area's young people.

The main problems are homelessness, poverty, mental illness and juvenile delinquency, the majority of such cases arising in the eastern sector or in the local authority housing estates to the west.

Within the western sector, one of the few families in local authority flats outside the housing estate is family X. They have been living in a three-bedroomed post-war flat on the sixth floor for nearly a year, having been rehoused from poor, unfurnished accommodation in the southern sector. The father is a fifty-year-old refuse collector, employed by the local authority for the last three years. The mother despondently classifies herself as a housewife of the same age, the engaged nineteen-year-old elder daughter is a waitress, a younger daughter aged twelve is at a comprehensive and the eleven-year-old son is in his last year at primary school.

The total family income amounts to £44 net per week, being

composed of the father's wage of £25, the elder daughter's wage of £18, and a £1 per week family allowance. The total contribution to household expenditure amounts to £30 of which the daughter contributes £6, regular outgoing expenditure amounts to £7 per week rent, £3 per week is spent on hire-purchase repayments, leaving a balance of £20 per week for food, clothes, fuel, household necessities and pleasure.

The father, Mr X, was referred to the social services department by the psychiatric unit in the local hospital for regular supervision of medication, the consultant psychiatrist having diagnosed chronic schizophrenia. From the psychiatrist's report it is gleaned that the man manages to keep his job going as a refuse collector, despite his current beliefs and problems. He sometimes, however, stops taking his medication and this results in severe depression and delusion, which in turn leads to readmission to hospital (seven previous admissions) if serious attempted suicide is to be avoided (two previous attempts). The last suicide attempt occurred shortly after the family was rehoused nearly a year ago, the last hospital admission was a two-month spell which ended two months ago.

From an interview with Mr X, it would seem that the problems were the pointlessness he felt about life, the school's annoyance at his younger daughter's absence, and many aspects of the wife's behaviour. Mrs X drinks far too heavily, helps create financial difficulties, neglects the house and her appearance, is always upset, nags him, complains about the neighbourhood and is frightened of going out alone.

Mrs X's perspective on family problems centres around the husband's role. He does nothing for the family, never says anything, isolates himself from everyone, rejects sex, is obsessed by the kill-joy religious sect called the Movement and thinks the world is about to come to an end so that life is not worth bothering about. She feels much worse since moving to the new flat and is now frightened of going out alone, relying on the children, or occasionally members of the Movement to accompany her. Her new neighbours are unfriendly and never talk, and she misses her old friends. She wishes she could get a factory job again as before, but cannot think what to do about travelling to and from it. She is angry with her elder daughter who is marrying next month because she is unexpectedly pregnant. She is worried about the younger daughter being 'sent away' through not going to school, while sympathizing, since she hated school herself.

The elder daughter sees the main problems as her father's depressing influence on the whole family, and her mother's heavy drinking which causes her to 'let things go'. She thinks the HP debt will go on mounting and that when she leaves no cleaning at all will get done and very bad cooking. She predicts that her sister will stop going to school completely, and will get into trouble with the police through her uninterrupted association with delinquent friends, and that her brother will become even more isolated from anyone of his own age (he never mixes with boys of his own age anyway), will get very worried about his family's problems, and will spend all his time helping his mother or doing chores for her.

The social worker's additional comments after preliminary investigations are that the GP is unhelpful, prescribing sodium amytal whenever husband or wife attends as he believes further referral of either to a psychiatrist or social worker is unnecessary; the school takes an increasingly punitive attitude to truancy as truancy rates soar; and the neighbourhood is highly unsupportive. Within the family, everyone takes it for granted that the father will not participate in decision-making and that the mother will rely on her son to help her out. The family seemed generally adrift, feeling outsiders from their community and its institutions, such as school and work.

We shall now review some of the possible case objectives to be considered by the worker in respect of the case. The references within square brackets, refer to the strategic objectives enumerated earlier on pp. 79—176

Possible Case Objectives
COMMUNITY-RELATED OBJECTIVES

To open up the social environment and stimulate a greater variety of communication and interaction in the western area, using the changing conception of the neighbourhood by family X and other similar families to monitor the effectiveness of this endeavour [C].

  (i) To foster neighbourhood social networks [B 13];
 (ii) to reduce the 'coldness' of the social environment by fostering relevant local interest groups (e.g. tenants' associations) [B 16];
(iii) to promote a spread of social services in the western part of the area [D 24];
 (iv) to reduce the hostility of the social environment by promoting more tolerant and understanding institutional attitudes, and modifying the primitive approaches of influential community figures (e.g. school attitudes towards truancy, GP attitudes towards family) [B 15];
  (v) to foster increased employment and occupational opportunities within the area [C 18].

FAMILY-RELATED OBJECTIVES
Immediate objectives:
1. To gain the family's confidence by demonstrating recognition of their anxiety and the practical relevance of social service intervention through the immediate action on felt problems of individual family members (e.g. claiming financial relief if debts are

caused by the father's hospital admissions) [D 25] .

2. In the course of (1) to relieve or dissipate the immediate felt pressures building up, so as to free the family to work through its own longer-term problems (e.g. ensuring all family's welfare rights are known and claimed if required) [B 12] .

Longer-term objective

3. To foster the increased social integration of family X with the neighbourhood, reducing its currently enclosed nature [C 20] .
    (i) To increase the number of significant interactions of family X with the similar socio-economic enclave in the western area whose life-style is similar [C 19] ;
    (ii) to provide information on and introduction to relevant community groups [A 5] ;
    (iii) to coordinate external supports for the family [D 25] .

Shorter-term objectives

4. To explore how the family might be helped to function more effectively through direct work with its members as a group [B 13; C 20] .
    (i) To gain agreement to work with them consciously as a group [A 7] ;
    (ii) to clarify and work through each member's relations with the others (e.g. husband-wife and wife-son relations) [C 17] ;
    (iii) to elucidate alternative ways the family might function effectively as a group (e.g. by building direct parental capacity as a primary support for the son, or arranging for multiple supports for the son via all available sources) [C 17] ;
    (iv) to improve internal family communications (e.g. about the effects of Mr X's illness) and help them share in decisions about each other [C 20; A 8] ;
    (v) to reinforce the parental role (e.g. by involving the parents in liaison with the school) [C 20; C 17] ;

5. To confront the whole family with its problems and to treat them as a whole [D 22] .

Emergency fail-safe objective

6. To explore the physical and emotional feasibility of the family moving to the eastern area as a contingency plan should other objectives fail, since the eastern area is more in line with its life-style, and the social climate would be more acceptable [B 13] .

INDIVIDUAL-RELATED OBJECTIVES

Mr X.

Immediate objective

1. To supervise Mr X's medication in a manner which will help to fortify his sense of responsibility towards himself in respect of this,

and eventually produce a more efficient medication regime for him [A 6].

Emergency objective

2. To provide Mr X with a long-stop in the case of future contemplated attempts at suicide (e.g. through contacts with the Samaritans) [B 12].

Longer-term objectives – rationality

3. To promote in Mr X a more rationally critical attitude towards the beliefs he has taken over without examination from the Movement, a wider view of alternative ways of acting sanctioned by such beliefs, and an increased ability to assess alternative values [A 2; A 6].

   (i) To make contact with the Movement in order to explore the specific nature of the beliefs involved, their implications, their knowledge and understanding of the effects on Mr X (and probably others like him), and what remedial action might be taken [A 2; A 6];

   (ii) to work through the consequences of Mr X's adherence to the Movement so as to open avenues for a more joyful communal life for the whole family (e.g. to help Mr X help his family more in the 'tail-end of life' to enjoy themselves, using positive reinforcements) [C 21];

   (iii) to help Mr X take an interest in other life activities, so far as this is consonant with his beliefs [B 16; C 21] (e.g. to explore the possibility of contacts with a number of specific alternative religious and philosophical groups and sects) [A 2; A 6];

   (iv) to promote more efficient and effective familial methods and supports for Mr X's mode of living [A 2; B 13];

   (v) to help improve Mr X's decision-making capacity [A 2];

Longer-term objective – emotional stability

4. To explore what emotional feelings Mr X may be trying to communicate via his behaviour (e.g. about how he sees himself) and to work through these with him [A 3].

Shorter-term objective

5. To encourage Mr X's support for his wife's efforts to extend her social contacts and take up employment [C 19].

Mrs X.

External contacts

1. To help the family learn more effective coping mechanisms by introducing a new influential element in its life via Mrs X's new community contacts [C 17; C 19].

   (i) To help Mrs X find new outlets for her social life through increased neighbourhood contacts with specific social interest, and possibly occupational groups [C 18; C 19];

   (ii) to promote an increased sense of her personal appearance and its effect on others [A 4] ;

(iii) to help Mrs X use her elder daughter as a role analogue [A 9; B 13] ;

(iv) to help Mrs X gain a more concrete and current sense of the external world, and foster her sense of her own normality [A 5].

Independence

2. To promote an increased sense of personal independence and initiative [A 7].

(i) To promote an increased interest in and ability to cope with H.P. debts by discussion and analysis of budgeting and, if necessary, by referral to domestic budgeting classes [C 17] ;

(ii) to promote an increased efficiency in household management by the discussion of methods and, if necessary, by referral to domestic management classes or a part-time home help for a short period [C 17] ;

(iii) to enlist Mrs X's support for her husband's ability to assume some familial responsibilities [B 13].

Parental Role

3. To promote an increased understanding of parental functions, child development and alternative methods of child rearing [C 17].

Occupational Effectuality

4. To assist Mrs X in attaining paid employment as a means to relieving her dependency on her husband, the pressure from her son's presence at home, and the frustration which she currently sublimates through drinking [C 18].

Elder Daughter

Emergency objective

1. To ensure that her current life plans are in no way impeded by the current family problems [A 7].

Short-term objectives

2. To build on and foster her continued interest in and support for her family [B 13].

3. To help her develop her new life situation as a model for the family from which she derives [B 13; C17].

4. To use her new situation to provide information to the family on available opportunities within the community for extended social contact [B 16].

Younger Daughter

Emergency objective

1. To ensure that the ill-consequences of her current modes of behaviour are minimized, primarily by appropriate education about drugs and sex, prescription of the Pill if necessary, and thence

development of a regime for taking it [C 20].

Other objectives

2. To promote an interest in the future [A 6].
3. To reduce the motivation for truancy [C 20].
4. To help her develop living habits which square with both her personal needs in relation to her family and with the school's demands on her [C 18; C 19; C 20].
5. To provide her with opportunities for talking out her feelings about her family and peer group situations [A 3; A5].
6. To provide her with the maximum number of attractive alternative peer group contacts to those she cultivates at present [B 16; C 21].
7. To help her remain in the home unless her situation and that of her family deteriorates [B 11].
8. To develop with her and her peer group a young people's centre for disturbed adolescent behaviour, beginning with direct contact with relevant street gangs [B 13].

Son

1. To promote increased independence by weaning him away from complete dependency on his mother [A 7].
2. To help him develop a strong personal identity by providing him with alternative male models to his father, through the medium of his school or through new neighbourhood contacts [A 4].
3. To provide him with alternative social outlets where a more relaxed atmosphere is possible, by promoting increased neighbourhood contacts with specific children's groups (e.g. adventure playgrounds, youth clubs, Boys Brigade) [C 19].
4. To counteract his ambivalence about his whole current environment, both home and school [A 5; A 6; A 8; A 9].
5. To reduce his feelings that he is totally different from all around him by forging links with peer groups and by generating a more realistic school attitude to his current problems [A 4; B 10].

PLANNING [D 22; D 25]

1. To assess the agency time and resources available in the light of the overall priority of the case and the problems of achieving change.
2. To order these objectives in some priority according to which of them are assessed as most likely to ward off immediate dangers and to have ramifying beneficial effects on the family as a whole in the longer term.
3. To take concrete action to achieve as many of these objectives as possible simultaneously, given the constraints of time and resources.
4. To evaluate the effectiveness of the action so taken, after a suitable time period, and revise the objectives accordingly.

Choice of Objective

In this, as in most other cases handled by social services agencies, the issues are complex, as is the choice, specification and balance of objectives.

One major issue is what should most appropriately be the target or targets of intervention? If the family as a whole is chosen as the primary target of intervention, this implies some belief that it is capable of functioning effectively, and possibly some value that traditional family institutions ought to be reinforced wherever possible, an assumption that followers of Edmund Leach might question. Some would see the marital relationship between husband and wife as pivotal, and work with this. Others would see the most likely hope of family salvation lying with one parent more than the other, thence working with that person individually and giving up on the other unless more time became available. One argument commonly put forward by those discussing the case is that even a slight improvement in the father would make a major difference to the whole family. Another is that to change the mother's world (e.g. through increased social contacts) would enable her to regather her energies so as to pull the family together. Some, particularly those who have no faith in either adult (especially given their age) or in the recuperative powers of the family as a whole (especially given their impending diminution) would choose to work directly with the children at risk – the second daughter and the son. Another group seemed to take a more or less exclusively community focus, concentrating on building a supportive local community environment and foresaking all attempts at direct family intervention except for putting members in contact with various groups. The systems approach opens an interesting new perspective in that the suggestion here was that the focus should neither be exclusively the individual client family (nor any of its members) nor exclusively the social environment, but the *interactions* between the family and its community.

Another issue is which social problem, or problem aspect, should be regarded as primary?

Broadly, the alternatives are as follows:

Physical Factors – inadequate housing, organic schizophrenia, alcoholism, etc.;

Psychological Factors – individual personality problems;

Social Psychological Factors – relations between family members, parent-child relations, marital relations, etc.;

Social Factors – isolation, job situation, neighbourhood intolerance, recreation etc.;

Institutional Factors – issues of debt, truancy, theft, child care, etc.;

Economic Factors – debt, financial problems, etc.;

Rational Factors – belief systems, logical consequences of beliefs, etc.;

Administrative Factors — budgeting, domestic management, personal appearance, etc.;

Planning Factors — liaison between services, welfare rights, etc.

3. Tactical Community Work Objectives

As a further example, we may list some tactical objectives of community work in a social services agency.

1. To define potential changes of facets of community life which might improve social conditions.
2. To locate through surveys unmet needs in the community relevant to such social changes such as:
   (i) lack of playspace;
   (ii) deterioration and poor housing maintenance by landlords;
   (iii) lack of activities for teenagers;
   (iv) isolation and lack of contacts.
3. To locate sources and issues of internal conflict central to the nature of the community which might cast light on or generate social problem conditions. These sources might include:
   (i) official community delegate groups (e.g. social committee, clergy);
   (ii) community members with similar problems unrepresented through any group;
   (iii) power interests of landlords;
   (iv) different 'generations' of community residents;
   (v) other affected interest groups.
4. To define the effects which community structure has on the lives of its members.
5. To locate target populations who are apparently coping and not obviously deprived (e.g. they possess basic economic, social and physical amenities), but who nevertheless have community problems and could benefit from community work.
6. To obtain a mandate for access to, cooperation with, and help for community members in respect of defined needs and agreed objectives for social changes.
7. To define support networks for implementing change both within the community and from groups with similar problems outside it.
8. To generate action to meet needs and achieve social changes by:
   (i) building coalitions of community members affected;
   (ii) gaining support from existing power groups by using any available leverage points;
   (iii) feeding-back results of surveys to gain understanding;
   (iv) enlisting services of community members contacted;
   (v) generating a climate and willingness to launch innovations

through press contacts;
- (vi) mobilizing relevant resources adjacent to the community involved;
- (vii) drawing on interested and concerned local people to help;
- (viii) illustrating the practicality of work by getting specific concrete results at an early point (e.g. mending a front door unfixed for a year) so as to prove commitment in the face of the community member's past experiences of being let down;
- (ix) building on particular interests of community members willing to give their time;
- (x) combining multiple complementary interests in one programme (e.g. play needs of children with isolation of mothers);
- (xi) orienting those interested to practical procedural issues about taking action;
- (xii) informing all those concerned about the relevant aspects of the action programme;
- (xiii) reviewing and adapting community members' conceptions of alternative courses of action;
- (xiv) safeguarding and clarifying specific outcomes (and their consequences) arising from meetings and the representation of interests not scheduled in the change programme;
- (xv) encouraging group formations and keeping relevant power and resources groups together;
- (xvi) building rapport and trust between workers and community members;
- (xvii) transferring the action plan to community members' possession;
- (xviii) maintaining the momentum of action taken;
- (xix) demonstrating community workers' support and commitment for the continuing work of community members;
- (xx) continuing the acquisition of relevant information by community workers.

4. Administrative Objectives

We have reviewed on pp. 219–227 above how the diverse professional objectives might relate to agency policy using one particular client case. Apart from such professional objectives, there are a range of administrative objectives relevant to social services operations. These are exemplified below in the specific terms of juvenile delinquency associated with the appearance of minors before the court and the requirement of liaison between the social services and the police under the provisions of the 1969 Children and Young Persons Act.[5]

Overall Social Objective

To reduce the prevalence, incidence and social malconsequences of juvenile delinquency in the community in so far as is possible by using existing administrative mechanisms for inter-organizational collaboration between social services, the police and the courts.

Overall Administrative Objective

To develop effective consultation between the police and social services departments in respect of the 1969 Children and Young Persons Act. (Under this Act, police are bound to provide information to and consult with social services departments in all cases under which children appear before the courts.)

Joint Agency Planning Targets

1. To establish and maintain viable communication channels between the social services and the police in respect of juvenile crime.
2. To establish a viable social services social records system as a basis for providing concrete, specific and relevant information to the police.
3. To establish with the police, agreed levels of social services priority to each type of case in view of current social services objectives and workloads.
4. To designate liaison officers from both social services and police agencies to clear up problem issues arising from inter-organizational liaison.

As a result of information obtained by the police a minor is suspected of having committed or been involved in an alleged offence. The police request for information from the social services department sets in motion the activities falling under this objective.

Intake Action Targets

1. To make as realistic an assessment as possible of the probable police view of and response to the case referred on the basis of discussion with the police.

There are perhaps five major alternatives:

    (i) probability of the police dropping the case through insufficient evidence or insufficient priority;
    (ii) probability of a caution being issued;
    (iii) probability of informal supervision being arranged;
    (iv) probability of the case being brought to trial;
    (v) probability of a conviction being obtained.

2. To determine whether the minor is known to the social services department by the inspection of records.
3. To determine whether the minor is known to other relevant agencies such as child guidance, probation, school welfare.

4. To decide the priority (hence approximate time allocation) to be attached to the case on the basis of available information and predicted police response.
5. To decide the nature of the observations with which the social services department shall provide the police.
   Once this target is determined, it leads to alternative courses of action:
   (i) A 'no observations' reply is sent to the police together with a statement of the reasons for this (e.g. person not known to the department and low priority attached to social services intervention at this point); the case is then closed.
   (ii) An immediate reply is sent providing relevant information on the basis of existing knowledge of the case, though no further action is taken by the department in respect of this episode;
   (iii) A reply is sent which mentions the probable date when observations will be sent by the department, and the case is allocated to a social worker.

Allocation of Action Targets
1. To determine which worker is best able to handle the case effectively, given the time available on the case, existing workloads of staff, the priority attached to this kind of case by the department and the distribution of skills among the team.
2. To agree with and hand over to the worker concerned full authority and accountability for the handling of this case henceforth.

Investigation Action Targets
1. To determine the nature and causes of the client's social problems or other aspects of his social situation which may be relevant to the department's observations and subsequent action on the basis of one or more social work visits to the client in his home situation.
2. To gain agreement from the client and client family where necessary on the desirability of exploring the social situation further.
3. To review alternative hypotheses in terms of available evidence specifically related to the client's situation and available general knowledge and evidence about relevant social variables.
4. To decide how much further social information would be relevant to the department's observations and what effects this might have in this case, in the light of existing evidence already acquired, the degree of probable accuracy and uncertainty of that evidence, an estimation of probable social consequences and degree or priority attached to this kind of social problem by the department.
5. To decide whether a request to postpone the target date is appropriate, and if so, to make such a request with relevant reasoning and evidence as a prelude to further investigation.

6. To formulate a decision on the recommendations and observations to be made by the social services department.

Report Targets

1. To provide a report on the case to the police which embodies recommendations and observations which take full account of the social issues involved, are well supported by social evidence and reasoned argument and which is designed to make some constructive practical impact on the client's social situation and problems.
2. To gain agreement on the social services department's recommendations and observations from all relevant parties — social worker, supervisor, area director and senior management levels in the department where necessary.
3. To deliver to the police a social services report which is as effective, relevant, accurate and agreed as is feasible on this case to within agreed target dates.

Post-Report Action Targets

1. To use the weekly meetings with the juvenile court liaison officer on difficult cases to gain support for an agreed social plan on the case.
2. To agree an alternative social plan on the case from all relevant parties.
3. To monitor police decisions on the case.
4. To undertake further inter-agency discussions in the event of disagreements on the case, gaining higher-level support within the department if necessary.
5. To submit a report on the social plan agreed by the agency in the event of the minor being found guilty at court.
6. To commission such social work and social services treatment as is necessary following the court decision.
7. To gain joint agreement with the police at whatever level is necessary on how to handle this case and similar case types.
8. To provide such follow-up work as is regarded as socially effective and relevant in terms of social services policy.
9. To review periodically the overall pattern of liaison of the social services with the police in the light of outcomes on specific cases.
   The terms in which this review might be evaluated might include:
   (i) degree of social services influence on police decisions;
   (ii) degree of police satisfaction with existing procedures;
   (iii) degree of joint criteria on cases accepted by both police and social services;
   (iv) reduction in the numbers of juveniles appearing before the court in relation to each type of offence, police juvenile crime detection levels, increases in numbers of reported juvenile offences, increases in juvenile population, varying degree of

social abhorrence of juvenile crime, etc.

(v) earliness of recognition of children in legal trouble by the social services department;

(vi) range of alternative usable service responses available to agencies concerned with illegal offences.

Part 2:
Action Towards Social Objectives

9 Programme of Implementation

The time has come to stretch blue-eyed Eden down
On earth like a chaste bride, and fill her full of seed . . .
Dreams yearn for bodies. Virgins long for sons.
And in all heads the unkissed and the shrunk ideas weep.
The mind has at last reached its ultimate task: the Act.
Kazantzakis. *The Odyssey: A Modern Sequel.*

Practical Relevance of Strategic Objectives

The social objectives pursued by the Social Services agency give rise to diverse programmes of implementation. These programmes may be arranged and organized around strategic agency objectives.

It may be argued that some of the strategic objectives outlined on pages 78 to 176 are irrevelant in that social services agencies are unable to influence them. In some cases local authority policies affecting their attainment are not the province of social services departments, in others, environmental circumstances exist which cannot be affected by social service or any other kind of local authority intervention.

This objection can be countered either by establishing the relevance of each to specific service programmes (a point we shall take up shortly), or by a demand that the social services agencies assume a genuine social planning role. All local authority policies, plans and operations have a social aspect. Moreover, agency effectiveness is conditioned by plans of allied departments, agencies and professions. Only in interaction with the service operations of others can agencies make any lasting social impact on the community.

Social planning studies[1] have shown that many circumstances previously considered unchangeable by social intervention may in fact be modified and changed by planned programmes undertaken within existing statutory powers. As one example, let us consider income-redistribution effects. All local authority programmes have some effect on the distribution of real income and wealth, both physical and human, sometimes explicitly, sometimes implicitly. Local authority resources allocated to social services tend by and large to redistribute in favour of lower socio-economic classes. It is less often realized that some local authority expenditures under other budgetary headings, such as mortgages for owner-occupier homes, may represent intentional or unintentional transfers in the other direction. The social services director has some responsibility in his social planning role on the Chief Executive Corporate Planning Committee, to articulate such effects. To do so he must be able to support his arguments, either with actual evidence or with some indication as to what would count as evidence.

Given that certain strategic social objectives have been agreed which are potentially realizable in practice, these objectives are pursued in certain specific contexts. The specific context of an objective is called its field of action, domain of application, or operational arena. It consists of the range of situations, cases or activities which are held to come within the purview of this objective. The field of action is summarized in an action programme. The strategic and tactical objectives outlined in Chapters 5 and 8 above are thus to be achieved by providing programmes of action of various kinds.

Programmes consist of an interrelated series of services, resources operations, provisions, procedures and activities which must be carried out, delivered or accomplished to achieve agency objectives, forming part of an interrelated structure of programmes. They are usually distinct from the present organizational placement of the service (e.g. residential division), conventional boundaries (e.g. casework services), classification by objects as in historical budgeting (e.g. items of equipment), or chronological sequences (e.g. diagnosis, treatment, evaluation). A programme structure is a directory of all the programmes and categories needed to achieve agency objectives, embodying an inventory of agency services and resources as related to these. The states of affairs indicated by the action programme should be such that those subscribing to the social objective can logically believe its attainment would make a favourable difference to the lives of community members and that it can feasibly or potentially be realized.

Objectives and Programmes

Several different programmes of action may be combined together in an overall strategy to achieve any one objective. Thus 'self-determination' may be fostered and maintained among clientele by a combination of casework, groupwork, community work, residential, domiciliary and day-care service activities. Action programmes have to be classified, therefore, in terms of the different types of agency response to the community social objectives they seek to achieve. An attempt was therefore made to list under each strategic objective some of the services which might comprise the action programmes aimed at its achievement.

However, the problem is less straightforward than management consultants often admit. For a start each strategic objective may enter as an element within any one service programme for a specified clientele, or indeed for any one community. What from one viewpoint is an end-to-be-served embodied in a strategic objective is from another a means. There can be no easy or rigid dichotomy between ends and means. A further remarkable and persistent feature of action programmes is how they develop a logic of their own based on the criterion of the optimal utilization of existing resources. For example a meals-on-wheels service may be primarily developed to attain the specific objectives of 'providing economic concessions for the poor' and 'providing meals for those physically unable to make them for themselves'. But once this provision has to be made, it may be desirable to make optimal, maximal use of it by developing the service so that it fulfils a secondary departmental objective of 'monitoring and maintaining nutritional levels of the community at a certain standard'. Identical considerations apply to the social worker who decides that his primary target in a particular case is to ameliorate deleterious family relations. In the course of his visits, however, he also gives advice on the family's subsidiary problems of domestic management which may not be directly relevant to his primary target focus. Thus when a service is being geared to achieve specific primary results, it must be decided how far that service will also be used to fulfil a range of subsidiary objectives.

In deciding on a standpoint of desired social outcomes, decision-makers therefore ask themselves: What are the action programmes most likely to achieve these desired states of affairs? They tend as a result to classify action programmes according to some classification of strategic agency objectives (as exemplified in Chapter 5). This allows them to decide allocations between different services based on an appraisal of community needs. If the strategic objectives outlined above really do adequately embody community demands on the social services, then those service programmes which fail to advance any of them can be considered as irrelevant and therefore closed down.

Once a set of action programmes exists on the ground and is running on a daily basis, decision-makers ask themselves how they can maximally utilize existing services and resources developed under current action programmes of the agency. In answering this, decision-makers tend to choose a second method of classifying action programmes based on principles of how best to use existing resources rather than on how best to realize social objectives (as exemplified on pp. 65 to 77). A service designed to fulfil several or all of the strategic objectives evidently has more potential and, in an overall way, would be more balanced. It is important in any programme structure to make clear at some point that in the allocation of resources decision-makers must choose between prevention and 'social casualty work', community and residential care, serving selection priority areas of greatest need and developing a heterogeneous mix of clientele from all areas of need, uncovering unknown new needs and responding to demand.

The reason for this is clear. To some degree, an agency's grasp of the effectiveness or otherwise of its programmes, services and operating methods moulds its objectives. Thus the social objective of reducing the pool of social problems of the community might only be realistic for those agencies who have profited from the introduction of systems technology into welfare planning, as this offers the promise of some method of counting the pool of such problems. Action programmes comprising resources, services, professional methods and technology have an influence on social objectives as well as the other way round. Objectives and resources (as embodied in action programmes) are part of a continuous loop in which each element interacts with the other.

What effect do such new developments as the use of behaviour-based or kinesiology-based approaches to treatment, or the use of new methods like conjoint family therapy, milieu therapy and various forms of community work have in changing the priority given to various agency objectives? How are the various agency objectives upgraded or downgraded? Hazard has made a start here by demonstrating how effective contraceptive technology will tend to upgrade the social objectives of individual pleasure, physical well-being, gratification, self-respect, comfort, self-fulfilment, love, affection, devotion to family, human dignity and reverence for life.[2]

This approach leads to alternative methods of classifying action programmes according to alternative principles.

Types of Programme Structure

Decision-makers have therefore to choose between alternative programme structures, or some combination of them, in terms of major fields of action falling under each objective. Some possible classifications are given below together with some simple examples:

1. Social Problem Syndromes

A classification by different types of social condition which may cut right across client groupings (e.g. alienation, deviance, inequality, homogeneity, dependency, adaptive inefficiency, personality inadequacies, etc.). These correspond to the strategic objectives outlined in Chapter 5 above.

EXAMPLE
Programme objective:
To reduce alienation and isolation in the community.

Programme definition:
- (i) Develop community life at neighbourhood level by providing and stimulating community activities and growth of social amenities.
- (ii) Increase opportunities for contact among isolated and alienated members of the community.

Programme elements and activities:
- (i) Sponsorship and payments to other agencies and groups.
- (ii) Community services (community centre for the general population; day centres and lunch clubs for old people and the physically handicapped; youth clubs; playgroups).
- (iii) Residential care in extreme cases.
- (iv) Groupwork services.
- (v) Casework services.
- (vi) Support services (home helps; meals-on-wheels; outings and holidays; visits by volunteers).

Field of Action:
- (i) General population: local clubs and amenities available to all.
- (ii) Specific target groups: old people; mentally ill; mentally subnormal; young people; physically handicapped; children.

2. Target Clientele

A classification by the different types of client in terms of characteristics which entitle the client to receive a certain amount of service (e.g. children, unsupported parents, the elderly, physically ill and handicapped, mentally ill and handicapped, homeless, unemployed, general population etc.).

EXAMPLE

Programme category:
Physically handicapped.

Programme objectives:
- (i) To help, sustain and develop social capacities;
- (ii) to mitigate deterioration of physical, mental or social well-being;
- (iii) to provide support for persons whose well-being is impaired, and/or for their families;
- (iv) to rehabilitate physically-handicapped clients.

Programme elements and activities:
- (i) Residential care (local authority homes; payments to other

local authorities and voluntary agencies to run homes).
   (ii) Day care (day centres; occupation centres; combined centres).
   (iii) Employment (own workshops; payments to other local authorities and voluntary agencies to run workshops).
   (iv) Domiciliary care (home helps; home adaptations and aids).
   (v) Support services (practical advice and assistance; short-term casework; long-term casework; groupwork; holidays; payments to other local authorities and voluntary agencies).

Field of action:
Physically handicapped; blind and partially sighted; deaf.

3. Service or Treatment Strategy
   A classification by different types of service or treatment strategy (e.g. social planning, social control, containment, prevention, protection, rehabilitation, amelioration, etc.).

4. Intervention or Service Methods
   A classification by different methods of intervention or service (e.g. intake, provision of material assistance, casework, groupwork, community work, residential work, domiciliary support, day care, social amenities, etc.).

5. Method of Service Delivery
   A classification by method of service delivery (e.g. on-demand services, outreach services, neighbourhood centre services, outposted services, referral services, treatment-prescribing services).

6. Agency Function
   A classification by agency function (e.g. administrative, protective, reformative, social planning, social action, etc.).

7. Agency Role
   A classification by agency role (e.g. diagnostic, treatment, advocacy etc.).

8. Effect of Service
   A classification by effect of service (e.g. basic, currently effective, predictably effective, developmental, repair, expedient, specialist, etc.).

Selecting Programme Classifications

Each of these types of programme classification will be reviewed later.

For the moment, it is worth noting the problems of how to relate these different kinds of classification along a single matrix. Administrative logic, local practice and needs-detection strategies may suggest certain programme combinations operationally. For instance, information services may usefully also include emergency practical assistance while community development services often include needs-detection and referral resources.

How does the mix of services affect access to them and the image of the agency while still deploying resources efficiently? It has been argued in the United States that it is now necessary to separate direct social service treatment from income maintenance, as in Britain, so that both types of service can develop without the traditional 'poor law' stigma.[3] Yet a combined social security-social services strategy at ministerial level is still to be developed in Britain. The abortive movement of social work away from practical assistance towards psychotherapeutically-based casework in the 1950s and 1960s may not have happened had income maintenance been part of total provisions available to British local authority social services.

The problem of how best to classify programmes is also important in that it determines the nature of agency specialisms, and ultimately of their organizational structures. It is unlikely that univeral answers as to how programmes can best be classified will be found for communities at various stages of social service development. Perhaps the best that can be said is that the optimal classification method is the one which will order information in the most helpful way for decision-making purposes, indicate clearly the essential choices and alternatives in policy and resource allocation and facilitate analysis of some of the major problems in the social services within the total, overall context. This probably means major action programme categories defined on the basis of strategic objectives, using for subordinate programmes, classifications based on resource utilization principles.

Classifying Programmes by Resource Utilization

Let us outline one further schema for action programmes based on the resource utilization principles.

1. Responsive Programmes: Satisfying Demands

Some agencies design programmes which will better articulate and satisfy certain community demands. The measure of effectiveness in achieving objectives is the degree to which clients feel satisfied with agency activities.

2. Idealist Programmes: Articulating and Satisfying Needs

Agencies may be pursuing idealistic or unattainable objectives. Their operations over specific time-spans are segments of an endless chain of approximations to an ideal. The measure of effectiveness is how far any one achievement at an earlier point in time facilitates the pursuit of a further objective at a later point in time more effectively. With this approach, an agency's objectives in any one time-span provide the optimal support for objectives in the next time-span. The agency survives only so long as it is construed as pursuing the same ideal.

3. Representative Programmes: Articulating and Satisfying Interests

Programmes of action may be designed so that the fullest possible expression is given to as wide a range and diversity of views and interest groups in a certain field as possible.

4. Remedial Programmes: Ameliorating and Resolving Problems

Some agency programmes are designed to resolve specific problems. The basic measure of effectiveness is the degree to which the problem is eliminated or ameliorated.

5. Replicative Programmes: Producing Outputs

Some agency programmes are designed to replicate outputs or products which meet a prescribed standard. For example, the objective of the meals-on-wheels service may be stated as: 'To produce and deliver each day a certain number of meals with a defined protein and calorie level at a standard degree of heat on delivery.' Since this type of objective is most common in industrial endeavours, it is not surprising to discover that it is also applicable to all occupational workshop programmes.

6. Growth Programmes: Acquiring Resources

At least one aspect of agency operations must be concerned with maintaining the flow of resources (including funds, personnel and information) which will allow it to carry out its basic activities. This may take two forms. Some agency programmes are aimed at growth, improvement, innovation, aggrandizement and extension. Others are designed so that a stable flow of resources is ensured, whereby essential operations may be maintained. Programmes concerned with growth will have the objective of improving the growth pattern of the organization by diversifying the range of services. The concept relates to diversification and heterogeneity.

Many agencies officially seek to pursue growth or aggrandizement objectives continuously. The leaders see their organization in terms of maximizing benefits and services along a potentially infinite scale. They seek to add incremental benefits endlessly. However, most success has a threshold, and there will be a limit to the feasibility of such an objective. Therefore it must be transformed at some point into a stability objective, which often happens in practice. For example, a local authority may achieve optimal service within the existing budget from direct levies and rate support grants or reach saturation point with one of its services, even though the leaders of the agency continue publicly to assert (usually for publicity purposes) that increased service growth is still the objective. To avoid obesity in the agency, perhaps it is an organic necessity to focus on new problems, not merely solve old ones, to create interest in new objectives and decrease interest in old ones.

7. Stability or Maintenance Programmes: Allocating Resources

The objective of this programme may be stated as follows: 'To maintain the agency's effective service under no matter what conditions or constraints.' This primarily involves sophisticated skills in allocating scarce resources.

8. Refinement Programmes: Resource Utilization

The objective here is to refine the agency's present capacity and performance. A social services agency may be more concerned to refine its present methods of intervention by better utilization of resources than to add new methods of intervention to its repertoire. Crucial elements are training and research programmes designed to develop agency skills and knowledge.

9. Administrative Programmes: Observing Codes

One aspect of agency operations will always relate to the observance of certain codes as established by administrative precedent or legal requirements. If this programme receives priority over all others, typical bureaucratic diseases set in.

Social Services Programme Structure

A comprehensive programme structure needs to be designed for the multi-purpose social services agency with constituent sub-elements, which will be helpful for decision-making on policy and resource allocation, and the analysis of some of the major problems. An example of such a programme is set out in Appendix 1 on pp. 359—385.

10 Agency Clientele

Clients may be regarded either as human resources who interact with agency workers to achieve certain social objectives, or as themselves the object of social service intervention. The two views lead to action programmes structured respectively on a social objective basis or on a client-group basis.

Clients as Resources

There may be good reasons for regarding agency clientele as resources. Without clients, agencies would not be in business. Furthermore, social work is based on a concept of client self-determination, which implies stimulating the client to make better use of his own internal resources in order to deal with problems he has been unable to cope with previously. In residential care, one aim is to encourage residents to use their own resources to run as much of their own lives — and even to take over as much of the running of the home itself — as possible.

The self-determination concept explicitly recognizes clients as human resources with whom staff collaborate to achieve certain results. The whole development of community work is arguably interpreted as mobilizing the community to help members achieve the kind of community which they themselves want.

Shortage of professional staff means there is little prospect of providing adequate help on a one-to-one basis for the number of children or other clients with behaviour problems. Instead of concentrating on direct service, it may be desirable to maximize the impact of professionals by using them to train and supervise parents and other members of the family in the home environment. Parents, friends and other members of the client system are likely to be therapeutically powerful because of their emotional significance to the client. They spend longer with the clients as compared with the professional therapist, which allows them potentially to make more impact. Client behaviour is influenced by community and environmental conditions which may be under the control of those close to them. To ameliorate behaviour problems it may be necessary for the client's family, friends, neighbours or peers to change these conditions. Problems to be overcome in using other members of the client system as therapists include obtaining their cooperation and increasing their contribution to reinforcing beneficial client behaviour.

If clients are regarded as resources, then target clientele or populations will logically be specified under each strategic objective, action programme and service.

Clients as the Object of Social Service Intervention

The achievement (indeed the very definition of) agency objectives is, however, crucially affected by who the client is and by the differing requirements and potentialities of various client groups. Moreover, if the client is not regarded as a resource then he (or his behaviour) will be regarded as part of the object of social service intervention, in which case objectives, action programmes and services will be allocated among clientele, rather than the other way round. This latter approach would result in a client-based programme structure, an example of which is given on p. 239, rather than a problem-based structure. While such a client-based programme is frequently of more direct use to fieldworkers, action programmes arranged around social objectives are of more direct use to policy-makers and managers.

Client Classifications

Whichever view is taken, it becomes necessary to group clients (or rather client behaviours) in terms which emphasize essential similarities and differences among these behaviours, as well as grouping them under the desired end results of interactions between clients and workers.

At first glance, the clientele of social services agencies may be quite simply denominated in terms of age and existing medical-administrative category: infants, juniors, juveniles, unsupported parents, spouses (with family problems), widowed and elderly, physically ill and handicapped, mentally ill and handicapped, emotionally disturbed, homeless, unemployed, addicts, legal offenders and the general population (in respect of certain services). However, some other more discriminating principle of the market for social services is needed. This is probably best provided in terms of degrees of pathology, vulnerability or severity of social problem affecting each of the categories as indicated along a five-point vertical scale indicating predisposition, impeded, impaired, deteriorated and collapsed. The 'Client Problem Dictionary' set out in Appendix 2, outlines a classification in these terms. This specifies the department's clientele, which consists of those types of persons exhibiting problematic social behaviour which an agency has to confront, classified into groups. Each group is built up from characteristic descriptions used in case records and social services literature and should represent elemental problem factors which, when combined, can be used to represent various multiple problem situations.

We may now say that the problems of any of these client groups will fall within one of the strategic objectives, action programmes or services analyzed previously. This allows workers to group individual cases within agency programmes and allocate resources accordingly. Alternatively, looking at the resource allocation procedure the other way round, we may say that one, several or all of the social problem elements indicated in the registry of strategic objectives may be involved to a greater or lesser degree in any one case, and practitioners must therefore choose which element they shall work on at the expense of others. Their cumulated choices will be decisively determining priorities among agency objectives. Conversely, any promulgated agency policies will set guidelines for practitioner choices of this kind on each individual case. In this way, each strategic objective should be related to each client, each neighbourhood or network of client relations, and to each interrelationship with which the agency is working. Strategic agency objectives may also be used as a basis for deciding which individuals, communities and individual-community interrelationships the agency should or should not work with given its limited resources.

Similarly, we may say that work with any one client discriminated under the classification of agency clientele will fall within one of the previously classified agency services. This provides a basis for aligning agency financial budgets classified by service with individual worker budgets classified by client or case. Policy-makers' choices between services on a financial resource basis can now be aligned with practitioners' choices between cases on a time basis.

Clientele may also be specified in other alternative terms, for example, as (i) recipients of the universal services; (ii) recipients of services for special need groups; or (iii) as residents of a socially deprived area which is benefiting from priority help. This classification can be used to define those services which are at one time or another experienced by most of the population (i.e. group i) so that no stigma is attached to their receipt, as opposed to the specialized, often stigmatizing services (i.e. groups ii and iii).

Evidently, specific tactical objectives and case targets may be set on the basis of the classification of clientele provided. Thus at field level, in respect of fieldwork, domiciliary and day care, and residential services, each objective could be arranged under the heading of each client group. The process of specifying case targets in this way for the individual case would take the following general form:

Client Group: Unsupported Mother With Child

1. To define specific problem areas under those of the variables (as previously defined generically) which are relevant:
    (i) depersonalization and loss of identity;
    (ii) insecurity;
    (iii) emotional tensions;
    (iv) regression and inhibition;
    (v) frustration and boredom;
    (vi) dependency;
    (vii) insentience;
    (viii) anomie;
    (ix) inarticulateness;
    (x) debilitative, hostile elements in client's social environment;
    (xi) homogeneity of environment;
    (xii) economic poverty;
    (xiii) deviance;
    (xiv) social inequality and lack of social opportunity;
    (xv) social malfunctioning;
    (xvi) social ineffectuality;
    (xvii) alienation and isolation;
    (xviii) irrational behaviour;
    (xix) stigmatization;
    (xx) ineffective agency interventions in client situation.
2. To define which of these problem areas should constitute a primary or priority target of intervention by the agency.
3. To define the specific target level of client improvement sought in each priority area.
4. To define alternative methods by which improvement may be achieved in these priority areas.
5. To define social criteria or indicators by which the effectiveness or otherwise of the intervention effort may be gauged.
6. To implement the chosen programme of action or intervention to achieve the target level of improvement in each of these priority problem areas.
7. To evaluate the effectiveness of the programme of action or intervention (defined under 6 above) in terms of the targets and criteria of success (defined under 3 and 5 above).

Specific Example

Let us take the example of a decision as to whether a child should or should not be taken into care. The worker analyzes the total family situation as summarized by the interrelationship between each element embodied in each of the strategic objectives. He then takes the decision most likely to realize these objectives effectively over the long and short term. From the child's standpoint, the worker must weigh up how far removal into care might have a depersonalizing effect on the child (for example, he may suffer loss of identity to some degree), and how long-lasting this effect might be. How far will the child's safety needs (food, shelter and clothing) remain unmet if he remains with the family? The worker must consider emotional tensions and stresses involved in either course of action, and which course of action is most likely to foster the child's emotional fulfilment in the longer term. How will growth, development and social learning be affected? What consequential effects of frustration and boredom are relevant? Will the child become more dependent in the longer term on external support, or will his own self-determination be fostered? The child's own awareness will be a pertinent factor, as will be the reduction of anomie and promotion of the child's sense of valuation in respect of himself, others and life generally. The impact on the child's present level of self-expression and articulateness cannot be ignored any more than his present poverty. Basic to the decision will be some estimate of the degree to which the child's present or alternative social environment is supportive or debilitative, so homogeneous as to preclude further child development or sufficiently stimulating as to provide the child with opportunities for further development.

How far will the child become more or less deviant or socially integrated? What are his life-chances in respect of the alternative courses of action? Will his present level of malfunctioning be improved or deteriorate further as a result of either course of action? Will the child's potential for social and occupational productiveness be improved, or will his present social ineffectuality deteriorate in either case? If the child is alienated or isolated, the effect of each alternative in terms of improved social participation will be estimated. The degree to which his behaviour is or is not likely to become more or less irrational is weighted. The degree to which he is at present tolerated or stigmatized and any likely changes in this social state are analyzed. A central feature is the agency's capacity for reducing or improving the child's problems by more extensive community care and intervention in the home situation or by fostering or residential care, given the present state of its resources.

Each of these elements will be considered by the skilled worker at every point in the developing situation anyway. The reason for arranging these diagnostic and treatment considerations under the headings suggested, is that we can begin to interrelate total agency objectives in the same terms. Having done so, coherent agency decisions on resource allocation can be made in every field of action and the resulting effects considered. The agency can begin to compare and evaluate decisions about the different amounts of time spent by the residential worker on one or other element in a resident's problem behaviour, about differential time allocations by caseworkers to various cases in terms of these variables, or about gearing up alternative agency treatment programmes and the manpower and physical resources needed to achieve these objectives in respect of the community which constitutes the agency's field of action. If a caseworker discovers that her work with many clients is continually being impeded by neighbourhood or school stigmatization of neglected children, for example, she can demand that more agency resources be ploughed into reducing stigmatization in the community by means of liaison with school authorities and neighbourhood groups, community work or improved publicity. If serious social planning or genuine operational integration of services is to mean anything at all, such comparative evaluations are both inevitable and indispensable.

11 | Agency Services

'If we genuinely serve men, we cannot by any hiding or stratagem escape the
remuneration"
Emerson, Sovereignty of Ethics.

Services differ in the type of effect they have in the course of inducing
desired programme benefits. If they are to be efficiently delivered, then
they themselves will generate various requirements which condition, to
some degree, which agency objectives are obtainable. The results of
service evaluations against desired objectives must be analyzed. For this
purpose, services may be considered in different groupings than those
formed when they are arranged in action programmes under strategic
objectives. For example, as basic, primary, futuristic, development,
defective, expedient and specialist services, all of which will be reviewed
below.

Cycles of Community Needs

Services are geared to client and community needs which are influenced
by social, cultural, economic and ethical changes. Local populations
change (e.g. through industrial developments), problems get bigger (e.g.
addiction) or are resolved (e.g. lack of clothing). Each service will
therefore have a limited life-cycle, and resource allocation should take
account of this factor. Service provision is therefore a dynamic process,
not the static affair which our budgetary systems often imply.

Three broad types of change recur. First, a service may undergo
change without any significant net effect on the overall level of client
needs met. For example, client needs may be met by a combination of
domiciliary and day care rather than through residential provision.
Secondly, a network of agency services may, over a long period of time,
become increasingly inadequate to make any impact on community
needs. Thirdly, services may develop in cycles or fluctuations in terms
of their relevance or irrelevance to community needs. For example,
practical assistance is once again becoming recognized as increasingly
relevant to community needs, whereas long-term, intensive
psycho-dynamic-based casework seems increasingly irrelevant to larger

portions of total community problems.

The need to enlarge resources does not vary with the *volume* of the demand by clients, but with the *rate* at which client demand is increasing. For allowance must be made for the fact that resources cannot be increased as rapidly as demand changes. Let us take residential places as an example. These may be unusually scarce to start with in any given period. Similarly, the need to reduce or maintain residential places at current levels varies with the *rate* at which client demand is decreasing, not with the decreasing *volume* of client demand. This means that the real need for more residential homes may be *decreasing* even though the volume of demand for residential places is still growing. This is called the acceleration principle.

Agency Services

Basic Services
Some social services are so basic as to merit elaborate organizational underpinnings. Examples are child protection services which guarantee to provide all feasible protection against child battering, and mental health admissions in which community protection is assured. In such fields, a minima is established for standards which must keep pace with community demands for raising the level of guarantee.

Primary Services
Some services are producing results by meeting current demands and needs, and this is probably where major agency resources are focused. Provision and operating methods are often standardized to certain levels. An example might be the home-help service or residential care for the elderly. The danger is that we might, by ploughing in ever more resources, try to make such services achieve more than they are really capable of, so that they all too easily end up by meeting yesterday's demands and needs. An example might be the exclusive use of residential homes for major elderly problems, a policy of which the limitations are now recognized. Sometimes this type of service requires some modification to meet changing community needs, as with the development of sheltered housing or of somewhat more specialized neighbourhood home helps, who, as well as doing the cleaning, consciously help relieve the isolation of some clients, or advise them on domestic and sometimes even income management.

Futuristic Services
A third type of resource is the kind which while already producing results is chiefly valuable because it is likely to meet predictable future needs most effectively. This kind of service may already be producing some client benefits, but is likely to produce still more and better

results in future. An example is the early-warning systems on rent arrears which attempt to mobilize the earliest possible social work support in preventing homelessness, and which in some areas have been established in the private housing sector as well as in conjunction with housing authorities. The problem with this kind of service is that precisely because it is doing so well, managers do not think they need additional support or extension (e.g. by developing similar early-warning systems via milkmen, gas and electric meter-collectors, road engineers, postmen, rent collectors, salesmen). Instead of developing such services so that they will be fully capable of meeting tomorrow's needs (e.g. of increasingly unintegrated neighbourhoods with shifting populations), resources are all too often diverted from them to prop up less effective services which are catering for yesterday's demands and needs.

Development Services
Another closely connected type of resource is the development service. This might include more extensive and intensive development of social planning activities, full-scale community centres, gestalt therapy, warden-assisted housing, liaison with public-utility companies, sentinel or concierge systems which use local volunteers to keep abreast of community problems. Development services have a large potential for meeting need, but often warrant intensive work by a small number of skilled staff. A typical problem is that some will inevitably turn out to be less effective than expected, but with so much effort and time already invested managers are reluctant to cut their losses and close the service. In this situation, they become purely an investment in management or staff ego, as with over-investment in intensive, extended casework.

Defective Services
It is always difficult to decide whether to plough more resources into a service which is not realizing anticipated benefits, or whether to cut any losses. For some services could be effective and make a strongly beneficial impact on many client problems if managers were to remedy one clearly definable defect which can be feasibly and practically corrected. An example of a potentially healthy and highly effective service which has needed some 'repair' has been the residential service. The over-concentration on physical at the expense of other forms of care which Townsend diagnosed in his research on residential homes,[1] is beginning to be rectified in many parts of the residential service. A practical working rule is often *not* 'try, try, try again' but 'try once more and then try something else' if you do not succeed first time. The outlook for a particular service does not necessarily improve the more you invest in it.

Expedient Services

Some services may be highly relevant as a temporary expedient pending the development of more adequate provision of a different kind. Thus some forms of residential care have been developed to tide over the gap in provision of effective therapy by field services, or in place of any effective advocacy for a change of policy in other services, such as housing. The important principle here is that the very effectiveness of the expedient service may create a disincentive or delay in investing in the more fundamental service which may require a larger investment. Thus it has been advocated that investment in such temporary expedients (e.g. the homeless family unit) should be limited in order to get the fundamental problems (e.g. homelessness) handled seriously, instead of delaying the day of reckoning.

Specialist Services

Another type of service may be called 'effective specialties'. These might include chiropody, baby-minders, playgroups, work with the deaf and many others. They are the services which serve a genuine function by making an effective impact on a limited and distinct social problem or clientele, and employ limited resources. Unfortunately, they all too easily become an unnecessary or unjustified speciality, at the expense of more urgent developments. Christmas, Easter and Whitsun parcels for the elderly are often cited as an example. More controversially, some social services personnel have argued against the continued intensive specialization in work with the blind by specialists trained in Braille or Moon, given the amount of unmet need in other areas.

Deprived or Sleeper Services

Lastly, we may mention deprived or sleeper services – those which might produce results if given a proper chance, but which have never really had the supply of resources they need. Employers contracted to take some physically handicapped, mentally ill, mentally subnormal or long-term unemployed clients, independently-run group homes and hostels, housing associations, subsidized holidays and groupwork have all been cited as examples. Sometimes it is easier to lobby for more deprived services, unless they are those primarily serving deviants.

Criteria for Service Development

Some of the principles that can be used to make the difficult decisions as to which services to develop and which to run down are discussed below. The essential criteria are:

1. What impact or effect does each service or method of intervention make on priority social problems and on the results the agency seeks to achieve in relation to each of these?

2. Do agency services make the attainment of priority results feasible?

3. How can existing resources and services be maximally utilized?

How far an effective impact is made on priority social problems depends on what resources are available or could be made available to meet them. Utopian solutions are worthless to managers. An objective is operational only to the extent that existing, feasible or anticipated resources of the organization can be geared to meet it. To decide what resources should be made available a directory must be compiled of all the potential services and methods of intervention analyzed by social objective or problem. This should constitute a specific, overall, logically coherent programme of all the things that need to be done if the objectives are to be achieved.

One viable approach to this is in terms of different methods of intervention — intake, screening, friendly visiting, counselling and environmental manipulation, brief and extended casework, groupwork, community work, residential care, domiciliary services, day-care services, recreational services and social amenities, practical help including financial concessions and matrimonial supplements, treatment services, comfort and diversional services, consumer participation, social planning. It then has to be decided on a basis of research or experienced judgement, how far each of these services will make an effect on the priority problems it is the agency's objective to reduce. As an example, adventure playgrounds have been shown to make more impact than youth clubs on children in areas of predominantly lower socio-economic class. The result is a set of decisions on how far to develop each service in terms of specific percentages of money, time and staff effort.

Objectives and Services

Emphasis on certain objectives may or may not in practice be accompanied by an equivalent emphasis on certain means or service-provision methods. Though objectives stated in terms of fulfilling citizen rights may imply universalist methods of provision by free access to all services, whilst objectives stated in terms of resolving certain community problems may imply selective methods of provision using eligibility clauses, these relationships do not necessarily hold in practice. This may be because decision-makers have inadequately formulated relations between objectives and service provisions. Or policy-makers may be trying to move the agency in new directions whilst service-provision methods follow historical precedents developed in different contexts. Or there may be a gap between what is desired (as expressed by objectives) and what is feasible in terms of what services staff are able to provide, or lastly, full use may not be made of improved service methods.

As professional methods of treatment and operation improve, so objectives change. Introducing behaviourist methods into social work treatment may facilitate our efforts to increase the numbers of persons able to live for increasingly longer periods of time in the community instead of being residentialized. It may allow us to increase our objectives of treating people in the community — with more consequential stress on self-determination, individualism, etc. — and reduce the amount of depersonalization, institutionalized dependency etc. Introducing kinesiological methods into social work increases workers' ability to use non-verbal methods of communication, thus helping to develop a far higher degree of social competence amongst a whole range of clients with low response to verbal communication, and may add a new dimension to the objective of promoting self-expression. Increasing acceptance of the pill, the coil and the loop allows workers to provide better advice on client problems of marital relations and sexual-emotional fulfillment, where before this objective may have been unattainable in many cases. Thus social objectives are sensitive to developing professional technology.

Taking the social objectives formulated earlier on pp. 79–176, an inventory can be made of specific social service activities required to meet them. In this 'Service Activity Inventory' which is set out in Appendix 3, pp. 403–437 each problem which the objective seeks to reduce is treated at the five distinct levels of social pathology or problem severity outlined on pp. 245–6 above, and the services commonly assigned at each level are listed.

12 | Agency Resources

We have reviewed approaches to agency clientele and services within the time-span indicated in programme targets or key results. One element which is lacking in the full specification of action programmes is the mobilizing, allocating and utilizing of agency resources in respect of these programmes.

Without resources being allocated to them, objectives are nothing more than pipe-dreams. Those who control the flow of agency resources thus also control the choice of social objectives and values.

What are Resources?

Resources are means to an end: available inputs, efforts, facilities and services which provide for and supply the needs to be met in the community. They can be viewed positively as strengths which can be built on so as to seize and exploit every available opportunity for improving performance and attaining agency objectives or desired end-results.

Three distinct types of resource can be enumerated: physical, human and structural. *Physical resources* include not only money, facilities, accommodation and equipment, but also time, space and information. *Human resources* include not only numbers of staff, volunteers and collaborators, but also their knowledge and skills. *Structural resources* refer to organizational patterns which are established in order to use and allocate human and financial resources more effectively. The organization should be viewed as a means or an instrument, never as an end-in-itself. Its survival and prestige cannot be paramount if it is to be an effective medium for achieving certain objectives. Moreover, structural resources include not only those staff on the agency pay-roll and their interrelationships, but also those staff of neighbouring agencies or departments whose resources of skill, time, expertise and information contribute directly or indirectly to the achievement of agency objectives, or may be indispensable to them. Thus the services and staff of external agencies such as education, planning, housing, clerks, treasurers and recreation departments, hospital, Department of Health and Social Security, other local authorities, universities and research institutes, probation, police and voluntary agencies may all form crucial resource elements for the agency's own programmes. Their resources are used and allocated through the medium of various mechanisms of interorganizational transactions. This definition of resources raises radical questions about conventional or traditional concepts of agency boundaries.

The wider view of the social services as a social planning agency implies the ultimate social goal of creating a caring, benevolent, integrated, healthy and happy community which makes provision for its weaker members. The aim is not simply the temporary alleviation of a specific client problem but the development of a community context and transactions between individual and community which prevent such problems arising in future for all members, so far as possible.

Developing the social planning perspective further, the agency itself, its organizational structure and the neighbouring related services with which it cooperates, may also be treated as resources which have to be geared to meet needs and resolve social problems. To take any other view is to designate the agency and its perpetuation as an end-in-itself, which is precisely what is meant when we talk pejoratively of bureaucratization and its attendant evils.

Is there a Problem?

Even given a relatively modest conception of social services, current projections of costs of existing national social goals will demand a substantially increased portion of the gross national product by 1980. Expenditures for the social services will be exceeded only by projected goals for consumer expenditures and urban development. Given the likelihood of new social service objectives and competing demands from other sectors careful choices will have to be made.

In one sense, all planning may be seen as a process of resource allocation, and many specific plans are occasioned by the need to make resource allocation decisions. Central and local authority treasury committees at all levels of government are responsive to a variety of political factors and precedents in making financial allocations. A planning process is set in motion and intellectual tools are developed for making decisions, which are consciously introduced and evolved through systematic, rational analysis.

There is a seemingly infinite gap between social objectives and the available resources to meet them. The real cost of achieving requisite objectives in terms of resources invested, is usually far higher than existing available (or mobilizable) resources. This demands some reallocation, reconsideration or re-ordering of priorities attached to objectives. A surfeit of any one particular resource usually indicates one of the following things: a temporary boom situation in respect of that resource; investment is being withheld from resources desperately needed in some other area; the agency's objectives are defined too narrowly or unambitiously; or overall resource reallocation is urgent.

With increasing frequency, scarce professional manpower needs to be budgeted as carefully as funds. Here the planner faces new questions such as: What mix of professional, pre-professional, specialist, non-professional and volunteer staffing will best achieve the objectives of the respective services? What training, recruitment, salary and general personnel policies are needed to advance the long-term manpower goals? What interrelationships among manpower programmes in different fields will increase effectiveness and help the realization of defined objectives?

One thing is clear. If all resources are completely tied up and committed already so that we have no mobility, then there are no decisions to make on priorities because all available resources have been allocated already. 'We require voluntary, not necessitated services', said Milton.[1] If social services agencies are to respond to changing community needs and cope with different demands from each rising generation, allocations must be reviewed and revised regularly so that they can be re-allocated in a way that will optimize the present situation. This may mean revising some commitments and dismantling some services in favour of others, as was done with the old Poor Law institutions. Where this is not immediately possible, longer-term decisions have to be made which will result in the re-allocation of resources to new priorities in the future. Unless this can be done, departments are not being managed. A manager reallocates resources to new objectives so as to optimize client benefits, and the only 'manageable' resources are those which can be made mobile enough to be shifted from one operation to another.

Insufficient Resources

How then can resources be made more mobile? If the agency lacks the resources to attain the objectives it has set itself, what are the practical alternatives open to it?

Formally Apply for More Resources

One response is to fight for more resources officially — a larger share of the local authority cake or a larger share of national priority. Typically, this will involve demands for an increase in the agency's workforce, which can be achieved by use of power. One implicit aim of the Seebohm merger may have been to acquire more resources for social services on the basis that increased economic power attaches to size. Or the case can be argued on the basis of the probable results of a more effective impact on community problems and the likely consequences of shirking these problems. Ways of assessing effectiveness are only just being devised and much can and still has to be done in this sphere.

Informally Acquire More Resources
A second response is to acquire more resources informally by more intensive and better use of volunteers, voluntary agencies and other neighbouring organizations. This involves developing more adequate exchange procedures with other agencies.

Redirect an Objective
Related to the above response is the idea of redirecting one or several of the objectives of the department by getting another agency to cooperate in or take over completely the pursuit of this objective. Some efforts currently being made to educate rent-collectors to spot social problems and advise problem tenants on income-management might exemplify this strategy.

Focus on the Maximally Effective
Alternatively, efforts might be concentrated on the achievement of one particular objective which will have a wide-ranging impact on total results, or services having ramifying benefits might be introduced. Arguments in favour of intensive preventive work in which the agency intervenes at the earliest possible stage of a client's problem propose just such a strategy.

Reducing Objectives
The size, scale or scope of a particular objective may be reduced, its realization being used to facilitate the attainment of larger objectives at a later period rather than some all-out effort being made to achieve the optimum in the shortest period of time. This really amounts to lowering all the 'levels' of objective in the overall ends-means schema, perhaps leaving many of the ambitious higher-level objectives unstated. In view of the interrelationship of social problems and of social services designed to cope with them, to reduce the number of objectives is a particularly problematic response, though the level of required attainment may be lowered over the whole range of objectives.

Enlarging Objectives
The size, scale or scope of the objective may be increased. Though it is rarely considered as an alternative, this can sometimes be equally effective. Its increased potential significance might cause those who were previously indifferent to sit up and take notice, or capture the

interest of others who might put pressure on the organization in favour of the idea. For example, to increase social service capacity to handle specific client housing problems, a move might be made into the area of social planning (calculating and presenting the social and financial costs of the local housing authority's policy of eviction and thence advocating that they contribute in various ways to preventive programmes), or into the area of social action by supporting squatters' groups.

Redirecting Resources
Resources from one kind of service might be redirected to another which meets the same objectives. This is done in three ways:

(i) *Substitution.* A less politically or financially expensive method of meeting a need or fulfilling a particular objective is substituted for more radical (hence costly) solutions. For example, home helps could be used instead of hospitals.

(ii) *Preparation.* Workers may prepare individuals to use other available services by information, advice and counselling

(iii) *Close down.* Or, more brutally, a service may simply be closed down, as a consequence of which unmet needs would manifest themselves in the form of demands for other types of service. Thus, closing down the service of free school milk led to increasing demands from less well-nourished families for meals-on-wheels in some areas.

Use Present Resources Better
A further response is the better utilization of present resources, which was a major objective of the Seebohm merger. Another aspect of this response is to introduce various labour-saving techniques and methods so as to invest manpower elsewhere. This can be done by amalgamating the tasks of those doing similar work, combining existing services and facilities, careful meshing of generic elements in professional expertise (e.g. casework practice as it applies across client groups), spreading overheads, avoiding unnecessary duplication, stimulating ventures into new services by housing all the capacity available under the same roof.

Only by constant critical analysis can savings be made in cost, time, effort and skill which can be used to better advantage elsewhere within the agency. Which operations could be eliminated with a minimal loss of benefits? For example, in one department, the cost of collecting client contributions amounted to twice the total receipts.

Some recent research[2] has shown that extended long-term casework has had far less effect than brief short-term target-oriented counselling over eight visits or so. Can one activity be advantageously substituted for another? Groupwork has proved more effective for some problems than casework, as well as more time-saving.

Can specialization help? If many of the administrative elements in social workers' activities are taken over by administrative auxiliaries, the social worker has more time available for contacting clients. Can an activity be routinized? Given the average, all-inclusive cost of £80 per committee report in some local authorities, vast resources can be made available by committee formulation and approval of specific policies and objectives which allows extensive increased delegation and decision-making within those policies and objectives, apart from defined exceptions. The same principle holds good at lower managerial levels.

Every social worker should ask himself of every piece of work: 'Who else could do this better or more conveniently? Is it necessary at all?' On the other hand, some activities fall between everyone's area of responsibility and no one will do these without prompting. This is avoided if everyone asks himself: 'What can I do now? What should be done which is just not being done?'

More Effective Methods

More speedily effective methods might be introduced which could hasten the attainment of some objectives. Thus new approaches to residential care, group, community and preventive work may be used. Or some existing resources could be consciously used to treat problems in a new way so that a professional breakthrough in which new skills are developed is achieved, as exemplified by the focus on family and community care. Although the development of new methods may be effective in attaining some social objectives, this policy also has a way of generating new wants, thus requiring that new social objectives be set.

Cut Internal Diseconomies

As the size and output of the agency increases from very small to very large, costs per unit of output fall, as a result of internal economies of scale. But when expansion beyond some critical point occurs, costs per unit of output increase owing to internal diseconomies of scale. This happens because managerial and staff resources of the agency cannot be increased in proportion to increases in the quantities of other resources available. Diminishing average returns to other resources cause costs per unit of output to rise. Alternatively, the operational unit producing results grows in complexity as it grows in size, leading to increasing difficulties of management and coordination. Internal diseconomies refer to those factors contributing to rising costs which stem from the agency's own activities.

External Diseconomies

External diseconomies are those factors contributing to rising costs which lie beyond the agency's direct control. As the agency's output of a service expands, demands for resources used in providing that service (e.g. trained social workers, residential workers, home helps) may increase. Beyond some point, these demands bring about rising resource costs (e.g. rising salaries for trained staff), which lead to rising costs per unit of service. The agency may thus deliberately decide to depress certain services despite evident need so as not to stimulate an accelerating demand to which it cannot respond.

Increase Workloads

Another approach is to increase critical aspects of workloads. Thus, with the revelation by national workload studies[3] that the largest percentage of social work time was occupied with administration and travel, efforts are now being made to increase client contact time by reducing time spent on these.

Disinvestment in Some Services

Despite all the emphasis lavished today on criteria for investment in new services, remarkably little attention is paid to criteria for disinvestment in ineffective services. A decision not to disinvest in an ineffective service is the same as a decision to invest in a potentially effective one with the capital cost represented by the opportunity cost of the benefits which could have been obtained from close down. An agency should logically apply the same criteria when considering whether or not to dispose of services as when appraising whether to start up new services. For example, if the agency requires a specific rate of client benefit before a new service obtains approval, it should demand the same rate of client benefit from its existing services. But, in practice, very few agencies actually treat investment and disinvestment in the same way. This is partly explained by the historical budgeting system which is based on the concept that a service once begun will continue into infinity, thus inhibiting the agency from closing down ineffective services. When a service's effective impact on community needs is decreasing, excuses are often made for retaining it. These excuses usually refer to continuity of operations, the difficulty of transferring resources already invested in one service to developing a new one, someone's fear of empire shrinking, staff fears, optimistic hopes that future changes in the community might provide new opportunities which would renew the value and appreciation of the service, fear of being swayed by professional fashions, expertise of staff in running the services. It should be recognized, however, that the disposal of a service often involves terminal costs such as staff retraining costs or capital expenditure elsewhere to replace some of the assets, and these should be added to the anticipated costs of developing a new service.

Rationing
Another response to a situation of insufficient resources is to ration them. This is the most distasteful and difficult, but also the most fundamental and unavoidable task of all. It does not involve a choice between good and bad, but between two or more 'goods' or 'client benefits'. Some objectives will have to be given priority over others; more time will have to be spent on some activities and services at the expense of others. Perhaps one of the most difficult and painful management decisions is to close down those services or treatment methods which prove to be ineffective.

Negative Resources

Resources not only make feasible the action which must be taken to achieve objectives, but also set the limits to this action. Every resource has a negative aspect in the form of some constraint or boundary which limits what can be done. Some constraints are external to the organization, such as the legislative powers and obligations, social, political and economic conditions which constitute the agency's environment. Others are internal, including the resources which are allocated to other competing services, the conflicting objectives of other parts of the local authority system, individual staff values and interests which may conflict with agency objectives, limitations of the current state of professional know-how, and so on.

The agency can be defined as the totality of processes used to convert its resources into results. The major point is that results and objectives lie *outside* the agency in the sense that they refer to some impact we want the agency to make on its clients or community. The essential planning task of deciding priorities can be defined as one of evolving the optimal feasible match between objectives and resources over a period of time.

This has radical implications for present resource allocation methods. Resources tend to be allocated on the basis of historical budgeting by which extra annual increments are simply added to what has been allocated previously. Precedent, political interest, current pressures, increased demand as assessed by the degree of vociferousness, quantity and level of service and costs are predominant factors. The result is a kind of self-perpetuating ennobilization of resources in which most of them are already committed to services whose effectiveness is seldom really tested in terms of their results and failures. This means minimum resource mobility, hence minimal management, hence minimal assessment of effectiveness. Resource allocation should be focused not on internal costs and activities but on external results, target social problems and effects of services in meeting or failing to meet them. This is the basic proposal behind planned programmed budgeting systems (PPBS) and the central concept of all effective planning.

Systematically Reallocating Resources

The agency seeks its objectives through the conversion of resources into services. Action absorbs resources, money gets spent, the organization structure becomes obsolete and hinders effective work, and staff are promoted, retire or need further training. Only if specific, concrete results are generated which justify further investment in replacement and renewal of resources will the agency become and remain effective. Without this systematic approach to resource allocation among priority results, the situation will continue to resemble that described by Lewis Carroll's Red Queen: 'Here, it takes all the running *you* can do to keep in the same place so that if you wanted to get somewhere else, you would have to run at least twice as fast as that.'

13 | Targets

"The time is short, the hour is late, the matter is urgent. It may not be incumbent upon us to complete the task. But neither are we free to desist from doing all we possibly can."
Ethics of the Fathers

Action programmes are essentially specified in terms of services, resources and clientele. They are not, however, normally mounted and maintained indefinitely. Key targets or results to be attained over specified time-spans have to be formulated if the agency is to assess what progress (or retrogress) these service or treatment operations are making in the steady achievement of objectives in respect of defined clientele. Targets or key results therefore consist of specific services, delivered by specified agency units or personnel having access to certain resources allocated to them for a specific clientele within a defined time-span, as part of a larger agency action programme to achieve certain social objectives on behalf of the community it serves.

Targets are thus practitioner objectives — specific, clear-cut, clarifying cues for action. They may be nothing more than the practitioner's check-list of the things that have to be done, and what he hopes to achieve by these, often being allocated to individual staff and sub-units on a month-by-month basis.

Allocation of Tasks

A crucial element in programming targets is the allocation of tasks to specific units or individuals. In terms of network planning, this is done by what is called 'loading'.

The available capacity is calculated in terms of the time and skills of the workers available to work on the particular operation. Here such factors as the usual skills needed for this type of operation, the usual level of efficiency and effectiveness in this type of job by the individuals involved, anticipated sickness or absenteeism, existing commitments, holidays and other limitations such as specified locations are taken into account.

In calculating how to load the different parts of the total operation onto the individual worker in terms of specific tasks the agency has to consider how to make the maximum use of the skills available among its staff, with the minimum delay in terms of carrying out vital tasks, and reducing the time in terms of cost and effort, as far as this is possible. In order to see how one job interacts with others, a histogram or vertical bar graph may be used. In a histogram of staff allocations, the length of the bar is made proportional to the load of work. The appropriate bar chart for the operation is drawn. We run down each time division and add up the usage of various resources (particularly staff time). The time needed in order to accomplish each sub-element of the operation is then inserted as a dotted line, the critical portion of the load being indicated by hatching.

Targets Within Strategic Objectives

There are good reasons why targets should be set within a framework or context provided by strategic agency objectives. Social decision-makers seek to gain some grasp of the total agency impact on its community so that resources may be allocated to broad programmes of action. To accomplish this, it is necessary to state objectives at the strategic level which refer to broadly conceived social states of the community, or to behavioural patterns or consistencies and broad predispositions towards certain responses by clients given certain types of treatment. If each case were so entirely distinct from every other that no generalization of this kind were possible, then each case would have to constitute a separate policy issue and might entail the extensive revision of agency resource allocations staff recruitment and training. Clearly, this would be an impossibility. In advance of clients presenting themselves to the agency, workers have in fact already categorized (at least by implication) agency objectives, problem syndromes and appropriate treatment alternatives. To the extent that any rational or systematic planning is possible, this procedure is necessary. The possibility of policy-making and planning implies some recognition of a pattern in the social system rather than a comprehensive refusal ever to judge any element except as unique to its own particular context. At the social planning level, the most helpful course may be to gear up resources and services to strategic objectives, with service programmes and client groups being arranged under each strategic objective in turn.

The relationship between strategic objectives, which may be crucial to social planning, and individual case targets, which determine the responsiveness of services to individualized problems, is complex and difficult. This complexity may well have given rise to the yawning gap between social policies and plans on the one hand, and treatments of individuals on the other.

It is evident that a social worker who merely treated any individual case by mechanically applying the broad agency objectives and treatment methods in which the agency has invested, would be unlikely to help the client effectively. Behaviour is specific to particular situations and its own particular context. For example, an apparently incompetent performer in some work activities might be a relatively competent performer in others and in arranging vocational adjustment, the worker obviously needs to take advantage of the client's specific abilities, rather than rely on any generalized categorization of his work status.

Social services focus much of their energy and attention on individuals who are specifically or relatively uniquely disadvantaged, handicapped or disabled in relation to the norm or average for individuals in the community. They are essentially concerned with significant discontinuities or exceptions to the norm or current national (perhaps international) average. The stress which is placed in social services operations, (e.g. in casework) on the diagnosis of behaviour *first* in relation to its place in the unique local context (be it role expectations of the individual, the individual's group, neighbourhood or community) is therefore particularly appropriate. This increases the difficulty of policy-making and planning, which depend essentially on the possibility of making comparative appraisals between cases, individuals or situations. These comparisons in turn depend on the definitions (at least for the sake of practical service delivery) of some characteristic socio-cultural patterns or personality systems in terms of needs and relationships which are relatively constant and common to all men, despite distinctive variations in each individual situation.

Objectives have a built-in generality, having some value and significance over and above the specific situations in which they are made manifest and which give them substantive, real-life form. This is why they constitute a suitable language for policy-making. When individual clients are valued for being the individuals they are, there is an obscure reference to the specific problem situations and behaviour with which they confront the agency. These the agency can contemplate and assess over a period of time and respond to with some degree of effectiveness, as a result of its analysis of similar variables (perhaps differently mixed) previously encountered in other situations. Workers extend to case B an attitude, skill and approach already directed to a closely similar case A, or generalize an attitude, skill or approach which was at first confined to a limited class of cases. On this basis, it is clear that in practice patterns of variables or typologies of problem syndromes are built up and responded to with *some* degree of consistency. These responses constitute professional policies and are embodied in strategic or tactical objectives.

There is also a linguistic element. Professional objectives for the social services are largely framed in dispositional words, signifying tendencies, capacities, liabilities or proneness to do various kinds of things when the need arises. On the other hand, actions are commonly expressed in episodic words, signifying actual occurrences and happenings. In developing a practical policy-making language, it is necessary to intersperse dispositional and episodic vocabularies consistently. Objectives are place-markers signalling concrete actions to be taken and tests of results achieved, instead of laboriously spelling out procedures detail by detail.

Effective policy-makers and planners must, at least to some degree, assume for the sake of planning, some degree of neo-determinism. Effective fieldworkers must assume for the sake of effective service delivery at least some degree of pluralism. The relationship may be sketched along the following scale:

<table>
<tr><td>Policy</td><td>Operations</td></tr>
<tr><td>Comparative
Patterns</td><td>Significant
Discontinuities</td></tr>
</table>

The social states referred to under the strategic objectives outlined on pp. 78–176 above represent generalizations about problems in the community, about aspects of various social problems which workers may be handling either separately or in combination, or about characteristics underlying their work throughout their caseloads. They are often similar to those referred to by clients in reporting various problems – tension, anxiety, fear, frustration, depression, guilt and inhibition. They necessarily refer to very different sets of objectively and subjectively observable emotional responses both by the same client on various occasions and by different clients.

To describe the normal biological programme as a precursor to 'promoting growth', is not necessarily to describe the actual developmental pattern of any one individual which will enable the worker to draw up an appropriate treatment programme.

At best, strategic objectives can provide no more than probabilistic statements in respect of the single individual. They are less useful for diagnostic than for managerial purposes, but represent a much more detailed specification than is comprised under such generic headings as 'children's problems', 'mental health problems', 'problems of the elderly', etc. Global methods of assessment and diagnosis are not helpful.

It is essential to interrelate the realm of objectives, values and theory on the one hand and operations, action and practice on the other. Too great an emphasis on the former leads to exaggerated expectations, illusion and fantasy. Too great an emphasis on the latter leads to blind, random and purposeless action for its own sake.

In further specifying the strategic and tactical programmes outlined in preceding chapters, the social worker's task is to define all relevant aspects of the client's problem behaviour so that a more verifiable assessment can be made of his emotional state at any time, and so that specific treatment targets can be set for the individual case. It therefore becomes necessary to state the general rule for formulating individual case targets, in such terms as these: To respond to and treat the specific problematic elements of client behaviour or situational dislocation which have caused exchanges, interactions or transactions between the client and his social environment to go awry. This covers the essential components of programme targets or key results as set out on p. 265. Let us take as an example of this process of target-setting in respect of each specific strategic social objective or problem the area of marital relations:

To Promote, Develop or Build on Marital Harmony Where Appropriate
To Reduce, Ameliorate or Resolve Marital Problems

A. Marital Relationship Itself

1. To promote a relationship which is supportive to the individual needs of each partner.
2. To help both partners complement their roles in the family in the way most suited to their respective personalities.
3. To define the personal needs of clients and the self-image they have of themselves as husband or wife.
4. To define perceptions of marital relationship partners bring from childhood and what expectations they have of each other.
5. To define conceptions of self-control which partners bring to marriage.
6. To define tensions arising from or degree of satisfaction in sexual relationships.
7. To define problems about contraception.
8. To define the significance which pregnancy and childbirth has for each partner.
9. To define methods and problems of communication with each other.
10. To define the roles performed in the family and the degree to which these are consonant with partners' self-images and expectations.
11. To define the impact the behaviour of each partner makes on the self-image of the other.
12. To define how the performance of each as parent, housekeeper or breadwinner affects their relationship.
13. To define how decisions affecting the family are taken, whether shared or hidden by one partner from another.
14. To define which partner deals with stress in the environment and

the emotions of each about this.

15. To define what capacity each partner has to acknowledge and examine problems including his own part in them.
16. To define the nature of partners' defences and emotional reactions.
17. To define the motivation in each partner to improve the relationship.
18. To define what the marriage offers each partner. What is the destructive impact on each?
19. To define the destructive and constructive impact on each partner.
20. To define the influence of relatives, friends, neighbours and other relations on the sexual nature of each partner.
21. To define the emotions about children born outside marriage and relations of each partner to them.
22. To define the probable effects of separation.

B. Family Planning
1. To assist in decisions on family planning.
2. To define whether either or both parents want to limit the family.
3. To define what having children means to each partner.
4. To define feelings of each partner about birth control (e.g. fears about religion, impact on their mental relationship and on themselves individually).
5. To define the capacity of parents to cope with increases in the family (e.g. mothering, physical care of children, material provision).
6. To define the probable impact on the mother's physical health of another pregnancy.
7. To define each partner's capacity to use differing forms of family planning.
8. To define fears partners have of clinics.
9. To define the relationship between mother and health visitor.

C. Separation Issues
1. To assist partners to take appropriate decisions on the continuance or ending of the marriage.
2. To enable such decisions to be taken in the least destructive way.
3. To define the motivation of each partner to preserve or to end the marriage.
4. To define how destructive the relationship is to parents and children.
5. To define the impact separation might have on each parent and on the children.
6. To define the probable consequences for the family of no decision being taken.

D. Overall

1. To define which, if any, of these are the key problems which will constitute target areas of intervention.
2. To explore and analyze alternative methods of resolving these problems.
3. To assist partners to take appropriate decisions in the full understanding of probable consequences.
4. To monitor and evaluate the results and effects of actions in accordance with these decisions.

14 | Agency Functions

We have now specified each of the possible strategic objectives pursued by social services agencies, together with alternative types of action programme. The alternative types of service, resource and clientele comprised in such programmes, and the targets or key results they are designed to achieve have been discussed. Once such programmes are in actual operation in the agency on a regular basis, they give rise to certain typical ongoing agency functions which are defined below. They consist of the contributions which a partial activity makes to the total activity of which it is a part.

Point of Intervention

One approach to defining functions is in terms of the point of intervention in the problem situation. In summary form, this may be sketched as follows:

Point of Problem Development	Type of Intervention
Pre-conditions	Social planning
Causes	Primary prevention
Effects	Secondary prevention
Consequences	Tertiary prevention

Pre-conditions are the circumstances from which social problems develop. *Social planning* involves intervention in these pre-conditions. *Causes* are the specific factors directly related to the problem. *Primary prevention* is intervention between pre-conditions and causes. *Effects* are specific symptoms indicating the problem's existence. *Secondary prevention* involves interaction between causes and effects. This may include preventing, avoiding or lessening the occurrence of typical reinforcing stimuli to problem behaviour arising. *Consequences* are longer-term secondary problem results. *Tertiary prevention* is intervention between effects and consequences.

Functions of the Social Services Department

Agencies not only differ in their objectives, or in the priority they give to each, but also in the functions they decide to perform. Social services functions are sanctioned by legislation. This legislation forms the official framework within which objectives may be set, though legislation does not itself provide substantive objectives (except in isolated clauses) since statutes are usually framed in such a manner as to allow a fairly wide measure of discretion in the interpretation and implementation of functions. Broadly, we may define six basic types of function or service which a social services department might alternatively or in combination carry out or provide. At a local level these service delivery systems may join together, integrate or offer entry into a number of different fields simultaneously.

1. **'Administrative' Functions**
   The social administration function refers to the administration of clear-cut services to eligible clientele. This is the role performed by social services departments in respect of services like registration, property management, cash collection duties, burials and cremations. Legislative references to this function include:
   1948 National Assistance Act (Sections 37 to 41 and 48);
   1958 Adoption Act (Section 40);
   1959 Mental Health Act (Sections 19 to 21);
   1968 Health Service and Public Health Act (Section 60);
   1970 Chronically Sick and Disabled Persons Act (Section 1).

2. **Protective Functions**
   The protective function refers to the department's role in protecting the community from the spiralling effects of client problems, or (to put it in Laingian terms) protecting specific, sensitive clients from the spiralling effects of community problems. The objective is: To protect the individual so that damage to self and others as a result of the intractable problem is minimized. This generally connotes some major alteration to or assistance with the client's living arrangements, often by means of residential-care services, boarding out and supervision, adoption and temporary accommodation.
   The function spills over into outright custodial or detention

functions such as are embodied in Section 32 of the 1969 Children and Young Persons Act, or liaison with other services in respect of detention, and including approved schools and committal to mental institutions. However, it is basically legislated for under the following residential-care provisions:

1948 National Assistance Act (Sections 21 to 27);
1948 Children's Act (Sections 1, 12, 15);
1958 Adoption Act (Sections 9, 28);
1959 Mental Health Act (Section 6);
1963 Children and Young Persons Act (Section 1);
1968 Health Services and Public Health Act (Section 12);
1969 Children and Young Persons Act (Sections 9, 19, 36, 38, 49, 51).

3. Reformative and Improving Functions

This function might be stated in terms of three sub-objectives.

(i) *Ameliorative:* To lessen the severity of individual client problems in an admittedly palliative manner. This objective has often been underemphasized at the expense of more ambitious and unrealistic curative objectives, resulting for example in the under-use of day centres and domiciliary care.

(ii) *Rehabilitative:* To make some improvement in the problem so that some degree of social function is restored. The social worker aims to reinforce the client's functional habits or expectations, and to decondition disfunctional habits or expectations.

(iii) *Curative:* To cure the problem by extinguishing or eliminating the problem behaviour or eliciting new forms of behaviour so that a situation of 'normality' is produced. This objective has often been overemphasized at the expense of ameliorative care, resulting for example in the over-use of hospitals and residential institutions.

The curative function covers general welfare counselling, day centres, domiciliary care and supervision, and is supported by a host of legislative provisions including:

1946 National Health Service Act (Section 22);
1948 National Assistance Act (Sections 29 to 31);
1958 Disabled Persons (Employment) Act (Section 3);
1959 Mental Health Act (Section 6);
1968 Health Services and Public Health Act (Sections 12 and 13);

1963 Children and Young Persons Act (Sections 1, 5 and 58);
1969 Children and Young Persons Act (Sections 9 and 14);
1958 Adoption Act (Section 38);
1960 Matrimonial Proceedings Act (Section 2);
1965 Matrimonial Causes Act (Section 2);
1969 Family Law Reform Act (Section 7);

4. Preventive Functions

Preventive functions relate to some earlier action taken to prevent problems of those at risk from becoming so unmanageable as to render them far more difficult or to preclude effective therapy and the restoration of normal social functioning. The objective is to avoid or postpone any deterioration of the situation which signals an increase in its social pathology by means of social planning, advocacy and social analysis. For example, extrapolating from present trends the population in need of residential care by 1980 can be predicted and alternative methods of attack which would prevent this need developing can then be planned.

This function has been most aptly sanctioned so far in terms of the sentinel and enquiry roles covered by several Acts. This implies a readiness to search out needs, investigate referred situations in which the person may be a danger either to himself or to the public and to take action if necessary, without recourse to a Court Order. Many of these activities have led to inevitable extensions of the custodial function mentioned previously. If the agency's powers or duties to investigate situations in which children are at risk are enlarged, the agency must have equivalent powers of action somewhere along the line to take such action as is necessary to remove the risk.

The relevant legislation is the following:
1948 National Assistance Act (Section 47);
1959 Mental Health Act (Section 6);
1963 Children and Young Persons Act;
1968 Health Services and Public Health Act (Section 12);
1969 Children and Young Persons Act (Section 2);
1970 Chronically Sick and Disabled Persons Act (Section 1).

5. Social Planning Functions

The social planning or broker function may perhaps be defined in terms of the objective: 'To help create a supportive community positively conducive to growth and the development of individuals', or the Seebohm objective 'To encourage development of community identity together with more active and widespread involvement in provision for need and in mutual aid'.

The broker function may be summed up as being to pressurize

other services to get more effective action in relation to social problems. The social planning function goes further, the aim being 'to collaborate with other local authority departments on the social planning of the community environment' as stated in Seebohm.[1] An important corollary underemphasized by the Seebohm Committee is the contribution of social information and analysis to economic plans.

In designating the social services director as a senior chief officer of the local authority and thus eligible for Maud-type chief executive planning committees, legislators of the 1970 Social Services Act legitimated this function to some degree. No such general clause as is embodied in the Scottish Act[2] ('to promote social welfare') favours English legislation. However, legislation like the 1968 Town and Country Planning Act is pointing the direction forward here.

6. Social Action Functions

Meanwhile, the function of social action is largely left to voluntary agencies and groups, or to the occasional community worker employed by local authorities. It may be described as 'trying to mobilize community resources, interests and activities in meeting need' and to quote Seebohm, to encourage 'maximum participation of individuals or groups in the community in the planning, organisation and provision of social services'. The strong support given in both the Skeffington[3] and Seebohm[4] reports for wider and more effective mechanisms for community participation in planning and the 1968 Race Relations Act under which community relations officers are employed by local authority community relations councils, provide some sanctions for the social action function.

On the basis of the six functions as outlined, target clientele may be defined thus:

Families and their children. 1933 Children and Young Persons Act; 1946 National Health Service Act; 1948 Children's Act; 1948 Nurseries and Child Minders Regulation Act; 1958 Adoption Act; 1958 Children and Young Persons Act; 1960 Matrimonial Proceedings (Magistrates' Courts) Act; 1963 Children and Young Persons Act; 1965 Matrimonial Causes Act; 1969 Children and Young Persons Act; 1969 Family Law Reform Act.

Old people, the physically handicapped and the homeless. 1946 National Health Service Act; 1948 National Assistance Act; 1958 Disabled Persons (Employment) Act; 1966 Ministry of Social Security Act; 1970 Chronically Sick and Disabled Persons Act.

Mentally ill and the mentally handicapped. 1959 Mental Health Act. *Chronically sick*. 1968 Health Services and Public Health Act.

15 | Agency Roles

Multi-Purpose Role

In regularly carrying out the administrative, protective, reformative, preventive, social planning and social action functions outlined in the previous chapter, a social services agency will be placed in a certain role in relation to the community and to other community agencies. It is most commonly seen as a multi-purpose organisation combining elements of all the roles and programmes listed below, seeking each to a certain degree and stressing the importance of achieving the most effective balance of objectives. Although most agencies opt for the last alternative, it does not absolve them from making the difficult value choices about how far they shall move in each direction. Departments will never have enough resources to pursue each of their objectives to a completely satisfactory end.

Diagnostic Role

How far should the agency's primary objective be expert diagnosis of social problems and the establishment of effective mechanisms for referring clients to others for specialist treatment? In the past this tended to be the pattern of social service developments in, for example, Kensington and Chelsea and in Kingston where voluntary services had been particularly well developed. Even where the treatment role is emphasized, the diagnostic element may continue in respect of one specific group of clientele, for example the blind and deaf, where a voluntary agency retains treatment responsibility.

Treatment Role

How far should the agency be mainly a treatment and rehabilitative agency, taking on problems others are unable or unwilling to tackle, developing and experimenting with new methods and strategies of treatment and intervention? Typically, this has been the policy of Coventry social services department, who were the first to take over medical social work, housing and education welfare from the hospitals, education and housing departments. This role normally entails a career-laddering structure allowing separate career progression for each type of treatment specialist and the development of a maximal number of alternative methods of intervention.

In residential situations, the treatment role manifests itself in the provision of specialized environments in which clients may explore new methods of relating to others, and staff are encouraged to experiment with new approaches to client problems. All too often, however, residential staff hold onto the illusion of having a treatment role to retain some hope that they are doing something constructive.

Social Control Role

Perhaps, as Wooten,[1] Laurie,[2] and others suggest, we are talking about what are primarily containment or social control agencies. The primary task is to contain those severest social problems which have proved unamenable to any effective treatment, prevent further deterioration so far as possible, and generally limit the spreading ill-effects of social problems through the community. Or it may be seen as socializing deviant individuals and groups into the community's common value system in the interests of maintaining the social order among its major social institutions. For example, residential institutions may be used as a receptacle for undesirable and awkward customers in the community, the object being to retain maximum quietness and orderliness. Certainly, departmental powers in respect of child neglect and compulsory mental-health admissions, provide some legislative sanction for this role, whilst many social workers emphasize good middle-class child-rearing practices. Some departments have been accused by more radical social workers of functioning rather like a social police force.

The basic conception of the social services is thus as an instrument for social stability in which welfare reduces deviancy and protects the social and economic stability of the community. This was the basis on which United States funds were ploughed into the Watts section of the Los Angeles Neighbourhood Youth Corps, in order to provide summer jobs for youths in urban ghettos.

Social Casualty Role

Some agencies primarily take on those severest social problems which are proving unamenable to treatment or cure by other agencies — those clients past all hope of cure. Here the primary function is that of a social ambulance service. In accordance with this policy, some agencies so arrange things that clients only visit them as a last resort. ('If they can find us they must have a *real* problem'.)

Family Substitution Role

Many workers in practice view the role of their agencies as, at least in part, that of a family substitute. Residential and day care can all be seen as surrogates for the family, being viewed as substitute homes for those having no abode. The individualized and case continuity approaches of the family caseworker can be seen as means of compensating individuals for deficiencies in emotional needs normally met through family support. The difficulty with this role is that staff are unable to view agency structures objectively, because to do so calls into question both their own professional skills and their personal 'goodness' as father or mother substitute, which constitutes an invasion of the person who performs the role.

Preventive Role

Alternatively, should the agency's primary aim be to prevent social problems arising or spreading by intervening on a community-wide scale at a sufficiently early point in time? The logical structural consequence of this approach is the development of planning, research and community-work in a multi-disciplinary team framework.

Advocacy Role

The community action or ombudsman model for the agency would be to make some impact on the socially deleterious policies of other agencies, generating pressure for social reforms, providing negative feedback to other agencies and asserting welfare rights. The Fabian approach of the Child Poverty Action Group might be cited.

Social Action Role

Some workers regard themselves as adversaries on behalf of the underclass. Agency workers assuming this role take various forms of direct action — confrontation, strikes, sit-ins, marches and subversion — against establishment institutions, in order to increase the power of this class and redraw establishment definitions of social situations. In extreme situations, this role may entail the underclass organizing its own social services, as occurred during Angola's revolutionary war, or as occurs in some black communities in the United States, or among drug-takers. Given the highly institutionalized setting of social work in Britain, this role is normally confined to small groups such as the Claimants' Union, or to workers 'working the system' covertly.

The underlying conflict model assumes that the interests of the social underclasses, which social workers have to some extent to represent — since most of their clients are underprivileged, unemployed, underfinanced, or in other ways disadvantaged — are irreconcilably at variance with the interests of established social institutions and those who run them.

Universalist Service Role

Some agencies endeavour to provide services which will meet the needs of all irrespective of socio-economic class, locale or problem. Where agency policy is concerned with the coverage of the total market of clientele, relatively little time will be spent by each worker with each client.

The assumption here is that welfare is a fundamental function having equal significance with economic functions of the community. What is the value of high economic productivity and prosperity if the social costs are so great as to render life socially intolerable for many? The environmentalists such as Ehrlich[3] argue that the only *point* of economic prosperity is to improve citizens' lives.

Selective Service Role

Some agencies endeavour to provide selective services which will meet the needs of those whose problems are of 'the severest kind, or for certain types of problems which are given priority. Typically, they may tend to concentrate on those manifesting the greatest degree of social pathology in respect of any of the major problem syndromes (as do the NSPCC), or on those people with any problems from one specific socio-economic group (as does Family Service Unit), or in one particularly run-down neighbourhood (as in Government-sponsored community projects)[4]. Where agency policy is focused on priority needs, workers will work intensively with selected cases, their average time spent on each contact will be longer and more time will be devoted to discussions, training and supervision.

Social Planning Role

Social services agencies emphasize different objectives if they build themselves on the corporate or physical planning model as basically social-planning agencies, systematically integrating social aspects of all community planning into a rational, effective framework.

Part of the social planning task is to understand the implicit conceptions of behaviour prevalent in the culture or sub-culture dealt with, so that a re-education or re-socialization programme may be mounted to modify lay community conceptions of certain behaviour in accordance with current knowledge and information. This includes investigation into how the community conceives social problems are resolved, and what potentiality exists for some change if this view were appropriate. The Cummings' Canadian experiment in mental health education[5] exemplifies this kind of programme.

Social Integration Role

The community settlement model for the agency is based on the objective of fostering the social integration of all elements of the community as an end in itself and stressing maximum community participation in bureaucratic processes. In carrying out this role, some social workers may deliberately pay little regard to how or whether it increases or decreases the efficiency of service delivery. Some demand that client groups should be brought into the daily running of the agency which implies either a completely unstructured agency or one in which the social services department's boundaries are broken at the maximum number of points.

This model is based on the consensus concept of communities. Social institutions are seen as essentially man-received rather than man-made, common interests binding diverse social groups to a set of central social objectives, so that it is the task of social workers to generate recognition of these common interests and values or in the absence of any central social values, to help develop them.

Administrative Role

Many departments are oriented to the more mundane task of public administration, providing statutory services to eligible clientele. These are usually the ones which trained social and community workers complain most bitterly about, and might be identified by their lack of interest in recruiting trained and qualified social work staff. The criteria for most decisions is ease of administration rather than client benefit, the structure usually reflecting the civil service approach, with administrators in charge and professionals giving them advice. The fact that social workers spend nationally 30 per cent of their time on desk jobs and administration (in some agencies as much as 60 per cent) shows the prevalence of this objective.

The underlying view here, as stated by E. Burns,[6] is that of the social services as burdensome. Past a certain threshold, the more that is paid out on welfare, the more the community's economic growth is overburdened.

Worker Roles

From these agency functions and roles, a variety of roles may be drawn up which social services personnel at various times occupy *vis-à-vis* their clientele depending on which service objective they are seeking to fulfil.

These roles may be grouped in terms of those in which some substitute services are provided (e.g. quasi-estate agent, quasi-employment agent, quasi-rent collector, etc.) which are not adequately provided by other specialists (e.g. Housing department, Department of Employment); those in which community or family substitutes are provided as supports (e.g. family-member-substitute, participant, cook); those which are unique to the specialist agency role *vis-à-vis* the clients (e.g. therapist, interviewer, counsellor); or those in which the agency functions as a medium through which client initiatives and demands may be articulated (e.g. representative, advocate, community worker).

Consumer Roles

Meanwhile, service consumers occupy a variety of roles at various times *vis-à-vis* their workers depending on which social need or problem they are demanding or receiving. These roles may be similarly differentiated in terms of those gaining or receiving substitute services unobtainable from other specialist sources (e.g. job applicant, rent-payer, petitioner, etc.), those gaining or receiving community or family substitute supports (e.g. 'disadvantaged person', 'scapegoat' etc.), those gaining or receiving services unique to social services agencies (e.g. client, resident, interviewee, etc.), or those using the agency as a medium through which they may articulate their own initiatives and demands (e.g. claimant, representative, negotiator, community participant, etc).

Role Relations

Policy-maker, worker and client normally occupy various roles *vis-à-vis* each other, depending on which of these agency roles is perceived to be appropriate in the particular situation. Some understanding and clarification of which role is adopted in which situations would clearly help to reduce confusions arising from role discord.

Positional Objectives

Individual roles may be specified in the form of a positional objective definition based on task targets. This will consist of a summary of relevant aspects of agency objectives from the standpoint of the role occupant. These will be translated into key targets to be achieved by the individual, obstacles and constraints to be overcome if these targets are to be achieved, and target action for improvement. An example is given in Appendix 5 in relation to the Personnel section of a Social Services agency. Sectional and positional objectives are either small-scale replicas of overall objectives or so constructed that by working towards its own interests and aspirations, the sub-unit or role-occupant contributes to the attainments of overall agency objectives as well.

16 Service Operations and Processes

'Man's vitality is only as great as his intentionality'
Paul Tillich

Service operations are chains of interconnected activities or tasks performed in the delivery of a service with some objective in view, producing at some defined end-point a state of affairs which has been changed in some way from the situation preceding the defined starting-point. Since the actual performance of operations often displaces the desired end-result, or in any case opens up new insights into possible objectives, operational processes must be analyzed not only as procedures generated by pre-defined objectives, but also in terms of the nature of these processes per se.

Content of Social Service Operations

What are the processes or mechanisms by which communities systematically influence and shape their social objectives? These can be conceived in terms of three interrelated community processes: benefits and rights distribution, resource development and task allocation.

1. **Benefits and Rights Distribution**
   This is the distribution to every community member and to social groups of specific rights to material and symbolic life-sustaining and life-enhancing resources, goods and services through rewards, entitlements and constraints. *Rewards* are rights provided in exchange for holding a position and performing an activity, for example salaries, wages, titles and other forms of prestige, expense accounts and job-linked pensions. *Entitlements* are rights assigned by virtue of membership in a total community or in a specified social group. Thus all members of a community may be entitled to free speech, public health, education, recreation, sanitation, etc.; all children to school meals. *Constraints* define the limits of the rights distributed to individuals and social groups as rewards or entitlements. Examples are zoning laws, which limit landowners' rights, taxation defining income limits and wealth transmission, and

fines, gaol sentences and other forms of penalties. Constraints tend to be distributed unequally in most communities.

2. Resource development

This entails developing material and symbolic life-sustaining and life-enhancing resources, goods and services, and relating community decisions and actions to the type, quality and quantity of these goods and services in terms of some relevant priority ordering. The resource development process comprises investment decisions on allocating resources to service production versus consumption, and storage of resources in the form of savings for future investment or consumption. The totality of rights (and rights-equivalents) available for distribution throughout a community depends on the aggregate of material and symbolic resources, goods and services generated. Thus, decisions and actions concerning resource development are of crucial importance for the levels and circumstances of living, having a significant impact on the overall quality of community life.

Resource development also involves generating symbolic resources, goods and services. As soon as essential subsistence-level material needs are met, people strive for a variety of non-essential goods and services like honours, titles and prestige symbols bestowed by governments and various groups in communities.

3. Task allocation

Task allocation entails the assignment or ascription of individuals and groups to specific tasks which must be performed in order to develop and distribute resources, goods and services throughout the community, thus assuring its survival and development. This process involves community decisions on the specialization of functions, the recruitment of people for specific tasks resulting from this, and the consequential attainment by individuals of various social and occupational positions in the community. Prestige is one of the rights distributed by the community as an inducement to, or reward for, incumbents of these positions. Any individual occupies usually more than one position within his or her community so that it is possible to describe a person's role in terms of the cluster of positions occupied at a given point in time and throughout his lifespan. Thus, a person may simultaneously hold the positions of local authority official, member of a professional association, community member and elector, family member, pressure group member, service recipient, and so on. Every community has its own methods of filling the various positions necessary for the total range of tasks to be performed and for allocating to each individual a specific combination of positions. These allocative processes tend to follow regular patterns: on the basis of biological characteristics such as sex, life-cycle stages, blood relations, size, physical characteristics; and on social criteria including skills assessment, patronage, merit systems, schooling and professional training. Major issues about status allocation arise over whether various positions are equally open to all community members, and which criteria determine the selection and allocation of individuals and groups to positions.

Life-Support Mechanisms

The above are some of the basic community social processes by which the individual's social life is shaped. Disjunctions and problems arising from the operation of these social processes give rise to one of several life-support mechanisms by which people gain access to valued ends.

1. Self-help
People help themselves on their own initiative (.e.g. retraining themselves for the job market).

2. Mutual aid
People associate together and freely help each other (e.g. baby-sitting).

3. Gratuitous help
People give help gratuitously or altruistically to others than themselves or their families, as with blood donorship or voluntary assistance.

4. Market-like transactions
The medium of exchange is money (or services in kind) paid for services or goods on a *quid pro quo* basis established by contract (e.g. payment for day-nursery services). A wide range of desired social amenities which cannot be provided are thus extracted from the market-place.

5. Social utilities
Some services are automatically provided for citizens (or stipulated sub-groups) without specific payment or qualification other than a capacity to utilize the service (e.g. care of minor lacking parents or parent substitutes).

6. Contributory services
Some services are freely bestowed by social organizations to secure benefits regarded as contributing to constructive human living (e.g. volunteers visiting those in residential homes).

Inventory of Social Services Operations

Social services agencies are essentially concerned with promoting and planning one or other of these life-support mechanisms. Several outlines of social services operations have already been given — in terms of specific programme targets falling under each strategic objective and of service activities falling under each problem and client group (see p. 79—176 and Appendix 3). Although the objectives social services agencies strive to achieve condition their operations, the operational activities also follow a certain temporal sequence from when a client problem is first recognized to when the agency closes the case. This temporal sequence of operations has a certain logic of its own and also partly conditions what is done. An attempt is made to define specific social services operations and associated decisions in terms of their temporal sequence by means of an 'Inventory of Social Services Operations' which is set out in Appendix 4 pp. 438—441. Each will throw up certain specific operational targets within the strategic objectives and programmes outlined earlier.

Objectives and Operations

The relation between objectives and operations can be complex. Each objective contains physical, mental, emotional and social elements. In relation to any one community or individual, they all have relevance to a greater or lesser degree and workers choose which elements they will pursue.

Clearly, in successfully taking any one course of action, workers may achieve several objectives simultaneously. Getting a plumber to lower the sink for a wheelchair-bound client not only improves his physical well-being, but may well have beneficial end-results in relation to other social states defined as desirable — for example, it may reduce frustration. Moreover, a task which helps fulfil an objective for one client may impede it for another. Thus collecting one client family's rent on pay-day may be the means to their independence as well as their economic security, for another, it will simply increase dependency on workers without achieving solvency. Conversely, any one objective may require many different kinds of operation for it to be realized. For example, to achieve a secure social situation for a client physically handicapped as a result of an accident, it may require some combination of therapeutic counselling to help him adjust to his situation, expert assessment of personal aids and home adaptations to ensure maximum physical mobility, meals-on-wheels to ensure nutritional needs are met, a home-help to keep the domestic situation functioning, and the mobilization of local handicapped groups for recreational activities. These five services are very different in their nature, methods and requirements of a social services agency. They range from forming a satisfactory relationship between social worker and client (which may require a climate in the agency in which workers are able to contemplate and review complex aspects of emotional functioning through community organization in the neighbourhood to promote lively recreational clubs), to a highly efficient logistics operation for preparing and delivering meals-on-wheels at the correct temperature.

Quite apart from the practical question of how objectives and operations tie up, further value issues arise about ends and means. Operations or activities may be undertaken which though regarded as disvaluable in themselves, nevertheless produce valued outcomes — for example, reducing the numbers of homeless by increasing an area's housing stock through cheap, high-rise flats. Conversely, highly valued activities may be employed within the context of undesirable end-states: the heroic cooperation of a family in the context of abject poverty, for instance.

Some workers so attach themselves to particular methods of operation, that they would rather leave the problems unresolved than employ other methods. Some workers would rather leave the client suffering than administer treatments without maximum client understanding and consent; or leave the day centre inefficient rather than improve its operation on any suggestions not originating from its members. At the other extreme, some workers are so oriented to resolving client problems that they place enormous strains on all their staff colleagues. The ideal may be the achievement of valued objectives by means of valued operational methods, but in most situations such an achievement is limited by values placed on the way activities are carried out, just as highly valued operational methods are of minimal relevance to many highly valued objectives.

This conflict manifests itself particularly in the area of consumer participation in planning. Highly effective plans relying on a sophisticated technology all too easily get overshadowed as the difficulties of communicating them to consumer participants mount. Conversely, consumer participation often gets overshadowed if the desired objectives are not achieved, either through delays which participation often entails, or through failure of schemes highly influenced by consumer demands. Resolving the implicit conflict between achievement and egalitarian values is a major task for most public-service operations in the next decade.

There is another issue worth posing in this context. Since most activities are complex responses to complex situations they tend to realize a range of multifarious conflicting values which motivate the agent and those influencing him. Most operations or activities are manifold, stimulating diversified states of affairs. The more this view is emphasized the more it becomes possible for multiple, possibly conflicting, values to influence the activity, and for people with diverse objectives to work together.

The Example of Homelessness

The interrelations between objectives and the operations can be illustrated by the example of homelessness. Some social services objectives in relation to this problem include: maintaining an overall view of the problem and problem development of homelessness within the community; tracking stage-by-stage the progress (or retrogress) of individuals or families who are in various problematic situations in respect of housing difficulty; and responding to each situation at each stage by providing effective services.

A temporal sequence of problem stages may be mapped in the form of a network which traces the alternative patterns of progressive (or retrogressive) development of the problem. On the basis of this sequence of problem development, the specific operational responses at each stage may be mapped in the form of a corresponding network. Both are illustrated in Appendix 5, pp. 442—446.

17 | Operational Effects

"You argue by results, as this world does,
To settle if an act be good or bad
You defer to fact; for every life and every act
Consequences of good and evil can be shown"
T.S. Eliot: Murder in the Cathedral

I. OVERALL OPERATIONAL EFFECTS

Evaluation of the overall effects and consequences of service operations consists of comparing the actual outcomes or results of action with the desired outcomes pre-formulated in the agency's objectives, and resource investments with the value assumptions of the plan.

An action is effective if it is adopted for the sake of some anticipated consequence which the agent values, and this expectation is verifiably borne out by the result of performing the act. Action is pointless unless the agent feels some assurance of a valuable result which it might realize. The anticipated result is sometimes decisively and finally verifiable: an enjoyable experience for instance. In other cases, the result is a state of affairs (e.g. participation) which cannot be tested directly, but only by way of certain indicators (e.g. numbers of policy-decisions reversed by consumer representatives). The following classification of results covers both intended and unintended changes, and the same action may produce several different results simultaneously.

Permutative Results
Permutative results are those which have produced some change or transformation in a situation, state of affairs, person or object. Some addition or subtraction is involved as between the initial, pre-action state of affairs and the later, post-action, target state of affairs.

For example, latch-key children in the neighbourhood have nowhere to go between the end of school and their mothers' belated return from work. An enterprising community worker therefore stimulates the formation of a neighbourhood children's playgroup, with the result that the children now have somewhere to go.

Preservative Results
Workers cause a situation, person or object to have the same properties,

elements or characteristics at the end of the given time period as it or he had at the beginning. For example, a client whose husband has died is given support from a social worker as a result of which she maintains good mental health despite her tragedy.

Preventive Results
Workers prevent a situation, person or object from acquiring a property, element or characteristic which it or he would otherwise have acquired had they not acted. For example, workers may establish a sentinel system involving milkmen, rent collectors, local GPs and others to ensure that old people who are at risk in various ways have their problems monitored well in advance of their reaching crisis proportions.

Constructive Results
A situation, person or object is provided with a property, element or characteristic which it or he did not previously possess before the change. Typically, workers may train people for new occupations or for reorientation into the work situation through an occupational workshop.

Destructive Results
The situation, person or object is deprived of a certain property, element or characteristic which it had before the change. For example, a client's problem behaviour is eliminated.

Reparative Results
A constructive result in the final stage of action is part of a preservative result at the initial stage of action. We restore in the final stage, the previous *status quo* at the initial stage, which is the essence of rehabilitative programmes.

Ineffective Outcomes
Many operations are simply ineffective. Ineffective outcomes are those which do not take the agency any nearer the longer-term objectives.

Unintended Consequences
Workers' motivations and commitments are intentionally directed towards some objective. Yet they also produce unintended consequences – events which are neither deliberately nor consciously desired.

Action-oriented planning is a highly dynamic process leading from one point of disequilibrium to another. Even the most able workers fail to anticipate certain new situations in advance. Most effective decisions and courses of action have at least some unanticipated consequences. It is therefore unwise to treat plans and decisions as blue-prints.

II. CRITERIA OF EFFECTIVENESS AND PROFESSIONAL STANDARDS

Criteria of effectiveness

These are specific statements telling workers what guidelines can be used to assess where they stand (i.e. the extent of their achievement) in relation to a specific objective. They define precisely what observable characteristics a situation must have if objectives are to be realized, show how the objective is applicable in concrete situations, and thus establish the specific aspects or dimensions in which objectives are to be evaluated.

They are used in determining what are the significant things to focus on in controlling work and in staff supervision and often function as the means by which several different objectives are interrelated and thus as reference points for comparison of information from diversified contexts.

Types of Criteria
We may define two types of criteria:

OUTCOME CRITERIA
define what sort of effects workers' actions should (desirably) have on the situation. They answer the questions:
   (i) What counts as success or failure in relation to this objective?
  (ii) How far has the agency achieved or failed to achieve its targets or goals?
 (iii) What specifically constitutes full achievement of an objective?
 (iv) How can the effectiveness of workers' efforts be assessed?
  (v) What are the intermediate degrees or stages of achievement between the extant situation and the requisite situation?

It is clear that if final outcome criteria are defined which specify the optimal situation the agency should like to attain, it may also be desirable to define criteria for intermediate targets which will indicate various stages of progress towards the optimal situation.

INPUT OR EFFORT CRITERIA
define the extent of effort, skill or resources which should (desirably) be expended in pursuit of a particular objective. They relate to how much work is, could be or should be done, given a trained or qualified worker working to certain outcome criteria, during a defined working period, under specific conditions, working to a specified and agreed method at a steady or normal working rate. They are the means by which a volume of output for various categories of work is agreed as 'fair' for the agency and the staff member. They answer the questions:

(i) What outlay of effort, skill or resources should be put into achieving this objective?

(ii) What are the small number of key tasks which would have a major impact on success?

(iii) What professional standards of work are appropriate?

(iv) What areas of present strength/skill would, if developed, have a major impact on achieving the objective?

(v) In what areas would poor performance threaten to damage the achievement of the objective?

(vi) What are the training implications of this, including on-the-job training?

How to Define Criteria

Criteria are essentially derived from further more detailed specification of objectives. To define criteria effectively we need to indicate:

(i) Where the agency stands now — the extant situation (e.g. a waiting list for service 'x' of 12 months).

(ii) Where the agency wants to get to — the requisite situation (e.g. a waiting list for service 'x' of 1 day).

(iii) Stages of progress towards the objective or requisite situation (e.g. a waiting list for service 'x' reduced to 6 months without major procedural changes).

This sounds simple, but it usually involves the following elements:

(i) SCALE
This is usually a five-point scale indicating different situations:

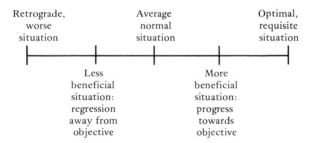

(ii) COMPLETION
What counts as completion of a task or the end of an operational cycle?

(iii) IMPROVEMENT TARGET
A prescription for improvement on the present situation.

(iv) MINIMUM ACCEPTABLE STANDARD
What are the minimum results necessary to ensure that basic functions are fulfilled? Here we must also consider constraints imposed by such aspects as available resources or possible future resources; the need to fulfil other requisite objectives by manifest (e.g. statutory regulations or central government policy) or assumed (e.g. personal staff) objectives.

(v) AN UPPER LIMIT
To define these, we need to establish: How far should the agency go in trying to achieve the objective? What constraints does it want to put on the extent to which this objective is achieved? Would full-scale achievement of this objective conflict with the achievement of other requisite objectives? Is there such a thing as *over*-achievement of this objective? For example, if the objective is to encourage interrelations among residents of an old people's home, this could be achieved so completely that all privacy is lost.

A further reason why upper limits need to be specified for social service criteria is that a cut-off point can be established for resource allocation. This is particularly important in that the consumption of a public service by one person does not necessarily lead to a subtraction of what is left over for consumption by other persons. Everyone in the community might sooner or later, directly or indirectly benefit from some community work services or efforts at social planning.

Vertical Alignment of Criteria
Since they correspond to objectives, criteria may be arranged in an equivalent hierarchy of levels. Higher-level, more gross criteria form a compound class of criteria into which sub-units or specific criteria fit. They are composite indexes using multiple factors which, on combination, yield the total measure. They make extensive use of aggregative indicators, cost-benefit ratios and summation scales. Lower-order criteria constitute further specifications of overall criteria, making extensive use of direct measures, supplementary measures and surrogates. They are simple indexes employing a single situational factor for observation. The levels are clearly related in that lesser, narrower traits or behavioural fragments may constitute trait-indicators for wider pieces of behaviour. Conversely, certain source-traits may constitute the underlying influence among (or cause of) observed correlations among trait-elements.

Horizontal Alignment of Criteria.
In aligning different streams of criteria, similar problems arise as are

confronted when aligning diverse streams of objectives. It is often difficult to decide which indicators are part of which objective, and which should be considered independent of or external to it. Is the crime rate to form an element in evaluation of community integration (or disintegration), or is it an external factor which might be predicted from some measure of community integration? In the absence of any verified sociological laws usable to relate such indicators, the mater is an open issue. Even if crime rates are excluded from evaluation of community integration, they might be so highly correlated (as a matter of empirical fact) that they could be used as a measure of integration if required. Where data on the indicators necessary to evaluate integration are unobtainable, this may be the best available expedient. To justify this process, we should need validating studies where crime rate is correlated with other integration indicators to establish that they are closely related, and to determine whether other non-integration factors so influence crime rates as to render any postulate correlations invalid. The problem is what relationships exist between one statistical series and another. In the absence of information from empirical research, decision-makers have to make the further decision as to whether to risk testing in use a possibly false set of indicators, and whether to do so would create more problems than the present use of intuitive indicators.

Professional Standards

Although a viable criteria scale may have been evolved in relation to an objective, how do we know how far we should be along the scale in either direction? The answer is given by specifying professional standards.

Professional standards are desirable yardsticks placed along criteria scales as targets for performance which it is expected shall be achieved. They are graduations by which we review the facilitation of an objective by action — the particular stages or progress points along the criteria scale leading from the extant situation to the requisite situation. By setting target standards, criteria of application are set for an objective by means of objectives and values that are actually applied in action. They function as assessment points against which the degree to which actual progress in relation to an objective keeps pace with expected progress can be gauged.

In using a standard against which to measure anything, we take a particular standard as the base line to be used. Other measures then function as substitutes which can be compared with our base line. Standards may also specify those upper and lower limits above or below which it would be highly undesirable for performance to fall. In this way, they may be regarded as control values around which variations in performance or its effects are minimized.

The setting of standards often demands that some stance be taken as between alternative theories in relation to concrete action. Thus a behavioural therapist may set as his professional standard of performance in relation to a problem family removing or inhibiting certain obvious symptoms — self-critical talk on key occasions, self-reliance in one family member — while reinforcing certain other stimuli — encouraging talk on selected occasions, a regime for drug-taking — for another family member. This might lead to the concrete action of applying drug therapy effectively through interdependence of family members so established. Meanwhile, someone taking a psycho-analytic approach might set his standard as the avoidance of symptom substitution. This may by contrast lead to the concrete action of establishing a psychotherapeutic relationship with the family as a whole and working with the total situational pattern.

How to Define Professional Standards

Relevant questions to ask in defining professional standards for any or each particular service include:

1. What *is* the agency's level of effectiveness now? Can it be defined specifically?

   Further questions related to such specification would include:
   - (i) Time: by when? how soon?
   - (ii) Cost: at what cost?
   - (iii) Quality: how well?
   - (iv) Quantity: how many?
   - (v) Method: in what manner?
   - (vi) Quota: how much need should be met and to what level?
   - (vii) Specification: how far has the problem been ameliorated?
   - (viii) Budget: how much money or time has been spent on this problem syndrome?
   - (ix) Schedule: at what stage should the agency withdraw and when should this be?
   - (x) Rate: at what rate of work can the worker appropriately handle this kind of problem?

2. What *could be* the agency's level of effectiveness without major procedural change?

3. What *should be* the agency's level of effectiveness if a systematic programme for service improvement was developed?

4. How does the agency's level of effectiveness compare with current national standards? (See Census, Ministry statistics, relevant research, etc.)

5. How does the agency's level of effectiveness compare with the best service standards in the country? (Visit any exemplary services).

6. How does the agency's level of effectiveness compare with the best

international service standards? (Review accounts of exemplary services in other countries).

7. How does the agency's level of effectiveness compare with that of other semi-analogous services? (Find points of comparison with other service standards).

Quantitative Standards.

Standards are quantitative to the extent that they may be measured, weighted or assigned probability ratios. In this case, they are expressible in such terms as numbers of case contact hours per week, numbers of placements per month, service cost levels, service valuation ratios, service cost client benefit ratios, per cent delay, and so on. Quantitative standards can often be developed where at first sight only subjective opinion appeared to be available, though quantitative standards are often used inappropriately. To take an obvious example, the numbers of cases visited per month tell us little about the amount of work done.

Qualitative Standards

Standards are qualitative to the extent that they are specific, though not at present expressible or directly measurable in quantitative terms. They can be verifiable or disconfirmable by judgement and empirical observation.

Quality is always more difficult to specify than quantity, but this can usually be done by describing the feature of quality concerned, providing examples of what is desirable, exhibits of all the problems which can occur at a given operation, together with the particulars of each problem under the appropriate heading.

Personal Standards

Personal standards are those standards or values which individual staff adhere to — an internalised series of do's and dont's which may conflict with agency standards.

Norms or Requisite Standards

Norms are theoretical concepts which may not be usable at the present time, but which are valuable for clarifying the philosophy and assumptions behind present work as paradigm cases, or as what may be attainable one day in the future. They signify the difference between what is actually being done and what *ought* to be done.

Manifest or Nominal Standards

A manifest standard consists of the minimum which is officially acceptable, whether defined by statute, central government dictate or derived (usually by devious routes) from local authority committees. At the level of staff relations we are in the area of mutual understanding between parties involved. Thus, if two staff members agree that a particular activity should be completed in a few days, this could mean that any sort of completion was acceptable provided that no more work was undertaken on it after this period. The relation between manifest and extant standards may thus be very complex.

Changing Standards

Standards continually change as more data from research and evaluation are acquired, when what was previously conceived qualitatively can be quantified or as we approach nearer to the requisite situation.

Criteria and Standards

These conceptions of criteria and standards can be illustrated in summary form as follows:

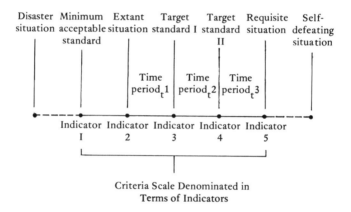

Criteria Scale Denominated in
Terms of Indicators

Having specified criteria of effectiveness in relation to an objective, specific measures and indicators can then be devised which will show whether these criteria are satisfied or not.

III. MEASUREMENT

Evaluation or measurement is a decision-making activity. It is the organizing of experiences so that they determine purposive decisions in a wide variety of contexts where the organizing process is subject to influence. Measures allow the adjustment of information from one situation to a whole set of situations, and thus facilitate the adjustment of our experience in widely different contexts. They are quantitative indices or yardsticks of socially significant conditions of society or of facets of reality which signal the social consequences of our policies.

Measurement is a method through which we are able to assert that 'x has property y under conditions z at time t', so that the assertion can be used in a wide variety of other conditions and times to enable many different kinds of people to take appropriate decisions.

Measurement as Comparison

Certain comparisons about the degree to which these states or characteristics are present or absent can be made. These comparisons are the basis of all measurement, since all measurement is relative. Broadly, these comparisons can be made in the following ways.

Comparison with Objectives

The effectiveness of any form of social service treatment must be evaluated by the extent to which it achieves specific objectives phrased in terms of client benefit.

Time Comparisons

The existence of the state from one time (e.g. the situation at some past date) to another (e.g. the situation in the present, or as predicted for the future) in respect of the same entity (e.g. client isolation) may be compared. These are called before-and-after studies.

Clientele Comparisons

The state of one client group (e.g. the isolation of the mentally ill) may be compared with that of another (e.g. the isolation of the elderly).

Problem Comparisons

The extent of one problem (e.g. isolation) may be compared with the extent of another (e.g. lack of privacy) within a defined context (e.g. a housing estate). Differences in the size, distribution and nature of the problems among clients receiving different types of service at the same time or over a period of time constitute the basic measures of effectiveness.

Prevalence Comparisons

The state of one element (e.g. one individual old person's isolation) may be compared with the wider whole of which that element is a part (e.g. the isolation felt by the over-seventies generally, in a particular community).

The framework for each measurement must thus either be the individual client (e.g. the socially disabled person), the client group (e.g.

the problem family), a local geographically-bounded community (e.g. the community living on a housing estate), or the interrelation between these.

Comparing Methods of Intervention
Evaluating the effectiveness of intervention includes the measurement of alternative methods of social treatment and intervention, especially as between various forms of residential and community care. Practitioners want to know whether, and in what circumstances, their professional intervention and treatment is effective. Social planners and welfare managers want hard data on the effectiveness or otherwise of intervention and treatment so as to place valuations on the different results or outputs and hopefully determine priorities at a macro-level. Randomized, controlled trials can provide the necessary data for both, so that the different approaches and interests of practitioners and researchers are likely to find a productive meeting-point.

Comparison Between Areas
One point which clearly emerges from available national statistics as well as from various descriptive studies[1] is the wide and apparently inexplicable variations between regions in all kinds of services. Variations between regions and between social services departments have been shown not to reflect different case mixes, client, sex/age structures and so on, but rather to reflect different service planners and practitioners responding in diverse ways when presented with the same kinds of problem situations. Most of the data needed to evaluate the results of differential intervention as between regions can only emerge from monitoring community conditions over a long period.

Institutional Comparisons
It is costly and difficult to try measuring one institutional framework *in toto* against another. Institutions are multifaceted bodies. We might find ourselves condemning residential homes in given circumstances or approving day-care centres, when in reality only one facet of the institution may be responsible for bad or good results. To convert such evaluation to manageable proportions and to avoid misleading results, we must define elemental aspects of institutions and find out the extent to which they are beneficial or detrimental to various client groups.

Measurement as a Comparison of Input and Output
Measurement is sometimes viewed as simply a comparison between (and consequential balancing of) service, social treatment or social intervention inputs with outputs defined in terms of client benefits or needs met.

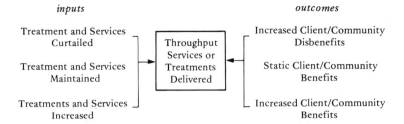

inputs

Treatment and Services
Curtailed

Treatment and Services
Maintained

Treatments and Services
Increased

Throughput
Services or
Treatments
Delivered

outcomes

Increased Client/Community
Disbenefits

Static Client/Community
Benefits

Increased Client/Community
Benefits

Measures as Thresholds

In pursuing certain objectives, other underivable social states may be created. For example, client institutionalization may be reduced at the expense of increased emotional stress on the client's relatives, social distress may be relieved through drugs or other forms of therapy at the expense of increasing drug- or therapy-dependence, therapeutic success rates may be improved at the expense of reducing inequalities in the distribution of attention and effort among clients, social participation and integration may be increased at the expense of individual privacy, and so on.

The resolution of such antinomies lies in so setting the criteria of effectiveness in relation to each objective that the criteria delineate a specific threshold-point of change. This is the point where treatment does not cause the client situation to pass from what is felt to be one undesirable social state into another equally undesirable social state by a process of problem substitution. In fact, in searching for criteria of effectiveness in a situation of multiple, conflicting agency objectives, the most fruitful search area is usually that borderland which distinguishes one undesirable social state from its contrary extreme. The principle is that of defining thresholds for each social condition beyond which nemesis sets in. We can only maximize one variable in a situation or system at any one time. Since most situations or systems consist of a great variety of interacting and self-checking variables, we can only at any one time optimize a certain range of variables, each to a certain degree. For every desideratum, there exists some counter-desideratum which is incompatible with and contrary to it. Therefore, in any viable system, no particular objective (however desirable) can be pursued to its maximum or minimum value. Measures denominate the point beyond which pursuit of an objective becomes self-defeating. Measures thus represent threshold or cut-off points — the line or boundary between what is acceptable and tolerable on the one hand, and what is unacceptable or intolerable on the other. Beyond the threshold, corrective action is needed. The threshold principle was illustrated by the example given on pp. 194–203 above.

Measures as Scales

Most of the situations and things managers and professionals may wish to measure, assume from time to time one of a range of possible values. Quantifiers of real-life situations are variable. Thus for managers and professionals, a number can never be a sharp point on a scale. It is therefore important to nominate the range of possible values and to quantify each value within this range by the probability of that value's occurrence.

Let us suppose it were true that distinctively human subject-matter is not subject to the use of ratio scales. Systematic study can be carried out using devices which are less precise than strict quantitative measurement, but far better than unaided individual judgement.

Measurement as Definition

Measurement is a matter of explicit definition and specification of a situation or an environment, the definitions excluding more than any earlier qualitative descriptions, and being to that extent more meaningful.

Measures as Symbols

A measure, an indicator or a surrogate is a symbol of reality. Sufficient approximate measures provide a language or model in which to conceptualize, speak of and manipulate reality. Testing out and experimentation can be done by means of discussion rather than on the reality itself. Measures constitute the planner's or manager's imaginative representation of the external world in mathematical symbolism, though hopefully a representation which has more verisimilitude than the allegorical fantasies constructed by the intuitive imagination of the untutored practitioner.

As the skull is pictorially used to symbolize death, so the infant mortality rate is used to represent the state of the community's health, and the equation $\log_2 x$ represents the variety of a certain situation. In the intuitive symbolism used by practitioners in their daily work, the process of evaluation and measurement is involuntary and unconscious, usually being accompanied by confusion of the measure and the phenomenon it measures, of the symbol and the reality. In the mathematical symbolism of researchers, the process of evaluation and measurement is made conscious, each measure being deliberately selected by reason of an observed affinity or correlation with the situation it represents. The province of measures and evaluation indicators used in managing and controlling the work process lies somewhere between these two poles.

The materials of the real-life situation are transmuted in the planner's or manager's mind via measures. The measures do not comprehend the totality of the real-life situation with complete precision, but always leave some margin for subjective interpretations.

Measurement as Distancing

Measurement always involves some distancing of the assessor from the situation, event or state under scrutiny. Typically, 'internal' facts which escape us are substituted by an external indicator which symbolizes them. The 'internal' facts are studied in the light of the external indicator. This distancing may be achieved through the following media — time, space, mode of self-perception, a meta-language.

Measurement through Time

An earlier objective (O^1 at time T^1) may be measured by the proportionate contribution it makes to the probable achievement of a later objective (O^2 at T^2). For example, the effectiveness with which current demands on the service are handled may be measured in terms of the preventive objective: To so contain existing demand that sufficient staff are freed to put into practice a preventive policy on the basis of clearly agreed priorities.

Measurement through Probabilistic Inference

All that workers have to go on in their diagnosis of clients' mental-emotional states is what people choose to tell them, their observed behaviour, and certain perceived patterns of responses. These inferences of mental-emotional states from observed behaviour can be tested by diagnosing the client's mental-emotional state, predicting its probable manifestations in subsequent client behaviour, then counting the occurrence of the predicted behaviour as evidence of the correctness of the worker's inference about the client's state. We are working with two probabilities — the probability of correctly inferring the mental-emotional state from observed behaviour, and the probability of this state giving rise to certain kinds of behaviour in future. These two probabilities double our chance of error and prevent us from deducing that the non-occurrence of predicted behaviour effects indicates either faulty prediction or faulty diagnosis.

There is no sure way of independently testing for the occurrence of certain criteria in terms of its behavioural manifestations and what these pieces of behaviour are criteria for. We have two practical courses of action open to us. All talk of mental-emotional states can be eschewed and we confine ourselves to observing chance connections between purely observable properties of behaviour such as sweating, specific motions, blushing, etc. which are favoured by behaviourists. The problem with this approach if taken alone, is that only external, overt features of behaviour can be learnt from it, and the motives and objectives which imbue behaviour with meaning elude us. Or we do what we can with probabilistic measures, building in such safeguards on their misapplication as may be necessary, and accepting the greater degree of uncertainty. (This is the programme advocated in this book.)

Measurement through the Modes of Self-Perception

The manner in which an agency takes account of itself in terms of what indicators, controls and reflective concepts it uses, is itself an indicator of the current state of agency effectiveness. The questions asked by supervisors are indicative. For example, if the major control question is 'How many cases do we have coming in per week?' this may be an indicator of input as opposed to an output orientation when unaccompanied by any concern about case closure.

Similarly, the manner in which a client takes account of himself and his progress as shown either in verbal self-evaluation or in terms of his actions over a period of time, is itself highly indicative of his current state and the effect of the worker's intervention. The fascination and value of consumer reaction studies is precisely the manner in which clients perceive the services as affecting them and which indicators they use of social worker effectiveness. For a situation or result may be measured by assessing participants' evaluations, including the number and range of elements they consider, the possibility of dis-confirmation or validation of their statements, and the congruence or discongruence of perceptions among several observers.

Measures of complex situations have to be taken by using human yardsticks in the form of human judges. Estimates are made by a panel of competent observers who together go through certain procedures which render their judgements more consistent, coherent, and hence (in a sense) 'expert'. Some suitable statistical combination of these is then taken as a measure of the situation in question. This measurement yields, as does all measurement, a relation between the situation being measured and other situations which serve as standards of measurement. In this case, the standards are other human beings. The measurement process in the social sciences does not yield, any more than does physical measurement, a relevation of properties intrinsic to the measured situation or object taken in isolation.

Meta-Measures

Meta-measures are measures of measures. They are measures used to evaluate, assess or weight the differential significance or value which are attached to the various measures we collect.

Thus, the variety of elements taken into account in the measures used, the sophistication of the measurement process employed, the level of accuracy, the practicality and convenience of use, the extent to which counter-intuitive information is supplied and the degree to which action is changed by measurement information form some of the highly relevant meta-measures of an agency's evaluation system.

IV. METHODS OF EVALUATING OUTCOMES

What is Evaluation?

Having classified the outcomes, the problem is how to evaluate them. Essentially, evaluation consists of eliciting by whatever objective means are feasible (or available), what is worth doing, what has the highest priority, and what are the cumulative effects of the agency's activities. How are we doing? Where do we stand? Are our activities relevant? Did we realize our objectives in practice? These are the basic questions put by managers, professional staff, administrators, planners, economists, psychologists, sociologists and operational researchers interested in welfare services.

The practitioner's (or operational researcher's) method of evaluation differs from that of the scientist or academic researcher, but for all of these specialisms evaluation involves reality-testing. Objectives are revised to some degree to accord with experience, theories to accord with new data, actions to accord with new stimuli.

Extant Evaluation

Perhaps a useful starting-point is to recognize that decision-makers are constantly evaluating and measuring albeit intuitively and semi-consciously.

There is a direct line of logical continuity from qualitative classification to the most rigorous forms of measurement by way of intermediate measurement devices such as systematic (or systematized) ratings, ranking scales, multi-dimensional classifications, typologies and simple quantitative indices. In this wider sense of measurement, social phenomena are being measured every day. Our assumptions about people's effectiveness are constantly indicated in our everyday language by evaluative but qualitive descriptions The first task is to transform these qualitative descriptions into quantitative measures. This is a semantic and logical task, not a metaphysical one. The history of science may be described in terms of rendering what were formerly considered to be qualitative phenomena in quantitative form, and thence re-interpreting quantified observations by more sophisticated qualitative descriptions and definitions.

If the quality, variety and specific components of treatment and care have been sufficiently specified and defined, some sort of rudimentary quantification of our specifications can be arrived at. We need to set quantities to the attributes applied in our qualitative evaluations. The first stage is to set quantification markers for defined qualitative factors (the formulation of criteria) and the second is to quantify in terms of actual observations (the application of indicators). In this way an appropriate quantitative scale which measures the qualitative elements we have observed in the situation is introduced. The important thing is to ensure that every aspect of the qualitative evaluation is covered with a corresponding quantitative descriptor.

In a recent case of a problem adolescent who had spent all his troubled life in care, the worker responsible raised the vexed question of his employment on leaving school. A senior supervisor endeavoured to open the rather desperate worker's mind to possible ways of helping this young person. In the course of this discussion, it was possible to list eight specific indicators which the supervisor was using to judge the worker's performance of this task.

   (i) Positive strengths in the client the worker pinpoints in the face of prior stigmatization or labelling of the client;

  (ii) action possibilities the worker evolves from diagnosis of the client's positive strengths;

 (iii) concrete opportunities the worker creates for the client in respect of these action possibilities;

 (iv) opportunities actually tried out by the client;

  (v) opportunities not realized;

 (vi) client re-trials in respect of each type of opportunity despite earlier failure;

(vii) additional supportive mechanisms used to help the client realize these opportunities;

(viii) successes and failures in job placement with clientele having different problems and interests.

This is quite a sophisticated list from a supervisor who was unaware of any usable evaluative criteria even though any experienced observer would undoubtedly seek to add more factors to this list.

Content of Evaluation

The major problem consists of defining a metric appropriate to measuring such aspects of life as need, demand, willingness and supply, and of obtaining measures which are up-to-date. To do this, the expected systemic behaviour manifested by the agency system in response to community stimuli has to be measured. One major difficulty is that people try to evaluate several very different (though interrelated) kinds of things simultaneously. Let us separate these out under the three headings of efficiency, effectiveness and efficacy of social service operations.

1. Agency Efficiency

Social efficiency refers to how far the agency is reaching its pre-defined social objectives with the minimum of social resources: how to get more out of less without lowering standards. Implicitly, it refers to the evaluation of inputs or effort.

When we talk of efficiency, we implicitly evaluate work from an internal agency perspective or standpoint. Efficiency relates to administrative objectives directed towards maintaining or achieving either standards of service quality or to minimizing costs in terms of financial, manpower or administrative effort.

We are interested in questions such as: How far are extant internal agency operations in line with agreed objectives and policies? How efficiently or otherwise are internal agency operations being organized and administered? Is the agency fulfilling its functions in the best way possible given invested resources? Is it delivering its services to the desired quantitative levels to the target clientele? How far are present agency workloads above or below average national workloads? How far is present staffing above or below average national staffing standards? How far is present agency practice quantitatively in line with current average national workloads?

WORKLOAD STUDIES

Various national workload studies[2] suggest some interesting approaches to the last three of these questions. Suppose agency policy is to equalize its amount of work with national performance standards. Given this policy, it can calculate by formula how many workers are needed to carry the average departmental workload at current national average work levels. Or keeping the numbers of workers constant, we can calculate how many case contacts could be made in a fortnight when every one was present, without any overtime.

This can be done by using as the base unit of time measurement, the mean time per worker's case contact. This is a stable measure which can be used to measure existing workloads and the numbers of people needed to carry them at existing standards of performance. National workload studies[3] have shown that the mean time for the average social work contact is 23 minutes. The mean time per contact-plus-supporting-activities is 75 minutes (1.25 hours). All we need to know to apply this formula are six easily discoverable figures:

(i)   number of social workers employed (S);
(ii) total case contacts workers perform over a fortnight (I);
(iii) time lost in hours over a fortnight (TL):
(iv) the contracted working week in hours (WW);
(v)   the contracted hours for the whole social work staff for a fortnight (S x 2WW);
(vi) the contracted hours for those staff actually working [(S x 2WW) - TL].

The formula for the number of workers (N) needed to carry the department's average annual workload equivalent to national standards without any overtime is calculated by multiplying social workers employed (S), total case interviews they perform over a fortnight (I), and mean national time per contact-plus-supporting-activities (1.25), and dividing the result by social workers employed (S), times the contracted working fortnight (2WW), minus total absences (TL).

$$N = \frac{S \times I \times 1.25}{(S \times 2WW) - TL/S}$$

This is simplified from:

$$\frac{S \times 2WW}{(S \times 2WW) - TL/S} \quad \text{x} \quad \frac{1 \times 1.25}{2WW}$$

The formula for the estimated total case contacts (I_E) which workers would have to make in a fortnight when everyone is present, if keeping to national performance levels, is obtainable using the following formula:

$$I_E = \frac{S \times (2WW - TL/S)}{1.25}$$

Using these formulae, we begin to get some idea of how much work the department is doing in relation to current national workloads. Such figures only tell us about service inputs, or mean national amounts of time spent on work. They tell us nothing about outputs or quality of service, desirable agency policies or methods, or desirable local or case variations.

What policy-makers can do, having determined priorities, is to translate these policies into desired mean times per contact-plus-supporting- activities for each problem syndrome. It would be bad management to lay down by rule how many contacts any one worker should make in a week. However, overall agency time commitments can be monitored throughout each problem syndrome to derive policy prescriptions of the following kind:

  (i) 'We are spending more time than we agreed on blind welfare at the expense of work with the mentally handicapped; let us reallocate our time accordingly.'

 (ii) 'One group of workers spend much less time than the national mean of 23 minutes on each case contact while another group spends well over this time. The first group must therefore be under severer pressure than average while the second group is working at a more intensive level, being under less pressure. If our agency policy is to give equal levels of service to all areas and clientele, we must balance up this service discrepancy. If, on the other hand, the second group are working in a depressed area which we have nominated as a key priority area of social need, and our policy is to give extra social service to such areas, the present imbalance will be about right.'

(iii) 'Our agency policy is to designate certain problem syndromes as priorities and work intensively with these selected priority cases, giving only token coverage to other problem syndromes. Therefore, we want people to work at a higher mean time of case-contacts than the national mean of 23 minutes.'

 (iv) 'Our agency policy is to designate certain problem syndromes as priorities throughout the area and to work intensively with these giving only token coverage to other problem syndromes. This means working intensively with selected priority cases. Therefore, we must work at a higher mean time of case-contact-plus-supporting activities than the national mean time of 75 minutes.'

COST STUDIES

The second approach to evaluating efficiency is cost comparison. This is stimulated by the interest which government always has in service costs. Without interfering with the principle of professional freedom, successive governments have exerted pressure to cut costs where possible.

The resource-saving effects of any programme include such things as the greater or smaller amount of social service resources which are consumed in total and indirect financial costs of lost working time as measured by such things as social sickness absence rates. We are concerned here with the cheapest forms (or methods of delivery) of treatment which will yield the same effects as at present.

TIME SERIES STUDIES

The third approach to evaluating efficiency is to collect time series statistics and show how they relate to an existing population. Thus information can be gathered over a period of time on the number of trained social work staff per populations at risk, numbers of residential beds per populations possibly requiring residential care, rates of staff turnover in relation to rates of clientele turnover, etc. These figures can then be compared with those of other analogous agencies elsewhere in the country.

LIMITATIONS OF EVALUATING EFFICIENCY

Although it is easy to calculate the cost of various welfare services, there is little that can be said about the benefit side of the cost-benefit equation. It has simply been assumed that whatever is done is a good thing — that any money spent on welfare is beneficial, or the reverse, depending on your political persuasion. The welfare services debates of the fifties and sixties were centred around the rather sterile political issues of sources and amounts of finance, with no-one really feeling able to say anything about what we actually got for our money.

The lack of data on outcomes is very evident. Economists discuss the social services in terms of welfare economics. They draw complicated tables on the economic cost of disability at so many million pounds. Without data on the effect of social service intervention on coping with disability (i.e. the output of actual intervention), these analyses do no more than awaken people to the magnitude of the costs of social problems and have no practical value in welfare service planning. Similarly, the practical use of Davies' classic econometric analysis of the social services[4] is limited by no equating output of welfare services with the number of cases treated by them. Unless historical trends are uncommonly clearcut, the throughput need bear no relation to real benefits to clients, which remain largely unmeasured.

To exemplify this, the advent of tranquillizers in the mental-health field coincided with a rapid reduction in long-term stays in mental hospitals, and large increases in sickness absence attributed to mental illness. It is not possible to demonstrate unambiguous gains across the board by historical analysis and correlation. More sensitive techniques are needed to identify cause and effect.

What inputs are needed (social workers, residential homes, etc.) must be derived from what outputs or outcomes are sought. Social outputs are valued in social terms. In taking their decisions, both planners and practitioners want to know the real benefits derived by clients in relation to service costs. How are the objectives of the welfare services defined? How are valuations put on the different objectives? How can outputs be defined and measured?

Instead of trying to undertake crude cost-benefit analyses on the shaky basis of historical data, perhaps we should seek to describe the welfare services and the way in which the socio-economic cost and benefits of welfare activities are generated, quantifying where possible, but recognizing the limitations of solely quantitative studies when there is rarely any hard evidence of the outcomes of the activities.

2. Agency Effectiveness

Effectiveness can be defined as productive intervention between an agency and its community, for we may be organizing and delivering very efficient social services which are completely irrelevant to real community needs. It relates to client- or community-oriented objectives directed towards decreasing social problems, or the distressful effects arising from these, and promoting habilitation or rehabilitation.

In evaluating agency effectiveness we are posing these questions: Supposing efficient services are being delivered, what impact are they making on the communities we serve? How effectively or ineffectively are services meeting the needs of clients and communities? What are the cumulative effects of all our services? Are we increasing or diminishing our returns (in terms of community benefit) in relation to service costs? From answers to these questions, we hope to answer the action question: How can we gear up and improve services to make greater impact? We have undertaken a programme of action research based on the technique of priority scaling, designed to formulate agency policies and priorities systematically and coherently, as a basis for evaluation.

The social services at present lack a consistent, coherent, practical, agreed language in which social service problems or cases on the one hand, and alternative methods of intervention on the other, can be appropriately formulated and compared. This makes it difficult to plan overall what resources in what quantities shall be allocated to which problem syndromes or clientele, and impossible to evaluate the results of these allocations in practice. How can a coherent decision be made between such diverse claims on limited agency resources as increasing residential places for maladjusted children, establishing sheltered workshops for those unable to work in open employment, hiring community workers, or increasing foster-parent boarding-out allowances? How can the agency think across its total generic caseload which might include such a diversity of cases as a family with gross housing inadequacy, severe mental breakdown with repercussions on children, an isolated elderly woman who is very depressed, the physically handicapped person whose home needs extensive adaptations, the neglected child? The basic requirement of any evaluation is to develop a language in which judgements are formulated, weighed against other evidence, then communicated with consistency, coherence, accuracy and understanding. A stable language involves a series of descriptions, variables, dimensions or characteristics which form the basis for rating or judging a situation and its changes through time. To begin to tackle these problems, a consistent language has begun to be devised for planning and evaluation which covers the whole field of problems which the social services department confronts. This is the language of the 'Client Problem Dictionary', outlined in Appendix 2, and provides a basis on which relevant information can be organized in devising agreed guidelines for which work to take on and which cannot be. Such a language is essential if information collected at one time and place is to be adjusted so that it is usable in another time and place, and if the effects of agency decisions and operations are to be evaluated. The language constitutes a standard or reference point for comparisons of information about different social services activities. Set against this inventory of target social problems, we also compiled a 'Service Activity Inventory' which is outlined in Appendix 3.

We end up with a matrix which relates the incidence and prevalence of each problem to the agency resources invested. As resource investments are varied (improving or increasing them to meet one set of needs, decreasing them elsewhere), concomitant variations in each problem are observed. If these fall out of line with the effects predicted when allocating resources, then the potential impact of a particular method of agency intervention on a particular need has been wrongly estimated. Until such interrelationships have been defined daily judgements about which intervention methods to use in coping with which social problems cannot be tested. Having defined them, interrelations between changing community problems and changing agency resource allocations through time can be monitored. Of course, this takes us no further in formulating the evaluation instruments in terms of which such interrelations can be monitored, and approaches to this problem will be considered shortly. Unless daily decision-making processes are systematized, their effects as an ongoing part of the management function cannot be evaluated.

RELATING EFFECTIVENESS AND EFFICIENCY
Let us illustrate how effectiveness and efficiency measures may

interrelate, taking an example from the hospital field.

With the aid of a computer, Dale and Hall[5] have been applying to their data a technique of auto-correlation which was previously used on the Concorde airliner tests to measure the rhythms of airflow over the parts of airframes. This test was adapted to measure the rates of fluctuation in serum protein in patients seen in an experimental pathology laboratory. Serum protein is usually determined monthly. On patients where the value was determined more frequently, computer studies showed that significant fluctuations occur within a month, so that monthly readings can be misleading and perhaps dangerous. Scientifically, this discovery has considerable interest where it is hoped to control the value therapeutically. But the management implications are also interesting. This test seemed to show that more resources will be required to provide a service at more frequent intervals. But Dale and Hall also implemented a technique which analyzed data to indicate the best sampling interval for other laboratory work (e.g. physiological data). Sampling of temperatures, pulse, respiration, blood pressure and so on can be examined by it. For some of these data, the optimum sampling period may be shorter than at present. For others it may be longer. This provided a key to resolving a range of clinical problems which have real implications for the level of staffing and equipment required in a hospital.

Similarly, referring back to our residential home experiment, increased staff participation in resident lives in terms of conversation, concern with mental and emotional factors, and so on may at first sight suggest a need for increased staffing of Homes. However, since this is combined with increased resident and community participation in the running of the Home and in helping each other, it is likely that many of the physical chores at present occupying the majority of staff time may be eliminated, so that no additional staff may be required. On the other hand, reliance on the recruitment of staff trained in nursing or domestic management might be reduced.

It would seem worth measuring the effect of each social service activity on such elements as:

(i) Changing expectation of adequate social functioning at various ages.

(ii) Pain, suffering, the quality of life in general, taking into account consumers' own assessments.

(iii) Absence from work, broken down by the length of absence so as to separate out the effect on chronic economic disability.

(iv) Other measures of personal and social functioning – e.g. indicators of stable inter-personal relationships.

(v) Those aspects of the professional practitioner's work which might be placed in the category of his social care function.

3. Agency Efficacy

Efficacy simply means continued effectiveness through time. For example, a short-term beneficial effect on the immediate present problem of homelessness may be made by ensuring that those in greatest need get flats on housing estates. But we may be doing nothing to prepare for tomorrow's problems by making a viable community life for those coming to live on the housing estates.

The relevant questions of efficacy are: Is the agency tackling significant community problems? Is its action making any impact on the key problem variables of community need? How can changes in community social conditions be described and evaluated?

Objectives

As has been suggested, the first problem in evaluating agency work is formulating specific agency objectives in terms of desired social outcomes, benefits and impacts, and the relative evaluation of these diverse benefits and and their interrelations. An inventory of social objectives was outlined earlier on p. 79–176 to help answer this problem. The widespread use of some such set of parameters is indispensable to any coherent evaluation of effectiveness. Deciding what the social services ought to be doing is what evaluation is all about. Comparability of statistics is half the battle in deciding between alternatives. Agreement on parameters might also be extended from management evaluation or *ad hoc* controlled trials, to the routine collection of statistics and record linkage studies. This would be an important advance since statistics as at present collected tend to use existing forms of recording irrespective of the use to which the information might be put in terms of effectiveness.

From the inventory of social objectives, summation objectives were compiled which summarized many of the diverse aims implied in the sub-objectives derived from case targets.

The first summation objective was to improve individuals' (or families') capacities to cope with their social environment. The second objective was to improve growth-inhibiting elements in the individual's social environment. The third was to promote a better match between individuals and their social environment. Primary emphasis was placed on a functional definition of social health and social ill-health — the extent to which treatment can eradicate social disability and restore clients to normal functioning in their social, economic and personal roles. All the statements of objectives or desired outputs related to improving social functioning in some way, or the minimization of social and emotional incapacity in chronic conditions.

As social distress thresholds differ widely, and individuals have an incentive to distort the picture, clients cannot provide reliable or complete information on intensities of social distress, though their judgements are significant and will contribute something. We must therefore attach numbers based on professional assessments which measure the degree of social distress attributed to a 'typical' or paradigm case suffering from a particular social problem. Professional practitioners customarily make such assessments anyway as part of their diagnostic or prognostic art in deciding priorities, forms of treatment, methods of intervention, etc.

Analogous numbers measuring the degree of social disability must be found, and then the degree of social distress and the degree of social disability needs to be combined into a single indicator. Is 25 social distress/10 social disability worse, better or the same as 10 social distress/25 social disability? Having compared various conditions in terms of social distress and social disability characteristics, a ranking can then be established and numbers attached to these combinations.

All of these measures could be combined to forecast the effect of any given service programme on the expectation of an active life free of social distress — to give measures of the extra quality of life offered by the programme. These numbers essentially form the welfare indicator itself. They are social judgements and are not necessarily or desirably made by the social services profession itself.

Subjective elements have played a large part in deriving welfare indicators. They cannot be eliminated, but must be made explicit. Third parties must evaluate the state or social condition of individuals. This evaluation is subjective but subjectivity is inherent in social aspects of living. Evaluation as such does not introduce subjectivity. Explicit social valuations must be introduced to combine the components of the indicator (e.g. social distress and social disability) and to assign numbers to the ranked degrees of social malfunctioning. These are equivalent to statements of social policy and should be recognized as such.

The next step is to formulate alternative methods decision-makers might use to assign differential values, weightings or priorities among these objectives, and make choices between alternative courses of action in the light of this valuation.

To illustrate this process let us consider one method sometimes used by various decision-making groups to decide systematically how extra resources for additional services for the elderly should be allocated. The example given is a case study of how the method was applied by one policy group in the social services.[6]

Assigning Values

Three objectives for the care of the aged were defined:

1. *Social Integration* (O^1)

   To reduce social isolation of the elderly — to give them the opportunity of a fuller life by increased social integration with the community.

2. *Independence* (O^2)

   To reduce depersonalization and dependency of the elderly — to preserve their identity and independence.

3. *Nurture* (O^3)

   To reduce the likelihood of physical illness of the elderly — to improve their physical well-being.

   To which of these three objectives did the group attach most value or weight, and in what proportions?

   First a ten-point value scale from zero to one was constructed:

The group tentatively estimated what weight along this scale they attached to each objective. They accepted this approach once it was recognized that in making major decisions in real life on what to do about a particular elderly person, we are often by implication evaluating the relative importance of these three objectives.

First Evaluation

A first rough evaluation was made in which 3 degrees of priority were allocated to the social integration objective, 5 degrees to the independence objective, and 8 degrees of priority to the nurture objective:

Social integration	(O^1) = 0.3 per cent priority
Independence	(O^2) = 0.5 per cent priority
Nurture	(O^3) = 0.8 per cent priority

Let us illustrate some of the many, though tentative, reasons for this first evaluation. Nurture is a primary physiological need without which independence or social integration would be impossible. Independence is the basis of our culture, and people seem willing to put up with social isolation because they would find the amount of social control needed to reduce social isolation and its effects intolerable. Social integration is a secondary need which is only sought after nurture and independence are secured.

Everyone was unhappy about this first valuation. How could this estimate be improved to make it more reliable?

First Check
'Nurture' on the one hand was compared with 'social integration' and 'independence' *in combination* on the other. Suppose we *had* to choose between them. Would it generally be worth giving up both independence and a full social life for the sake of maintaining full physical agility? The group's unequivocal answer was 'no'. 'Social integration' and 'independence' taken together were therefore selected in preference to 'nurture' alone.

Such choices demand extensive and clear statements of reasons and there is plenty of room for discussion and argument. But in formulating a policy, making a decision or taking some action decision-makers cannot avoid taking some definite standpoint on values (even if only implicitly) and thence assigning relatively more importance to one value than another.

What were the group's reasons for such a choice? A fully integrated social life, in which identity and independence is fully preserved, in a sense supplies our very motivation for preserving physical well-being. Lacking any form of independence or social integration or the prospect of such, we might well begin to question the very purpose of continuing to live at all. The group therefore argued that 'social integration' and 'independence' are higher-level values. When taken together, they should influence decision-making more than the primary value 'nurture' on its own. Social services agencies can no longer address themselves exclusively to physiological needs. On the basis of such reasoning, 'social integration' plus 'independence' were selected in preference to 'nurture' alone.

Yet in the original valuation, the group had valued 'social integration' plus 'independence' together $(O^1 + O^2)$ as of *equal* significance $(0.3 + 0.5$ degrees$)$ to 'nurture' (O^3) alone at 0.8 degrees priority. The original valuation was therefore adjusted so that 'independence' plus 'social integration' were greater than the value of 'nurture' alone:

Social integration	(O^1) = 0.4 per cent
Independence	(O^2) = 0.5 per cent
Nurture	(O^3) = 0.8 per cent

Second Check
The group was still not happy about its valuation. So further checks were made by going on to compare 'social integration' and 'nurture' against 'independence'. The question was posed: Is it appropriate that together 'nurture' and 'social integration' should represent more than double the value of 'independence'?

Basis for Decisions
From several successive checks* the group concluded with a final valuation of 'social integration' at 4 degrees, 'independence' at 5 degrees, and 'nurture' at 8 degrees of priority:

Social integration (O^1) = 0.4 per cent
Independence (O^2) = 0.5 per cent
Nurture (O^3) = 0.8 per cent

These final valuations were converted into percentages by 'normalizing' them, i.e. dividing each estimate by the sum total of the three estimates together. In this case, each estimate was divided in turn by 1.7 (i.e. 0.4 + 0.5 + 0.8).
The result was as follows:

Social integration (O^1) = $\frac{0.4}{1.7}$ = 0.2 = 20 per cent

Independence (O^2) = $\frac{0.5}{1.7}$ = 0.3 = 30 per cent

Nurture (O^3) = $\frac{0.8}{1.7}$ = 0.5 = 50 per cent

The resulting percentage told the group what proportion of resources they ought to allocate each objective, given their successive estimations. Examining existing resource allocations in the light of overall results, the group found that actual agency priorities were not at all as any decision-makers thought they should be

The group decided that the desirable next stage would be to introduce into the discussion representatives of those elderly social service consumers whose lives were being influenced by its decisions, so that consensus on objectives would be broader-based and so that consumer participation in decision-making was increased. This would entail formulating choices and supplying information in such a clear

* Though changes were made to the result produced after the first check, further changes made in subsequent checks eventually produced a final check which coincided with the results produced after the first check.

manner that elderly consumers, some of whom are confused, could bring to bear the consumer's view standpoint in making such choices. In a similar way, the decision-making group might be extended to include political representatives (i.e. members of social services committees) and planners of neighbouring services.

Underlying Principle

The underlying principle of the process is this. When a decision-maker is presented with choices between different outcomes, his preferences give some information about the value basis for his decisions. They tell us something about the real value the agency places on these outcomes. Each successive choice is used as a basis for improving the decision-maker's original valuations since his second set of judgements have some potentiality for revising the first set. Each successive choice gives us more information about the agency's real valuation of the outcomes.

This principle can be justified in terms of its success in many areas of work where it has been put to the test. It has been used, for instance, in the extremely difficult areas of measuring consumer attitudes about various product qualities where its success has been clearly established by accurate predictions of consumer purchase patterns.

Alternative Courses of Action

Having placed some sort of value on the different outcomes, the decision-making group has then to evaluate the merits of alternative activities or investments.

If results of evaluative trials suggest benefits normally go in the same direction, an increased expectation of adequate social functioning being accompanied by positive benefits in all other areas too, then there is less pressing need for reducing the outcomes to common terms by making overt valuations of trade-offs between two or more outcomes. However, where this is not validated, the following procedure may be used.

By the same method used above in evaluating outcomes, the group then compared the efficiency of various alternative courses of action for example developing better community care (C^1) as against developing better residential care (C^2), and assessed how far each might contribute towards the objectives previously weighted: social integration, independence, nurture.

The group reckoned that good community care potentially contributed considerably more than good residential care to the social integration of the elderly within the community. This was still more the case if we are seeking to preserve independence of the aged, since residential care involves at the very least an abandonment of residential independence. On the other hand, they estimated that nurture is more adequately ensured by residential care (where old people are under constant surveillance) than by community care (where the health visitor's half-hour visit may be the only surveillance).

On the basis of such reasoning, the relative values of community care (C^1) and residential care (C^2) were evaluated in relation to each objective. The result looked something like this:

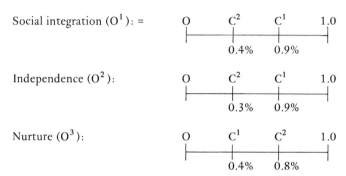

C \ O	O^1	O^2	O^3
C^1	0.9	0.9	0.4
C^2	0.4	0.3	0.8

At this point, people often point out that 'nurture' (O^3) had been evaluated as more important than preserving 'independence' (O^2) which in turn was evaluated as more important than 'social integration' (O^1). Therefore, we should go all out for 'nurture' and take whatever course of action will further this end. This would have meant developing residential care (C^2). For it was estimated that residential care contributes most to the most highly evaluated objective of 'nurture'.

However, no one was interested in pursuing the nurture objective *exclusively*. The group wished to pursue 'nurture' *in conjunction with* 'independence' and 'social integration'. To choose whether developing community care or developing residential care is the most effective, *both* courses of action in relation to the group's valuation of *all three* objectives had to be considered.

The evaluation therefore had to combine valuation of the objectives — social integration, independence, nurture — with valuation of the courses of action — community or residential care.

C \ O	O^1	O^2	O^3	TOTAL
C^1	0.2 x 0.9	0.3 x 0.9	0.5 x 0.4	0.65
C^2	0.2 x 0.4	0.3 x 0.2	0.5 x 0.8	0.54

From this, it is possible to work out percentage valuation of each course of action by 'normalizing' the totals (i.e. by dividing each total in turn by their sum which is 1.19). The result was 60 per cent to community care (C^1) and 40 per cent to residential care C^2).

On this basis, and in view of the valuation of the three objectives of social integration, independence and nurture, the group allocation of further increases in resources between community care and residential would be in the proportion of 60 per cent to 40 per cent. Clearly, additional objectives may be incorporated into the equation, as may other alternative services. Moreover, it may be important to specify both the objectives and the services in more detail (e.g. in terms of the 'Client Problem Dictionary' and 'Inventory of Special Social Service Activities', set out in Appendices 2 and 3) if decisions are to be made between more detailed alternatives.

Along such lines, a method begins to evolve by which we might decide between alternative courses of agency action and resource allocation, in accordance with our evaluation of objectives. This approach potentially allows us to tackle the extremely difficult problem of weighting various benefits as well as intangible psychological costs in the final cost-benefit equation of overall agency effectiveness which we are pursuing.

Indicators or Measures

The second stage of development was to take each objective in turn and to define specific social indicators by which we could evaluate how far it had been attained. If we begin to collect such a range of information, what different types of quantitative measure or indicator would result? What alternative assumptions might we make to those outlined earlier, which might help us to break through the generally gloomy picture and make some progress in measuring effectiveness?

Essentially there are two ways of measuring. We either measure by qualitatively assigning characteristics to classes (i.e. by classification) or by assigning quantities to characteristics. Either way we must fall back on one of the following alternative evaluation methods in support of this overall evaluation strategy:

    (i) ongoing statistics;
    (ii) surrogates or substitute measures;
    (iii) ranking;

(iv) specifying criteria;

(v) social indicators.

Most work outputs are in principle measurable, using one or several of these types of measure. Let us look at each in turn with an example of how they are being tried out in research.

1. Ongoing Statistics

If we are measuring events which can be directly observed or counted, then an intelligence system can be set up to get the counting done in the form of statistics. We can then answer such questions as 'How are agency resources being distributed over different client groups'? 'What proportion of children in care are boarded out in foster homes?' etc. In this way, the ongoing trend of events can be monitored.

This approach has been used by Davies.[7] He first correlated indices of services resources such as gross expenditure on social services per population, numbers of staff per population, qualifications of staff per area, numbers of people in residential care, expenditure on homes, etc. He then reviewed social conditions in terms of such facilities as housing, income, employment, expenditure on domestic goods, people registered under different categories of need, etc. On the basis of available statistical evidence, he compared trends variations and correlations between the extensiveness of service provision in different areas as weighted by existing social conditions. This approach allows departments whose services fall below national standards of provision, to argue for more resources on the basis of territorial justice.

However, Davies' work at no point moves (nor did he intend it to do so) outside the area of what can be deduced within the framework of current available statistical information. It was not his objective to question existing statistics, but simply to use these to the maximum advantage in evaluating levels of service provision.

Statistical surveys are not vehicles for making fine distinctions. Many questions relating to the effectiveness or otherwise of our services still have to be decided. This can only be done by asking fundamental questions about which indices or statistics it would be most helpful and relevant to collect — in short, by exploring which indices would be necessary is we are to compile an evaluative social report.

Perhaps because of scepticism about how far existing statistical returns picture relevant changes in social conditions and the impact social service agencies are making on them, Davies' work has been less used in practical daily planning and management of the social services than it deserves to be.

2. Substitute Measures

Some of the information which we require about complex human problems is not provided directly by available statistics. Some important conditions are not directly observable. The degree of social pathology for example, cannot be pharmaceutically measured. However, we may infer something about such matters by using a quantitative or quantifiable substitute item which *is* observable or measurable to stand-in, represent or do duty for the unobservable characteristic.

A surrogate is a substitute, symbolic, indirect or proxy measure. It is obviously impossible to observe the amount of self-respect an old lady has, or a social worker's valuation of the comparative significance of social problems. The amount of time he spends on a case may however, constitute a surrogate for this evaluation. To this extent surrogates constitute a measure of objectives implicit in action. There is no such observable state as the old lady's self-respect, but we may determine something about this by observing such things as how much of her personal money she spends on her personal appearance. Similarly, observable symptoms (e.g. sweating, tensed facial muscles) are used as surrogates for unobservable aspects of personality (e.g. nervousness).

A more sophisticated example is the use of perceptual field-dependency as an indicator of potential delinquency or criminality. Prisoners' reactions to a simple perceptual exercise may indicate their criminal tendencies, as shown by H. Marriage, a senior psychologist in the prison service.[8] He has described an exercise in measuring the criminal subject's 'field dependence', i.e. the degree to which he is affected by external influences. Similar experiments[9] have shown that children become more perceptually independent as they grow up, that more intelligent people are more field independent, and that upbringing can affect field dependence. If the child is encouraged to solve problems for himself, he will tend to be field independent; if on the other hand, the parent is overprotective, and varies between indulgence and extreme punishment, the child tends to be field dependent.

It is here we begin to pick up the criminality aspect, for this second pattern is often found in delinquent backgrounds. It looks as though the conditions which produce field dependency are similar to those which give rise to delinquency. If we then look for some of the characteristics of field-dependent people — heavily dependent on external cues, particularly influenced by immediate situations, prefering short-term gains to larger, long-term gains — then a pattern of similarity emerges between the offender and the field-dependent person.

Even with a small sample, the expected relationships appeared between field dependence and a range of criminal variables such as average sentence and the number and rate of convictions. All the relationships indicated that the more criminally inclined men were the more field dependent. It was found they fell into the patterns of being old with lots of convictions and sentences, a high rate of offending, and they were unmarried.

It is often impossible to manipulate directly the phenomena or entities we wish to measure. We therefore manipulate other phenomena which are directly manipulable, and on the strength of these correlations, conclude certain things about the comparable phenomena which are not directly susceptible to measurement. We may not have direct access to a person's feeling of privacy when ensconced in an old person's home, but *do* have direct access to the number of people who knock on that person's room before entering. We also have access to the number of suggestions by residents of old people's homes in response to questionnaires, that they feel a greater sense of privacy when people knock on their doors before entering.

The major difficulty about using surrogates is the danger of assuming a linear relation between the phenomena evaluated (e.g. magnitude of need satisfied) and the substitute measure itself (e.g. the amount of money allocated to the need by agencies). This relation may sometimes be justifiable in practice to the extent that it provides a better means of reducing evaluative uncertainty than any alternative assumption to date, or to the extent that it provides a means of making explicit existing assumptions for testing, thus focusing research and data-collection on a relevant field. *All* indicators are relative and have no more than a probability relation to the phenomenon evaluated. All measurements are indirect in one sense or another.

Surrogates themselves are essentially ascertained by predicting what observations would have occurred had they been made under a 'standard' controlled set of conditions. They themselves represent interim targets to be aimed at for the sake of improving present operations until a programme of more scientific and systematic measures can be set up as a result of empirical research findings. As such, it is usually more useful to evaluate a situation by means of several surrogates used in conjunction rather than to rely on one surrogate to do duty for many variables simultaneously.

3. Ranking

Such phenomena as brutality and reason, misery and happiness, ignorance and knowledge, impotence and power cannot be compared without acquiring the ideas of better and worse, excellent and imperfect, effective and ineffective. In this way, criteria ranking scales are formed. Values and disvalues, benefits and disbenefits, healthy and unhealthy situations admit of comparison. Scales of degree can be applied to them but tend to be vague — infinite at opposite poles with a common area of 'indifference' between.

Where quantities cannot be assigned to characteristics, we may be able to assign the latter to fairly precisely defined classes. Though unable to quantify directly the degree of social pathology of one problem family compared with another, we may nevertheless rank both problems along one scale in relation to a precisely defined set of factors.

SITUATIONAL SCALE

This can be done by making a scale showing five degrees of social pathology or problem severity, ranging from no problem at one end to extremely complex problematic situations at the other.*

Norm	Minimal Problem	Moderately Severe	Very Severe	Extremely Severe
1	2	3	4	5

Either things remain much the same as they are, which is indicated by the central point on the scale (point three). Or they become very much better or very much worse than at the time of initial referral, which is represented by the two extreme ends of the scale (points one and five). Or they become just a little bit better or a little worse than when the case started, which is represented by the two intervening points (points two and four).

In real terms, this scale can be translated, for example, into the field of homeless families in five stages of decline:

---

* This is the type of scale used to indicate degrees of social pathology in the 'Client Problem Dictionary', Appendix 2, after the current average position is defined:

Current   Predisposition   Impeded   Improved   Deteriorated   Collapsed
average

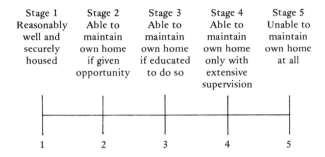

Stage 1	Stage 2	Stage 3	Stage 4	Stage 5
Reasonably	Able to	Able to	Able to	Unable to
well and	maintain	maintain	maintain	maintain
securely	own home	own home	own home	own home
housed	if given	if educated	only with	at all
	opportunity	to do so	extensive	
			supervision	

Of course, we may wish to elaborate this scale to include additional relevant factors like domestic management, family unity, health-care considerations, rent arrears, security of tenure, and so on.

The 'Client Problem Dictionary' (See Appendix 2) may in one sense be seen as a comprehensive set of scales covering the range of client problems confronting a social services department. Each problem syndrome is defined by descriptor phrases indicating varying degrees of severity along a ranked scale.

On referral, it can be assessed where any one client's problems fall on such a scale of social pathology, and the agency can then intervene in whatever way is appropriate. Having treated the problems, their position on the scale can be re-assessed. This gives some indication of whether the situation has changed for better or for worse, or stayed the same. If the problems move from point four on referral day to point one on the last visit, the situation has improved. If they move to point five, it will have deteriorated.

In one sense, it may not matter whether agency intervention, environmental influences or chance factors caused the improvement. Chance and extraneous factors will sometimes work for us, in which case so much the better, sometimes against, in which case we are out of luck. The important thing is whether the improvement happens or not, irrespective of means. If the family is about to move to point five, efforts must be intensified. If they have moved to point one, the case can be closed. Need and its fulfilment are only evaluated as a cue for further action or closure.

PERFORMANCE SCALES

If we want to critically compare different methods of intervention or how well the individual caseworker performs, then some performance measurement are required in addition to these measures of social condition.

Special problems arise where we want to measure not only what the situation is at several points in time, but also the degree of change or movement from one point in time to another. Thus, in casework we may need to assess not simply what type of problem the client has, how serious it is and what treatment is given, but also the changes that take place in the client during and after the treatment process.

Here a five-point scale of case movement might be used for evaluating performance which looks something like this:

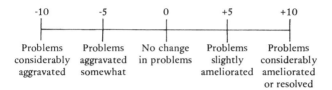

Applying this scale to improvements in a multi-problem situation, we might evaluate that over a year's period they showed considerable improvement. They may have moved from a severe degree of social pathology (point four on our social pathology scale) at the point of referral, to a minimal degree of pathology (point two on the social pathology scale). This improvement is evaluated on the case movement scale as having considerably alleviated the problem (+10 valuation of case movement). Retrogression or stasis may be similarly indicated.

Against such situational scales, equivalent performance scales can be placed in terms of client benefit per agency input:

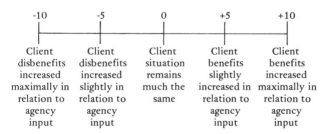

These two elements of evaluation involve monitoring changing social problems in terms of situational criteria and monitoring changing effects which differential services and methods of intervention make on social problems in terms of performance criteria. Unless we constantly monitor both by means of empirical research and agency evaluation, we are likely to go far astray.

Having understood the problems of a community more clearly,

what action should then be taken? The very fact that we have defined social problems more closely, throws new responsibilities onto practitioners in terms of how to make decisions on resource allocation, and new responsibilities onto research to provide information which will help them to take these decisions. This research must relate to what impact on the community problems different planning strategies might have, and an assessment of these as opposed to collecting more and more data about problems. It must provide indicators relating to the effectiveness or ineffectiveness of alternative services. Improved evaluation of social problems inevitably stimulates improved evaluation of the service impact on these problems.

These scales may seem crude instruments for evaluation. Yet in practical terms, this may not matter. Changes in clients or social conditions are made in the face of massive inertia – inertia embodied in the client's background and development, his socio-cultural situation, the rigid institutional structures he interacts with, or a few traditional limited treatment programmes available. The behaviour patterns dealt with are by and large so stable that subtle changes have little effect on results. Consequently, a simple five-point scale will usually offer enough discrimination to define the sorts of change we are concerned with.

There are several tendencies to be avoided in constructing evaluative scales. One is the tendency for descriptions at midpoints on any particular evaluative scale to be written in terms of what both extremes (above and below the mode, average or middle point) lack. This is avoided if a full narrative report is made, using all midpoint descriptions to determine whether it is so phrased as to be meaningful, and thus exclusive of other possibilities. Another is the tendency to make the two extreme points on the scale refer to situations which are so rare as to be seldom exemplified in reality. A third tendency is to group together at each point of the scale an arbitrary combination of three diverse characteristics which are rarely found in combination in reality. This usually results from futile efforts at being precise about a particular variable or aspect of reality by adding additional related (though uncorrelated) variables. It is usually best to provide a different scale for each distinguishable variable. The five critical points or bench-marks on the evaluative scales must be defined as precisely as possible, with examples. Among many other experiments, the Finkle and Jones study[10] on the Standard Oil Company of Ohio gave evidence of the increased reliability of situational and performance assessments which were based on this type of scaling procedure.

Whether the 'high', 'low' or 'middle' point on the scale is counted as the optimal one will, to a large extent, depend on the situation.

Since most human situations are best modelled in terms of a range of interrelated variables, the interrelationship between the various indications on each scale are likely to be of more significance than the evaluation of any one factor or element. Most of the things decision-makers will wish to measure, may for a large variety of reasons assume from time to time one of a range of possible values. It is therefore important to nominate that range by a scale and to quantify each value within it by the probability of that value's occurrence.

4. Specifying Criteria

Another approach is to specify an objective and the criteria for its achievement so precisely that participants can readily determine whether the observable indicative factors are present or not.

This can be illustrated by reference to an action project undertaken by the author in an old people's residential home.[11] With staff, residents and management ways of improving the life-situation in the home were discussed. A key objective was defined which if pursued successfully, would, in everyone's opinion, make a major impact: 'To encourage interrelations among people in the home which would better meet their emotional needs for social integration'. A consequential programme of action was then devised. How could staff know whether and how far this objective was realized? The approach was to define criteria of effectiveness quite specifically by analyzing exactly what was meant by key phrases used in the objective.

RESIDENTIAL CRITERIA

'Emotional needs for social integration' was the key phrase used for one of the final outcome criteria. What types of social integration needs were we trying to fulfil? Staff obviously cannot meet all social integration needs of all the old people. It would be undesirable to meet any need which was pathological, such as the quasi-sadistic needs of one old lady who nearly disrupted the whole home.

The key phrase referring to intermediate action criteria was: 'Interrelations among old people in the home'. What types of interrelation should staff aim to achieve? There was no desire to encourage interrelations which resulted in the old people becoming emotionally distraught. The phrase 'to encourage' referred to input or effort criteria. Only certain methods and styles of encouragement are appropriate in trying to achieve this objective. Some methods — such as physical force — would be wholly inappropriate.

Staff then compiled an inventory of all the factors which were relevant to the need for social integration, the nature of the interrelations they hoped to encourage, and the methods of encouragement to be used.

SOCIAL INTEGRATION
The inventory of factors of social integration included elements like:
Group permissiveness of expression of fears needs and concerns by all residents;

ability of all residents to make and accept interpretations by and about others;

residents' ability to collect and use appropriate information about themselves;

sharing informal leadership functions;

achieving mutual sensitivity to the different styles of participation by different residents in the life in the home, distinguishing between contributions which different members have to make to home life;

distinguishing distinct personality characteristics of others;

assimilating new ideas without anxiety;

assimilating new residents in a way which strengthens rather than disrupts the home, profiting from success experiences and learning from failure experiences;

setting realistic goals;

making constructive use of internal conflicts;

ability of residents to inform themselves and to think straight about their own problems;

ability of residents to use the full contribution potential of others;

residents' ability to create new functions and sub-groups as necessary.

From this inventory, staff derived scales related to:
Adequate mechanisms for getting feedback among residents;

adequacy of resident decision-making procedures;

degree of resident cohesion as a group or groups;

degree of flexibility of group organization and procedure among residents;

use of resident resources;

degree and clarity of communications among residents;

clarity of goals and intentions accepted by residents in relation to specific activities;

feelings of inter-dependence among residents;

shared participation among residents in the leadership function;

acceptance of minority views and persons.

On the one hand, staff began to distinguish *mere social presence* where a resident grasped little of what was happening in the home, regarding its events and inhabitants as alien to herself. On the other, they distinguisged *genuine social integration*, where a resident knew almost everything happening to everyone, identifying with events and other residents in a familial way. Residents' information and concern about what was happening to whom thus became a key indicator of social integration.

INTERRELATIONS
The staff made a similar inventory of interrelations in terms of their number, frequency, type, compatibility and range. They were concerned to foster:

a large number of interactions between all old people in the home;

more initiators of interactions with others;

a greater variety of interaction in terms of instruction, information, advice, chat, argument, joint activity, and joint decisions;

more frequent interaction, for example at different times of day and in different locations in the home;

greater depth of interaction so that, for example, those people with similar interests and personalities were matched;

a wider range of interactional topics;

a greater degree of understanding between residents.

For each factor in the inventory criteria scales were derived covering the degree of interaction among residents. For example, the degree of total interactions were indicated on a five-point scale ranging from virtually no interaction at one end to optimal overall interaction at the other end. This was evaluated in terms of the numbers of interactions between residents within their own groups, outside their own groups, and outside the home. Similar scales were derived which related to the frequency of interaction, the number of initiators of interactions, various sub-group orientations, types of interaction, depth of interaction, range of topics of interaction, staff ability to recognize the significance of such interactions within the home, and various silent interactions which occured.

On the one side was the current situation of *mere contact,* where one resident neither understood nor responded to messages others tried to communicate. On the other was the prospective requisite situation of *genuine interaction* in which messages were understood, and positive or negative responses were made. The residents' degree of responsiveness to initiated contacts became the key indicator for resident interaction.

With staff participation an inventory was made of styles of encouragement which would be appropriate in relation to this objective. We began to distinguish between *imposition* in which various forms of overt or covert pressure was used by management on staff and by staff on residents, and *genuine encouragement* in which informing, questioning, providing example, proposing and inculcation through resident participation was the order of the day. All forms of commanding or ordering of staff by management, or of residents by staff, was ruled out as an impermissible way of encouraging interactions. The degree of participation became the key indicator for genuine encouragement.

From the criteria for evaluating attainment of the objective, a series of ranking scales were then derived against which progress in achieving or failing to achieve the objectives could be evaluated. The present Home situation was evaluated in terms of each criteria scale. Targets were set on each scale indicating by what stages staff hoped to improve the situation, synthesizing them into an overall plan for achieving the overall objective. Questionnaires were then designed translating each of these very specific criteria into colloquial language so as to elicit from residents how far they felt life in the Home was becoming more sociable. Having allowed time for the programme of action to take effect, staff were able to evaluate achievement of the objective in very specific terms.

5. Social Indicators

Where it would be too big a job to evaluate all the factors involved in a situation by the methods previously outlined, it may be helpful to take two or three key indicators to do duty for all the measures we cannot make. Thus, in pursuing the residential objective previously quoted in other homes, it is possible to work exclusively with the three key indicators of residents' information about what was happening to whom, residents' degree of responsiveness to initiated contacts, and the degree of participation.

Social indicators are interrelated, aggregate figures (not congeries of statistical data) telling us about situations as wholes (rather than about situational elements). They give a reading on progressive and regressive social trends in some segment of the community, and summarize a variety of correlated changes in a set of meaningful numbers, allowing us to aggregate a large number of factors into one state, and to compare this aggregate with other similar aggregates. They are combinations of several surrogates (or items) in one measure embodying rules according to which various factors will be considered equivalent under certain circumstances. Indicators are not absolutes. They only have a probability relation to the underlying concept of the phenomenon to be evaluated. They facilitate concise, holistic and informed decisions about agency action which will make some difference to the community condition. They are ways of analyzing a large, confusing array of data, such as the state of a community. Having applied indicators, supplementary measures may thereafter be necessary for specific analytic purposes, refinements and correctives to make the basic measures more feasible and applicable, and to provide better understanding of their limitations and meaning.

The potentialities of certian indicators can be shown, for example, by the use which can be made of census data on a person's origins. A person's origins can indicate to some degree whether he is more or less likely to be born prematurely, to survive the first month or year of life, to have numerous brothers and sisters or to be the only child, to live in conditions of overcrowding, to do well in intelligence tests, to remain at school beyond the age of compulsory attendance, to go to a university, to maintain or improve on his father's occupational status, to succumb to various diseases, to enjoy a longer or shorter life.

WHAT INDICATORS
Rational decision-making demands either knowledge or informed guesses about:

(i) The output of welfare operations or action consequences, as clients only go to social services departments because they potentially get some help from them.

(ii) The evaluation of these consequences in terms of good or bad: placing social and humanitarian values on various rates of output of any welfare service or operation.

(iii) The resources or means needed to effect these consequences: the professional implications necessarily implied by any service or operation.

(iv) Assessments of the value of these resources in view of the best alternative uses to which they could be put: social costs of any service or its operation.

Several attempts have been made to derive social service indicators. One approach uses the following line of reasoning. Welfare increases whenever the aspiration-gap (between what the client or community aspires to and what it actually gets) is reduced. The higher the aspiration level and the lower the real income, the lower is economic welfare. This occurs, for example, when an increase in incomes is greater than the rise in the standard of taste, or vice versa. The same may be applied to social welfare. The higher the aspiration level for social benefits and the lower the real satisfaction of these aspirations, the lower is the social welfare. In the absence of any such sophisticated general measure of effectiveness which covers the multitude of social service objectives, impartial criteria are needed to assess the degree to which specific objectives are being achieved.

The major problem consists of defining a metric appropriate to measuring such aspects of life as need, demand, willingness, effectiveness and supply, and of obtaining measures which are up-to-date.

The approach outlined, in which the full implications of specific states of affairs are delineated by specific criteria, may well prove fruitful for a whole range of social phenomena. Take the client problem of inhibition. Inhibition blocks the articulation of a tension set up by the individual's needs and drives. Given the amount of tension generated by needs, the degree to which a need is articulated can be analyzed as a function of the strength of the inhibiting barrier. The total strength of a particular need or drive can therefore in principle be calculated from the amount of internally and externally inhibited activity associated with that need. Some indication of this might be given by defining those activities which a person would undertake if not inhibited by denominated internal or external constraints. On this basis, the amount of inhibited tension could potentially be estimated. The next step would be to begin to devise techniques whereby these indicators would be conveniently monitored in a range of individual cases.

18 | Priority Objectives and Strategies

I. PRIORITY OBJECTIVES

Many political and ethical philosophers have attempted to establish by rational argument that various values or objectives of the kind outlined earlier are more primary than others which derive from them. For example, Hocking[1] attempted to establish most of them on the basis of an egalitarian postulate, Radbruch[2] from a tolerance principle and MacIver[3] from a gratification standpoint. Most philosophical attempts at establishing hierarchies among these values, run into insuperable difficulties since they all seem so closely interlinked.

Social services agencies endeavour to make varied impacts on a complex and richly interactive community situation. They have to choose between a complex range of objectives which we have endeavoured to enumerate at various levels of conceptualization.

At each level, the nature of the choice varies in that different kinds of variables operate. Our choice of agency objectives both conditions and is conditioned by the amount and range of actually or potentially available agency resources, and vice versa. Similar interactions characterize all the other elements and levels, which is why the classification system for each level is divergent from the others. This also to some extent explains the conceptual divergence of different schools of management theory. Thus rationalists or synopticists like Dror,[4] develop their characteristic approach by viewing the work process from the standpoint of higher-level objectives. Action programmes, services, resources, clientele, functions, operations and roles are subsumed under these. By contrast, incrementalists like Braybrook and Lindblom,[5] or opportunists like Drucker,[6] view the work process on the basis of the resource utilization principle. Objectives, programmes, functions, operations and roles being geared accordingly. Meanwhile, operationalists like Weick[7] and Etzioni[8] start at the level of agency operations, and having derived the other elements from these, interpret the work process accordingly.

It is not surprising that social services agencies have found difficulty in formulating objectives given the incredible range and complexity of choice which characterizes the work process and the variables which enter daily decisions. The difficulty of the choice depends on the degree of conflict over objectives which obtains in the agency.

Degree of Conflict

The degree of homogeneity or diversity of agency objectives varies from agency to agency — indeed, from community to community. Although factors influencing this have been covered in earlier sections, four additional elements not previously considered are given below.

1. Recruitment Procedures

An organization consisting entirely of accountants will obviously be more homogeneous and attain more overall agreement on its objectives than a local authority containing architects, town planners, valuers, lawyers, accountants, operational researchers, engineers, educationalists, and so on.

Thus, recruitment procedures can be used indirectly to determine preference objectives and to tailor how much conflict or conformity to objectives is acceptable. The kind of preference objectives ultimately selected are determined very much by the source of recruitment. The more diverse the recruitment sources, the greater is the potential conflict over preference objectives, and the greater the danger of the organization falling apart. This has occurred in many community organizations. Therefore, the more recruitment procedures are tied into agreement by applicants on stated organizational objectives the less the conflict in formulating objectives subsequently. However, if an organization reaches a point where it is unable to recruit members of an adequate level of skill owing to its existing objectives, it may have to enlarge the base of its objectives to embrace a wider range of trained personnel. This happened with many large organizations when they first began to recruit graduates.

2. Reference Group Affiliations

Reference group identifications may be more or less strong within the organization. Differentiation of sub-unit objectives is a sign of organizational maturation, though it throws up new problems of coordination.

3. Intra-Organizational Competition

Individuals or groups compete for scarce resources. The environment within which the organization operates is turbulent. In this situation, the organization as a whole is impelled to resolve the relative merits of sub-unit claims, and debates on priorities become paramount and critical. Relations among sub-units and individuals tend to resemble a strictly competitive game, and both inter-individual and inter-group conflict increases.

On the other hand, more adequate resources and a benign environment within which to operate usually gives the organization sufficient slack to both satisfy explicit, manifest overall objectives and have excess resources or energy to satisfy individual or sub-unit objectives not directly related to overall objectives. At these points in time, there is less conflict since sub-unit objectives can all be met within the same programme and are therefore rarely challenged. This is a time for greater differentiation and diversification of sub-unit objectives.

4. Allocational Decisions

One would expect that the organization pays for those skills it values most. What then tends to happen is that the objective for which the organization is paying more, tends to get preferential treatment in certain situations, even though the viability and effectiveness of the organization may demand a reverse allocation of priorities. The result inevitably is increased diversification of and conflict over objectives.

Value-Conflict Resolution

Some conflict over objectives within an organization is probably desirable in that it keeps the organization self-critical and therefore capable of development. Too much conflict can pull an agency in so many diverse directions that it loses its stability and identity as an organism, and is either torn apart or becomes a loose federation of independent kingdoms, as is exemplified by countless mergers which have taken place among outfits which lack any common unifying theme. Conflict among agency objectives, however desirable in principle, has its own attainment threshold.

Some resolution of such conflicts among strategic objectives is necessary to balance out such conflicting demands at the operational level as: many services versus a few selectively intensive ones; specialist 'light' caseloads versus 'heavy' heterogeneous caseloads; number of cases and speed of handling with proportion of deteriorated problems; interests and standards of administrative sections (e.g. in keeping down costs) versus interests and standards of workers (e.g. in providing high quality services), and so on.

In resolving such conflicts, priorities have to be established.

Social Values, Objectives and Action

Deciding Between Objectives

In real-life situations, decision-makers are called upon to choose, as consciously as they know how, which among the wide variety of possible social objectives to give precedence to, assigning weights between them, and which to postpone. Only thus can eventual congruence among agency objectives be established, though even when fully aware of the power of conciliation, every value cannot be taken into account simultaneously.

Selecting an objective is the first series of choices in planning. The organization has at any moment of time alternative objectives which it can adopt. In the following situations, decisions as between one objective and another become particularly acute:

(i) when it is proposed that two objectives are being pursued which are to some degree incompatible;

(ii) when limited resources demand that choices be made on the relative priorities to be attached to different objectives;

(iii) when a situation of limited resources demands that choices should be made as to the degree of attainment of each objective, and priorities allocated in these terms.

In any comprehensive or adequate objectives-structure, these three situations will be pervasive.

In practical work situations, practitioners must decide which mix of possible objectives are most significant for each individual client, client group, or community, and which shall regrettably count as subsidiary objectives on which work cannot be done directly. They must decide which shall be limited, specific, key priority or preference objectives. Scarce resources resulting in lack of available time, may well demand that hopes for achieving other subsidiary targets are pinned on the ramifying or avalanche effects gained by achieving the key objectives.

Setting preference or priority objectives demands that the key variables in the community situation which the agency seeks to influence shall be delineated. In making the choice, we run the risk of inevitably complex objectives being used as hedges against unsatisfactory performance. The principle of choice has been delineated in the often-quoted maxim of Pareto[9] — that 80 per cent of our effective results are produced by 20 per cent of our daily activities.

Social problems may be defined using the 'Client Problem Dictionary' (See Appendix 2) or may be developed using elements of the kind embodied in the strategic objectives like alienation, deviance, inequality, dependency, economic dislocation, behavioural dislocation, and so on. Either way, decision-makers must rank these problems according to the priority they shall attach to meeting them. If they do not do this consciously, they will do it unconsciously, by implication, in terms of the way they differentially invest in services and what they spend their time on in the working situation. In making these choices, decision-makers are making value judgements about how far demand reflects genuine need. If they are unsure as to how far it does, then they must test their value judgements and one of the aims of community participation in this situation might well be to stimulate demand so that it reflects genuine need. The next step is to make corresponding choices amongst services which are judged to have the capability of supplying this demand or need with services which make some effective impact on priority social problems.

In making such choices decision-makers are subjected to influences from all directions. How much weight should they give to the various demands of pressure groups, professional bodies, other neighbouring services and departments, vocal staff, committee and councillors, ratepayer groups, bureaucrats, client and client family, all of whom probably desire a different future for the agency? Decision-makers have the task of finding their way around these conflicting values to gain legitimation and sanction for certain preference objectives if any effective action is to be taken at all.

Primary Objectives

The objectives chosen will be described as in some way primary, dominant, major, key or critical, though they may embody a greater or lesser number of secondary aspects or sub-objectives. Primary objectives will consist of the key states of affairs we most wish to achieve, even though this may mean forfeiting the attainment of other desirable objectives, or the central characteristics or aspects of a state of affairs which we wish to attain, even though secondary subsidiary aspects may be disregarded.

This process embodies subjective estimates of feasibility and the assumption that the key objectives can be achieved. Primary objectives will not form a completely utopian scheme (as would be the case if they were based exclusively on the ideal, requisite situation). Nor will the choice amount simply to a reaffirmation of the *status quo* (as would be the case if primary objectives were based entirely on a projection of the extant situation). They will, however, present some sort of innovation or initiative for the agency. Secondary objectives relate to those results subsidiary to the key results which may be undesirable or inevitable concomitants, or desirable, auxiliary concomitants. A particular objective can be irrelevant when action on it no longer produces the benefits it used to, or malign when action on it begins to produce more harm than good.

The process of deciding between objectives involves comparison of different values held by conflicting decision-makers; analysis of the grounds for holding these different values; evaluating competing objectives or values in advance of action by the survey of relevant research; and evaluating competing objectives or values after they have been put to the test in terms of concrete action. If no resolution is possible through analytic comparisons, then a straightforward bargaining process ensues in which participants trade off degrees of attainment of different objectives.

It is inevitable that the agency will not be able to achieve all it should like to. Objectives may thus have to be more or less compatible; relate more to a unique maximum than to a unique minimum, or vice versa; be achieved with more or less precision; be achieved more or less comprehensively; more or less facilitate other objectives; be achieved with fewer or more undesirable concomitants; or be achieved to a quantitively greater or lesser extent.

Decision Elements in Selecting Objectives

In ranking objectives, decision-makers may be influenced by the following aspects:

1. Current State
The current state of agency aspirations is reviewed, embodying explicit and implicit objectives established in the last policy declarations and still operative at present. The nature, structure and dynamics of the organization provides indicators here, as do historical trends descriptive of its past.

2. Projected State
Let us assume for a moment that the internal situation, the external environment and the extant objectives remain the same. If this is the case, how would things develop in future? Current trends indicative of the organization's probable future are relevant.

3. External Factors
These include potentialities and limitations of socio-economic, institutional, cultural, professional and technological factors helping to determine the agency's future.

4. Modifications of Current State
Certain features which are virtually unavoidable are likely to emerge in both the internal and external environments of the agency. If these are incorporated into the statement of objectives a partial picture of probable change in objectives is given. Also included here are commitments for the future established by previous actions and events

5. The Unexpected

The *kinds* of unexpected events which might occur and the sort of response mechanism necessary for the agency to develop further should be looked at.

6. Personnel Objectives

These refer to future states which the relevant personnel wish to pursue.

7. Range of Possible Developments

There are certain alternatives in the development of objectives. If things go exceptionally well and a range of favourable circumstances occur, certain optimistic developments would become likely. If things go exceptionally badly and a range of adverse circumstances occur, certain rather pessimistic developments would become likely. Taken together, the optimistic and pessimistic pictures of what might happen to change our aspirations represent the complete range of possible aspirations for the future.

8. Ideal

Those objectives which although perhaps ultimately unattainable can be approached to some degree need to be represented.

9. Interconnected Objectives

Casual interconnections between desirable states of affairs formulated in the agency's objectives must be evaluated. To pursue one objective may commit it unavoidably to the pursuit of other interconnected objectives. Some of these interconnections were explored earlier (See pp. 157—212).

We are relying on a mixture of three types of judgement: personal axioms about what the agency should be doing, based on the individual's professional training and experience, personal values and beliefs; calculations of cause and effect based on evidence; and political decisions or directions to be pursued by the community.

The decision involves a mixture of rational calculation from evidence and intuitive judgements of merit. Having taken into account the variables enumerated above, the final decisions on priorities will result in the following elements being ranked in order of significance. They may be ranked either directly or by implication in the way resources are actually allocated as between varying community problems:

1. Fundamental Cause

In choosing priority objectives, the decision may be made to define and work with the fundamental, underlying variables causing problem client (or community) behaviour. These are sometimes referred to by social psychologists as 'source traits'. A source trait is the underlying influence in (and cause of) observed correlations between behavioural elements. This strategy will normally imply a longer-term strategy of the kind often favoured in deep intensive casework with a psycho-dynamic base, or by longer-term community work.

2. Resource Capability

It may be decided instead to work with those problem variables which the workers' skills or intervention methods are most likely to make some impact on. Thus, a worker whose skills are predominantly in the area of marital counselling will tend to focus primarily on marital problems if these constitute one of the major problems and a choice has to be made.

3. Most Feasible Point of Intervention

If the client is sceptical about treatment, the worker may well choose to work first with those of his or her problems on which they are most likely to achieve together some initial, tangible success.

4. Probability of Treatment Success

The chosen priority objective may be to work with those areas of problem behaviour in which most movement (or improvement) is viable. This approach is often favoured by behaviour therapists.

5. Probablity of Client Satisfaction

If the client is resistant to treatment of certain of his or her problems, it may be advisable to focus on those for which he is demanding help and willing to accept some form of intervention. This latter treatment strategy is particularly important in that many clients object that social workers avoid and fail to deal directly with the problem they came about, in favour of some other area of concern which they do not perceive as relevant or do not agree shall be the focus for the worker's intervention.

6. Agency Credibility

Those objectives where failure would jeopardize the viability or credibility of the agency as a whole, with its consumers, rate-payers or constituency may be chosen. This approach to the decision is favoured by those taking a public relations view, but also by committee members.

7. Critical Variable

The choice may be a problem element which is in some way the key to several other areas of problem behaviour when success with this key variable might provide the most wide-ranging client benefits with minimal intervention. This strategy is very much that of those who take a systems approach to social work.

8. Agency Feasibility

Lastly, the choice of objective may be guided by constraints or limitations on the field of agency action. These are defined and circumscribed by:

(i) FIELD OF AGENCY ACTION

Decisions must be made as to what sphere of action shall be covered by the agency, defined in terms of:

immediate client-presenting problems;

underlying client problems;

problems of the client system and reference groups;

problems of the local neighbourhood;

problems of impinging institutions and agencies;

problems of the interaction between the client and his social environment.

(ii) TIME-SPAN OF AGENCY ACTION

Decisions must be made as to what time-span or horizon of action shall be covered by the agency, defined in terms of how far each of the following shall be pursued:

Demand Policy — work with existing clients whose need has been translated into demand;

Social Casualty Policy — work with clients with severest social need;

Preventive Policy — work with potential clients whose social needs and problems are as yet undetected or are only predicted.

(iii) OPPORTUNITIES AND CONSTRAINTS

Each objective is specified in terms of the opportunities and constraints on agency action arising in respect of each of the following elements:

problem identification;

client motivation, capacity, skills and resources;

resistance to treatment;

necessity for treatment;

attitudes of other relevant reference groups in the situation;

policies and resources of other agencies;

resource availability of the agency (including worker skills and time);

alternative possible treatment methods;

agreement with the client on decision and action;

evaluation of the effectiveness or ineffectiveness or the programme of action or intervention.

Upgrading and Downgrading

As a result of such processes, objectives are changed (i.e. upgraded, downgraded or replaced) in various ways. They may be acquired, in the sense that the person, group or agency begins to subscribe or adhere to an objective for the first time, or diffused more extensively over those involved, gaining more adherents. They may be rescaled, in that there is an increase in the intensity of their adherents' commitment to them or redeployed in the sense that they are applied over a wider context, field of action or domain of application. They may be re-emphasized in that certain changes in the situation may force them to our attention. The standards according to which an objective is assessed to have been attained may be raised, or additional standards for its attainment may be included. Or the interim targets or target dates necessary for the achievement of an objective may be given a more prominent place on the priority schedule.

A Note on Voluntary Agency Priorities

We have presented a range of alternative objectives, action programmes, services, functions and roles which might be said to apply either to public or voluntary social services agencies. It might be relevant at this point to define some priority objectives which seem to be emerging for voluntary agencies in the post-Seebohm situation:

1. To develop client advocacy functions which local authority services fail to provide.
2. To test sophisticated and expensive means of the evaluation of impact.
3. To experiment with and innovate new services, especially those which have yet to win broad-based public acceptance, or which are difficult — even illegal — for the public sector to mount.
4. To supplement services and programmes which are neglected by public sector services or allocated low priority.
5. To provide a continuous community-based perspective on social problems.

Basis for Selection

Evidently, if the banner goal of 'promoting community development' is chosen as the preference or priority objective, all kinds of other choices follow at each level. The agency will tend to be interested at the missions level either in sociological change by improving the present social situation and conditions in the community, or in the process type of objective where the aim is to develop community integration. If the former is chosen, the agency will tend to take the social planning perspective at the systems level so that the strategic objective becomes 'to reduce growth-inhibiting and promote growth-inducing elements in the individual's social environment'.

This can be translated in terms of strategic objectives as: reducing debilitative and homogeneous aspects of the social environment, economic poverty, social inequality, insecurity, stigmatization and the effects of breakdown.

Further choices than have to be made at the level of agency function and role between developing either social planning or social action functions and roles. Suppose it is decided to adopt a social action role and function. If the condition of the community is particularly acute, an emergency social action programme would be adopted as many United States social action groups have opted for. If time is on our side, a preventive strategy may be adopted, or if the times bode well, a developmental strategy aiming to develop community self-help and self-determination in the course of achieving concrete concessions from the establishment, Alinsky-style[10].

Let us assume the emergency strategy is chosen. Inevitably, this involves the community work area of service or intervention. Thence the priority choices for a hypothetical agency might follow this pattern:

Banner Goal: Promote community development.

Mission: Sociological change.

Systems Objective: To change the social environment.

Strategic Objective: To reduce growth-inhibiting elements in the individual's social environment.

Tactical Objective: To reduce debilitative aspects of the environment.

To reduce economic poverty.

To reduce social insecurity.

To reduce the effects of breakdown.

Key Service: Community work.

Agency Function and Role: Social action.

Agency Strategy: Emergency.

Similar patterns of choice may be worked out for different agencies. For example, one local authority social services department was clearly oriented as follows:

Banner Goal: Alleviate undesirable social conditions.

Mission: To deliver certain services efficiently to eligible clientele.

Systems Objective: To help the individual remove those major constraining factors which radically inhibit or reduce his ability to fulfil his fundamental needs and negotiate reality effectively.

Strategic Objective: To reduce individual's incapacities to cope with their social environment.

Tactical Objectives: To reduce agency inefficiency.

To reduce effects of breakdown.

To reduce deviance.

To reduce social malfunctioning.

Agency Clientele: A concentration on children and elderly.

Agency Services: Practical assistance.

Routine visiting.

Custodial care.

Agency Functions and Role: Administrative.

Agency Strategy: Emergency.

Priorities among objectives are sometimes signalled by the inclusion of clauses such as these: 'particularly in "high-need" areas of the community', 'especially where the disadvantaged, deprived or underprivileged are concerned'. Islington Social Services Department's programme objectives can be cited as one such example, where the concentration has been on twilight zones and depressed areas of the borough and on those clients manifesting the severest forms of social pathology.

II. STRATEGIES

Alternative Strategies

The choice of priority objectives is intimately related to the choice between emergency, preventive and development strategies at the level of political objectives. In making such complex choices at each level, decision-makers will tend to opt for various strategies which are classified below:

1. Short-Range Planning Strategy

The alternative is chosen which is the most immediately feasible to obtain, has the greatest pay-off in the short-term and deals with problems of the immediate situation adequately. This strategy is the one most likely to give initial, though perhaps limited, success.

2. Long-Range Planning Strategy

The alternative is chosen which would, if attained, be most likely to achieve optimal overall benefits in the total situation and help to resolve some fundamental, underlying problems. This strategy is the one most likely to give greater, though longer-term, success.

3. Maximizing Benefits Strategy

The alternative is chosen which produces the greatest amount of benefit as qualified by the likelihood of its succeeding in practice. This strategy is usually best where the consequences of alternative courses of action can be predicted with reasonable certainty.

4. Maximin Strategy

The worst possible outcome likely to result from each alternative (i.e. the lowest pay-off from each) is predicted, and then the alternative chosen which would give the best of these, minimize the risk of a particularly bad outcome and give the decision the greatest possible level of security. This strategy is usually best where is is difficult to predict results of any action taken. It is favoured by the pessimist and the cautious man who wishes to risk as little as possible.

5. Maximax Strategy

Alternatively, the best possible outcomes (i.e. the highest possible pay-off), likely to result from each alternative are predicted, and then the alternative chosen which would give the best of these and thus capitalize on the chances of a particularly good outcome. This is the strategy of the optimist and the bold man who goes for all or nothing.

6. Mix Strategy

The mix strategy is simply a consciously adopted combination of two or more of the above strategies.

7. Minimax Regret

The best and worst possible outcomes likely to result from each alternative (i.e. the highest and lowest pay-offs) are predicted. Suppose one of the alternatives has both the best pay-off possible if it succeeds and the worst pay-off possible if it fails and this is chosen in preference to others. If in practice it succeeds, we will be very glad to have chosen it since it had the highest pay-off. If it fails, we will very much regret our choice since it has the worst possible outcome.

Now if the difference between the highest possible pay-off and the lowest possible pay-off for this alternative had been estimated in advance, we would have shown how regretful we would be if it failed. An estimate of regret is thus placed against each alternative and then the alternative chosen which involves the least regret. This is the minimax regret strategy.

Illustration of Strategies

Let us exemplify these different strategies. A senior social worker knows from bitter experience that she cannot take on more than one additional case at this time. She therefore has to choose between two possible clients. One client has previously been dealt with by an experienced, trained social worker who has just left and has written: 'a hopeless case, completely unresponsive to casework and going from bad to worse'. Yet the current worker feels that, given time, some help could be provided especially if a new approach were tried. The other client has been dealt with by an untrained inexperienced social worker who has put in a request for another worker to help. The client's problems do not seem very great and a little, really expert help is probably all that is needed to set her on her feet again. The staff supervisor described the case as 'almost preventive work'. A third alternative is not to take on any new clients, but to do some groupwork of which she has had experience. Assuming these assessments are true, then if the current senior social worker chooses the first case, she will probably be adopting a strategy which is long-range and maximax, for if she is to succeed she will have to attempt to handle the total client situation and is aiming for a spectacular outcome. If she chooses the second case, she will probably be adopting a strategy which is short-range and maximin, since success seems most immediately feasible to obtain and there is less likelihood of failure. If, however, she chooses to do groupwork, she is probably adopting a 'maximize benefits' strategy since it would probably produce the greatest amount of benefit with some likelihood of success, thanks to her past experience.

Selecting Objectives

The final process of selecting may involve the following steps:
1. Interpret and diagnose the genesis or cause of need.
2. Project the probable consequences of the adoption of objectives and interventions necessary.
3. Tentatively select or amalgamate several of the most desirable and feasible objectives.
4. Try out allocations of resources and operations to these, making whatever modifications are necessary in the process.
5. Finalize objectives in the light of resource and operational constraints. It must also be recognized that there is a limit to how systematic we can afford to be in defining objectives. Our planning needs to converge towards some sort of resolution by the time action is required.
6. Implement objectives.
7. Determine after action has occurred whether the needs and objectives were actually met and whether some improvement in the problem area has taken place. The more such demonstration research studies are made, the more concrete evidence we have to support

chosen objectives, and the more they become matters of calculation rather than being decided axiomatically.

8. Revise the objectives in the light of reviewed action.

Conclusion:
Integrated Managing, Planning and Action Systems

'Here past and future are compared and reconciled' . . .
T.S. Eliot.

The approach to analyzing and implementing social services objectives which has been illustrated in this work, is suggestive of an integrated managing, planning and action system (I.M.P.A.C.T.S.). This is a process or methodology designed to achieve some junction of theory with action, policy with practice, plans with daily operations, professional work with administrative methods, decision-makers' intentions with situational constraints. 'Comprehensive planning', 'systems planning' or 'macro-rational decision-making' are terms sometimes used to describe the philosophy underlying this method, as outlined by Dror,[1] Lasswell,[2] and Etzioni,[3] among others.

The integrated managing, planning and action system (I.M.P.A.C.T.S.) embraces many specific stages and techniques. Some of these have been packaged by management consultants under such titles as management by objectives (M.B.O.), planned programming budgetting systems (P.P.B.S.), programme analysis and review (P.A.R.), priority scaling, input-output analysis, and manpower planning.

However, the process embodied in I.M.P.A.C.T.S. is distinct from these primarily administrative approaches in that the substantive professional content and methods used in the work area reviewed is fully integrated with administrative components. The process is not built out of the existing organizational framework of departments, divisions, sections, ranks and roles. Distinctions between levels of objectives are not based exclusively on perceptions deriving from the organizational hierarchy of policy-makers, managers, supervisors and operative staff. Instead it is based on a logical analysis of how objectives, resources and operations may be matched, with the implication that organizational structures may be adjusted to or rebuilt around the logic of the work process thus analyzed. Applied to the social services, the aim is to translate community social goals into effective service programmes. Other features of such a system have been outlined by Dror: "Comprehensive planning occupies an intermediate position between policy-making and operational planning . . . The noun 'comprehensiveness' refers to two interrelated characteristics, namely, attention to multiple dimensions of a system and an interdisciplinary approach . . . Sensitivity to both rational and extrarational components, to value assumptions and to political implications of social action must be added to the features of effective comprehensive planning . . . Beyond the various discrete features, effective comprehensive planning must be self-aware, self-evaluative and continuously self-developing."

The stages of integrated managing, planning and action systems (I.M.P.A.C.T.S.), may be outlined in the following general form. A commitment to agency planning is generated among all relevant groups, which may include the fund-supplying sources, consumer groups, professionals, community representatives and affected interest groups. A range of alternative possible objectives are suggested by each group. Information is gathered from all groups on trends, interests, preferences and other factors influencing the choice of objectives.

The total spectrum of possible agency objectives is reviewed. The optimal feasible objectives are selected. The full range of objectives are integrated into a unified system. They are aligned vertically, at different levels of abstraction and specificity. The general concern to promote individuality and reduce depersonalization is linked with such specific procedures as staff in an old persons' home knocking on the bedroom door and not entering unless invited, instead of barging straight in with visitors in tow. Objectives are aligned horizontally across several different streams of interest and concern. The aim of increasing social interaction among residents of homes is balanced against the aim of increasing privacy and non-intrusion. Objectives implicit in the current mode of operating (extant objectives) are compared with those avowed desirable (requisite objectives). Thus block toiletting in an old persons' home induces institutionalization, contradicting the avowed value that each resident should be treated as an individual. Objectives are aligned through time by establishing interim milestone targets which might lead from the extant through to the requisite situation (e.g. the toiletting process is not confined to a particular period during the day). Objectives to which agency personnel are personally committed (through vocational interests or on the basis of what is perceived and assumed appropriate to agency functioning) are aligned with objectives deemed to define agency interests and effectiveness.

Various methods are used to handle built-in tensions and conflicts which manifest themselves when varied objectives are thus delineated — some have been explored in this work. Priority objectives are agreed in the light of group assessment of interests, trends, problems, social values, and awareness of wider implications. Sanction is gained for priority objectives from relevant groups, and the sanctioned objectives are promulgated to all concerned. Agreed objectives are translated into specific programmes of action at different levels. Consequences are evaluated after action has been taken to achieve the objectives. Revisions are made to agreed objectives accordingly, and the planning process is recycled.

Planning Implementation
There are several approaches to implementing integrated managing, planning and action systems (I.M.P.A.C.T.S.). Individual staff participate in planning seminars, thereafter applying the principles within their own areas of discretion. The approach spreads outwards from this base as effectiveness is demonstrated by the trained 'change-agents'. Thus, objectives formulated in planning seminars by fieldwork managers have been used to implement area offices' planning systems, afterwards being adopted as overall agency objectives.

One-to-one implementation occurs when manager-staff relations begin to be regulated along principles implicit in integrated planning systems. These form role relationship models for other sections. Groups of staff may apply the approach to their own areas as teams, using project group methods.

Corporate implementation occurs when all agency staff endeavour to implement the integrated planning system together. Periods of reorganization, for example, 1970 Social Services Act or 1974 Local Government reorganization, often provide the occasion. Inter-agency implementation occurs when different agencies jointly act to achieve agreed objectives; for example, some social services departments and hospital boards have jointly agreed compatible programmes to increase community rather than residential care for various client groups.

Lastly, in conjunction with community workers of a social services agency, various community groups may form coalitions to implement various objectives, for example, to improve levels of maintenance of dwellings by housing authorities. Agreement of planning methods precedes agreement on objective.

Planning embraces on the one hand, step-by-step, time-phased schedules of action — e.g. a network map for moving a day centre from one locale to another. On the other, it includes comprehensive sets of alternative systems of valuation, analysis, prediction, allocation and operation — e.g. comprehensive simulation of community social processes. Prefix the word 'social', and the range of concern covers anything from planning an entire social system like a new town, to evolving specific task targets for day nursery workers.

Social planning is a process of systematic social development to achieve given social objectives in the interest of a given population with given problems or concerns. It is a continuous, conscious activity aimed at objectives which are progressively realized through sequences of means-ends and cause-effect relations. Planning involves adjustment to circumstances, possibilities, resistances, stimulating and countervailing forces. It involves clarifying objectives, pointing up positive or negative consequences of alternative solutions, using foresight to achieve predetermined goals, applying values, and continuous evaluation to improve strategies. Planning usually addresses new problems and needs, not limiting itself to accumulated past interventions and responses, and ushering in a series of guides to future action.

Genuine planning is marked by several aspects. Decision-makers try to match values, resources, knowledge and action. They do not merely think ahead to the next thing to be done (e.g. calling a tenants' meeting on an estate). They anticipate probable resistances (e.g. the social committee may oppose the tenants' meeting), and envisage appropriate responses which might help overcome such resistances (e.g. engineer alternative support for the tenants' meeting). As in chess, planning involves thinking and working at least three moves ahead, including how to cope with contingencies and counteractions. It involves considering pros and cons of several alternatives (e.g. written, verbal, individual, small group, formal or informal contact with tenants) rather than fixing on one action course. Moreover, planning entails envisaging proposed developments of the current situation (e.g. establishing a tenants' association) in the context of the wider system in which we are intervening (e.g. the social structure of life on the estate) so as to take account of ramifying consequences (e.g. effects on housing authority relations) through an extended time-span (e.g. minimally a year). We need to think at least one dimension beyond the current problem situation (e.g. to the community's power over the pattern of its own social life).

Resources are mobilized (e.g. tenants supply time and expertise while the Council supplies facilities). A major element distinguishing planning from blueprinting is plan adjustment. Feedback from action taken casts light on infeasibilities, errors and gaps in original plans (e.g. those uncovered when tenants show that lack of play space and social facilities poses a more urgent requirement than petitioning housing authorities for improved maintenance). Some attempt is made to control chance, to set some pattern on otherwise random events through conscious, willed intention (e.g. the tenants do not simply trust themselves to the goodwill and efficiency of housing authorities).

Effective planning has some impact on the environment (e.g. the estate becomes more habitable), not simply on the planners. One effect will be some redistribution of power or resources (e.g. balance of power tipped to favour tenants more than housing authorities have hitherto allowed). This in turn means several interest-groups are enlisted in the programme (the poorly housed, the isolated, the bored, the housing authority, wardens, the social committee, adjacent neighbours, etc.). Nor can any of this occur without informal or formal organizational groupings having some authority and accountability to progress the plan through (e.g. tenant groups having legal rights, housing authorities having property ownership). Lastly, planning entails that the system will at the end of the day, structure and regulate itself independently of further planning interventions (e.g. tenants' associations, once effectively established, may no longer need the support of community workers).

Outcomes of effective social planning may include: new policies (e.g. preventive policies); new programmes (e.g. day-care centres for mixed clientele); programme coordination (e.g. of community and residential care allowing easier client transfer between them); service integration (e.g. through intake teams); programme and service innovations (e.g. introduction of brief, short-term casework); new priorities for allocating resources (e.g. more priority to the social problem of homelessness); new professional and administrative decisions (e.g. on criteria for entry to residential homes).

Instead of customary definitions, it may be more helpful to say what planning should *not* be. It should not be unconscious, non-deliberate, unsystematic, unimplemented, chaotic, a one-shot leap-in-the-dark, local in scope, lacking authority, lacking redistributive effects, without influence on the environment, divorced from real-world happenings, unevaluated, chance-dependent, lacking explicit evaluations, unconcerned with causes. Something may be said to be planned if an affirmative answer can be given to one or several of the questions:

    (i) Have options and their possible consequences been reviewed?
   (ii) Have objectives and resources been matched systematically?
  (iii) Have outcomes been monitored causing objectives to be redefined?
  (iv) Has the course of events changed in ways which would not have occurred with pre-design?
   (v) Have some powers or resources been redistributed?
  (vi) Have ramifying interactions of variables been monitored?
 (vii) Have several interest groups been related?
(viii) Have accountability structures been established to progress through appropriate action?
  (ix) Have we envisaged effects over a time span of at least one year?
   (x) Have values underlying action been made explicit?
  (xi) Have interconnections with the wider system or context been explored?
 (xii) Have any specific problems been resolved through plan-implementation?
(xiii) Have resistances and responses to them been anticipated?
(xiv) Are causes being addressed rather than their later

manifestations?

(xv) Have things been set on a course which will have its own momentum, not requiring continuous intervention?

Appendices

Appendix 1:
Social Services Programme Structure

I. SAMPLE PROGRAMME STRUCTURE BY CLIENT GROUP*

Services for Socially Handicapped

To plan and provide social support and care for socially-handicapped families and individuals.

A. Community Care
1. Practical assistance and material aid, including assistance for legally sanctioned cases
2. Advisory services
3. Practical treatment services
    (a) Nursing
    (b) Physiotherapy
    (c) Specialist instruction
    (d) Recuperative holidays
    (c) Clothing
    (f) Heating
    (g) Bedding
4. Domestic services
    (a) Home helps
    (b) Meals-on-wheels
    (c) Sitting-in services
    (d) Nurseries
    (e) Playgroups
    (f) Occupational therapy

* Similar programmes may be developed for other groups such as addicts, unemployed, unsupported parents, young people, couples with marital relations problems, ex-offenders, and so on.

   (g) holidays to relieve family
 5. Diversional services
   (a) Handicraft courses
   (b) Leisure services, including grants to playgroups
 6. Comfort services — practical aids
 7. Therapeutic and problem-solving services
   (a) Brief casework
   (b) Extended casework
   (c) Conjoint family therapy
   (d) Groupwork
   (e) Community work
   (f) Behavioural therapy
   (g) Reality therapy
   (h) Milieu therapy
   (i) Crisis therapy
 8. Support for voluntary agencies
 9. Prevention of illness
10. Clinic services
11. Midwifery services
12. Nutritional services
13. Family-planning services
14. Temporary accommodation
15. Short-term residential treatment

B. Residential Care

Services for Children

To plan and provide social support and care to problematic children through counselling, domiciliary, day or residential services.

A. Community Care
 1. Preventive services for children at risk
 2. Advising and befriending children who have gone out of care
 3. Financial assistance for children who have gone out of care
 4. Service to the courts, probation and Home Office
 5. Fostering services
 6. Supervision of child-minding arrangements, privately fostered children and day-care arrangements
 7. After-care supervision and evaluation of ex-approved school children
 8. Adoption services
 9. Joint service planning and provision with juvenile bureaux
10. Joint service planning and provision with youth employment
11. Joint service planning with youth groups

12. Clinic services
13. Social services in schools
14. Guidance services
15. Joint service planning and provision with health services

B. **Residential Care**
1. Reception into care
2. Rehabilitation
3. Assumption of parental rights
4. Acceptance into care as without parents
5. Treatment of children in care — reception home, boarding out, adoption, remand homes and other residential accommodation
6. Reviewing children in care

Services for Physically Ill and Handicapped

1. To provide support other than medical or nursing skills to persons who are ill, recovering from illness, handicapped or adjusting to handicap.
2. To plan and provide social support and care to the chronic sick, the physically-handicapped and their families by counselling, domiciliary, day-care and residential services and particularly by the provision of aids, appliances, adaptation, teaching, employment and workshops.

A. **Community Care**

FOR BOTH MOBILE DISABLED AND THE HOUSEBOUND HANDICAPPED
1. Access to buildings
2. Aids and adaptations
3. Rehabilitation
4. Employment
5. Recreation
6. Holidays
7. Sheltered employment
8. Treatment services
9. Domestic services
10. Comfort services
11. Employment agency services

B. **Residential Care**

Services for the Elderly

To plan and provide social support and care for the elderly and the family of which they are members through counselling, domiciliary, day or residential services.

A. Community Care
 1. Practical assistance
 2. Financial aid
 3. Advisory services
 4. Treatment services
 5. Domestic services
 6. Diversional services
 7. Comfort services
 8. Day centres
 9. Work centres
10. Nutritional services
11. Foot clinics
12. Employment-agency services
13. Service for incontinence

B. Residential Care

Services for Mentally Ill and Handicapped

 1. To plan and provide social support and care to mentally-ill people, alcoholics, drug addicts, etc. and support to their families through the mental-health programme and by the provision of hostels, schools, workshops, etc.
 2. To plan and provide social support and care to mentally handicapped people and support to their families through the mental health programme and by the provision of day care, hostels, workshops, clubs, etc.

A. Community Care
 1. Junior training centres
 2. Adult training centres
 3. Day centres
 4. Brief casework
 5. Extended casework
 6. Treatment services
 7. Sheltered employment
 8. Group homes
 9. Advisory services
10. Practical assistance
11. Domestic services
12. Diversional services
13. Comfort services

14. Employment-agency services

B. **Residential Homes**

Services for the Population Generally

1. Practical assistance
2. Advisory services
3. Day centres
4. Community work
5. Short-term support services

II. EXAMPLES OF SUB-PROGRAMME STRUCTURE

Investigation and Development Services

1. Investigate prevalence and incidence of need and demand for each agency service.
2. Identify those in need of a service.
3. Adjust criteria for service delivery to changing demands and needs.
4. Plan extension of service provision accordingly.
5. Incorporate new professional and technological developments into service provision.

Intake Services

To process enquiries or requests or to render brief service on behalf of clientele to determine whether the agency is able to meet the client's needs through its services or not.
Start-Point: An enquiry or request.
End-Point: A decision to refer; not accept; accept with clearly defined and mutually understood goals; or client withdrawal.
Time-Limit: Every effort must be made to complete the process within thirty days; a sixty-day period should be sufficient for any but the most exceptional case.

THE INTAKE PROCESS

Step 1	Step 2	Step 3
1. Enquiry	Answer enquiry	Investigation and study
2. Request (a) client	Accept or reject for further study	Department intake decision (a) Case accepted

Step 1	Step 2	Step 3
(b) agency referral		(i) Reach with client clearly defined and mutually understood plan for assistance, care or other services (ii) Confirmation to client
3. Complaint or report	Validate complaint or report and assign for study	(b) Case not accepted (i) Denial (ii) Withdrawn (iii) Referral
4. Court Order	Accept Court Order	Court intake decision (a) Dismiss (b) Waiver (c) Referral (d) Process on petition (e) Process without petition

Definitions

An *enquiry* is the seeking of information about the service in general rather than expressing a desire that service be provided.

A *request for service* is an expressed desire made by a person on behalf of himself or by some other person acting on his behalf.

Referral is a request made by one agency to another to provide a service.

A *complaint* or *report* is an expression or concern that becomes a request of the agency.

A *Court Order* is a specific court mandate relative to a person within the service function of the agency.

Screening Services

Definition: To process an enquiry or request for service to determine if an answer can be provided to the enquiry; if further study is needed; if a referral should be made elsewhere; or if the request is not to be accepted.

Start-point: An enquiry or a request.

End-point: An enquiry is answered; a decision is made that further study is needed; a referral to another resource is made; a decision is made not to accept; or when the request is withdrawn.

Study Services*

Definition: To determine if the agency, through its services, is able to meet the needs of the client and, if so, to establish a plan.

Start-point: A decision is reached that a study is necessary.

End-point: The agency and client reach a defined and mutually understood plan for assistance; care and/or service; with referral to another agency; with agency denial; with a determination that the client has the ability to meet his need; or with the client's withdrawal.

A. Study Services for other Agencies

1. To evaluate the family, relative or foster home of a child or children who are about to move or who have moved to the area.
2. To evaluate homes of relatives as a resource for an infant whose mother is unable to take care of the child.
3. To gather social history for adoptive or other purposes when parents or a mother are living in one place, while their child is living elsewhere.
4. To process a consent for adoption, or ascertain the mother's or parents' willingness to allow an existing consent elsewhere to be acted upon.
5. To contact the child's alleged father to ascertain social history and/or possible financial support.

B. Study for Protective Services

Definition: To determine the nature and reasons for a child's neglect and whether the parents can themselves take the necessary steps to correct the neglect, whether the parents, with agency help, can effect the necessary change, or whether action is necessary to remove the children from a harmful environment.

Start-point: Neglect or possible neglect has been validated.

End-point: A mutual decision is made by the client and agency to work on problems; the client seeks to use other resources; the problem is resolved during the study process; or the client rejects help and the agency seeks court intervention.

(i) FOSTER-CARE RECRUITMENT

Definition: To undertake promotional activities designed to secure prospective foster-parent applications.

(ii) FOSTER-CARE SCREENING

Definition: To process an enquiry or request to determine the advisability of further study of foster-care applicants.

---

*Study services may, of course, be provided for any service which warrants this procedure.

Start-point: Receipt of enquiry or request.
End-point: Answering enquiry; withdrawal or rejection of request; or assignment for further study.

(iii) BOARDING CARE STUDY

Definition: To determine the suitability of adoptive and foster-home applicants.
Start-point: A decision for a study.
End-point: The written report of the study is approved; the applicant's request is accepted or rejected.

(iv) RE-EVALUATION

Definition: To determine the continuing suitability of foster family.
Start-point: With complaint; request for change of licence; or need for annual re-evaluation.
End-point: With decision to continue, modify or discontinue use.

Consultation

Definition: To increase the knowledge, understanding and effectiveness of personnel in other divisions of the Department and to other community agencies concerned with the social problems of clients which confront the department.
Start-point: A request by personnel in other departmental divisions or other agencies for information or for help in formulating a plan to meet the needs of the family and handicapped child.
End-point: The consultation is concluded by mutual agreement; or the request is withdrawn.

Support for Voluntary Agencies

1. Grants to voluntary agencies.
   To enable voluntary agencies to carry out general or particular tasks either directly or on behalf of the Council, in line with or as an augmentation of Council policy.
2. Grants to Playgroups.
   To provide financial assistance to voluntary playgroups offering day-care facilities, requiring places on medical and/or social grounds.

Child Protection Services

Definition: To assure the health, well-being and safety of the children and the integrity of the family in cases when, according to community standards, the children are abused, exploited or receiving inadequate care.

Start-point: On completion of the intake process with cases for which the agency assumes responsibility.

End-point: When the protection of the children is assured through adequate family functioning; the date of the Court Order; or voluntary agreement for the removal of the children from the neglectful situation.

A. Community Care

(i) SERVICES TO HANDICAPPED CHILDREN IN THEIR OWN HOMES

Definition: To improve the children's functioning and the parents' ability to cope effectively when the children are retarded, emotionally disturbed or physically handicapped and are not receiving this service elsewhere in the department.

Start-point: Completion of the intake process for cases for which the agency assumes responsibility.

End-point: The assurance of the welfare and optimum health of the child and of parental acceptance of the child's limitations; or the decision that no further service is needed.

(ii) SERVICES TO PARENTS AND HANDICAPPED CHILD

Definition: To enable parents and child to make use of out-patient rehabilitative, educational and/or remedial facilities to improve the child's functioning; to evaluate and enhance parental ability to accept and to deal effectively with the problem; and to help the child realize his potentials for self-care, education and adjustment within the family and in the community.

Start-point: On completion of the intake process for those cases accepted by the agency for service; or when a mutual decision has been reached by parents, child and the agency that help in the home setting is the appropriate means to meet the problem.

End-point: When parents and child have demonstrated their ability to meet mutual needs without further services from the agency; when it is determined that service to parents and the child in their own home does not meet his needs; with referral to another resource; or withdrawal by parents and child.

(iii) PARENTAL CARE SERVICE

Definition: To enable parents to give acceptable care to meet their children's needs, including helping them to change behaviour and attitudes which impair their parental role.

Start-point: A mutual decision is made by the client and agency to work on the problem.

End-point: Parents are giving adequate care to their children; or service is ineffective in eliminating the neglect and the court decision or voluntary agreement is made to remove the children from their home.

(iv) UNSUPPORTED PARENTS SERVICES
Definition: To help resolve the physical, emotional and other problems of unmarried parenthood.
Start-point: Acceptance of case for on-going service.
End-point: The health and welfare of mother and child are assured; or the client withdraws.

(v) LIAISON WITH JUVENILE BUREAUX
Definition: To provide information and advice to the bureaux on all children charged with offences who are known to the department.

B. Residential Care

(i) PLACEMENT AND FOLLOW-UP
Definition: To place children in foster or institutional care and provide service to foster parents, institutional personnel and children, particularly during the first three months since this is a particularly crucial time in terms of success or failure of placement.
Start-point: Placement into foster or institutional care.
End-point: After first three months of placement.

(ii) CONTINUED SUPERVISION
Definition: To provide on-going service of care and advice to foster parents, institution personnel and to children subsequent to the first three months.
Start-point: The beginning of the fourth month of placement.
End-point: The termination of custody; termination of voluntary agreement; conclusion of guardianship; or when by department and/or court plan the child returns to his own home and custody remains with the agency.

(iii) COORDINATION OF EXTERNAL RECEIVING HOMES
Definition: To supervise the receiving home parents, in controlling intake and serving as liaison between these parents and the department.
Start-point: Assignment of the coordination responsibility.
End-point: Closing of the home; or continued settlement of children in home.

(iv) SERVICES TO PARENTS OF CHILDREN IN CARE
Definition: (a) To help parents meet their responsibilities while their child is in care; (b) To work with the parents towards the return to their own home of children for whose care the department has

responsibility by reason of custody or voluntary agreement.

Start-point: With custody or voluntary agreement, and assignment of responsibility for service to such parents.

End-point: The child returns home; parent abandons child; another agency assumes responsibility; or the department terminates service.

(v) PREPARATION FOR CHILD'S PLACEMENT

Definition: To provide services to parents, prior to placement or replacement, to help them understand and accept the reasons for placement and, when possible, to enable them to participate in the process of placement.

Start-point: Date of legal custody of child, date of voluntary agreement for placement or assignment of responsibility for service to such parents.

End-point: Placement.

(vi) ADOPTION SERVICES

Definition: (a) To board out children to foster parents who are prepared to consider accepting them as a full member of their family wherever this is possible; (b) To arrange adoption of children where necessary under the provisions of the Adoption Act 1958, acting as welfare authority for protected children, as guardian *ad litem* agent appointed by the Court, as adoption agency, as respondent to enquiries from other local authorities; (c) To give the child a new set of legal parents by matching, placement and supervisory services to a child legally free for adoption and to his adoptive parents.

Start-point: Completion of the intake process for the child and study process for the adoptive applicants.

End-point: The Court Order of legal adoption, or with the decision of non-adoptability of child.

(vii) SUPERVISION OF ADOPTIVE PLACEMENT

Definition: To supervise the child in adoptive placement, evaluate his adjustment, counsel adoptive parents, and carry through the court process which does not culminate in legal adoption.

Start-point: Placement of the child in the adoptive home.

End-point: Granting or denying the legal adoption by the court.

(viii) AFTER-CARE SERVICES

Definition: To provide services to the child and his parents after his return home, when this is the permanent plan.

Start-point: The child returns home.

End-point: The termination of custody, or when the parents and department agree that services are no longer needed.

Fieldwork Services*

To provide community support services in order to safeguard people at risk, maintain them within their chosen homes and neighbourhoods, and to prevent further social problems and consequential suffering.

A. Advisory Services
To provide information, literature, referral and suggestions to individuals and groups who require it on specific problems.

B. Brief Service
1. To provide emergency service or referral of short duration (e.g. less than thirty days).
2. To provide minor financial assistance in a crisis.
3. To provide immediate practical assistance and advice in the short term.

C. Casework Services
To provide skilled casework support for families and individuals having personal, social or material difficulties, living in or coming under the responsibility of the local authority social services department.
1. To build a relationship between worker and client as a means of enabling the client to identify his problems, adopt appropriate attitudes, develop appropriate skills and then to resolve his problems.
2. To call upon, as necessary, the present statutory and voluntary resources available, so that the client may operate at an adequate level and function in society.

D. Groupwork Services
To form and maintain effective client groups which help each individual member meet his own needs, improve his emotional health, or help organize services so as better to meet his needs.

To use groups to help break down social isolation; to bring certain clients into the social community; to help reduce stigmatization; to help achieve certain changes through social action; to help individual participants learn new modes of adaptive social behaviour via their group membership.

E. Community Work and Development Services
To discover, encourage and assist community participation in the development of the social services, to interpret Council policy in the community, to feed back the views of the community as a guide to

*Sub-programmes may be analogously developed for other types of services.

future policy.

1. To encourage the development of community identity through clubs, play centres, associations, etc. and by the provision of professional support, information, stimulation and grant aid.
2. To help the development of social and physical environment by involvement in social planning.
3. To assist local groups to clarify their needs and to take collective action to meet these needs.
4. To encourage community organizations to evaluate the quality of service provided.
5. To provide adequate information services on the range of social services available to the community.
6. To provide support to voluntary organizations.
7. To enlist the services of volunteers to complement professional staff.
8. To liaise with other planning agencies of the community.

F. Service to the Courts
To provide a service to the courts as specified under the Adoption Act 1958, the Matrimonial Causes Act, the Matrimonial Proceedings Magistrates Court Act 1960, the Family Law Reform Act 1969, Children and Young Persons Acts.

G. Administrative Services
1. Administration, personnel and clerical support for delivery of other services.
2. Specific provision of some services (e.g. access to buildings, registration, receivership, burials and cremations etc.).
   (a) To provide social assessment for housing allocation system.
   (b) To participate in identifying needs for special housing provision for the elderly and handicapped.
   (c) To liaise with housing managers.
   (d) To provide after-care services for special schools.
   (e) To liaise with education services and education welfare.
   (f) To liaise with the Supplementary Benefits Commission.
   (g) To improve the effectiveness of the social care content of Health Care Programmes.

III. EXAMPLES OF SERVICE TARGETS

Fieldwork Services

A. Fieldwork Time
1. To reduce by half the total number of cases which are both

unvisited and unclosed within the next month, and completely within the next four months.

2. To reduce mean client waiting time of 2 weeks before the first visit to 1 week within the next month, and to 2 days within the next four months.

3. To reduce within the next two months the mean delay of 2 months between first and second client visit to 1 month wherever a brief casework sequence of eight visits is planned.

4. To reduce within the next two months the mean number of visits for a planned long-term casework sequence from 32 to 24 for 80 per cent of longer-term cases.

5. To analyze all cases within the next month in terms of problem syndromes as defined in the diagnostic handbook, and calculate the mean amount of time spent on each problem syndrome.

6. To close, within the next month; all cases unvisited for six months by re-referral, suggestion to client or to client family or by supply of alternative support mechanisms.

B. Fieldwork Quality

1. To record a preliminary diagnosis on the first visit of each new case (in which ongoing visits will occur) in terms of the problem syndromes defined in the diagnostic handbook (e.g. of the kind illustrated on pp. 385—402) in terms of additional relevant problems variables.

2. To record on the first visit the fieldwork prediction of the probable development of the problem diagnosed.

3. To record on the first visit the specific targets for the individual case and the time period for a review of the achievement or non-achievement of these targets.

4. To record on the first visit the specific methods of intervention which will probably or actually be used on the particular case to achieve the target objective.

5. To record on each subsequent visit, revisions to preliminary diagnosis, prediction, case targets and methods of intervention, or additional evidence in support of the original diagnosis, prediction, case targets or methods of intervention.

6. To review with the supervisor any case on which diagnosis, prediction, case targets and methods of intervention have been revised on more than three successive visits or more than seven times.

7. To improve client's overall situation:

From	To
Problem syndromes E	Problem syndromes D
D	C
C	B
B	A
A	norm

Over the next four months to redistribute the overall amount of time spent on cases analyzed by problem syndrome as follows:

Syndrome	From Old Priority	To New Priority
1A	41	40
1B	3	1
1C	2	21
1D	1	31
1E	31	11
2A	42	41
2B	6	2
2C	5	22
2D	4	32
2E	32	12
3A	43	43
	etc.	

C. Fieldwork Content
1. To refer through a case to another agency within one day of contact.
2. To produce a social history report for the court within a fortnight.
3. To provide an escort for a child.
4. To act as an interpreter of the client's situation in respect of the court.
5. To obtain for the client a service from another agency (e.g. a grant for a school uniform, reconnection of the electricity or gas supply from public utility companies, nursery or residential placement for a client) within the next month or two.
6. To supplement the parental role (e.g. in respect of domestic or sex education) within the next six months.
7. To help a mother to be able to undertake part-time employment within the next six months.
8. To ensure within the next nine months that a child in care is settled in work and accommodation as near to the time of leaving school as possible.
9. To help a client newly suffering from a physical handicap (e.g. blindness) to make a primary adjustment to his changed condition

within the space of the next eight months.

10. To establish a dependent person or family (e.g. an unsupported parent and children) in the community as a self-supporting entity within the next year.

11. To develop and test out interpersonal relationships with clients as part of an evaluation of the suitability of the clients to obtain legal guardianship of a child or infant in care with the next year.

12. To help a chronic depressive establish her own identity and independence from her present neurotic dependence on other community figures within the next year.

13. Within the space of eighteen months, to help a married couple clarify and understand the strengths in their relationship and gain insight into the dynamics of their mutual behaviour so as to live together more harmoniously.

Day Care and Domiciliary Services

A. Day Care Services

To provide care and attention during the day for those unable to cope adequately at home or to ease the burden of others caring for such persons and thus reduce the demand on permanent residential accommodation, and delay the need for permanent care in individual cases.

(i) PREVENTIVE

To contribute to a total supportive environment for certain of the socially disabled, enabling them to be cared for, maintained or helped through a time of difficulty or crisis without having to be removed from their own home to a local-authority-maintained institution of some kind, and thus retaining a higher level of self-determination and self-care.

(ii) REHABILITATIVE

To contribute to a more adequate level of independent social, occupational and physical functioning and productiveness, perhaps even to the point where (ideally) the client becomes a fully productive member of society.

(iii) CURATIVE

To provide opportunities for social interaction and reduce loneliness and emptiness which so often characterizes the lives of the socially handicapped, while enabling them to remain in their own home.

(iv) AMELIORATIVE

To provide some relief to relatives who find the care of severely disabled family members extremely burdensome, and some expert and varied physical treatment for those who need this.

(v) DAY NURSERY SERVICES
To provide for the day care of children under five in certain priority classes.

(vi) LUNCHEON CLUB SERVICES
To provide a cheap mid-day meal seven days a week in comfortable surroundings and at a reasonable distance from their home for those elderly, physically or mentally handicapped persons wishing to avail themselves of this service and to provide transport to the club where nesessary.

(vii) WORK CENTRE SERVICES
To provide group employment in sheltered conditions and for modest rewards so as to encourage old people and the physically and mentally handicapped to participate in useful and self-fulfilling communal activities.

(viii) SPECIAL SCHOOLS
To provide care and training for children aged 5—16 who, because of their mental handicap, have been found unsuitable for education in schools within the educational system.

(ix) ADULT TRAINING CENTRES
To provide daily care, training and occupation for adults who, because of their handicaps, are unable to survive in open employment.

(x) RECREATIONAL SERVICES
To encourage social intercourse between socially handicapped, elderly, physically and mentally handicapped persons to prevent them from becoming isolated. To give them opportunities of enjoying their lives despite physical, mental or social constraints, and to stimulate a sense of involvement with and contribution to the community through recreational activities in their own homes, at day centres, through outings, or elsewhere in the community.

(xi) EMPLOYMENT SERVICES
To assist the unemployed to obtain suitable employment in open or sheltered industry as appropriate, and to provide employment for those unable to achieve this.

(xii) REHABILITATIVE SERVICES
To assist physically or mentally disabled people to overcome the

adverse effects of their disabilities and encourage them to achieve the maximum degree of independence and make a useful contribution to society.

B. Domiciliary Services
To provide domiciliary help for households where household maintenance is impossible or difficult owing to illness or incapacitation.

(i) HOLIDAY SERVICES
To provide annual holidays at a nominal charge to as many socially and recreationally deprived people as possible, so that the quality of their lives is enhanced.

(ii) AIDS AND ADAPTATION SERVICES
To provide aids to daily living and to carry out adaptations to homes which will enable the elderly, physically and mentally handicapped people to achieve a greater degree of independence in their personal care and domestic activities.

(iii) HOME HELP SERVICES
To provide daily home care services to compensate for incapacities to cope with household management.

Residential Services and Specific Residential Targets

1. To provide residential treatment and care for those who are unable effectively to support themselves (or be supported) in the community.
2. To concentrate small-unit residential services in or near the community from which the residents come so as to maintain contact with friends, familial contacts and familiar localities, and to use these services for treatment in providing a fresh start for some people and as the ultimate form of care for others, for whom the only alternative would be hospitalization.

(i) ASSESSMENT
To provide an environment in which some client problems can be diagnosed and assessed before they are referred through to the appropriate treatment programme.

(ii) SHELTER
To enable certain clients to live out part of their lives for a period of time, sheltered from the strains which would otherwise be too much for them in the wider community.

(iii) THERAPY

To provide for certain clients an environment which is conducive to carrying out a specific, time-delimited therapeutic programme, which is of sufficiently short duration for the focus to be on how the client will live in the community after the programme is complete.

(iv) CUSTODIAL

To provide protection for certain clients or to protect the community from them.

A. Residential Services

(i) TEMPORARY ACCOMMODATION SERVICES

To provide temporary accommodation to homeless persons suited to the needs of individual circumstances.
1. To ensure adequate accommodation for unsupported mothers immediately preceding or following confinement.
2. To provide adequate facilities for the rehabilitation of families with special problems.
3. To provide temporary accommodation for single persons with social or psychological disabilities.

(ii) REHABILITATION OF PERSONS IN RESIDENTIAL CARE

To diminish the need to keep people in residential care by offering advice, guidance and assistance.

(iii) RECEPTION INTO CARE

To receive into care children under 15 with no parent or guardian, or whose parents or guardians are permanently or temporarily prevented from providing proper care and up-bringing.

(iv) ASSUMPTION OF PARENTAL RIGHTS

To assume parental rights in circumstances where parents are mentally unfit or have persistently failed to discharge their obligations as parents.

(v) ACCEPTANCE INTO CARE UNDER A CARE ORDER

To receive into care all those children committed to the care of the local authority under the Children and Young Persons Act 1969.

(vi) TREATMENT OF PEOPLE IN RESIDENTIAL CARE

To provide appropriate care for each person in residential homes, so as to further his or her total mental or emotional physical well-being.

(vii) BOARDING OUT SERVICES

To afford children and others in care the maximum opportunity for development of their potentialities by boarding them out in foster homes where these are available and appropriate.

(viii) PROVISION FOR PRIVATELY FOSTERED CHILDREN
To review progress and well-being of foster children according to specified criteria.

(ix) REVIEWING PERSONS IN CARE
To review the progress of every person in residential care every six months.

(x) ADVISING AND BEFRIENDING CHILDREN WHO HAVE GONE OUT OF CARE
To advise and befriend any people over compulsory school age but under eighteen, who have been in local authority care, providing financial assistance, under the Children and Young Persons Act 1963, Section 58, as necessary.

(xi) PROPERTY AND RECEIVERSHIP SERVICES
To protect the moveable property of persons admitted to residential and hospital care under Section 47 of the National Assistance Act 1948, and to act as receiver for people in such care, who are unable to manage their affairs.

(xii) REGISTRATION AND PROVISION SERVICES
To ensure adequate standards are maintained at establishments managed by voluntary or private organizations which are registered by the Council under statute, and to register annually any society making arrangements for the adoption of children when its administration centre is situated within the community covered by the bureau.

(xiii) TRANSPORT SERVICES
To provide such transport services as are necessary for the carrying out of the services listed above.

B. Specific Residential Targets

(i) COMMUNITY CHILDREN'S HOMES
Within the next 2 years to provide 70 extra places estimated as needed owing to the trends towards increasing temporary and permanent family break-down and dislocation in the community, the increasing population and the failure of improved community support programme (including foster care) to keep pace with preventive work or alternative provisions for care.
1. Home A: To have closed and sold, redistributing residents among

other more suitable homes.

2. Home B: To link with local foster homes to provide greater continuity of care.
3. Home C: To enlarge by the purchase of the next-door home.
4. Home D: To create a long-stay home for 15 disturbed adolescent girls with improved staff quarters.
5. Home E: To nominate 20 places for day care, occasional overnight and weekend stay.
6. Home F: To provide an additional building in the existing grounds as a half-way house for younger children awaiting placement after assessment.
7. Home G: To replace this with a new home split into three sub-units denominated on an age basis.
8. To complete 5 new homes covering disturbed, long-stay children and a half-way house for children awaiting return to community.
9. To complete provision of a 5-day week for all staff by increasing the number of staff-children ratios appropriately.

(ii) DAY NURSERIES

Within the next 2 years, to provide 300 extra places estimated as needed owing to the growing numbers of unsupported parents having to work during to day.

1. To complete the building of a new day nursery with 100 places.
2. To extend day-nursery provisions attaching to existing old people's homes by an overall total of 50 places.
3. To contract the provision of a further 150 places in private nurseries.
4. To close Day Nursery B and replace with the purchase of a new day building capable of conversion.

(iii) OLD PEOPLE'S HOMES

Within the next two years to provide 200 extra places estimated as needed owing to the growing population of the elderly, the increasing breakdown of family support for the elderly and the failure of warden-assisted, sheltered housing and elderly fostering programmes to keep pace with these increases.

1. Home A: To convert home into bedsitting-room units providing semi-independence.
2. Home B: To be coverted into a home providing short breaks for people normally living independently in the community, or with relatives.
3. Home C: To convert into a convalescent home for the elderly and to obtain an enlarged contribution of an additional 10 per cent from hospital funds.
4. Home D: To improve and enlarge staff quarters by adding an extra

storey to the existing building.

5. Home E & F: To accelerate completion and opening by 6 months in both cases, one to cover the geriatric elderly, the other to cover those active elderly unlikely to return to the community.

6. To mount a programme of research to determine whether present estimates of need are over-pessimistic and whether the building of two scheduled homes can be postponed or cancelled.

7. To complete professional training of 80 per cent of the existing residential staff and all new staff.

8. To improve overall the provision of rehabilitative services by making places available to all residents on the programmes of groupwork, physiotherapy, occupational therapy and day care.

9. To achieve full-scale resident participation in all non-geriatric homes.

10. To recruit twenty more nursing-trained staff and twenty married couples to run homes.

(iv) HOMES FOR THE PHYSICALLY HANDICAPPED

Within the next year, to have built a multi-purpose centre for the handicapped which will include residential provision for forty people.

(v) GROUP HOMES FOR THE MENTALLY ILL

1. Within the next 2 years to provide 40—50 places for the mentally ill in group homes or other residential accommodation.

2. To provide 30—40 places for the mentally ill in 5 group homes for 5 to 6 residents each at a cost of £10,000 each.

3. To provide 10 place on the upper floors for existing day nurseries for those mentally ill and in temporary need (e.g. on discharge from hospital).

4. To complete a programme of research designed to predict the needs for group homes in the subsequent 5 years.

(vi) HOMES FOR THE MENTALLY HANDICAPPED

Within the next 2 years, to provide one new home for up to 40 mentally handicapped by conversion of Children's Home F.

(vii) HOMELESS FAMILY UNITS

1. Within the next 2 years to provide for two additional homeless family units catering for an estimated additional 40 families which will emerge as a result of redevelopment problems.

2. To convert Homeless Family Unit A into one capable of taking complete (i.e. husband, wife and children) families, which will involve conversion of the existing building.

(viii) FOSTER HOMES

1. To mount an intensive campaign for the recruitment of 80 more foster parents within the next 2 years.
2. To mount a campaign aimed at fostering 20 elderly within the next 2 years.

(ix) TRANSPORT

To improve transport facilities for all homes by an increase of 25 per cent of present availability by a combination of the following methods:

1. Purchase of more vehicles for transporting residents.
2. Recruiting more drivers willing to do shift work for existing vehicles.
3. Increasing the overtime of existing drivers.
4. Developing a transportation model for the area allowing swifter transport between one location and another.
5. Contracting private transport firms for any duties not covered by the above programme.

(x) CHILDREN'S RECEPTION CENTRE

1. To provide residential care for such temporary period as is necessary for all children not immediately placed in foster homes or who, for reasons of 'unruly behaviour' have immediate needs that cannot be met in an 'open' establishment.
2. To provide a residential service of help to parents, the courts and the police.
3. To return all children to their own homes or into the care of relatives as soon as possible, and to indicate the best alternative care for all children who do not return home.
4. To identify how the needs can best be met within present resources.

Reception

1. To comprehensively plan the reception of children to meet individual and statutory needs covering: special reception; reception under Children's Act 1948, Section 1; specialist referrals; short-stay children; committals and place of safety orders.
2. To provide staff with the fullest possible relevant information on significant features of the children's background.
3. To identify any elements in the child's need which might suggest previous categorization is stigmatization.
4. To give assessors access to multiple-source referrals to ensure more balanced assessment on the degrees of seriousness of social problems.
5. To identify those children experiencing greatest loss or threat of loss.

6. To provide full consultancy service for staff so that facts, opinions and theories on delinquency are constantly reviewed.
7. To establish the policy on appropriate or alternative groups which the child might join.
8. To provide maximum information for the child.

Diagnosis
1. To identify certain specific needs of the child in terms of his behaviour components and motivation.
2. To plot the child's ego strengths and adaptive responses pinpointing where further learning might take place.
3. To apply principles of human growth and development in practice.

Mental Needs
4. To provide a wider range of varied, interesting and mentally stimulating activities.

Physical Needs
5. To provide a range of diversified and interesting means of physical expression and outlets for physical energy.
6. To make maximum physical comfort possible in respect of carrying out each activity.
7. To provide activities demanding the use of fine motor skills.

Social Needs
8. To identify social and anti-social responses in specific areas of functioning.

Emotional Needs
9. To identify the points at which the child needs to be relieved of pressures from people and situations.
10. To ensure that all children have regular face-to-face contact with at least one staff member.

Analysis
1. To encourage informal discussions in which analysis of alternative questioning of hypotheses and deductions from evidence is highly valued.
2. To continuously use home situations as a medium for staff development and training.
3. To develop a more systematic approach by all staff in evaluating behaviour on a continuous basis.
4. To use individual staff interviews, meetings and case conferences as a medium for pooling information and evidence on the child's behaviour from as many varied sources as possible.

5. To define the degree to which a child grasps his real-life situation.
6. To define areas for further enquiry and observation.
7. To ensure that information on the child's behaviour spans the full range of different sub-environments provided by the home setting and the full range of time-samples (e.g. behaviour at different periods of the day or week).
8. To document and present information in a form which will be valuable to future caring agents in implementing treatment objectives and methods.
9. To record such additional information as is statutorily required.
10. To define specific treatment objectives and strategies for each child.
11. To match the child's needs with children's for foster-home facilities.
12. To identify changes necessary in homes so that they are better adapted to the children's needs.

Treatment in Home
1. To use the residential environment as a treatment centre in which physical, mental and emotional needs of children are met.
2. To provide children with the maximum freedom of action within constraints which are unavoidable if the home is to function effectively.
3. To design or convert accommodation so that it better contributes towards meeting the children's individual needs.
4. To establish individual, personal clothing as the norm in the home.
5. To maintain a high standard of nourishment provided by food.
6. To create a framework in which children and their parents feel they are accepted.
7. To develop a more varied and interesting diet.
8. To create an environment through peer group behaviour.
9. To treat all children as individuals, with equal rights and as worthy of equal respect.
10. To accept and recognize risks and possible consequences of unsupervised activity.
11. To use supervision as an opportunity for building relationships rather than as an attendant or control function.
12. To establish the most liberal possible norms of tolerance of non-conforming behaviour.
13. To agree available controls, sanctions and punishments and appropriate occasions for their use.
14. To place particular priority on sensitive handling of the child at the point of his initial impact.
15. To avoid neglect of any one child.
16. To use staff-child contacts to establish genuine communication

with the child.

17. To plan regular face-to-face contacts with each child by at least one member of staff.
18. To use the child's present situation in the home to stimulate his expression of expectations and fears.
19. To use a varied range of communications media to establish the relationship with the child (i.e. not only verbal exchange).
20. To maintain those relationships the child has with family and friends in the external environment (e.g. by financing the visits of friends).

External Liaison

1. To identify changes in the family situation necessary for the child to be able to return home.
2. To work with the parents so that the child's absence is used as an opportunity for establishing a fresh attitude and approach to problematic aspects of the situation.
3. To link with fieldwork staff to establish integrated objectives and strategy for each child.
4. To liaise with psychiatrist, educational psychologists and headmasters to gather relevant information on the child's behaviour from these sources.

Administration

1. To meet cost and quality standards in respect of food, accommodation and clothing.
2. To meet necessary efficiency standards in the running of the homes.

Appendix 2:
A Client Problem Dictionary

I. Family Socio-Emotional Problems

These cover problems listed separately under client groups : children, young people, unsupported parents, marital relations, elderly.

Ideal
1. Happy, warm, close, yet unrestricted family and social life.
2. Harmonious marital, parent-child (including elderly parents and adult children), sibling, or other close interpersonal relationships.
3. Fulfils community expectations of the family effectively.
4. Family environment generally life-enhancing.
5. Highly effective alternative to family mechanisms may provide equivalent socio-emotional supports.

Average Functioning
1. Generally positive family and other interpersonal relationships though not without tensions and conflict.
2. Societal functions of family fulfilled adequately.
3. Family environment sustaining.
4. Effective alternative to family mechanisms may provide equivalent socio-emotional supports.

A. Predisposition
1. Family reasonably stable as unit despite some dislocating strains and stresses.
2. Interpersonal relationships often tense and stressful though remediable within the family's own resources.
3. Family environment intermittently sustaining.
4. Societal functions of family just about fulfilled though not without some cost to its members.
5. Dependent family members generally well supported provided advice and help is given on problem issues.

B. Impeded
1. Family goes through unstable and dislocative periods.
2. Dependent family members just about hold their own within the existing family structure.
3. Some pressure, tension and stress generated within the family over specific issues and situations.
4. Societal expectations of family intermittently fulfilled at marked cost to its members.

C. Impaired
1. Continued survival of family as a family is precarious and open to doubt in the longer term.
2. Dependent family members in need of some protective support and occasional short-term substitute care, to ensure their situation does not deteriorate further.
3. Family situation far from stable and a source of some strong socio-emotional pressures on its members which are generalized over several aspects of functioning.
4. Family does not fulfil societal expectations adequately.

D. Deteriorated
1. The family is near dissolution or locked into a family situation which is having deleterious consequences for all the members.
2. Dependent family members in need of protective support and perhaps substitute care for a period.
3. Family situation generally debilitative and retrogressive.
4. Family does not fulfil even minimum societal expectations adequately.

E. Collapsed
1. The family is either completely dissolved or existing relationships are extremely damaging and dangerous to some or all members.
2. Dependent family members in need of protection and substitute care on a very long-term and perhaps permanent basis.
3. Interpersonal relations between any two family members either very debilitating or exacerbating the total problem situation of the family.
4. Family situation itself dislocates all aspects of its members' societal functioning.

II. Children's Problems

Ideal
1. Fully protected and cared for by any standards, though not over-protected to the point of dependency.

2. Parental figures successful, understanding and loving without over-dominance.
3. Belongingness, independence and self-esteem, excellently though realistically catered for.

Average Functioning
1. Adequately protected and cared for given the situation.
2. Parental figures reasonably proficient and essentially warm.
3. Belongingness, independence and self-esteem reasonably well catered for.

A. Predisposition
1. Temporary separation with adequate parental substitutes.
2. Parent soon returns from absences.
3. Very much over-indulged child.
4. Consistent, just adequate parental care with strictly temporary impairment of parental function.

B. Impeded
1. Periodically deprived of emotional needs.
2. Periodically feels unwanted.
3. Parental figures interrelate reasonably well with each other, but not with child.
4. Inconsistent and apathetic parental care.

C. Impaired
1. Often deprived of emotional needs and security with repeated periodic separation.
2. Parental figures provide chancy and haphazard care.
3. Unstable parental care (e.g. marital breakdown, mentally disturbed parent).

D. Deteriorated
1. Neglected, rejected, needing care and protection.
2. Parental figures largely ignore child despite danger.
3. Consistently inadequate or deleterious parental care.

E. Collapsed
1. Abandoned or battered or severely maladjusted (e.g. autistic child with extensive ill-effects on others).
2. Complete irreparable family breakdown.
3. Extensive effects of child's problems on all other aspects of family living.

III. Young People's Problems (including delinquents)

Ideal

1. Excellently adjusted to the maturation process.
2. Belongingness, esteem, self-fulfillment needs fully catered for without any unrealistic or artificial inducement.
3. Negotiated relationship with authority figures which is satisfactory on all sides on justifiable grounds.
4. Complete acceptance by peers on fully justifiable grounds.
5. Adjusts to changes positively through personal coping mechanisms even when preparation and support less than adequate.
6. Law-abidingness established on rational grounds.

Average Functioning

1. Reasonably adjusted to the maturation process given customary difficulties.
2. Belongingness, esteem, self-fulfilment needs adequately catered for all in all given situational constraints.
3. Some contained friction with parents and other authority figures within normal limits, which is worked through adequately by those involved.
4. Accepted by peers to a degree adequate for daily functioning.
5. Adjusts to changes positively given relevant preparations and support.
6. Law-abidingness established as intrinsic value.

A. Predisposition

1. Growing pains or rebellion causing anxiety.
2. Alienated against self.
3. Some peer support.
4. Variance with authority figures though not with self.
5. Swings of mood.
6. Parental anxiety and friction.
7. Minimal referrals from juvenile bureaux in area.
8. No appearance before court.
9. Wide community tolerance and flexible community norms.

B. Impeded

1. Strong rebellion against parents on all fronts, despite reasonable parental responses.
2. Inadequate parent-adolescent relations.
3. At variance with authority figures on variable grounds.
4. Misunderstanding and friction frequent in many situations.
5. Poor relationships within family and peer group.

C. Impaired
1. Major relationship problems with peer group.
2. At variance with all authority in principle.
3. Radical conflicts in family or peer group.
4. Member of law-breaking gang.
5. Negative relations with specific authority figures.

D. Deteriorated
1. Law-breaking, beyond any parental control.
2. Negative and destructive to all authority of any kind or in any form.
3. No peer or community relations provide any satisfaction.

E. Collapsed
1. Involuntary drop-outs.
2. Rebel against local community, lacking any self-supporting basis for sustaining or justifying the rebellion.
3. Severe problems with self and community at large.
4. Criminal law-breaking.
5. Unable to obtain work.
6. Totally rejected by family.
7. Many referrals from juvenile bureaux.
8. Contempt of Juvenile Courts.
9. Strong community intolerance and highly enforced community norms.
10. Large numbers of community affected by behaviour.

IV. Marital Relations Problems

Ideal
1. Happy domestic life without exclusiveness and well-developed capability of coping with externally-posed problems.
2. Belongingness, esteem and self-fulfilment needs fully realized within marital situation without exclusion of others or development of unrealistic responses to external world.
3. Fully capable of coping with changes in marital situation without any consequential devaluation of marital harmony.

Average Functioning
1. Reasonable adjustment to domestic life.
2. Belongingness, esteem and self-fulfilment needs met to adequate degree within marital situation.
3. Reasonably able to cope with changes in marital situation.

A. Predisposition
1. Some marital disharmony.
2. Fear, coolness, involuntarily going separate ways.
3. 'Doormat' behaviour by either partner.
4. Husband continuously occupies leisure periods outside the house.
5. Periodic miscommunication leading to quarrels and bickering.
6. Significantly different attitudes towards parenthood.

B. Impeded
1. Periodic separation based on marital conflict situation.
2. Symptoms recognized by community as approaching virtual breakdown (e.g. continuous quarrels, separate beds, affairs, separate money or sexual distance).
3. Partners' mutual needs and expectations unmet.

C. Impaired
1. Emotional separation with alienative effects.
2. Marriage continues as a matter of social convenience.
3. Adjusted to acknowledged separation or divorce, though difficulties being worked through.

D. Deteriorated
1. Marital breakdown — total emotional mental and physical separation with alienative effects.
2. Bitter disagreement and other severe marital breakdowns with repercussions on children or divorced spouse.

E. Collapsed
1. Long bitter disagreement and violently quarrelling partners.
2. Spouse battering or emotional withdrawal with severe effects on children who are being 'used' as instruments in marital disputes.
3. Divorce or legal separation pending, with major complications (such as custody disputes).

V. Unsupported Parent Problems

Ideal
Parent well-supported in parental role by another or by others.

Average Functioning
In as reasonably happy and self-sufficient state as other happy family situations.

A. Predisposition
1. Able to support self and child reasonably adequately at present,

though difficulties may emerge.
2. Infrequent stigmatizing effects on child, which are well handled by all parties.

B. Impeded
1. Just able to support self and child, with dependence on others and some intermittent stress.
2. Some specific stigmatization in certain areas of living.

C. Impaired
1. Support of self and child, leading to some continuous stress and intermittent ill-health.
2. Specific stigmatization by some key figures from time to time.

D. Deteriorated
1. Unable to support self and child without continuous support from others of all kinds.
2. Specific stigmatization by all key figures in social environment continuously.

E. Collapsed
1. No prospect of being able to keep child if self and child are not to suffer severe stress and ill-health.
2. Maximum stigmatization at every turn by all persons of any significance.

VI. Elderly and Widowed Problems.

Ideal
1. Well supported and cared for in all aspects of living.
2. Belongingness, esteem and independence excellently catered for by any standards.
3. Socially well integrated with community.
4. Excellent health despite age.

Average Functioning
1. Adequately supported and cared for in major aspects of living.
2. Belongingness, esteem and independence reasonably well established given constraints of situation.
3. Socially integrated with neighbourhood without loss of independence.
4. Reasonably good health considering age.

A. Predisposition
1. Adapted to living alone or with family or others' support.

2. Some dependence on family and/or external agencies.
3. Family group generally supportive, though some domestic tensions emerge occasionally.

B. Impeded
1. Intermittent physical crises or isolation.
2. Unsympathetic family and/or neighbours.
3. Family group inconsistently supportive.

C. Impaired
1 Ill or disabled or severely isolated.
2. Bereaved, feels unwanted and useless.
3. Grudging family support.

D. Deteriorated
1. Severely ill or disabled.
2. Very dependent, feeling unwanted and useless.
3. Completely isolated socially.
4. Rejection by family.
5. No support available and/or accepted.

E. Collapsed
1. Chronically ill or disabled (e.g. needs total care).
2. Constant attendance and nursing needed.
3. No possibility of any support outside local authority or health service.

VII. Physically Ill and Handicapped Problems (including Blind and Deaf)

Ideal
1. Excellent physical health.
2. The person is not only free of any illness but has a high level of strength, energy and coordination.
3. Completely adjusted to an able to compensate for condition.

Average Functioning
1. Generally good physical health.
2. Adequate support.
3. Adequately adjusted to condition.
4. No serious illnesses or handicaps, or able to maximize existing strengths.
5. Physical capacity adequate for most normal tasks.

A Predisposition
1. Slight continuing incapacity owing to disabling condition.
2. Requires some treatment and rehabilitation.
3. Currently adequate home care.
4. Mildly depressed owing to condition.
5. Temporary social incapacity due to illness.
6. Responsive to medical treatment with mild effect on social functioning (e.g. temporary unemployment or inability to care for children).
7. Minimal hindrance (e.g. clumsiness).
8. Realistic ability to come to terms with, and appraise handicap.
9. Satisfactory compensation for physical impairment.
10. Recently contracted or diagnosed progressive condition.

B. Impeded
1. Some problems in functioning through disabling condition, with intermittent need for outside help.
2. Some dependence on family or others (e.g. family no longer free to go out when they wish without making special arrangements).
3. Relief but no cure available from treatment.
4. Unsympathetic family.
5. Intermittent crises.
6. Chronic but not severe handicap (e.g. partial sight or mild heart disease necessitating some care).
7. Over-sensitive, sometimes afraid.
8. Intermittently depressed and frightened about condition.
9. Some circumstances create temporary departures from stability.

C. Impaired
1. Able to function within community with extensive external help and support, despite all problems.
2. Frequent crises which are half-contained or clumsily handled.
3. Second handicap complicates adjustment.
4. Constantly depressed to some degree about physical condition – upset by minor stress.
5. Severe handicap which is only contained in community because nursed by relative with maximum domiciliary services and formal support.
6. Family or others find it very difficult to have a break.
7. No known treatment or relief.
8. Easily manoeuvred to manifest behavioural characteristics typical of them.
9. Some personality or developmental lag resulting from handicap – personal equilibrium brittle.
10. Environmental circumstances unhelpful to physical condition.

11. Adjustment to handicap causes severe identity problems and associated relationship difficulties.

D. Deteriorated

1. Progressive, severe illness established, possibly with multiple handicaps.
2. Severe incapacity requiring continuous protective care by family or hospital.
3. Family not coping, or person completely isolated.
4. Needing to be coaxed and weaned into cooperation.
5. Large personality and developmental lag resulting from handicap.
6. Environmental circumstances seriously and extensively aggravate physical condition.
7. Handicap precludes participation in or positive response to many social activities.
8. Efforts to adjust to handicap result in personality breakdown and associated relationship difficulties.
9. Seriously depressed and fearful about own condition.
10. Frequent dangerous crises which are badly handled.

E. Collapsed

1. Chronic incapacity with total care necessary by family or hospital.
2. A critical crisis point of catastrophic dimensions.
3. Terminal illness or malignant physical condition requiring constant attendance and nursing.
4. Complete rejection by family or friends.
5. Handicap creates extreme disturbances, obtuseness, hostility, indolence, rendering client incapable of accepting necessary services.
6. Handicap precludes participation in or positive response to most social contacts.
7. Nil attempt to adjust to handicap and self-rejection.

VIII. Addiction Problems (including alcoholics, drug-addicts and gamblers)

Ideal
Completely non-addictive.

Average Functioning:
Occasional minor experiments with harmless drugs, occasional 'hearty' drinking or the occasional 'flutter' in appropriate social conditions without repercussions or continuance.

A. **Predisposition**
1. An addictive personality in occasional tempting situations in relation to drugs, alcohol or gambling.
2. Life-supports may not sustain any increase in drug-taking, alcohol consumption or gambling.
3. Drug use and familiarity.
4. Varying awareness of dangers of addiction.

B. **Impeded**
1. Heavy drinkers.
2. Indulging in drug-taking though not addicted.
3. Gambling out of proportion to income.
4. Drug misuse.
5. Unaware of dangers of addiction.

C. **Impaired**
1. On-the-road to alcoholism.
2. Life-supports currently sustained despite addiction.
3. Hooked on soft drugs.
4. Gambling consumes leisure activities.
5. Psychological dependence.
6. Asserts benefits, drama and pleasures of drinking, drugs or gambling in an unrealistic manner.

D. **Deteriorated**
1. Clearly alcoholic or drug-addicted though not incurable.
2. Some life-supports remaining.
3. Other interests intermittently or marginally sustained.
4. Gambling after all but basic necessities are met.
5. Physical dependency or habituation.
6. Has joined the alcoholic, drug or gambling sub-culture.
7. Continuous experiments with hard drugs.

E. **Collapsed**
1. Maximum possible alcoholism, gambling, addiction to hard drugs.
2. No life-supports remaining.
3. Completely at the mercy of addiction which consumes whole life.
4. No social contacts apart from those connected with addiction.
5. Feels unable to interrupt alcohol consumption, drug taking or gambling at any point.

IX. Mentally Ill and/or Emotionally Disturbed Problems (including neurotic and psychotic illness)

Ideal:
1. Reasonably happy person with feeling of well-being.
2. Capacity to develop close interpersonal relations.
3. Able consistently to perceive reality objectively rather than in terms of own perspective.
4. Productive within capacity with a realistic sense of constraints in various fields of living, though able to reduce constraints by planned progress.

Average Functioning
1. Reasonably good interpersonal relations though not without conflicts with others.
2. Some anxiety which is not debilitating.
3. Able to contain and use internal conflict and anxiety.

A. Predisposition
1. Mild or re-active depression.
2. Indications of bizarre thoughts etc.
3. Temporary illness responsive to medical treatment with mild effect on social functioning (e.g. temporary unemployment or inability to care for children).
4. Able to work and occupy themselves.
5. Dependence on family or others, though no professionally identified pathogenic relationships.
6. Symptoms minimally affect daily living.
7. Able to maintain relations reasonably well.
8. No ill-effects on family.
9. Financially secure.
10. Rather rigid, highly defended personality.
11. Recent or immediate social crisis with some resources available to reestablish personal equilibrium.
12. Stress or organic factors create predisposition to mental illness.

B. Impeded
1. Chronic or recurring illness but not severe (e.g. depression necessitating some care).
2. Incipient affective obsessional states; mild phobias.
3. Manifest anxiety and worry by individual, family or others in relation to condition.
4. Problem no longer contained by established family methods of coping.
5. Unable to work regularly, though usually able to occupy self.

6. Considerably adjusted to own state, though lacking significant insight into this state.
7. Financially unstable.
8. Symptoms affect daily living to some extent.
9. Physical environment places stress on individual and is pathogenic.
10. Relations with others maintained with difficulty.

C. Impaired
1. Severe mental illness medically diagnosed.
2. Unpredictable behaviour (e.g. schizophrenia, depression, dependent on care of relatives with support of day centre, severe phobias).
3. Comparatively mild depression which extends to family or others.
4. Daily living inhibited by symptoms.
5. Little adjustment to own state.
6. Occasionally able to do simple work.
7. Negative relations with others which are only rectified through external supports.
8. Emotional-social environment places stress on individual.
9. Seen by others as deluded.

D. Deteriorated
1. Chronic and severe mental illness and depression medically diagnosed.
2. Uncontainable in community (e.g. serious family or neighbourhood crisis necessitating professional intervention).
3. Hospitalization alternating with vagrancy.
4. Normal life impossible (e.g. breakdown of family relations).
5. Rather paranoid individual living alone.
6. Severe depression reflected in family or others.
7. Deeply unobjective in relation to several aspects of reality, and unadjusted to consequences of this.
8. Never able to occupy themselves without help.
9. Daily living seriously distorted by symptoms.
10. Never able to work.
11. Relations never made without traumas.
12. Significant and unmalleable alienative factors in environment.
13. Rigid and established scapegoating procedure in family.

E. Collapsed
1. Genuinely suicidal; violent homicidal tendencies.
2. Complete incapacitation and total withdrawal.
3. Symptoms causing breakdown in family or others.
4. Pattern of deviance seen as totally unacceptable by community.
5. All aspects of environment conspiring to reinforce illness and its consequential problems.

6. Passive resistance to treatment on grounds which are seen as totally unreasonable by family and by professionals.
7. Perceives reality completely unfeasibly and entirely in terms of own perspective without any objective orientation.
8. Denies or lacks any sense of interrelationship even when in contact with others.
9. Extreme danger to self and others.
10. Incapacity for self-care.
11. Even mere contacts with others present major difficulties.
12. Symptoms have completely taken over individual's whole life.

X. Mentally Handicapped Problems

Ideal:
Above average intelligence and well adapted to the consequences of this situation.

Average Functioning
Average intelligence.

A. Predisposition
1. Dependence on family or others.
2. Socially and vocationally adequate, though needing supervision and guidance in adverse social and economic conditions.
3. Substitute care available for relief of family intermittently.

B. Impeded
1. Mildly handicapped.
2. Able to work under supervision in unskilled employment.
3. Capable of unskilled jobs.
4. Needing supervision and guidance in times of social or economic stress or in unfamiliar social situations.
5. No substitute care available other than local authority or hospital.

C. Impaired
1. Family resents strains and limitations imposed by handicapped member.
2. Significant strain on family.
3. Needs permanent guidance and supervision, although able to look after himself to some extent.
4. Contributes to self-support in sheltered environment.

D. Deteriorated
1. Severe strain on family with periodic breakdown as support system.

2. Frequently uncontainable in community as a result of behavioural difficulties.
3. Hospitalization or residential care frequent.
4. Unable to attend to own personal needs.
5. Shows severe retardation in all respects from babyhood.
6. Requires constant nursing care or complete supervision.
7. Trained to feed, wash and dress self under supervision and execute simple remunerative work.
8. Stigmatization experienced by self and family with consequent distress.

E. Collapsed
1. Unable to function at any level – total care required.
2. Maximal incapacity (e.g. vegetation, severely subnormal).
3. Need constant, complete, uninterrupted nursing care throughout life.
4. Only able to walk, feed or toilet themselves with maximum help.
5. Family totally unable to cope or totally rejecting.

XI. Adult Legal Offenders' Problems
Ideal
1. Law-abiding with high ethical standards.
2. Takes responsibilities as a citizen seriously.
3. Makes a positive contribution to the well-being of his community.

Average Functioning
1. Reasonably honest and law-abiding though not totally free of conflict with constituted authorities, including parents and teachers and not above 'cutting corners'.
2. Does relatively little in the citizen role beyond voting and performing adequately in work role.

A. Predisposition
1. Environment tending to encourage anti-social behaviour.
2. Development of criminal behaviour probably as a result of influences, but no pattern of offences yet emerged.
3. Variable response to social control (e.g. parental)
4. Small thefts from shops.

B. Impeded
1. Pre-prison (e.g. suspended sentence).
2. Probation instead of sentence.
3. Conviction to detention centre or committal to local authority.
4. A pattern of minor offences beginning to emerge.

5. Anti-social attitudes not yet completely internalized.
6. Good chance of positive response to non-authoritarian approach to treatment aimed at helping the offender to meet his needs more effectively without resorting to anti-social behaviour.

C. Impaired
1. A clear pattern of anti-social and illegal behaviour.
2. Official punitive action necessary as a sanction.
3. Some hopeful signs for a positive response in the community (e.g. conviction with post-prison sentence on licence).

D. Deteriorated
1. Short-term prisoners.
2. A clear pattern of ingrained anti-social and illegal behaviour.
3. Official punitive action necessary for protection of society but occasional hopeful signs for a positive response to a rehabilitation programme in a correctional institution.

E. Collapsed
1. An established pattern of anti-social and illegal behaviour.
2. No signs of hope that pattern can be reversed.
3. Long-term incarceration necessary for protection of community.
4. Long-term or life prisoners.
5. Recidivists.
6. Violent offenders.

XII. Homeless and Housing Stress Problems

Ideal
1. Person or family comfortably and attractively housed.
2. Income allows discretionary spending on household repairs and appliances.
3. Neighbourhood network of relations well established.

Average Functioning
Person or family adequately housed.

A. Predisposition
1. Inadequate or unacceptable housing (e.g. caravans).
2. Small rent arrears occasionally.

B. Impeded
1. Periodically homeless or gross housing inadequacy.
2. No discretionary spending on household repairs and appliances possible.

3. Unable to find somewhere to live.

C. Impaired.
1. Voluntarily homeless.
2. Heavy rent arrears.
3. Eviction immanent.
4. Major complaints from neighbours.

D. Deteriorated.
1. Involuntarily homeless.
2. Suffered constant evictions.
3. Part of non-rent-paying sub-culture.
4. Evicted without evident alternatives.
5. Formal protests from neighbours.

E. Collapsed
1. Requires emergency housing in interest of person or family health and safety.
2. Permanent resident in reception centre.
3. Unable to adjust to permanent house.
4. Intolerable as neighbours.
5. Hard-core, inadequate families who are homeless despite all help.

XIII. Financial Problems including problems of the unemployed

Ideal
1. Person or family comfortably and attractively fed and clothed.
2. Income allows discretionary spending on car, household appliances, recreation, additional educational and health care insurance, and for most future contingencies.
3. Expert budgetary skills.

Average Functioning
1. Limited surplus of discretionary spending.
2. Limited resources for future contingencies.
3. Reasonable security established.
4. Person or family adequately fed and clothed.
5. Belongingness, esteem, self-fulfilment established.
6. Budgetary skills adequate to most circumstances.

A. Predisposition
1. Income covers basic essentials at present but maintenance at current level uncertain.

2. Inadequate use of current income.
3. Unanticipated experience liable to create serious hardship.
4. Uncertainty or instability of income (e.g. substantial change in financial circumstances immanent through retirement, birth of child etc.).
5. Difficulty in planning for future contingencies in view of current contingencies or poor budgeting skills.

B. Impeded
1. Income covers only barest essentials.
2. No surplus for discretionary spending.
3. Any unanticipated experience liable to create desperate hardship.
4. Periodic interruptions of income and reliance on state benefits.
5. Debt accumulation with considerable pressure from creditors resulting in panic budgeting.

C. Impaired
1. Unemployed though diagnosed as fit for work.
2. Income does not quite cover bare essentials.
3. No sense of budgeting whatever.
4. Hardship evident, though person or family is 'just' coping somehow.
5. Situation is bound to deteriorate unless help forthcoming.
6. Individual or family can envisage little possibility of paying debts or making ends meet in foreseeable future.
7. Total reliance on state benefits for extended period.

D. Deteriorated
1. Involuntarily unemployed.
2. Financial resources used entirely irresponsibly.
3. Financial resources completely inadequate.
4. Person or family not coping at all.

E. Collapsed
1. Financial resources nil.
2. Requires emergency relief or protective care in interest of person or family health and safety.
3. Categorized and regarded as unemployable by self and others.
4. Total loss of initiative and self-respect (e.g. depressed, apathetic reaction to situation).

Appendix 3:
A Service Activity Inventory

I. Objective: Reduce Effects of Physical Malfunctioning or Breakdown.

A. **Predisposition Services**

1. Safeguarding access to thorough and appropriate treatment by medical specialists.
2. Detection of pathological body changes before their overt manifestation.
3. Housework aids.
4. Rendering relevant technological advances available to the handicapped.
5. Fostering the spread of amenities and resources through the community.

---

* No Social Services agency would have the full repertoire of service activities listed here. Each agency has developed its own range of service activities according to assessed need and agency policy. To be of practical use, the inventory requires to be tailored to the specific local conditions of each agency concerned.

Moreover, the service activities and tasks listed under their headings, are not regarded as uniquely appropriate to the specific problem or problem addressed by the objective. Generally, any service activity which is assessed as potentially appropriate at less severe levels of social pathology (e.g. at level A 'predisposition') may also be used at more severe levels (e.g. at level B 'impaired functioning') if this is assessed as relevant in the specific client or community situation concerned. No one-to-one correspondence between problems and service activities is postulated.

Lastly, some references are made to practice methods and techniques which are unfamiliar in current Social Services practice (e.g. to kinesiological therapy, logotherapy and Frostig programmes). These are included with references to appropriate literature, partly because they have often been suggested as viable and effective approaches for handling some of the social problems confronted by workers, and partly because they refer to a range of practices which many would argue are already employed by many workers, albeit in a less systematic and conscious manner than is advocated by their primary exponents.

6. Aids to daily living provided.
7. Adaptations to dwellings.
8. Domestic equipment (e.g. household appliances).
9. Local linkmen for handicapped.
10. At risk, handicapped, unemployment and observation registers.
11. Assessment centres.
12. Liaison with voluntary agencies (e.g. Disablement Income Group, Disablement Resettlement organizations, Council for Health Education etc).
13. Liaison with occupational therapists, hospitals, medical services, G.P.s, physiotherapy, health visitors etc.
14. Sponsor the enforcement of legislation on access to public buildings, pavings, crossings.
15. Voluntary helpers.
16. Public education programmes *vis-à-vis* the handicapped (e.g. through mass media).
17. Support for medical screening and community health programmes.
18. Prepare client psychologically for consequences of illness.
19. Monitoring reactions to chemotherapy.
20. Dietary education.
21. Liaison with factory and other health inspectors, industrial welfare officers, etc.
22. Genetic counselling.
23. Sponsoring disability insurance.

B. **Services for Impeded Functioning**
1. Nutritional counselling.
2. Budgeting for impairment.
3. Social intervention to prepare family or client for handicap and its acceptance.
4. Handicap centres.
5. Transportation facilities.
6. Friendly visiting.
7. Adventure holidays.
8. Teaching (e.g. braille, sign language, etc).
9. Daily help (e.g. dressing).
10. Aids to mobility and learning (e.g. transport, garage adaptations, plumbing adaptations).
11. Individual, personal short-term casework.
12. Escort services.
13. Stimulate use of public facilities without fear.
14. Arrange visiting nurses.
15. Counselling for rehabilitation.
16. Groupwork with special interest groups.
17. Medical social work services.

C. Services for Impaired Functioning
1. Physical aids to daily living.
2. Home adaptations.
3. Household gadgets and appliances.
4. Amenities and physical conveniences.
5. Specialized therapy ensured.
6. Individual outings (e.g. with voluntary agencies).
7. Purpose-built transport.
8. Home helps.
9. Subsidized holidays.
10. Specialized equipment (e.g. talking books, Optacon reading aids, robot limbs, foot-operated typewriters).
11. Boarding out.
12. Mobility assistance and training.
13. Meals-on-wheels for special diets.
14. Home visits by occupational therapists.
15. Group homes.
16. Emergency housekeepers.
17. Night sitters-in.
18. Laundry service.
19. Remedial instruction programmes.
20. Encourage use of appropriate medication.
21. Chiropody services.
22. Behavioural modification to extinguish reinforcers of illness and sickness.
23. Inculcate adjustment to changed role through role theory-based therapy.
24. Sponsorship of medical and industrial rehabilitation units.

D. Services for Deteriorated Functioning
1. Support and guidance for relatives.
2. Meals-on-wheels to safeguard nutritional levels.
3. Sentinel system to avoid physical catastrophe.
4. Securing resistant client agreement to necessary treatment.
5. Provision of highly specialist aids and training in their use assured.
6. Short-term residential therapy.
7. Temporary adoption schemes.
8. Rehousing arranged.
9. Specialized building.
10. Physical rehabilitation arranged — physiotherapy, hydrotherapy.
11. Handicraft classes.
12. Recuperative holidays.
13. Short-term hospital admissions arranged.
14. Group outings.
15. Sheltered environment (e.g. Papworth model village, Enhamelain[1]).

16. Foster G.P. involvement in medication regimes.
17. Coordinated home care programmes.
18. Intensive physical skills training.

E. Services for Collapsed Functioning
1. Referral to appropriate health specialists.
2. Counselling relatives and clients (e.g. on death).
3. Client advocacy with specialist services.
4. Residential care — possibly long-term to safeguard survival.
5. Geriatric hospital long-term admissions arranged.
6. Terminal hospital bed.
7. Support in adjustment to hospital.
8. Planning of personal circumstances in conjunction with relatives and friends.
9. Burial and cremation arrangements.
10. Voluntary friendly visiting.
11. Discharge planning from hospital.
12. Hairdressing service.
13. Supervised medication.
14. Multi-disciplinary consultation on patient's progress.
15. Support hospitalization with temporary fostering or emergency mothers.
16. Foster improved social climate in hospitals.
17. Highly specialised therapy (e.g. kinesiological therapy[2]).

II. Objective: Reduce Mental Instability and Breakdown

A. Predisposition Services
1. Safeguarding access to thorough and appropriate treatment by psychiatric specialists.
2. Development of client cognitive skills.
3. Review of unanticipated action consequences.
4. Insight learning methods.
5. Role model for systematic problem-solving.
6. Spread relevant information.
7. At risk, handicapped and observation registers.
8. Local linkmen for handicapped.
9. Assessment centres.
10. Liaison with psychiatric units, special education etc.
11. Exploration-ventilation-description therapy.
12. Identify and re-state client problems.
13. Supportive treatment and sustainment.
14. Voluntary supportive visitors.
15. Worker detection of pathological mental illnesses and changes

before manifestation overt.
16. Public education programme *vis-à-vis* mental illness and handicap.

B. Services for Impeded Functioning
1. Exposure of logical incompatibilities.
2. Negatively reinforce thoughtless, over-impulsive behaviour.
3. Replace behavioural distortions with adaptive responses.
4. Develop know-how and information.
5. Develop calculative and deliberate capacities.
6. Develop intellectual resources.
7. Supportive help in relation to institutions (e.g. school, work).
8. Modifying treatment and direct influence.
9. Individual personal short-term casework.
10. Social intervention to gain family or client acceptance of illness or handicap.
11. Groupwork with those under mental stress.

C. Services for Impaired Functioning
1. Revise inaccurate client perceptions.
2. Special classes — remedial instruction.
3. Supervised open hospital.
4. Short-stay mixed homes with supervision.
5. Reflection on client's personality pattern and dynamics.
6. Group homes and hostels.
7. Boarding-out.
8. Liaison with health services.
9. Liaison with special education and remedial programmes.
10. Behavioural modification to extinguish external reinforcers of illness and sickness.
11. Inculcate acceptance of changed role through role theory-based therapy.

D. Services for Deteriorated Functioning
1. Use of a therapeutic community setting.
2. Spasmodic residential care.
3. Intensive explorations of intra-psychic processes.
4. Reflections on early life.
5. Meals-on-wheels for reducing effects of mental derangement on health.
6. Recuperative holidays.
7. Group outings.
8. Sheltered environment.
9. Counter-conditioning regimes.
10. Psycho-geriatric day care.
11. Escort services.

12. Logotherapy.[3]
13. Deconditioning phobias.
14. Intensive skill training.

E. Services for Collapsed Functioning
1. Programmes to develop minimal skills of literacy, numeracy and logic.
2. Permanent custodial care to safeguard survival.
3. Intensive behavioural therapy – drugs, etc.
4. Compulsory admissions.
5. Use of personality simulation models.[10]
6. Foster improved social climate in hospitals.
7. Support hospitalization with emergency mother or temporary fostering.
8. Liaison with Samaritans and similar organizations.
9. Protective custody.
10. Gestalt therapy.[4]

III. Objective: Reduce Emotional Stress

A. Predisposition Services
1. Reinforcing client problem-solving capacities.
2. Build on emotional strengths.
3. Specialized day centres.
4. Exploration-ventilation-description therapy.
5. Identify and re-state client problems.
6. Supportive treatment and sustainment.
7. Voluntary supportive visitors.
8. Anticipatory guidance.
9. Liaison with marriage guidance councils.

B. Services for Impeded Functioning
1. Helping clients recognize proximate causes of emotional tensions.
2. Purposeful relief of feelings.
3. Provide opportunities for release of pent-up feelings.
4. Build up client resilience to stress.
5. Generate confidence.
6. Manipulate conditions generating stress.
7. Behavioural modifying treatment and direct influence on client behaviour.
8. Work with interpersonal relations.
9. Groupwork with those under emotional stress.

C. Services for Impaired Functioning
1. Helping clients recognize origins of emotional tensions.

2. Provide cathartic experiences.
3. Help client off-load feelings onto worker and other forms of tension discharge.
4. Help clients resist panic at onset of stress.
5. Help clients develop stable responses to unwelcome emotions and impulses.
6. Sustaining procedures.
7. Evoke pleasant emotional responses.
8. Reflections on client personality pattern.
9. Short-term conjoint family therapy.

D. **Services for Deteriorated Functioning**
   1. Counter-conditioning regimes.
   2. Extended longer-term casework.
   3. Building client support network anew.
   4. Long-term conjoint family therapy.
   5. Long-term fostering to relieve emotional stress on children.
   6. Emergency mothers' service.
   7. Subsidized holidays to relieve stress.
   8. Help client manage affect and delimit spread of tension.

E. **Services for Collapsed Functioning**
   1. Intensive milieu therapy.[8]
   2. Adoption services to relieve emotional stress on children.
   3. Residential care to relieve stress on children.
   4. Ban on amphetamines prescription.
   5. Use of personality simulation models.[10]
   6. Foster improved social climate in hospitals.
   7. Support hospitalization with emergency mother or temporary fostering.
   8. De-sensitization regimes.
   9. Liaison with Samaritans and similar organizations.

IV. Objective: Reduce Depersonalization

A. **Predisposition Services**
   1. Information on citizen rights through advertisement and publicity.
   2. Fortify social statuses and anchorages through anticipation.
   3. Assist client to understand and handle formal organizations and their mechanisms.
   4. Strengthen particular interests and successes.
   5. Aid client self-evaluation through casework.
   6. Develop belief of individual as end-in-himself through positive reinforcement.
   7. Protect freedom of dissent from social policies and majority views

through community work.
8. Safeguard opportunities to influence policies.
9. Liaison with other services to promote individualized service delivery methods, personalization of provision and reduced formalism.
10. Reinforce sense of personal adequacy.
11. Leadership training.

B. **Services for Impeded Functioning**
1. Fortify client sense of identity through consumer participation, self-regard and uniqueness.
2. Strengthen client assertion of predelictions.
3. Reinforce client autonomy in respect of his own social space.
4. Encourage development of private selves.
5. Reduce pressures to conformism through community work and environmental manipulation.
6. Create opportunities to influence social policies through consumer participation.
7. Render human service units smaller through reorganization.
8. Differentiated style of service delivery.
9. Hopefulness of problem resolution expressed by worker.
10. Questioning official decisions.
11. Educating neighbouring professions in consumer rights.
12. Groupwork with persons with special needs.

C. **Services for Impaired Functioning**
1. Reinforce coherent system of client responses through rehearsal of client situations.
2. Restore individual to full status in his community through community work action.
3. Correct distorted self-image through behavioural evaluation.
4. Aid applicants at tribunals, etc.
5. Reinforce client autonomy in respect of mental space.

D. **Services for Deteriorated Functioning**
1. Develop coherent system of client response.
2. Build client social status.
3. Preserve client sense of roots.
4. Reinforce client autonomy in respect of emotional space.
5. De-routinization of activities.
6. Worker sensitivity to individual differences.
7. Demeaning and crippling self-images modified.
8. Help clients review relevant past experiences to elicit lost pride and self-confidence.

E. **Services for Collapsed Functioning**
   1. Build client social anchorages through environmental manipulation.
   2. Establish client autonomy in respect of physical space.
   3. De-standardization of activities.
   4. Individualized treatment in Homes.
   5. Facilitate communication of genuine feeling.

V. Objective: Reduce Insentience

A. **Predisposition Services**
   1. Dissemination of information on services.
   2. Dissemination of policy.
   3. Increasing knowledge of how to use provisions.
   4. Propagating understanding of community power structures.
   5. Client engagement in diagnosis of own problems.
   6. Provide alternative viewpoints, interpretations, frames of reference.
   7. Verbal labels used to help discrimination.
   8. Interpretation, clarification and cognitive restructuring of problem.
   9. Liaison with other services to foster awareness of their availability by relevant consumers.
   10. Liaison with Citizens Advice Bureaux.
   11. Liaison with education authorities.
   12. Help consumers collect relevant information.

B. **Services for Impeded Functioning**
   1. Divergent expectations of community resources.
   2. Client engagement in treatment of own problems.
   3. Direct advice and guidance with reasons.
   4. Symbolic re-enactment of responses.
   5. Positive reinforcement of objective reality.
   6. Recall of relevant earlier experiences.
   7. Reflection on personality dynamics.
   8. Communication of current socio-cultural norms.
   9. Help client retain problems in consciousness.
   10. Formulate cognitive resolutions of problem.
   11. Groupwork with persons with special needs.

C. **Services for Impaired Functioning**
   1. Client engagement in study of own problems — clarify nature of problem by explanation.
   2. Symbolic re-enactment of problem.
   3. Negative reinforcement of subjective fantasies.
   4. Confrontation techniques.
   5. Interpretation and assessment of medical information on client condition.

6. Reduce client aspirations to realistic levels.
7. Help client manage affect arising from awareness of problem situation.

D. Services for Deteriorated Functioning
1. Reality therapy techniques.[6]
2. Review consequences of client action.
3. Develop family and neighbourhood insight into illness and its behavioural effects.
4. Insight therapy techniques — examine effect of past on current situation.
5. Reduce client expectations to realistic levels.
6. Gestalt therapy.
7. Stimulate emergency problem-solving mechanisms.

E. Services for Collapsed Functioning
1. Intensive reality therapy techniques.
2. Use of situational simulation models.
3. Role-playing methods of instruction.
4. Remedial instruction.
5. Development of or referral to Frostig programmes of diagnosis and therapy.[5]
6. Planned crisis creation.
7. Help client redefine problems and needs.

VI. Objective: Reduce Anomie

A. Predisposition Services
1. Client ventilation.
2. Increased ego-involvement.
3. Improving feedback of action consequences.
4. Ensuring service delivery without belittlement.
5. Social accounting services.
6. Fostering citizen responsibilities.
7. Promoting dialogue with relevant external critics of agency services.
8. Value propagation.
9. Consumer education programmes.
10. Develop and promulgate service priorities.
11. Elicit, explicate and publish community social values.

B. Services for Impeded Functioning
1. Abreactive casework techniques.
2. Increasing investment in values.
3. Stimulating client revaluations of own situations.

4. Ensuring services delivered in acceptable ways.
5. Developing sensitivity to others through groupwork.

C. Services for Impaired Functioning
1. Reducing anti-social effects of significant sub-cultures.
2. Foster sense of care for relevant dependants.
3. Restore sense of goal-seeking activity.
4. Reawaken sense of positive elements in environment.
5. Helping client reach decision.
6. Help clients or client groups decide on their stance on significant issues.
7. Logotherapy.[3]

D. Services for Deteriorated Functioning
1. Reality therapy techniques.[6]
2. Casework centred on ethical evaluation.
3. Review of client obligations.
4. Develop realistic client objectives.
5. Develop sensitivity to others through groups.
6. Articulate advantages and benefits of certain items, persons and situations as normally perceived by client groups.
7. Assist client appreciation of comparative costs and benefits, constraints and inducements.
8. Help client envisage something to look forward to with hope.
9. Help clients decide what they want — develop personal goals and aspirations.

E. Services for Collapsed Functioning
1. Intensive reality therapy techniques.[6]
2. Groupwork programmes centred on developing client's valuational skills.
3. Build on client's capacities to appreciate and value certain items, persons and benefits.
4. Assist clients in formulating what a better personal future would look like.
5. Reawaken community debate on values.
6. Help clients discover meanings and congruences in their lives as individuals.

VII. Problem: Reduce Dependency

A. Predisposition Services
1. Helping groups and individuals to plead their own cause.
2. Helping citizens to take up their choices.
3. Stimulating citizens to influence community development.

4. Extend positive freedom from interference in decisions.
5. Sponsor community action groups.
6. Help client use personal resources.
7. Assist client control of external situations.
8. Client and resident participation in treatment and service delivery decisions.
9. Liaison with consumer councils.
10. Consumer education programmes.
11. Reduce powerlessness of service recipients.
12. Reduce service-giver power.
13. Leadership training.

B. Services for Impeded Functioning
1. Community organization programmes.
2. Developing consumer participation in decision-making.
3. Evolving concrete action from protest.
4. Develop personal resources.
5. Approval of independent behaviour and disapproval of dependent behaviour.
6. Assist self-steering, corrective action within problem situation.
7. Child nurseries for parental relief.
8. Welfare loans programmes.
9. Extend and articulate range of choice in life situations.
10. Reduce pressure of group bonds on the individual.
11. Family placement for elderly.

C. Services for Impaired Functioning
1. Social action programmes.
2. Systematically modify dependency-reinforcing practices using deep positive and negative reinforcers.
3. Patient operator selector-mechanisms provided.
4. Daily minders for parental relief.
5. Sheltered housing for maintaining independence.
6. Explore available choices open to client.
7. Groupwork with dependent persons.

D. Services for Deteriorated Functioning
1. Milieu therapy reducing dependency-inducing elements in environment.[8]
2. Stimulate client motivation towards self-help and self-choice.
3. Present at least one genuine service alternative to client.
4. Provide substitute 'parenting' in community care setting.

E. Services for Collapsed Functioning
1. Intensive milieu therapy generating self-help programmes.

2. Sponsored consumer cooperatives.
3. Resident participation in Homes.
4. Escort services.
5. Provide substitute 'parenting' in residential settings.

VIII. Objective: Reduce Inarticulateness

A. Predisposition Services
1. Develop verbal communications.
2. Freer expression of emotions facilitated, including negative feelings and hostility.
3. Facilitate unburdening of problems.
4. Casework relations used as a forum for free and open expression of feelings.
5. Ventilation techniques.
6. Use of verbal labels to increase discrimination.

B. Services for Impeded Functioning
1. Develop verbalized attitudes.
2. Release interpersonal communication.
3. Elaboration of restricted speech codes.
4. Casework relation used as a testing ground for more adequate modes of expression.
5. Facilitate expression of positive feelings.
6. Use of verbal labels as behavioural guidance cues.
7. Groupwork with friendship groups.

C. Services for Impaired Functioning
1. Develop expression of feelings and emotions.
2. Training in interpersonal communication.
3. Develop alternative outlets for expression other than violence.
4. Develop alternative means for sharing problems.
5. Casework relation used as a model for self-expression.
6. Restructuring family communications patterns.

D. Services for Deteriorated Functioning
1. Find substitute means for release of tensions and relief of pressures.
2. Exposure to others as expressive models.
3. Provocation of verbal responsiveness.
4. Communications therapy.

E. Services for Collapsed Functioning
1. Educational therapy.
2. Develop non-verbal communications.

3. Encounter groups.[9]
4. Linguistic therapy.

IX. Objective: Reduce Stultification, Regression, Retardation and Decline

A. **Predisposition Services**
1. Stimulate renewed social learning.
2. Promote positive attitudes towards schooling, training and re-training.
3. New Town developments.
4. Socio-cultural development programmes.
5. Diversifying community amenities.
6. Articulation of consequences of major social changes.
7. Information on community facilities.
8. Provide socio-physical environment adequate for maturation.
9. Set a limit on excessive anxiety about learning when this inhibits learning by producing distracting emotional states.
10. Develop intrinsic motivation for client learning.
11. Liaison with education services.

B. **Services for Impeded Functioning**
1. Develop adaptive attitudes.
2. Help clients reflect on influential factors in developmental pattern.
3. Help transference of client experiences across analagous situations and through time from earlier to later situations.
4. Community development programmes.
5. Assistance in use of opportunities and resources.
6. Fostering participation in civic affairs.
7. Social education of parents in child-rearing practices.
8. Replace punishment controls with reward controls in stimulating learning.
9. Help individual set realistic learning goals.
10. Provide information about the nature of effective performance.
11. Groupwork with persons with special needs.

C. **Services for Impaired Functioning**
1. Preserve and develop repressed behaviours.
2. Reinforce adaptive responses.
3. Community reconstruction programmes.
4. Training in learning procedures.
5. Development of community resources and amenities.
6. Short-term fostering services for child development.
7. Planned crisis-creation for sake of learning.

8. Use of growth-oriented groups on model of primary groups.
9. Build a backlog of success in learning as a basis for client toleration of failure.

D. Services for Deteriorated Functioning
1. Decondition regressive, infantile reactions.
2. Advocacy programmes.
3. Regional priority area programmes.
4. Educational therapy.
5. Long-term fostering services for child development.
6. Regressed behaviour regimes to recover earlier emotional experiences which partially or symbolically block development.
7. Develop client capacities to learn through doing, and through active participation.

E. Services for Collapsed Functioning
1. Locality development programmes.
2. Frostig programmes.
3. Reality therapy techniques.[6]
4. Adoption services for child development.
5. Regressed behaviour regimes.
6. Change behaviour by positive/negative reinforcements.
7. Provide specialized socio-physical environment restorative of maturation processes.

X. Objective: Reduce Insecurity

A. Predisposition Services
1. Propagate precautionary measures to dangers and discomfitures.
2. Develop realistic appreciation of anxiety-provoking situations and their consequences.
3. Objective appraisal of threats.
4. Provide social securities, supports, contacts and outlets for interests.
5. Reinforce security of continued supply of psychological needs.
6. Liaison and advocacy with housing authorities to develop housing as a social service.
7. Disciplined housing policy on rents.
8. Extension of mortgage arrangements.
9. Housing advice centres.
10. Liaison with Citizens Advice Bureau on rent rebates, legal and technical advice.
11. Liaison with consumer councils.
12. Consumer education programmes.

13. Sentinel systems to locate clients in insecure situations.
14. Integrated information system to prevent inadvertent client 'drop-outs'.

B. Services for Impeded Functioning
1. Financially-assisted career programmes.
2. Fostering influences generating social security.
3. Help reduce client sense of threat as basis for action.
4. **Provide** mental securities and supports — self-esteem, confidence, etc.
5. Sentinel system — early warning arrangements on rent arrears.
6. Education and liaison with rent collectors on social issues.
7. Liaison with insurance and debt-collection companies.
8. Skilled rent-collection techniques — culturally acceptable payment methods arranged.
9. Support, financial encouragement and advice to housing associations, co-ownerships, etc.
10. Exchange tenancy schemes especially between Councils.
11. Meals-on-Wheels service.
12. Sponsorship of tenants' associations.

C. Services for Impaired Functioning
1. Assuring access to basic services.
2. Reinforce protective influences.
3. Establish effective responses to antagonistic anxiety-provoking behaviour.
4. Permissive psycho-drama and group therapy.
5. Build on clients' coping capacities in response to threats.
6. Provide emotional securities and supports — affection, love, care.
7. Reinforce sense that disabilities will not endanger immediate security.
8. Temporary accommodation under rehousing schemes.
9. Rent subsidies and guarantees.
10. Special rent payment arrangements.
11. Planned eviction strategies.
12. Rehousing.
13. Short-stay and mixed homes.
14. Sheltered and warden-assisted housing.
15. Short-term fostering services.
16. Advice on health fears.

D. Services for Deteriorated Functioning
1. Assisting claims for income entitlements.
2. Adaptation of services to most vulnerable.
3. Protection of clients from hazardous environments.

4. Systematic desensitization to irrational fears.
5. Maintain physiological securities.
6. Consolidation orders.
7. Housing subsidies encouraged.
8. Establishment of caravan sites encouraged.
9. Provision for homeless in homeless family units.
10. Hotel-type residential homes.
11. Boarding out of elderly.
12. Home help service.
13. Sponsored consumer cooperatives.
14. Accommodation bureau register.
15. Long-term fostering services for family security.
16. Family support unit.
17. Arrange for housing subsidy.
18. Nutritional counselling.

E. **Services for Collapsed Functioning**
1. Protection of clients from dangerous environments.
2. Provide physiological securities of food, shelter, warmth and health.
3. Sheltered housing for homeless.
4. Adaptation and patch repair of old properties.
5. Use of properties pending development.
6. Liaison with squatters' groups.
7. Residential social worker attached to special accommodation units.
8. Semi-geriatric residential homes.
9. Support in adjustment to residential situation.
10. Discharge planning for residential care.
11. Rents subsidies.
12. Adoption services for family security.
13. Life care retirement residences.
14. Sponsoring private residential care.
15. Escort services.
16. Direct admission to patch repair property.
17. Liaison with Simon Community, Salvation Army, the Spike and similar agencies.
18. Family systems therapy.[7]

XI. Objective: Reduce Economic Poverty

A. **Predisposition Services**
1. Securing income through employment or insurance.
2. Sponsoring income increases.
3. Encouraging ownership and management of property.
4. Job counselling and career guidance.

5. Financial advice.
6. Income planning.
7. Economic concessions — reduced fees for transport, recreation, holidays, food, etc.
8. Subsidized transport facilities.
9. Subsidized heating.
10. Christmas, Easter and Whitsun parcels.
11. Consumer cooperatives sponsored.
12. Consumer education programmes.
13. Advice on all financial entitlements.
14. Liaison with Department of Employment and Youth Employment service.
15. Advice on curtailment of leisure activity and reduced social activity.
16. Social education in home budgeting.
17. Advice on financial rights and their take-up (e.g. rent and rate rebate schemes, family allowances).
18. Sponsoring credit unions.

B. Services for Impeded Functioning
1. Securing income through fiscal welfare policies.
2. Improving service take-up.
3. Help with compensations for income mismanagement errors.
4. Programmes to utilize client earning capacities.
5. Job-finding services.
6. Counselling on family income management.
7. Direct liaison with utility companies, landlords, building societies, etc., to secure relief schemes.
8. Grants from trusts and voluntary agencies.
9. Community work at block level.
10. Revision of family financial control system.
11. Help maintenance of coherent pattern of activity despite economic deprivation.
12. Groupwork with financially deprived groups.

C. Services for Impaired Functioning
1. Ensuring income through social security.
2. Reimbursement for services programmes.
3. Negotiating claims to benefits on behalf of clients.
4. Safeguarding priority for essential client commitments.
5. Training in household and income budgeting.
6. Programmes to develop clients' earning potential.
7. Explore and develop clients' attitudes towards money.
8. Reception Centre support and training with whole families.
9. Special arrangements for direct rent payments.

10. Assistance in managing tangible assets.
11. Assistance in longer-term planning of client's economic future.
12. Discourage sale of key tangible assets.
13. Pressure on DHSS for discretionary grants.
14. Liaison with Claimants' Unions.
15. Assistance at redundancy tribunals.

D. Services for Deteriorated Functioning
1. Ensuring economic security through financial concessions and services.
2. Clarification of and regulated provision for client's essential commitments.
3. Specialist help with family budgeting procedures.
4. Spread responsibility and benefits of income among family.
5. Contracted accountants to provide specialist personal advice to clients.
6. Special arrangements with utility companies for payment.
7. Rent subsidies.
8. Nutritional counselling.
9. Discourage sale of tangible assets.
10. Encourage sale of saleable and unnecessary goods.
11. Transport vouchers.
12. Pressure on Department of Employment for concrete results.
13. Special arrangements for direct payments of income supplement entitlements.
14. Arrange for housing subsidy.

E. Services for Collapsed Functioning
1. Programmes redistributing economic benefits in favour of lowest income group.
2. Maximum selectivity of service.
3. Insurance of regular income provision.
4. Providing a floor to possible economic disaster.
5. Ensuring income through direct protection.
6. Financial assistance under 1963 Children and Young Person's Act.
7. Supplementation programmes (e.g. for clothing).
8. Ensure exceptional needs grants given.
9. Special arrangements for non-statutory income supplements.

XII. Objective: Reduce Effects of Breakdown

A. Predisposition Services
1. Build repertoire of client responses to reduce susceptibility to future breakdown.
2. Assist anticipation and prevention of crises.

3. Sentinel systems arranged through use of milkmen, gas men, rent collectors, postmen, highway maintenance men etc.
4. Liaison with marriage guidance council in respect of marital breakdown.
5. Sponsoring disability insurance.

B. Services for Impeded Functioning
1. Preparing clients and client groups for future crises.
2. Strengthen positive influences in client environment.
3. Working through feelings of guilt and aggression.
4. Groupwork with people in crisis situations.

C. Services for Impaired Functioning
1. Priority areas programmes.
2. Reinforcing survival techniques for coping with crisis.
3. Use of crisis as catalyst for longer-term changes.
4. Depress negative influences in client environment.
5. Short-term fostering and shelter care to relieve crisis.
6. Temporary care by local authority to relieve crisis.

D. Services for Deteriorated Functioning
1. Mobilization of community to cope with crises (e.g. floods).
2. Help achieve peaceful crisis resolution rather than all-round exhaustion.
3. Long-term fostering to compensate for family breakdown.
4. Subsidized holidays to relieve breakdown.
5. Use role theory approaches to inculcate acceptance of role changes.
6. Provide client with skills rendering his condition less catastrophic.

E. Services for Collapsed Functioning.
1. Intensive crisis therapy.
2. Adoption services to compensate for family breakdown.
3. Escort services.
4. Sponsoring and collaborating with disaster relief services.
5. Family and community systems therapy.

XIII. Problem: Reduce Debilitative Elements in the Social Environment.

A. Predisposition Services
1. Social planning of integrated work and leisure facilities.
2. Encouraging cooperation on problems among family members.
3. Fostering nurturant family relations.
4. Immigrant settlement schemes.

5. Liaison with agencies representing minority groups.
6. Disseminate information on debilitative conditions.
7. Consumer associations liaison.
8. Consumer cooperatives sponsored.
9. Consumer education programmes.
10. Liaison with marriage guidance councils.
11. Parental education centres fostered.
12. Liaison with and reference to education, health, youth, environmental health, voluntary agencies, child guidance, police, town planning services in respect of environmental services.
13. Liaison with Citizens Advice Bureaux.
14. Recruit volunteers from among clients.
15. Support and reinforce person's current adequate behaviour in face of environmental pressures.
16. Liaison with town planning on land-use controls.
17. Liaison with housing department on planned tenant selection policies.
18. Education for improved urban planning.
19. Leadership training.

B. Services for Impeded Functioning
1. Use of situational contingencies to reinforce treatment.
2. Define usable family and community resources.
3. Broker activities between public services.
4. Fostering receptiveness to others in community sub-cultures.
5. Short-term conjoint family therapy.
6. Outward bound clubs fostered.
7. Youth clubs fostered.
8. Sponsored adventure playgrounds.
9. Pre-school playgroups.
10. Community and neighbourhood development work.
11. Develop neighbourhood support networks.
12. Develop intrafamilial cooperation.
13. Family life education.

C. Services for Impaired Functioning
1. Open up therapeutic possibilities of clients' own social networks.
2. Foster sense of caring among client contacts.
3. Environmental manipulation.
4. Social action on specific disabling elements in social environment.
5. Sponsor voluntary agencies representing specific minority needs.
6. Long-term conjoint family therapy.
7. Before-and-after school playgroups.
8. Nursery groups.
9. Daily child minders.

10. Homemaking classes.
11. Build associational institutions.
12. Re-structuring family role relations.

D. Services for Deteriorated Functioning
1. Recruiting professionals to live in and service slums.
2. Reducing risk to individual from environment.
3. Create voluntary agencies representing and geared to specific minority needs.
4. Milieu therapy.[8]
5. Liaison with school transport service.
6. Motherhood classes.
7. Develop mutual aid schemes.
8. Develop multi-laterality of social relations.
9. Mediation of client relations with agencies.
10. Relocate person in less debilitative neighbourhood.
11. Foster care for unmarried mothers.

E. Services for Collapsed Functioning
1. Protective custody of the vulnerable from dangers of environment (e.g. by protective residential care or boarding out).
2. Intensive milieu therapy.[8]
3. Intensive urban renewal programmes encouraged.
4. Liaison with schools to cater for parental needs.
5. Transport to work (e.g. for unsupported mothers).
6. Parent education centres.
7. Emergency mothers' service.
8. Liaison with police on institution of relevant legal proceedings.
9. Children's Homes to protect children from dangers of environment.
10. Adoption services
11. Disaster relief services.

XIV. Objective: Reduce Inequality of Life-chances

A. Predisposition Services
1. Helping clients to claim their rights.
2. Training of social work and allied services in knowledge of citizen rights.
3. Promulgate universal standards of provision.
4. Social planning reducing unevenness and lag in service availability between neighbourhoods.
5. Articulating needs of underprivileged in community planning.
6. Reduce distinction between givers and receivers of service in service delivery.
7. Political education.

8. Foster power of client representative groups.
9. Establish legally enforceable rights in court.
10. Ensure availability of free legal aid at required level of quality.
11. Ensure rights fulfilled at required levels of service quality.
12. Establish territorial justice by equality of provision enforced between different regions.
13. Educate other services regarding consumer needs.
14. Establishing eligibility requirements.
15. Planning location of community facilities to achieve territorial justice.
16. Leadership training.

B. Services for Impeded Functioning
1. Support of client's case in disputes with officialdom.
2. Spread of relevant information to underprivileged.
3. Assisting client self-advocacy.
4. Increase self-confidence of client representative groups.
5. Extend citizen rights by using the tribunal and appeals system against use of discretion in application of law to individual cases.
6. Rectify wrong application of eligibility rules through advocacy.
7. Mediation of client relations with agencies.
8. Bargaining for resource reallocations on behalf of consumers.
9. Groupwork with neighbourhood groups.

C. Services for Impaired Functioning
1. Programmes reducing artificial differences in power, status and privilege.
2. Developing political skills of underprivileged.
3. Increase knowledge, information and understanding of representative client groups.
4. Inform low-income groups of their legal and administrative rights.
5. Publicize results of legal test cases.
6. Use legal processes for legal review of way administrative processes work.
7. Groupwork with underprivileged groups.

D. Services for Deteriorated Functioning
1. Programmes reducing influence of key factors causing past inequalities of power, status and privilege.
2. Increase use of high-cost services by low-income groups.
3. Free and subsidized holidays.
4. Intensive client advocacy programmes.
5. Organize representative client groups.
6. Modify overtly stigmatizing and punitive community actions and pressures.

7. Test cases in law on behalf of individuals to establish rights not obtained.
8. Establish take-up of rarely used rights (e.g. on evictions from furnished tenancies).
9. Providing legal advice to clients in support of their situation.

E. **Services for Collapsed Functioning**
1. Highly selective and concentrated services for underprivileged, deprived, etc.
2. Open up areas where legal rights are not established.
3. Ensure clients are receiving rights to which they are entitled.
4. Enforcing clients' entitlement to their state rights.
5. Intensive milieu therapy.[8]
6. Take test cases to court to establish rights.
7. Establish sequences of social action by consumers.
8. Patient advocacy in hospitals.
9. Social action programmes.

XV. Objective: Reduce Stigmatization

A. **Predisposition Services**
1. Public education about minority groups by talks and leaflets.
2. Disseminating public information, knowledge and understanding of handicaps.
3. Revise social labels used to refer to handicaps.
4. Stigma-reinforcing planning devices (e.g. planning permissions) checked.
5. Published agency policies of non-stigmatization.
6. Liaison with consumer associations.
7. Liaison with external services to prevent stigmatization of client groups.
8. Promoting intercultural understanding.
9. Liaison with Race and Community Relations Boards.

B. **Services for Impeded Functioning**
1. Interpreting problems of stigmatized to agitators.
2. Canvassing community support for stigmatized groups.
3. Mixed day centres based on skill.
4. Legal advice.
5. Reinforce sense of personal adequacy.
6. Groupwork with neighbourhood groups.

C. **Services for Impaired Functioning**
1. Revise agency classification of clients.
2. Revise definitions of client problems.

3. Develop mix of clients under each service.
4. Counselling family to extend tolerance.

D. Services for Deteriorated Functioning
1. Social action and influence generated in opposition to organized stigma-reinforcing protests.
2. Milieu therapy techniques.[8]
3. Neighbourhood resident counselling to extend tolerance.
4. Develop client confrontation skills (e.g. Alinsky-type confrontation with employers).
5. Reduce or eliminate means tests.
6. Rebuild sense of personal adequacy.
7. Groupwork with stigmatized groups.

E. Services for Collapsed Functioning
1. Intensive milieu therapy.[8]
2. Sponsored consumer cooperatives.
3. Sponsored legal aid and assistance.
4. Develop community tolerance of specific handicaps by specific persons (e.g. employers' tolerance of pain and unsightliness, co-patients' tolerance of each other).
5. Relocation programmes.
6. Lessen rigour of means test applications.
7. Increase and develop community tolerance of others' pain and of unsightliness.
8. Social action programmes.
9. Specific negative reinforcement of scapegoating.
10. Protection against discrimination.

XVI. Objective: Reduce Socio-cultural Deprivation

A. Predisposition Services
1. Expose clients to alternative values and beliefs.
2. Locate area offices on border between disadvantaged and prosperous areas.
3. Planning for balanced communities of heterogeneous composition.
4. Full account taken of social background variations in family assessments.
5. Universalist service policy.
6. Establish recognition of need for and uses of constructive conflict.
7. Community planning for diversified activities.
8. Liaison with town planning department on land-use controls.
9. Planning optimal location of community facilities.
10. Planned tenant selection policies.
11. Education for improved urban planning.

12. Leadership training.

B. Services for Impeded Functioning
1. Expose clients to alternative problem resolutions.
2. Help clients cope with conflict.
3. Help clients adjust to their variable social roles.
4. Social planning for non-place communities.
5. Environmental manipulation to increase options open to the client.
6. Provide client with varied experiences.
7. Community and neighbourhood development.
8. Groupwork with interrelated and opposed interest groups in neighbourhoods.

C. Services for Impaired Functioning
1. Sympathetically rehearse in thought alternative responses to problems.
2. Promote behaviour in others which reinforces changes in client behaviour.
3. Stimulation of client's interest in community activities.
4. Stimulate increased client contact outside immediate locale.
5. Transportation schemes.
6. Sponsored community social clubs and activities.
7. Provide client with novel experiences.
8. Initiating task-oriented interest groups modelled on official groupings.

D. Services for Deteriorated Functioning
1. Sponsored holidays.
2. Negative reinforcement of learned and stereotyped responses.
3. Expose clients to new contacts.
4. 'Mixed' intake into residential homes and day centres.
5. Milieu therapy.[8]
6. Initiating growth-oriented interest groups.

E. Services for Collapsed Functioning
1. Multi-level, intensive community development 'priority area' programmes.
2. Slum-clearance planning encouraged.
3. Urban-renewal schemes encouraged.
4. Intensive milieu therapy.[8]

XVII. Objective: Reduce Social Malfunctioning

A. Predisposition Services
1. Non-directive institutional programmes.

2. Publicize and disseminate available community resources.
3. Instructional job counselling.
4. Broad social education programmes.
5. Liaison with consumer councils.
6. Review with clients what is feasible.
7. Reinforce sense of social competence.

B. Services for Impeded Functioning
1. Non-directive occupational training programmes.
2. Ensure feedback of results of performance to clients.
3. Sheltered employment.
4. Diagnose and communicate gaps in client's use of community resources, and selection of resources.
5. Reinforce client's learning.
6. Modify client's behaviour towards worker as substitute figure.
7. Instruction on income management.
8. Advice on significant home-care and child-rearing problems.
9. Worker acts as a role model.
10. Groupwork with social education and development groups.

C. Services for Impaired Functioning
1. Directive instructional training programmes.
2. Supplement capacities to cope with family functioning.
3. Sheltered housing.
4. Sheltered workshop and occupation units.
5. Diagnosis of distinctive ways an individual uses his resources.
6. Help provide client with a wider repertoire of responses.
7. Review client's relevant past experience.
8. Symbolically reorganize client's 'felt' experiences.
9. Demonstrate viable behaviour to client.
10. Instruction on home care and child-rearing.
11. Sponsored consumer cooperatives.
12. Liaison with special schools and remedial education services.

D. Services for Deteriorated Functioning
1. Directive occupational programmes.
2. Halfway hostels.
3. Rehabilitation units and programmes.
4. Supplement client experience with additional information.
5. Develop imitative learning in client through role-analogue methods.
6. Aids for learning for physically handicapped.
7. Groupwork for sharing and transmission of skills.
8. Remedial instruction programmes.
9. Behavioural modification therapy to increase amount of social communication.

10. Sensitivity training.
11. Family systems therapy.[7]

E. **Services for Collapsed Functioning**
   1. Intensive social education.
   2. Highly directive social training programmes.
   3. Protected community.
   4. Special care units.
   5. Urban renewal schemes encouraged.
   6. Milieu therapy.[8]
   7. Motherhood classes.
   8. Parental education centres.
   9. Behavioural change therapy.
   10. Behavioural rehearsal and structured role-play.
   11. Skills analysis and development.

XVIII. Obective: Reduce Occupational Ineffectuality

A. **Predisposition Services**
   1. Work advice centres and employment counselling.
   2. Work placements.
   3. Light industrial work provided.
   4. Foster job-enrichment schemes in industry.
   5. Foster applications of behavioural science knowledge in companies.
   6. Outreach programmes.
   7. Regional development programmes.
   8. Investments in modernizing industrial capacity.
   9. Social planning in respect of industrial location.
   10. Investment in social infrastructure (e.g. communications, civic facilities).
   11. Social and economic community development.
   12. Job-guidance counselling programmes.
   13. Liaison with Department of Health and Social Security and Department of Employment.
   14. Promoting the welfare function and social responsibilities of firms.
   15. Specialized employment groups contacted.
   16. Foster employee participation in industry.
   17. Foster industrial welfare schemes.

B. **Services for Impeded Functioning**
   1. Retraining programmes.
   2. Employment placement.
   3. Sheltered employment.
   4. Contracted employers.
   5. Help clients understand organizational context of work.

6. Industrial social work.
7. Promoting job-enrichment opportunities.
8. Job-enrichment techniques.
9. Upgrading schemes for unqualified workers.
10. Client counselling in potential work satisfactions.
11. Work through client relationship problems in work situations.
12. Liaison with industrial training units.
13. Encourage voluntary occupational activity by unemployed clients.
14. Help maintain some pattern of life.
15. Facilitate consideration of alternative courses of action.
16. Groupwork with occupational groups.

C. **Services for Impaired Functioning**
1. Sheltered workshops and work centres.
2. Productive-oriented workshops with bonus payments.
3. Intensive search for industrial outwork.
4. Advocacy with social security.
5. Use of club settings for job placement.
6. Job simplification techniques.
7. Work reorganization procedures to open jobs to more persons.
8. Work through impact of client's work situation on domestic and social relations and situations.
9. Rehabilitative and retraining units.
10. Promoting an active orientation to new developments in work methods.
11. Liaison with industrial welfare workers.

D. **Services for Deteriorated Functioning**
1. Contracted home employment.
2. Attempts to change the 'no work' ethic of delinquent sub-cultures.
3. Using clubs to selectively reinforce constructive work activities.
4. Craftswork and sewing.
5. Training in social habits (e.g. after stroke).
6. Induction and training in daily living (e.g. toiletting, cleaning teeth).
7. Provoke imitative client learning on basis of worker's own competence and prestigious position.
8. Use client's sense of need to repay worker for efforts.
9. Help clients order financial rewards and penalties for work.
10. Motivate clients to improve life situation and status.
11. Sponsored workers' cooperatives.
12. Transport-to-work services (e.g. for unmarried mothers).
13. Stimulate motivation to gainful employment and independence.
14. Stimulate motivation to gainful employment.
15. Recruit volunteers from among clients.

16. Homebound employment schemes.

E. Services for Collapsed Functioning
 1. Substitute occupational diversions.
 2. Day nurseries to relieve relatives.
 3. Day centres to relieve relatives.
 4. Outings and entertainments.
 5. Pressure on Department of Employment for discretionary grants.
 6. Work-relief schemes.
 7. Promote client activities of any kind which provide opportunities for further experience.
 8. Skills analysis and development training.

XIX. Objective: Reduce Social Alienation

A. Predisposition Services
 1. Client representatives on agency planning groups.
 2. Conscious trust of consumer by welfare administrators.
 3. Articulating social consequences of physical plans (e.g. motorways, one-way schemes).
 4. Provision of services as of right.
 5. Voluntary associations for exercising client influences.
 6. Mutual aid schemes.
 7. Schemes for developing responsive services.
 8. Youth clubs.
 9. Increased decentralization and delegation of decision-making.
10. Search and outreach programmes.
11. Telephone contacts developed (e.g. dial-a-friend scheme).
12. Sponsored consumer cooperatives.
13. Liaison with other services to foster consumer participation (e.g. parent-teacher associations, tenants' associations).
14. Foster worker participation in industry.
15. Information services on community social activities.
16. Social education in committee procedure.
17. Promoting support of neighbourhood through social networks.
18. Public relations programme to secure public cooperation in reporting cases.
19. Planning optimal location of community facilities.
20. Developing increased community control of services.
21. Volunteer counselling under supervision.
22. Groupwork with friendship and membership groups.
23. Leadership training.

B. Services for Impeded Functioning
 1. Recreational clubs for similar age brackets and interests.

2. Provisions for redress against bureaucracies.
3. Area offices as neighbourhood multi-service centres.
4. Complaints procedures.
5. Periodic consumer surveys on successive services and issues.
6. Adventure playgrounds.
7. Friendly visiting.
8. Luncheon, senior citizen and church clubs.
9. Information to clients on local community.
10. Encourage social contacts.
11. Develop reciprocation in community social relations.
12. Social education in literacy, letter-writing, form-filling.
13. Promoting support of extended family in its various forms.
14. Encounter-group therapy.[9]

C. **Services for Impaired Functioning**
  1. Good neighbour schemes.
  2. Volunteer visiting schemes.
  3. Social contact bureaux.
  4. Informal communication networks which feed client reactions back to staff.
  5. Fostering among clients objective attitudes to services.
  6. Elected client delegates to transmit specific service complaints.
  7. Groupwork with clients and client families.
  8. Telephone installation subsidies.
  9. Specialized clubs (e.g. for unsupported mothers).
  10. Socialization therapy.
  11. Encourage development of earlier interests.
  12. Pairing in accommodation.
  13. Promoting support of immediate nuclear family.
  14. Re-locate person in more communitarian or accustomed environment.
  15. Special council housing (e.g. old people's flatlets, warden-assisted housing etc.)
  16. Increase group support for individual via groupwork.

D. **Services for Deteriorated Functioning**
  1. 'Laboratory' social clubs.
  2. Specialist social clubs.
  3. Agency ombudsman.
  4. Client advocates.
  5. Improvement of administrative law to enlarge client and citizen protection.
  6. Practice fieldwork induction of newly qualified planners in twilight zones as social workers and spokesmen for the poor.
  7. Neighbourhood action plans.

8. Selectively reinforce behaviour incompatible with isolation.
9. Milieu therapy techniques.[8]
10. Group therapy with clients.
11. Daily child-minders.
12. Night sitter-in services.
13. Recuperative holidays.
14. Communications therapy.
15. Counsel on job changes and transfers.
16. Sensitivity training.
17. Examine effect of past relationships on current situation.
18. Promoting support of spouse.
19. Examine and resuscitate former interests.
20. Transport provision by vouchers.
21. Establishment of home-alarm system.
22. Role theory-based therapy to stimulate participation.

E. **Services for Collapsed Functioning**
1. Psycho-therapy directed at fostering some capacity to make significant relationships.
2. Operant conditioning regimes beginning with motor responses.
3. Drama therapy.
4. Actively therapeutic residential treatment.
5. Intensive milieu therapy.[8]
6. Liaison with marriage bureaux.
7. Standard symbol-designed route maps.
8. Communications equipment and devices.
9. Escort services.
10. Regular reports on condition by visitors.
11. Transport vouchers.
12. Inaugurate sense of interdependence through groupwork.
13. Linguistic therapy.

XX. Objective: Reduce Deviance

A. **Predisposition Services**
1. Programmes designed to render services more responsive to needs.
2. Negotiating compromises between conflicting community groups.
3. Value propagation.
4. Outreach programmes.
5. Sponsored and supervised adventure playgrounds.
6. Liaison with educational authorities.
7. Elicit, explicate and publish community values and their implications.
8. Develop community mechanisms for harmonious resolution of conflicts.

9. Articulate bases of value divergencies between community groups.
10. Liaison with probation services.

B. Services for Impeded Functioning
1. Reduce intolerance of groups and community so as to declassify deviance.
2. Help client adjust impulses and fantasies to reality.
3. Modify overt community pressures against deviant behaviour which harms nobody.
4. Assist the process of acculturation.
5. Protection of individuals from stigmatizing bureaucratic behaviour which is unable to cope with exceptions.
6. Develop client awareness of current community social norms.
7. Groupwork with neighbourhood groups.

C. Services for Impaired Functioning
1. Teach client more sophisticated and discreet methods of fulfilling deviant personal impulses and drives.
2. Positive reinforcers presented to facilitate more integrative client behaviour.
3. Reshaping client attitudes, impressions and images about how others live.
4. Increase client's sensitivity to effects on others.
5. Establish contacts between clients who may be able to assist each other.
6. Specialized youth clubs.
7. Work with street gangs.
8. Court-work services.
9. Help client envisage consequences of norm-rejection (e.g. punitive neighbours).
10. Help clients incorporate norms into behaviour which they positively seek to accept (e.g. through training in child-rearing practices).
11. Assist viable living despite norm rejection.
12. Assist consciously deviant client to seek alternative modes of securing social approbation if he seeks it.
13. Worker acts as a role model.

D. Services for Deteriorated Functioning
1. Modify client's extreme negative attitudes towards all authority figures.
2. Modify socio-cultural norms of unemployed or non rent-paying sub-cultures.
3. Help client relinquish self-destructive social traits in favour of more adaptive responses.

4. Verbal labelling to generate anxiety *vis-à-vis* maladaptive behaviour.
5. Sheltered environment.
6. Short-term residential care.
7. Halfway houses.
8. Milieu therapy techniques.[8]
9. Liaison with community schools.
10. Liaison with remand homes.
11. Inspection of reported cases of child neglect or ill-treatment.
12. Temporary care by local authority.
13. Behavioural modification therapy.
14. Develop mutual-aid schemes.
15. Restructuring family-role relations.
16. Help client develop internalized controls which avoid punitive responses from external authority.
17. Family systems therapy.

E. Services for Collapsed Functioning
1. Negative reinforcers presented to suppress deviant responses.
2. Elimination of problematic behaviour by aversion or shock therapy.
3. Longer-term 'custodial' residential care.
4. Intensive milieu therapy.[8]
5. Parent-education centres.
6. Children removed into care.
7. Legal proceedings on grounds of child neglect or ill-treatment.
8. Children's Homes services to prevent offences against children.
9. Behavioural change therapy.
10. Develop client's ability to relate to surroundings.
11. Liaison with police.
12. Protective custody.

XXI. Objective: Reduce Social Ennui and Boredom

A. Predisposition Services
1. Promoting socio-cultural aspects of housing programmes.
2. Adventure Playground.
3. Sponsorship of commercial enterprises (e.g. bingo halls, dances etc.).
4. Liaison with parks, recreation, baths, arts and libraries departments and authorities, in respect of integrated recreational and leisure services.
5. Education programmes on leisure-use and retirement.
6. Volunteer counselling under supervision.

B. Services for Impeded Functioning

1. Helping clients achieve personal satisfaction and enjoyment from activities.
2. Provision of recreational activities in clubs and societies.
3. Planning of commercial entertainment facilities.
4. Groupwork with special interest groups.

C. Services for Impaired Functioning

1. Provision of recreational activities in day centres.
2. Subsidized holidays.
3. Explore and encourage development of former interests.
4. Recreational hostels.

D. Services for Deteriorated Functioning

1. Encouraging and sponsoring commercial entertainments.
2. Sponsoring improvements in physical appearance of immediate environments.
3. Milieu therapy techniques.[8]
4. Sponsored holidays.

E. Services for Collapsed Functioning

1. Intensive milieu therapy techniques.[8]
2. Liaison with marriage bureaux.
3. Sponsorship of specialized cultural facilities.

Appendix 4:
An Inventory of Social Services Operations

I. Detecting Problem and Needs
1. Receiving referrals.
2. Developing community contacts.
3. Direct observation of needs.
4. Stimulation of needs.
5. Search models.
6. Outreach policies and procedures.

II. Screening and Intake
1. Problem syndrome pinpointed.
2. Degree of agency priority assessed.
3. Associated treatment opportunities reorganized.
4. Contracts with clients made.

III. Diagnosis: Goal Selection

A. INFLUENCES ON GOAL SELECTION
1. Wishes of clients.
2. Rights and responsibilities of agency.
3. Degree of client distress.
4. Detrimental consequences to client or community.
5. Availability of services.
6. New responses to problems mounted by agency.
7. Inducements and constraints to service take-up.

B. TREATMENT TARGETS AND GOALS SELECTED
1. Modification of underlying problem causes.
2. Common theme of several client problems.
3. Concurrent treatment of different problems.
4. Ramifying beneficial consequences from treating key variable.
5. Spin-off effects from 'generalized' treatment relationship.

IV. Treatment Planning

A. FOCUS OF INTERVENTION
  1. Clients.
     (a) Inner needs.
     (b) External needs.
  2. Relevant client environment.
  3. Client-environment interactions.
     (a) Remove stimuli reinforcing 'undesirable' behaviour.
     (b) Strengthen stimuli reinforcing 'desirable' behaviour.
     (c) Model situations presented.

B. USE OF AVAILABLE RESOURCES AND SERVICES
  1. Services effectively meeting present community needs.
  2. Services likely to meet future community needs.
  3. Developmental services: those which would be effective if developed.
  4. Repair services: those which need slight 'repair' of one feature.
  5. Cinderella services: neglected and under-capitalized services.

C. RESPONSES TO RESOURCE INSUFFICIENCY
  1. Resources sufficient for all needs.
  2. Resources partially sufficient — adequate for priority needs.
  3. Insufficient resources: stimulate one of the following responses:
     (a) Fight for more resources;
     (b) Ration resources by priority scaling;
     (c) Redirect the objective: reduce expectations;
     (d) Use other agencies' resources to own ends;
     (e) Use internal resources better by improved efficiency methods;
     (f) Articulate 'posteriorities' or non-priorities.

D. CHOICE OF SERVICE PATTERN
  1. User-initiative social utilities.
  2. Age-specific services.
  3. Problem-specific services.
  4. Case-selected services.
  5. Purchaseable services.
  6. Income transfers.

E. CHOICE OF SERVICE TYPE
  1. Brief casework.
  2. Extended casework.
  3. Conjoint family therapy.
  4. Groupwork.
  5. Community work.

6. Community development.
7. Broker services.
8. Day care.
9. Domiciliary care.
10. Residential treatment.
11. Residential care.
12. Intelligence services.
13. Advocacy services.
14. Social planning services.

V. Intervention

A. METHODS OF CASE ALLOCATION
1. Assignment.
2. Allocation by objectives.
3. Allocation by available resources or skills.
4. Allocation by task.
5. Self- or group-assignment.
6. Positional assignment.

B. METHODS OF SERVICE DELIVERY
1. Flexibility of service.
2. Specificity of service outcome.
3. Duration of service.
4. Degree of self-containment of service.
5. Eligibility for service.
6. Service availability.
7. Conduciveness of service environment to clients' physical, psychological and social comfort.
8. Commensurability of client and service targets.
9. Service quality.
10. Client preferences met.

VI. Closure

A. CASE CLOSURE CRITERIA
1. Problem resolved.
2. Alternative support provided.
3. Client network stabilized.
4. Successful prevention or preparation established.
5. 'Protection' guaranteed.
6. Social worker's skill developed.
7. Sentinel or re-referral system established.
8. Problem abandoned because:
    (a) a non-priority;

  (b) factors uncontrollable;
  (c) no progress made.
9. Problem redefined.

B. CASE CLOSURE STRATEGIES
1. Discouraging referrals.
2. Discouraging office callers.
3. Avoiding relationship.
4. Inadvertence.
5. Rendering service ineffectively.
6. Limiting resources allocated.
7. Publishing priority criteria.
8. Referring to other agencies.
9. Referral to volunteers.
10. Referral to case closure specialist.
11. Saying 'no' acceptably and diplomatically.
12. Establish contact only.
13. Establish queues for service informing clients of waiting period.
14. Establish client claims to other services.

VII. Evaluation of Results

A. TYPE OF RESULT
1. *Permutative*
  (a) Immediate change.
  (b) Permanent self-reinforcing through: (i) client capacity; (ii) greater range of circumstances coped with than before.
2. *Preservative*
  (a) stabilization of situation to allow client's present coping capacities to operate;
  (b) stabilization of client in new circumstances.
3. *Client Satisfaction or Dissatisfaction.*

B. TYPE OF IMPACT MADE
Evaluation of effectiveness in terms of specific criteria and indicators.

Appendix 5:
Defining Postional Objectives

PERSONNEL SECTION

Operational Area

Staff resources — to ensure provision of sufficient staff resources throughout the agency to enable qualitative and quantitative achievement of defined agency objectives.

Key Targets

1. Staffing Needs
To assess, establish and thereafter control staffing needs in relation to changing agency objectives, workload and content, on the basis of agreed yardsticks:

(i) to quantify current and anticipated agency workloads;

(ii) to specify current and anticipated work-methods;

(iii) to formulate yardsticks and indicators for staff numbers, grades, qualifications and skills needed to achieve defined objectives;

(iv) to revise defined objectives to make them more realistic if this is necessary as a result of staffing reviews under (i) to (iii) above;

(v) to coordinate information into long- and short-term staffing plans related to long- and short-term agency objectives;

(vi) to review and update staffing plans at agreed intervals;

(vii) to review and update the organization of staff as changing objectives bring changes in working methods;

(viii) to ensure manpower budgets are consistent with agreed yardsticks;

(ix) to forecast staff needs more accurately on the basis of changing workloads, staff turnover, market availability and staff succession;

    (x) to continuously monitor actual staff employed against staff authorized in manpower budgets;

   (xi) to establish procedures for achieving each key result to replace current methods unrelated to key results;

  (xii) to allocate responsibilities for these procedures among existing staff to replace existing responsibilities which are unrelated to key results.

Deadline: Total programme for assessment and establishment of staffing needs to have been completed within six months. Further deadlines for each activity within this programme to be agreed at lower levels.

2. Staff Provision

(a) To secure agreement of relevant committees to provision of defined staffing needs, or alternatively to appropriate revision of agency objectives to match staff availability.

(b) To recruit, develop and retain enough staff with appropriate skills to meet identified needs.

(c) To control staff recruitment and development thereafter to meet changing needs.

    (i) to analyze available market skills to meet staffing needs;

   (ii) to define agency's points of attraction for recruiting required personnel;

  (iii) to analyze potential motivations of needed personnel for joining agency;

  (iv) to develop more sophisticated methods of recruiting needed personnel;

   (v) to develop a sufficient establishment not to be at the mercy of market forces in recruiting personnel;

  (vi) to recruit staff up to predictions of forthcoming and future staffing needs;

 (vii) to provide training and staff development programmes to bring existing and newly-recruited staff up to required skill levels.

Blockages and Constraints

1. Lack of operational agency objectives.
2. Insufficient agency linkage between objectives and staff resources.
3. Personnel section underinvolved in wider issues of staff resources and allocation.
4. Personnel section seen as uninterested in and ignorant of qualitative aspects of work and staffing.
5. Line staff felt to underplay quantitative aspects of workload and feasibility of staffing yardsticks.
6. Personnel section uninformed on changing objectives, nature and

problems of work.

7. Line staff underinvolved in assessment and planning of staffing needs.
8. Lower-level staff insufficiently involved in briefing and advising top management on present and probable future staffing needs.
9. Personnel section's ability to agree staffing needs with line staff limited by lack of status or delegated authority by which firm agreements could be made.
10. Meaningful staffing yardsticks non-existent and difficult to formulate.
11. Present grading system militates against defining and subsequently providing types of staff required.
12. Manpower planning and staff development skills lacking.
13. Recruitment methods inadequate and recruitment skills lacking.
14. Insufficient promotion and transfer opportunities for talented staff within pay and grading structure.
15. Misuse of staff — wrong placing, inadequate movement, recognition — leads to high staff turnover through boredom and job dissatisfaction, and to inadequate performance.
16. Lack of staff awareness of service conditions, prospects, training and development methods leading to low morale through mistaken impressions and invalid assumptions.
17. Negative attitudes towards salary administration through inflexible pay and grading structures which fail to reward the able sufficiently while cosseting the inefficient and less able.
18. Salary administration adversely affected by absence of reliable information on pay and other rewards in comparable employment, and on market trends.
19. Recruitment tied to current establishment rather than predicted needs in view of market factors and staff turnover.
20. Recruitment methods limited to traditional advertisement.

Action to Improve Results

1. Extend management by objectives exercise to personnel work.
2. Second staff members (from personnel and planning) to short courses in modern methods of manpower planning, staff development, staff recruitment, job evaluation, staffing ratios, staff turnover.
3. Seconded staff prepare detailed improvement proposals for achieving key results supported with reasoning, implementing their proposals after discussion with relevant staff.
4. Seconded staff secure agreement and cooperation with the Clerks Department (Establishments) for implementing schemes.
5. Seconded staff conduct seminars for other relevant staff,

communicating substance of their external training.

6. Personnel section to propose to policy group specific increases in delegated responsibility on personnel matters, together with specification of existing responsibilities.
7. Social work staff to respond to specific proposals made under 3 and 5 above, with written suggestions for incorporation into proposals.
8. One member of Personnel in conjunction with one field and one residential staff member to collect information on yardsticks used and job values established in other social services agencies and relevant research data. Proposals incorporated into report under 3 above.
9. Personnel review with Clerks Department (Establishments) of pay and grading system, compiling evidence from other local authorities of measures used to increase flexibility.
10. Personnel pursue early allocation of central computer time for computerization of staff information and records, integrating this with salaries and wages scheme.
11. Personnel investigate findings of existing market research, or conduct its own with help of Clerks Department (Establishments), into recruitment trends in respect of different types and levels of staff.
12. Social Services Director to agree with Chief Executive, needs and desirability for increased support from Establishments in respect of these developments.
13. One Training Section member to attend short course on recruitment methods, effective advertising, selection methods, thereafter training relevant agency staff in these areas.
14. Planning section to inaugurate personnel interviews with all staff on future development on basis of staff development and personnel objectives. Agency objectives to be modified to take account of personnel objectives at each six-monthly review meeting.
15. Planning section, in conjunction with Personnel, to apply results of behavioural science research into factors relevant to effective staff deployment in terms of motivation, reward, environmental constraints, human relations and avoidable staff turnover.
16. Training section to establish staff induction schemes in consultation with all relevant staff.
17. Personnel section to produce well-presented booklets for distribution to all staff, giving information on pay, prospects, service conditions, training and development.
18. Social Services Director, with preparatory work and help from the Personnel, to produce report to Chief Executive, proposing urgent overhaul of present pay and grading structure so as to relate pay to correct value of each job and increase flexibility of structure so as

to reward individual ability.

19. Training section to investigate opportunities for planned 'skylighting' among staff, both as additional methods of reward, additional incentives to staff morale and a means of improving agency public relations.

20. Recruitment methods to include executive search techniques.

Appendix 6:
A Network Analysis
of Homelessness

What are the actual phases through which housing stress in the community manifests itself and what are the resulting agency operations undertaken in response to each phase?

Clearly the answer to these questions will differ from community to community and from agency to agency. However, a general picture of the alternative ways the problem develops and of the alternative possible agency responses to the problem begin to emerge from some analyses made in several local authority situations. This general picture is represented below in the form of a network analysis of homelessness. It is not presented as a definitive map of the processes involved, but rather as an initial attempt at an overview of these processes which needs to be revised and developed in the light of research and adopted to local situations.

I. The Development of Homelessness

The development of homeless problems can be tracked through seven phases: causal origins, starting points, referral points, pre-reception alternatives, homeless family units, routes out of units, levels of resettlement after the problem. Each phase may contain several possible alternatives. Thus a family may proceed through the seven phases by any one of a number of different courses. The particular course which the development of any one family's problem may take will define that family's problem in terms of its 'genetic development'. The experiences of this family will often be very different from the experiences of some other family for whom the problem has taken a different course. By tracking the different courses taken by different families through the seven phases, we begin to discriminate the different types of problem in terms of their development and the different conditions associated with each phase. Thus, the possible developments of homelessness problems may be mapped in the form of a network. We shall now outline some of the alternatives at each phase.

Causal Origins

Before the problem begins, the family is housed more or less satisfactorily. Yet the causal origins of the problem are already present and the problem may be simmering. Some of these causal origins may include:

1. An insufficient stock of cheap houses or accommodation in the local community;
2. Low family income and poor budgetary management;
3. Unacceptability of family to landlord as tenants;
4. Living in sub-standard housing;
5. Health risks;
6. Fire risks;
7. Flood risks;
8. Strong family antagonisms;
9. Lack of adequate home supports;
10. Difficulty in maintaining home;
11. Unacceptability to neighbours.

At some point in time, at least one of these causes becomes operative in some way, which leads through to the next phase.

Starting Points

This phase begins with the event or set of events, which provides the occasion for the onset of the problem. By the end of this phase, the problem impinges so drastically that action can no longer be postponed. Some of the alternative occasions may be:

1. Notice to quit;
2. Unauthorized occupation;
3. Eviction from accommodation;
4. Inability to find accommodation;
5. Speculative migration to a new area;
6. Mortgage failure;
7. Fire or flood;
8. Family break-up;
9. Breakdown of home maintenance;
10. Unacceptability to neighbours
11. Financial breakdown.

In one sense, eviction or loss of home followed by an inability to find accommodation may be seen as the consequential result of some of the other elements such as financial breakdown. However, they are listed together in this phase since they each describe the actual onset of the problem in terms of what prompts action on the client's part. Precipitate eviction will mark the onset of the problems for one family, whereas for another family financial breakdown which has yet to lead to eviction will prompt action in response to the family's recognition of the seriousness of their situation.

At some point in time, at least one of these occasions leads to the family's first contact with the social services agency.

Referral Points
This phase concerns the mode through which the client contacts or is referred to the social services agency which has often been shown to be significant. The process of reaching the agency may take a shorter or a longer period of time. Some of the alternatives seem to be:
1. Self-referral by client direct;
2. Voluntary agency;
3. Housing Authority;
4. Courts;
5. Citizens' Advice Bureau;
6. Health visitor;
7. Private landlord;
8. Town Planning Agency;
9. Neighbours;
10. Relatives;
11. Discovery by social services agency investigation.

Pre-Reception
As a result of referral via one of the referral points mentioned, the client or client family makes contact with the social services agency. A number of alternatives are usually explored, all of which are designed to prevent or delay reception into a homeless family unit. The consequential states of affairs may include one or more of the following:
1. Help with rent arrears;
2. Alternative private or publicly owned accommodation found;
3. Rent or mortgage guarantees;
4. Psychological – social support;
5. Financial assistance (e.g. grants from trusts, intervention with Social Security);
6. Revision of mortgage arrangements;
7. Arranging help from client's employees;
8. Stay of execution of eviction by landlord;
9. Residential placements or subsidized boarding house accommodation;
10. Accommodation with relatives;
11. Improved financial position through change of employment;
12. Community action with neighbours.

Homeless Family Unit (HFU)
If all these alternatives fail, or only succeed in delaying what often begins to appear as the 'inevitable' development of the problem,

reception into a homeless family unit and the family's experiences therein constitute the next stage of problem development. If there is time, the family will be helped to prepare for their entry into a homeless family unit in various ways. Once admitted, several alternative states of affairs may ensue. For example, the family may:

1. Remain self-supportive within the HFU context and make strenuous efforts to leave it;
2. Receive additional supports in the HFU setting;
3. Resign themselves to the HFU setting as though it were permanent;
4. Undergo a major deterioration in morale;
5. Disintegrate completely within the HFU setting.

Routes from Homeless Family Unit

There are several routes which a family may take out of the homeless family unit. Some of these include:

1. Family rehoused by Local Authority;
2. New tenancy under a private landlord;
3. Return to accommodation with family, relatives or friends;
4. Rehoused by housing trust;
5. Rehoused under housing association scheme;
6. Family splits up and finds separate accommodation individually;
7. Family rehoused in temporary squatters' accommodation;
8. Family moves to another area.

Outcomes

There are several alternative outcomes of the problem. The family's problem may be permanently resolved by settling them into satisfactory new accommodation, temporarily resolved in that temporary accommodation is found which is satisfactory for at least a short period of time, or after some temporary move from the homeless family unit, the whole cycle might begin again.

II. Agency Responses

For each phase through which the homeless problem proceeds the social services agency has the possibility of some kind of response. Parallel to the map of the alternative ways homeless problems develop just outlined, a network of how alternative agency homeless services are (or may be) successively introduced in response to these problems can be developed.

Primary Prevention

The agency begins with a situation of being geared up to some extent to respond to agency problems. At the very first phase where the causal origins of the problems begin to manifest themselves, the agency may engage in various kinds of primary prevention. Roughly, the alternatives may be seen in these terms:

1. Joint social policy and planning with Housing Authorities;
2. Liaison with rent collectors and insurance debt collectors;
3. Adaptation of old properties;
4. Special rent-paying arrangements agreed;
5. Early referral arrangements;
6. Lists of willing landlords with available accommodation;
7. Development of systematic and flexible Housing Authority rent-paying policies;
8. Rent subsidies;
9. Exchange tenancy schemes;
10. Income-planning and financial advice services;
11. Objective appraisal of threats to client's shelter;
12. Provision of social securities, supports, contacts and outlets for interests;
13. Extension of mortgage arrangements;
14. Consumer education in housing matters.

Secondary Prevention

All the alternative modes of primary prevention mentioned above are concerned with gaining recognition of the housing stress problems either by client, neighbourhood, or one of the agencies involved and nipping the problem in the bud if at all possible. Once the problem has been recognized, secondary prevention responses come into play if the problem has not been prevented from arising at the outset. The responses under this heading may include:

1. Early-warning arrangements or rent arrears;
2. Rent guarantees provided or negotiated with other agencies;
3. Mortgage guarantees provided or negotiated with other agencies;
4. Rehabilitative programmes;
5. Supportive work.

Tertiary Prevention

Where secondary prevention is inadequate, a range of tertiary prevention responses may be made. These might include:

1. Analysis of family's situation;
2. Consultation and advice to referral bodies in how to handle the problem;
3. Encouragement of the family to exploit its own alternatives;
4. Encouragement of appropriate client action;
5. Help by contacting relatives, neighbours, friends or other agencies on the client's behalf.

Pre-Homeless Unit Reception

Prior to taking the decision that there is no alternative to a family entering a homeless family unit, a range of agency responses may be made at the stage when pre-reception alternatives are explored:

1. Agreement made with the rent officer on how to handle rent arrears;
2. Financial assistance or loans may be made;
3. Relatives may be contacted;
4. Housing-ownership schemes may be fostered;
5. Rent or mortgage guarantees;
6. Housing Trusts may be contacted;
7. Long-term rehabilitative measure may be undertaken;
8. Solicitors contacted on the issues of instalment rent-payments;
9. Employers may be contacted to provide help.

Supervising Entry into Homeless Family Unit

Once the entry of the family into a homeless family unit has become inevitable, the focus of the worker's attention is on supervising and supporting the family's entry into the unit. Some of the alternatives, many of which occur in succession one after another, include:

1. Ascertain that eviction is inevitable;
2. Investigate availability of HFU vacancies;
3. Board out family in guest house as a temporary measure;
4. Investigate whether HFU is really necessary;
5. Add family to HFU waiting list, giving earliest and latest possible entry times;
6. Prepare family for nature of HFU situation;
7. Accompany family on visit to HFU;
8. Attend eviction if necessary;
9. Settle family into HFU;
10. Make necessary associated administrative arrangements (e.g. change of schools etc);
11. Use of residential placements.

Treatment in Homeless Family Unit

It is often pointless merely to use homeless family units as though they were old-style residential homes for the elderly. The aim is to use the HFU situation as a forum for treatment and rehabilitation. The very first condition for such an approach is the provision of HFUs which are usable in a flexible manner. The alternative possible agency responses to the family once it has arrived in the HFU include:

1. Support for family attempts at re-entry into the community;
2. Increase family's points rating on housing list;
3. Support family relations within HFU setting;
4. Support family in its contacts with others in HFU setting;

5. Stimulate family connections with others outside HFU setting;
6. Monthly case reviews;
7. Admit family to rehabilitation centre;
8. Admit family to longer-term HFU;
9. Admit children to Local Authority care;
10. Continue to explore alternatives to HFU;
11. Supervise family's re-entry into new accommodation.

After Care and Follow-Up
Once the family has left the homeless family unit, the agency worker maintains contact with the client and the relevant Housing Authority or private landlord to ensure that the client's improved situation is mentioned. Without some continued support, the family may repeat the same pattern of behaviour so that the whole cycle begins again.

Using the Homelessness Network Analysis

The map of the development of homelessness can obviously be detailed further. However, it provides a general picture of the alternative pattern which homelessness may take. Any one family's problems may of course jump any one of the phases mentioned. Many families, for example, are able to progress straight from a situation of mortgage failure through to some more or less satisfactory rehousing. Other families may, having experienced the process once, go through the whole process a second time.

One advantage workers have found in using such a map is that it helps them to analyze and track the development of a particular family's problem and share this insight with the client, instead of regarding the whole history as though it were some picaresque novel in which event succeeds event unpredictably and haphazardly.

Similarly, the network of agency responses which correspond to the various phases of a homeless problem may be thought through by the worker in advance of the actual need for them, so that a clear picture emerges of what may be needed to be done and when. This enables all agency workers to warn agency planners in advance of probable and possible future demands on service, which in turn may provide the agency with sufficient time to pre-plan services and prevent some of the emergencies which arise with such disastrous consequences in connection with homeless problems.

In using this type of network for managing daily operations within a specific agency situation, various pieces of specific information are necessary. For example, the numbers of people in each alternative stream should be monitored, those who are homeless as a result of eviction, what happens to those homeless through eviction at later points in time and the type of accommodation in which they end up.

This enables the agency to answer the question: do people who are homeless through eviction tend typically to end up in one type of accommodation rather than another? Is this correlation caused through any specific agency procedure or does it reflect certain community trends and structures? If the former, would a change in agency procedure help? If the latter, has the agency some responsibility for changing community trends and structures via social-planning activities community-worker advocacy, or other kinds of social action?

Correlations between different stages of problem development may be noted. For instance, there may be some correlation between those whose problem is caused through local authority eviction following rent arrears and/or possession orders and those whose problem is finally resolved by the local housing authority rehousing them again. Correlations may also occur over time between the development of problems and their resolution. For instance, the occurrence of homelessness in the private sector may typically lead to rehousing of the family in the local authority sector and vice versa. This correlation could lead us to conclude in particular situations that the net effect of social services policies *vis-à-vis* homelessness amounts to little more *in toto* than a gigantic swop between the poorest, most insecure families in the public sector with the poorest, most insecure families in the private sector. There seems to be evidence supporting this analysis in some communities, though the research has not been done which demonstrates the analysis conclusively.

Correlations may become evident between different types of homelessness, agency responses to each type and the final outcomes of each problem. If established, such correlations would enable the social services agency to predict from its early contacts, such relevant items as probable numbers requiring homeless family unit accommodation, the probable length of their stay in such units, numbers of local authority buildings to be provided for particular types of clients, and so on. Such information would be of inestimable help to local authority planning. This would allow the agency potentially to improve their purchase on the homeless situation through systematic planning based on more systematic prediction. An audit may be made of numbers of homeless or potentially homeless persons at each stage of development and numbers currently consuming agency resources. Assessments are made of the number of persons who are expected at various times to move through to the next stage of development in the light of the homelessness treatment plan for each client. The average loss of clients at each stage for reasons other than progress or retrogress through agency services (e.g. through disaffiliation with the agency's services, removal from the area, death etc.) is calculated. Given this information, it then becomes possible to predict the probable claims on services at each stage for future time periods. We can then view the existing flow of demand for homeless services at different stages.

If we were interested in the difference between existing demands for homeless services and potential need, it would be necessary to mount a community audit. Factors could be reviewed which might cause the existing flow to increase or decrease (e.g. probability of increased housing stress through redevelopment, unemployment etc.) and future demands predicted accordingly. By comparing the probable future availability of homeless services in respect of future periods of time, we can begin to define the existing and future gaps between demand for homeless services and their availability. On this basis, rational plans for the agency's homeless services can begin to be made.

Managers may seek to expand homeless services to meet predicted demands, increase utilization of existing homeless services by the development of alternative means of meeting the needs of the homeless within the community, or begin to make more explicit priorities for the allocation of scarce homeless services among those demanding them. Such an integrated planning system for homeless services requires more explicit case opening and case closure criteria on the basis of which homeless services are provided, as well as clearer social indicators of what conditions are likely to delay or propel a family's problem from one stage to another.

Glossary

All definitions are framed with reference to the subject-matter of this text.

Activity. A particular thing a person actually does or performs, by which input resources are utilized to achieve outcome results.

Activity Network. A diagram of a particular combination of activities, connected by arrows to show their sequential relationships.

Administration. The process of interpreting policy and translating it into action.

Agology. Study of change processes.

Alienation. Distance, separation, withdrawal, isolation, anonymity and inaccessibility among community members.

Alignment. Interrelating and meshing of objectives of different levels, streams or time-horizons to form a coherent, interconnected and logical system.

Anomie. Personal and group disorganization and disorientation through desocialization and retreat by the individual into his own ego or the group into group consciousness.

Assumed Objective. An objective as variously assumed or perceived by staff or clients of an organization.

Autism. Cognitive processes in which there is a turning point away from reality, so that inner life dominates.

Awareness. Reflective mental attitudes enabling individuals and groups to understand themselves and their environments with varying degrees of clarity.

Axiology. The study of values and their impacts on living.

Breakdown. Disintegration of the stable equilibrium of a personality or of a situation, as in personal or social emergencies, crises or disasters.

Cinderella Services. Neglected services potentially capable of meeting a distinct need effectively if properly developed.

Community. A system or collectivity wherein supra-unit relations and norms, which bind the sub-units and regulate their relations, are more powerful than intra- or inter- sub-unit bonds. Its members are potentially capable of acting in unison by appeal to common normative bonds.

Community Settlement Agency. An agency whose primary task is fostering social integration of all community groups and forces.

Compulsion. An irresistible impulse to perform some act contrary to one's better judgement or will.

Conflict Theory. The view of objectives as specific irreconcilable commitments between opposed interest groups.

Consciousness. A generalized capacity to be aware, to pay attention.

Consensus. Congruence of perspective among a set of actors.

Consensus-Formation. The process by which the perspectives of organizational or community members are transmitted upwards to the controlling management and downwards to change-implementers, differences among them being reduced.

Constraint. A factor limiting freedom of choice in objectives set, sanctioned or pursued.

Containment Agency. An agency specializing in preventing deterioration of problems which have proved unamenable to treatment elsewhere.

Control. The process of revising on-going processes and correcting errors to reduce the distance from agreed objectives and prevent situations getting out of hand.

Corporate Planning. Periodic intensive meetings attended by the organization's management group to develop long range objectives jointly.

Cost Benefit. The ratio of community or client benefits obtained, to agency or service costs.

Cost-Benefit Analysis. A process used to evaluate the socio-economic costs and benefits of a programme, service, or project.

Cost Effectiveness. A process for deciding the optimal feasible way of providing services, the value of which cannot be measured in money terms.

Critical Path Analysis. Acitvities necessary to carry out operations are mapped in terms of a graphical model comprising logical and temporal interconnections, costs and times for each constituent task. The model is analyzed, times determining overall project time and cost extracted, and relative significance of each constituent task calculated.

Cybernetics The science of analyzing and improving management, communication and control processes by which systems operate.

Debilitative Environment. An environment in which social elements predominate which are inimical to individual growth, development, stability.

Decision. The actual selection from a range of possible alternatives of a course of action designed to achieve a particular objective. A conscious choice between two or more alternatives.

Decision-maker. Anyone whose choices influence outcomes of what is done or achieved by an agency.

Dependency. The individual's or group's reliance on others' resources to achieve their own ends.

Depersonalization. The individual's or group's loss of identity through institutionalization, collectivism, groupism, bureaucratisation, self-devaluation, self-diffusion and self-deprecation. The process of being dissolved, of losing the identity, personality, the "I". A mental phenomenon characterized by loss of the sense of the reality of oneself. It often carries with it loss of the sense of the reality of others and of the environment.

Depression. A complex feeling, ranging from unhappiness to deep dejection and hopelessness; often accompanied by more or less absurd feelings of guilt, failure, and unworthiness, as well as by self-destructive tendencies. Its physical concomitants are usually disturbances of sleep and appetite and a general slowing-down of many physiological processes.

Determinism. An approach in which predicted futures are seen as following inevitably upon what is currently the case.

Development. Reconstruction and upgrading of individuals and groups to do better justice to potentialities of human nature.

Developmental Services. Services with a large potential for meeting need though still in the process of introduction.

Deviance. Social disorganization or digressive behaviour within a given milieu, which so intensively or persistently departs from or conflicts with socially, culturally or ethically accepted norms, codes or expectations that it comprehensively or permanently disturbes the equilibrium and possibility of viable interaction continuing.

Diagnostic Agency. An agency tending to specialize in expert diagnosis of client problems followed by referral through to specialist treatment for other agencies.

Directionality. Apparent purposiveness or directedness of an agency system.

Discretion. The relative freedom and authority to decide or pursue a particular objective according to one's own judgement and decision, rather than according to another's decision.

Economic Security. Fulfilment of individual and group rights to sufficient money to pay for food, shelter and clothing, and to an income sufficient to support basic human passions.

Effectiveness. The extent to which an agency makes an impact on its community, a service makes an impact on needs it was designed to fulfil, a staff member achieves the output or outcome requirements of his position.

Effectiveness Areas. Those key areas in which successful results would make an extremely large contribution to the work of the agency and which we cannot afford to neglect at any price. General output requirements of a managerial position.

Effectiveness Standards. Specific output requirements and measurement criteria of a managerial position.

Emotional Stress. Debilitative emotional pressures, tensions, strains, frustration and suffering.

Equality. Evenness of life chances of individuals, groups and communities.

Expectation. Level of goal-achievement demanded and anticipated.

Extant Objective. Objective actually pursued or implied in action or method of work as revealed by systematic exploration and analysis.

Field of Action (of an objective). A set of cases taken to lie within the purview or domain of application of an objective. Subscription to the objective calls for a certain position or stance in regard to these cases.

Frustration. Temporary or permanent obstruction and thwarting of felt needs and drives by interruption of goal-seeking behaviour.

Fulfilment. Satisfaction of felt needs and drives, discharge of tensions as they arise, and gratification which accompanies activities which accord with individual impulses or goal achievement.

Futuristic Services. Services chiefly valuable for their potentiality in meeting the community needs which predictably will arise in the future.

Goal. Synonymous with objective.

Growth. Development of the individual's ego and capacities so that they are integrated with the timetable of his organic needs and the structure of his social environment. Developing socio-cultural accumulation in which new cultural elements or traits are progressively and cumulatively added to those already present.

Heterogeneous Environment. A social environment containing a heterogeneous and stimulating range of activities and functions, supported by and supporting varied occupation or leisure groups resulting in variety, richness, experiment, spontaneity and socio-cultural variation.

Homogeneous Environment. A social environment producing uniformity among community members.

Horizontal Alignment. Interrelating and meshing objectives relating to different streams of need, service or activity, so that they form a coherent and logical system.

Hysteria. A neurotic condition characterized by the conversion of emotional conflicts into physical manifestations — e.g. pain, anesthesia, paralysis, chronic spasms — without actual physical impairment of the afflicted organ or organs.

Idealist Objectives. All short-run objectives are viewed as degrees of approximation to an unattainable, ideal goal.

Implementation. Performing activities necessary to achieve objectives.

Inarticulateness. Impulses, thoughts, wishes or feelings blocked from consciousness or verbalised expression through neurotic inhibitions, guilt or repression.

Individualization. The individual's sense of his own unique personal identity, integrity and continuity of self; his particular interests, aversions, needs and predelictions. A clear intact conception of self-hood.

Inequality. Social under-privilege arising from inequities and injustices of life chances.

Influence. The encouragement of a course of action which is in line with the preferences of the actors involved.

Input. The effort, energy, skills, knowledge, personnel or other resources which provide the basis on which action may take place. Inputs provide the material, personnel, clients or situations which action will in some way affect.

Input-Output Analysis. A process of describing, in quantitative terms, the transactions which take place during a specified period of time, between a number of entities. A comparison of the inputs in their initial state prior to action, and the outputs or outcomes in their later state after action has occurred.

Insecurity. The individual's or group's non-fulfilment or uncertainty of meeting their basic physiological needs of food, shelter and clothing, emotional needs for belongingness and reward, gratification, and mental needs for intellectual vitamins and nourishment.

Insentience. Lack of awareness of shared societal expectations, or utilization of role-taking skills, in structuring and interpreting relations meaningfully, resulting in insensitivity, lack of information, ignorance and avoidance of problems.

Integrated Managing, Planning, and Action System (IMPACTS). A coherent, systematic approach to planning and managing work processes, based on matching objectives-resources-operations-structures, in ways which integrate professional and administrative methods and concerns.

Intention. A subjective determination to act in a particular manner designed to produce a certain result.

Issue Analysis. Various versions of the systematic problem-solving or decision-making process applied to particular topics or problems on which a decision between alternative courses of action must be taken in order to achieve a given objective.

Job Effectiveness Description. A written statement specifying the effectiveness areas, effectiveness standards and authority of a particular managerial position.

Key Targets. Those specific critical objectives or end results to which we attach priority in virtue of their critical importance in terms of overall effectiveness.

Life Chances. The individual's or group's supply of goods, external living conditions and personal life experiences, or increased opportunity of attaining these irrespective of the starting point.

Management.
1. Applying principles of effective action and interaction to improve things in the working situation.
2. Deciding between alternative ways of gearing up work processes to achieve more beneficial results for communities and clients.

3. Deciding what to do and getting it done.

Management by Objectives. A process of formulating overall agency objectives and deriving from these sub-unit objectives which are either small-scale replicas of overall objectives or are set in such a way that by working towards them the sub-unit fulfils its own objectives.

Manager. A person who takes some part in planning, executing and controlling the work of others.

Managerial Effectiveness. The extent to which a manager achieves the output requirements of his position.

Manifest Objective. An objective as it is officially reported to be or approved in the organization's constitutions, creeds, legislative sanctions, operating manuals and official statements.

Manpower Planning. A process used for assessing the future staff requirements of an organization in relation to its objectives. A wide range of factors are weighed up and a comprehensive plan for selection and training devised for all levels over the following few years to ensure a flow of staff adequate to achieve long-term agency objectives.

Measurement Method. The way in which the degree of attainment of an objective is to be determined.

Mental Instability. Disorder among the individual's or group's emergent emotions, beliefs, perceptions or activities — disbalance between the individual's or group's responses as a whole to internal or external stimulation in relation to their past experience and future expectations — irrationality, neurosis, prejudice and mental aberration in which choice is exclusively dominated by emotions, drives, instincts and impulses.

Mental Stability. The organized

totality of the individual's or group's emergent emotions, beliefs, perceptions and activities — the balancing of the individual's or group's responses as a whole to internal or external stimulation in relation to their past experience and future expectations.

Meta—. A prefix meaning "changed in position", "beyond", "higher", "transcending", etc. Used generally as referring to the body of knowledge *about* a body of knowledge or field of study, e.g. metamathematics, metacommunications.

Model. A map or representation of a complex real-life situation in which certain symbols are used to stand in or do duty for certain aspects of the real-life situation. A map of organizational objectives constitutes one such model.

Negative Feedback. Pinpointing, at time of evaluation and review, what has gone wrong, and the feeding back of this information into the working process so that corrections can be made.

Network Analysis. A pictorial model which maps the interrelations between activities and events in the process of achieving an end objective. Variants include Critical Path Analysis (C.P.A.) and Programme Evaluation and Review Technique (P.E.R.T.).

Objective. A preferred state of affairs, end result, feasible outcome, benefit sought, value to be realized, to which resources and operations are directed.

Objectives Abandonment. A person, group, or agency, ceases to adhere to objectives to which they previously subscribed.

Objectives Distribution. Pattern of adherence to an objective as diffused amongst a group or agency.

Objectives Redeployment. Change in

boundaries of field of action of an objective (e.g. of political equality to include Asians).

Objectives Redistribution. Change in pattern of distribution of an objective within a group or agency.

Objectives Scale. Comparative ordering of objectives by greater or lesser priority.

Objectives Subscription. A person, group or agency holds, accepts, subscribes or adheres to a certain objective.

Occupational Mobilization. Increasing, diversifying, and releasing latent energy of individuals and groups, hence of community social assets or of a particular under-privileged group.

Occupational Technology. Technology of effectively performing operations.

Operations Research. Application of scientific methods and techniques to a system's functioning so as to provide decision-makers with optimum feasible resolutions of problems.

Optimum — Optimal. The best possible resolution of a problem in view of the many varied factors in the situation.

Organization. All the factors which influence behaviour within a social system that are common to essentially unrelated positions.

Organization Structure. The way work processes and roles are structured to get agency objectives achieved.

Output. The results, outcome or effects of our operations or activities.

Participation. Staff and/or consumers share in processes of formulating objectives, defining problems, analyzing alternatives, gathering information, formulating decisions, implementing and evaluating changes in relation either to community, agency, or individual development.

Performance Appraisal. Review of the effectiveness or otherwise of the work of staff.

Personal Effectiveness. The extent to which a manager achieves his own private objectives.

Personnel Objectives. The sum total of vocational aims of staff based on their perceptions of agency objectives and personal needs.

Phobia. A morbid fear associated either with a specific object or a specific situation.

Physical Malfunctioning. Impairment, defectiveness, and disturbances of function resulting in incapacity for physical self-care, physical pain and discomfort, and associated subjective feelings.

Physical Wellbeing. Internal bodily equipoise and adaptation to environment.

Planning. The process of selecting and valuing objectives, policies and priorities, and the programmes and procedures for achieving them, by looking ahead and postulating a requisite situation to be attained.

Planning Meta-Language. This is a higher-order language which we use to talk *about* and conceptualize reality — to comment on the *structure* of activities, situations, and on the daily action language we use. It is the language of theory, of research work, of training, of philosophy, of planning and policy-making.

Planning — Programming — Budgeting Systems (P.P.B.S.). A system aimed at helping management make better decisions on the allocation of resources among alternative ways of obtaining objectives. It focuses on identifying the fundamental objectives of the agency and then relating all activities to these regardless of their organizational placement.

Policy. The total set of objectives and priorities adopted by the organization or its members.

Policy Sciences. Sciences and technologies, especially cybernetics, relevant to policy formation.

Posteriority. A non-priority.

Poverty. Income, housing or social deprivation, insufficiency, dislocation or dis-economy.

Power. A term which defines the strength or intensity of influence that a person or body is potentially capable of exerting regardless either of the role assumed or authority carried. The capacity to introduce change in the face of resistance; a capacity to overcome part or all of the resistance.

Power, Political. The capacity to control the state and other downward political processes.

Power, Societal. The capacity of a societal unit to gain its way in the face of resistance by other societal units.

Praxiology. Study of the principles of action.

Prediction. Forecast outcome.

Predictive Objective. An objective based on a prediction rather than a plan.

Preventive Agency. An agency placing primary emphasis on preventive policies.

Preventive Policies. Expansion of operations in an 'anterior' direction so that, through various preventive measures, we may begin to make some impact on causes or earlier manifestations of social problems.

Primary Services. Services which are effectively meeting current, primary needs and demands of the community.

Priority. The degree of significance (as measured in money, time, energy, attention, skill, or some other value) attached to one of a number of objectives, problems, services, or courses of action. We should in principle, like to accomplish all the objectives, resolve all the problems, provide all the services, or undertake all the courses of action considered, given sufficient resources or time. But given the normal work situation of scarce resources, we are obliged to make choices between them.

Priority Scaling. A systematic process for analyzing and agreeing an integrated, coherent set of priorities for action in terms of objectives, resources and operations at every level of the organization.

Procedure. A defined method of handling an activity or work process which details the sequence in which this activity is accomplished.

Programme. A complex of policies, resources, procedures, operations, task assignments and other elements necessary to achieve a defined objective.

Project. A concerted effort which entails the focusing of energy and comparatively intensive and guided activity related to limited and specified tasks.

Project Groups. Project groups are teams whose members are brought together in one team from several levels and functions, to spend their whole time resolving and implementing solutions to problems which cut across all operating line units.

Psychopathology. A generic term denoting emotional and/or mental illnesses or disturbances, or the branch of medicine dealing with these conditions.

Psychotic. Pertaining to the psychoses, i.e. psychiatric conditions of either organic or functional (− psychogenic) nature of such a degree that the patient's individual, intellectual, professional, social, etc. functioning is severely impaired, while in the − psychoneurotic patient this impairment is only partial and limited to certain areas of his life.

Public Administration Agency. An agency primarily emphasising provision of statutory services for eligible clientele.

Purpose. What is desired and viewed as possible, even though no specific method of affecting this result is formulated.

Ratchet Principle. Setting a slightly higher objective than the one previously attained.

Rational Behaviour. Synonomous with mental stability.

Regression. Return to earlier, less developed patterns of behaviour or stages of ego or community development.

Requisite Objective. The optimal recommended or desired objective. The objectives which the agency would have to pursue to meet a defined range of needs and values most appropriately.

Rescaling Objectives. Reordering of priority among objectives comprising an objectives scale.

Resources. The means or wherewithal to accomplish action and achieve objectives which may consist of money, materials, equipment, information, staff time, space, clients or other inputs.

Responsibility. A staff member's sense of obligation to do a specified piece of work or to endeavour to achieve a particular objective.

Responsiveness. That which takes into account the needs of the units involved.

Retardation. Decline in individual or community capacities.

Retargeting. A change in interim targets set for implementing the objective, or of related target dates.

Role. The position of an agency (or person) in relation to others in the same field, taking into account his social as well as his formal working relations with others.

Safety Needs. Basic physiological needs of food, shelter and clothing, emotional needs for belongingness and reward gratification, and mental needs for intellectual vitamins and nourishment. Immunity of individuals and groups from apprehensions, anxieties and insecurities, ranging from uneasiness to complete panic in reaction to either real or symbolic, actual or potential dangers, hazards, risks, nuisance and threats.

Sanction. Sufficient formal or informal support for a particular objective (or set of objectives) for it to be consciously pursued.

Schedule. A plan with timings.

Schizophrenia. A psychiatric condition accounting for about half the patients in mental hospitals and about one quarter of all hospital patients in the United States. The term was coined by the Swiss psychiatrist E. Bleuler and denotes a psychosis marked by fundamental disturbances in the patient's perceptions of reality, concept formations, affects, and

consequently, his behaviour in general. Depending on the specific symptomatology, schizophrenia is usually divided into various subgroups, e.g. the paranoid, hebephrenic, catatonic, and simple forms.

Self-Determination. The individual's or community's actual exercise of freedom by purposeful, willed behaviour in the direction of their own choosing, resulting in self-help, self-direction, assertiveness, self-sufficiency and autonomy.

Self-Expression. Articulation and verbalization of the individual's or group's emotions feelings and thoughts.

Situational Objectives. Goals evolved as a result of environmental conditioning of agency work.

Social Casualty Service. Expansion of operations in a 'forwards' direction towards the most socially disabled clients or towards a universalist service.

Social Competence. Adaptive efficiency in response to environmental changes and behavioural equilibrium; capacity and ability of individual, group or community to understand, master, orient themselves to and participate in the prevailing customs, habits and behaviour of society.

Social Ennui. Boredom and restlessness in relation to social life and leisure.

Social Environment. System of spatial and temporal regularities of human structure which influences biological and behavioural processes of the population as a whole and of individuals.

Social Gratification. Pleasurable activities; optimal use of leisure; outlets for individual and group interests.

Social Ineffectuality. Apathy — the

reluctance to act – the inability or lack of opportunity to perform useful occupational activities.

Social Integration. Cohesion, interconnectedness, consensus or concern for others, among its diverse members so that members of different interests or reference groups, social classes, income brackets, and races, can live together harmoniously.

Social Malfunctioning. Incapacity and inability of individual, group or community to understand, master, orient themselves to and participate in the prevailing customs, habits and behaviour of society.

Social Participation. Inclusion, responsiveness and authentic involvement by individuals in the processes which shape their social behaviour, and the investment of energy and ego-involvement in those activities, persons, events and situations which the individual finds significant for himself.

Social Planning. Study and management of systematic social development to achieve given social objectives in the interests of a given population with given problems or concerns.

Social Planning Agency. An agency primarily concerned with integrating all social aspects of community planning into a rational, effective framework.

Speciality Services. Services which make a limited and distinct impact on one aspect of a specific social problem and employ limited resources to accomplish this.

Specific Effectiveness Areas. Effectiveness areas specific to particular managerial positions rather than common to all.

Standard. Guideline for measuring or evaluating the extent to which an objective is attained in particular cases within its domain of application.

Stigmatization. Discrimination, discredit, scapegoating and victimization attaching to a variety of individual deviations from norms and expectations. Unfavourable treatment or attributions of inferiority to certain categories of people on arbitrary or irrational grounds which have little to do with the actual behaviour of those stigmatized.

Strategy. A stage-by-stage plan for achieving long-term targets and objectives.

Structures. Mechanisms for assigning problems to the most qualified, informed or experienced person.

Supportive Environment. A social environment which is growth inducing and restorative in respect of physical, social and cultural elements and their interrelations.

Supportive Services. Services necessary to accomplish the primary results the agency seeks, though not directly contributing to them.

Surrogate. A substitute or proxy measure of something tangible which stands in or does duty for a less tangible, qualitative phenomenon which cannot be measured directly.

Synthesis. The organization of bits into contexts.

System. An entity which consists of interrelated, interacting or interdependent parts manifesting coherence, pattern, directionality and dynamism.

Systems Technology. The technologies for managing social and organizational systems.

Systems Theory. Principles and hypotheses about interrelations between parts of a system.

Tactics. A stage-by-stage plan for achieving short-term targets and objectives.

Target. That part of the intent for the sake of which specific actions were adopted.

Technique. A method or process for systematically analyzing and resolving a specific type of work problem or achieving a specific kind of objective.

Temporal Alignment. Interrelating and meshing objectives through time (i.e. extant and requisite objectives) so that they form a coherent and logical system.

Time Span. The length of time which elapses before the results of work are evaluated or reviewed by others.

Tolerance. Permissiveness or acceptance of deviations from social norms, which implies a greater variety and heterogeneity of social behaviour.

Transformation. The actual process of change by which an initial situation is rendered different by our action, by which resources are used to produce results.

Treatment Agency. An agency tending to expand the variety of its methods of treatment and therapy, perhaps relying on other's diagnosis.

Universalist Service. Service catering for the full variety of potential client need covering all families, not just those within defined problem groups.

Valuation. Coordinated conception of comparative relevance and desirability of various things in relation to human attitudes, needs and desires.

Value Theory. A theory about how values, hence objectives, are evolved.

Values. Excellence, significance, desirability, attributed to states, situations, behaviours, etc.

Variety. The number of discrete elements or aspects which may be delineated in a situation.

Vertical Alignment. Interrelating and meshing objectives of different levels of generality and specificity (i.e. higher-order and lower-order objectives) so that they form a coherent and logical system.

Work. Utilization of resources in carrying out activities to achieve optimal feasible objectives.

References

Chapter 1

1. *Chronically Sick and Disabled Persons Act 1970*, HMSO, 1970
2. *Report of the Committee on the Local Authority and Allied Personal Social Services* (Seebohm Report), Cmnd 3703, HMSO, 1968

Chapter 2

1. *Manifesto of Columbus South Side Settlement*, Columbus, Ohio, U.S.A., 1972
2. *Seebohm Report*, op cit
3. For example see — Royal Borough of Kingston-Upon-Thames, 'Social Services Committee Proceedings', 1970
4. N Dalkey, *The Delphi Method*, Rand Corporation, 1969
5. C Morris, *Management Science*, Prentice-Hall, 1969
6. J Algie, 'Evaluation and Social Services Departments', in *Evaluation in the Health Services*, W A Laing (ed), Office of Health Economics, 1972
7. D Bannister & J Mair, *The Evaluation of Personal Constructs*, Academic Press, 1968
8. J Boissevain, *Friends of Friends*, Basil Blackwell, 1974
9. European Social Development Programme, *Seminar on Nordic Approaches to Social Planning*, Copenhagen, 1972, UN, 1973
10. W Williams & J Evans, 'The Politics of Evaluation: the Case of Head Start', in *Annals of American Academy of Political and Social Science*, 385, 1969
11. O Helmer, 'Simulating the Values of the Future', in K Baier & N Rescher (eds), *Values and the Future*, NY Free Press, 1969
12. See Appendix 2
13. Chronically Sick and Disabled Persons Act 1970

14. J Algie, 'Management and Organization of the Social Services', in *British Hospital Journal and Social Service Review,* 80, No 4184, 26.6.70

15. See Appendix 2

16. J Algie, 'Evaluation and Social Services Departments', in
&17. *Evaluation of the Health Services,* op cit

18. Office of Population Censuses and Surveys, *Handicapped and Impaired in Great Britain, Part I,* by Amelia Harris, HMSO, 1971

19. *Integrated Client and Community Information Systems,* unpublished training manual by J Algie and A Kromholz, National Institute for Social Work, 1972

20. J Forrester, *Urban Dynamics,* Wright-Allen, 1962

21. J Coleman, *Simulating Social Processes,* Prentice-Hall, 1962

22. G Mallen, *SIMPOL: A Simulation of Police Activities,* Home Office and SSRC Research Document, 1967

23. W Eicker, *HAWSIM Manual: A Health and Welfare Simulation,* Applied Human Service Systems, Brandeis University, 1971

24. W Eicker, J Wulff & M Joshi, *DESIM Manual: A Health and Welfare Decision Simulation,* Applied Human Service Systems, Brandeis University, 1972
   J Algie, *SODESIM: A Social Decision Simulation,* unpublished training document, NISW, 1972

25. K G Lockyer, *An Introduction to Network Analysis,* Pitman, 1964

26. M North, *Personality Assessment through Movement,* MacDonald & Evans, 1972

Chapter 3

1. This analysis follows Maslow's famous hierarchy of needs in A H Maslow, *Motivation and Personality,* Harper & Row, 1954

2. Chronically Sick and Disabled Persons Act 1970, op cit

Chapter 4

1. S Alinsky, *Rules for radicals,* Random House, 1971

2. Seebohm Report, op cit

3. Seebohm Report, op cit

Chapter 5

1. H A Murray (ed), *Explorations in Personality,* Oxford University Press, 1938

2. R Mayer, *Social Planning and Social Change,* Prentice-Hall, 1972

3. D Gill, *Unravelling Social Policy,* Schenkman Publishing Co, 1973

4. R Warren, *Truth, Love and Social Change*, Rand McNally, 1971
5. R Uhlig, *A Study in Social Service Values and Priorities*, Pittsburg Health and Welfare Council, 1956
6. G Hartmann, 'Six differences in Valuational Attitudes', in *Journal of Social Psychology*, 5, 1934
   'Value as the Unifying Concept of the Social Sciences', in *Journal of Social Psychology*, 10, 1939
7. F Brentano, *Ueber die Zuknuft der Philosophie*, Germany, 1893
8. A Meinong, *Psychologisch Ettische Untersuchungen zur Wertheogie*, Graz, 1894
9. J Findlay, *Axiology*, Prentice-Hall, 1970
10. R S Downie, *Roles and Values*, Methuen, 1971
11. H D Lasswell, *A Preview of Policy Sciences*, Elsevier, 1971
12. A Brecht, *Political Theory*, Princeton University Press, 1959
13. J Friedman, 'The Study and Practice of Planning', in *International Social Science Journal*, 11, No 3, 1959
14. W Reid & L Epstein, *Task Centred Casework*, Columbia University Press, 1972
15. O von Mering, *A Grammar of Values*, University of Pittsburg Press, 1961
16. H Spencer, *Systems of Synthetic Philosophy*, London 1862–92
17. C M Kluckhohn, 'The Evolution of Contemporary American Values', in *Daedalus*, 87, 1958
    C M Kluckhohn, 'Towards a Comparision of Value Emphases in Different Cultures', in L White, *The State of the Social Sciences*, Chicago University Press
18. *Nordic Approach to Social Planning:* Report of Seminar held in Rungstedgaard, Copenhagen, United Nations, 1973
19. G Blum, *A Model of the Mind*, Wiley, 1961
20. E B Hunt and C I Hovland, 'Programming a Model of Human Concept Formulation', in E Fiegenbaum and J Feldman (eds) *Computers and Thought*, McGraw-Hill, 1963
21. A Rosenblatt, 'Perception Experience', in *Proceedings of the IRE*, Vol 48, March 1960
22. L Uhr and C Vossler, 'A Pattern-recognition Program that Generates, Evaluates and Adjusts its own Operators', in E Feigenbaum and J Feldman (eds) *Computers and Thought*, op cit
23. J T and J E Gullahorn, 'A Computer Model of Elementary Behaviour', in E Feigenbaum and J Feldman, (eds) *Computers and Thought*, McGraw-Hill, 1963
24. K M Colby, 'Experimental Treatment of Neurotic Computer Programmes', in *Archives of General Psychiatry*, American Medical Association, 1964
    K M Colby, J B Watt and J P Gilbert, 'A Computer Method of

Psychotherapy', in *Journal of Nervous and Mental Disease,* 142, 1966

25. J C Loehlin, *Computer Models of Personality,* Random House, 1968
26. H A Murray, (ed) *Explorations in Personality,* op cit
27. K Baier and N Rescher, (eds) *Values and the Future,* NY Free Press, 1969
28. L Hazard, 'Can we Afford Our National Goals?' in *Harvard Business Review,* June 1972
29. Baier, *Values and the Future,* op cit
30. G W Allport, P E Vernon and G Lindsey, *Manual for the Study of Values,* Boston, 1960
31. H Hyman, 'The Value Systems of Different Classes', in Bendix, Reinhard and Lipset (eds) *Class, Status and Power,* Glencoe Free Press, 1953
32. S M Lipset, 'The Value Patterns of Democracy: A Case Study in Comparative Analysis', in *American Sociological Review,* Vol 28, 1963
33. E Spranger, Ueber die Stellung der Werturtheile in der Nationalokonomie, Munich, 1914
    E Spranger, *Types of Men,* Houghton Mifflin, 1960
34. G Hartmann, Articles in *Journal of Social Psychology,* op cit
35. J Findlay, *Axiology,* op cit
36. O von Mering, *A Grammar of Values,* op cit
37. K Baier and N Rescher, (eds) *Values and the Future,* op cit
38. J P Powelson, 'Economic Attitudes in Latin America and the United States', in K Baier and N Rescher (eds) *Values and the Future,* op cit
39. L Hazard, Article in *Harvard Business Review,* op cit
40. Baier, op cit
41. W Reid & L Epstein, *Task Centred Casework,* Columbia University Press, 1972
42. H Stein and R Cloward, *The Impact of Value on Practice: Social Perspectives on Behaviour,* Glencoe Free Press, 1963
43. H H Perlman, *Social Casework, a Problem Solving Process,* Chicago University Press, 1960
44. N Gilbert & H Specht, *Dimensions of Social Welfare Policy,* Prentice-Hall, 1974
45. H D Lasswell, *A Preview of Policy Sciences,* op cit
46. J Friedman, 'The Study and Practice of Planning, in *International Social Science Journal,* 11, No 3, 1959
47. H Goldstein, *Social Work Practice: a Unitary Approach,* University of South Carolina Press, 1973
48. Brecht, op cit
49. See — J Speigel and D Walker (eds) *Information Systems Sciences,*

Spartan Books, 1965

50. J Burckhardt, *Civilisation of the Renaissance in Italy*, Phaidon, 1945

51. M Croft, *Red Carpet to China*, Longmans, 1965

52. R Bales, *Interaction Process Analysis*, Addison Wesley, 1950

53. T Marmor, M Rein, & S van Til, 'Post-War European experience with cash transfers', in *The President's Commission on Income Maintenance Programs*, US Government Printing Office, 1970

54. A Gouldner, 'Secrets of Organization', *National Conference on Social Welfare — The Social Welfare Forum, 1963 Official Proceedings*, Columbia University Press, 1963 (161–177)

55. G Leibnitz, *Leibnitz Selections*, ed P Weiner, Scribner, 1951
Philosophical Writings, trans, Morris Everyman, Dent, 1934

56. H H Aptekar, *The Dynamics of Community Work and Counselling*, Houghton Mifflin, 1955

57. D Miller, *Effectiveness of Social Services to AFDC Recipients*, San Francisco Social Psychiatry Research Association, October 1968
D Miller, 'New Definition of our Poor', in *New York Times*, 21 April, 1963

58. J E Mayer and N Timms, *The Client Speaks*, Routledge and Kegan Paul, 1970

59. H Strupp, R Fox and K Lessler, *Patients view their Psychotherapy*, John Hopkins Press, 1969

60. S Lipkin, 'Client's Feelings and Attitudes in Relation to the Outcome of Client Centred Therapy', in *Psychological Monographs*, Vol 68, No 1, 1954

61. S Briar, 'Welfare from Below: Recipients' Views of the Public Welfare System', in *California Law Review*, May, 1966
S Briar, 'Family Services', in H Maas (ed) *Five Fields of Social Service*, NASW, 1966

62. R Roberts, K Wiltse and B Griswold, 'Unmarried Mothers' Perceptions of the AFDC Experience', in *Mandate for Research*, American Public Welfare Association, 1965

63. S Alinsky, *Rules for Radicals*, op cit

64. D S Howard, *Social Welfare Values, Means and Ends*, Random House, 1969

65. E H Erikson, 'Identity and the Life Cycle', *Psychological Issues*, 1959, 1, No 1, Monograph 1, International University Press, 1959

66. A Gesell and F L Ilg, *The Child from 5 to 10*, Hamilton, 1946

67. F L Ilg and L B Ames, *Child Behaviour*, Harper, 1955

68. J Piaget, *The Construction of Reality in the Child*, Basic Books, 1954
J Piaget, *The Language and Thought of the Child*, 3rd edition, Routledge, 1959

69. H S Sullivan, *The Interpersonal Theory of Psychiatry*, W W Norton, 1953
70. M Frostig and D Hearne, *The Frostig Program for the Development of Visual Perception*, Follett, 1964
    M Frostig, 'An Approach to the Treatment of Children with Learning Difficulties', in J Hellmuth (ed) *Learning Disorders*, Vol 1, Special Child Publications, Seattle, 1965
71. S Alinsky, *Rules for Radicals,* op cit
72. Mayer and Timms, *The Client Speaks,* op cit
73. R Ballard and E Mudd, 'Some Sources of Differences Between Client and Agency Evaluation of Effectiveness of Counselling', *Social Casework*, Vol 39, No 1, 1958
74. R Pomeroy, H Yahr and L Podell, *Studies in Public Welfare*, City University of New York, 1967
75. P Silverman, *The Client who Drops Out*, Heller School for Advanced Studies in Social Welfare, Brandeis University, 1968
76. *Nordic Approach to Social Planning*, Report of Seminar held in Rungstedgaard, Copenhagen, UN, 1973
77. F Redl, 'Strategy and Technique of the Life-space Interview', *American Journal of Orthopsychiatry*, 1959, 29, No 1, (1–18)
78. W Bateman, 'Assessing Program Effectiveness' in, *Welfare in Review*, Vol 6, No 1, January 1968
79. E H Erikson, 'Identity and the Life Cycle', *Psychological Issues*, 1959, 1, No 1, Monograph 1, International University Press, 1959
80. A Kushlick, 'A Method of Evaluating the Effectiveness of a Community Health Service', *Social and Economic Administration*, 1967, 1, No 4 (29–48)
81. E Pavenstedt (ed) *The Drifters*, Little, Brown & Co, 1967
82. Kushlick, op cit
83. M Buber, *I and Thou: A New Translation,* T & T Clark, 1970
84. D McConaghy, *Another Chance for Cities: SNAP 69–72*, Shelter and Neighbourhood Action Project, 1973
85. Housing Act 1969, Chapter 33, HMSO, 1969
86. D Reisman, *The Lonely Crowd*, Yale University Press, 1961
87. J Dumazedier, *Toward a Society of Leisure*, Collier-Macmillan, 1967
88. A Gouldner, op cit
89. A Etzioni, *The Active Society: A Theory of Societal and Political Processes*, Free Press, 1968
90. G Caplan, *An Approach to Community Mental Health*, Tavistock, 1961
    Principles of Preventive Psychiatry, Tavistock, 1964
    Theory and Practice of Mental Health Consultation, Tavistock, 1970
91. Alinsky, op cit

92. R N Titmuss, *The Gift Relationship*, Allen & Unwin, 1970
93. Titmuss, op cit
94. D Novick, *Program Budgetting*, Harvard University Press, 1967
95. W J Reddin, *Effective MBO*, McGraw-Hill, 1971
96. J Galbraith, *The Affluent Society*, New American Library, 1958
97. Seebohm Report, op cit
98. 'The Area Social Work Team Concept in Islington' by Bob Deacon and Crescy Cannan (North Western Polytechnic) in *Social and Economic Administration*, 4, 1970
99. Gouldner, op cit D S Howard,
100. D S Howard, *Social Welfare Values, Means and Ends*, Random House, 1969

Chapter 6

1. K Mannheim, *Ideology and Utopia: an Introduction to the Sociology of Knowledge*, Routledge, 1960
2. F C Amos, *Social Malaise in Liverpool*, Liverpool Corporation, 1970
3. D Jehu et al, *Behaviour Modification in Social Work*, Wiley, 1972
   D Jehu, *Learning Theory and Social Work*, Routledge & Kegan Paul, 1967
4. M Rosenberg, E Suchman and R Goldsen, *Occupational Values*, Glencoe, 1952
5. K Baier & N Rescher, op cit
6. H Marcuse, *Eros and Civilisation*, Sphere Books, 1969
7. J Dollard, N Miller, L Doob, O Mowrer and L Sears, *Frustration and Aggression*, Yale University Press, 1961
   R Sears, J Whiting and H Howlis, 'Anticedents of Aggression and Dependancy', in *Genetic Psychology Monographs*, Vol 47, 1953
8. E Durkheim, *Professional Ethics and Civic Morals*, Routledge, 1957
9. W Schroeder, *Lowell Dynamics*, MIT, 1972
10. E Fromm, *The Fear of Freedom*, Routledge & Kegan Paul, 1960
11. S Johansson, *Investigation into the Standard of Living Conditions*, Stockholm, 1970
12. H Simon and A Ando, 'Aggregation of Variables in Dynamic Systems', in *Econometrica*, Vol 29, 1961
13. D Braybrooke, 'Private Production of Public Goods', in K Baier and N Rescher (eds) *Values and the Future*, op cit
14. J Algie, *Applying Management by Objectives in an Old Peoples Residential Home*, Unpublished Research Document, NISW, 1970
15. H Marcuse, op cit
16. C Silberman, *Crisis in Black and White*, Random House, 1967

17. M Maruyama, 'The Second Cybernetics', in *American Scientist,* Vol 51, 1963

Chapter 7

1. H Marcuse, op cit
2. W Woolfe, *Values and Personality: An Existential Psychology of Crises,* Little, Brown and Co, 1957

Chapter 8

1. W Reid and A Shyne, *Brief and Extended Casework,* Columbia University Press, 1969
2. W Reid & L Epstein, op cit
3. D Jehu, op cit
4. E M Goldberg et al, *Helping the Aged,* Allen and Unwin, 1970
5. Children and Young Persons Act 1969, HMSO, 1969

Chapter 9

1. A Kahn, *Studies in Social Policy and Planning,* Russell Sage, 1969
2. L Hazard, 'Challenges for Urban Policy', in K Baier & N Rescher, op cit
3. R Morris (ed), *Centrally Planned Change,* NASW, 1964

Chapter 11

1. P Townsend, *The Last Refuge,* Routledge, 1962

Chapter 12

1. J Milton, *Paradise Lost,* Book V
2. W Reid & A Shyne, and W Reid & L Epstein, op cit
3. E Grey, *Workloads in Children's Departments,* Home Office, Research Studies No 1, HMSO, 1969
   V Carver, *Social Workers and their Workloads,* NISW, 1972

Chapter 14

1. Seebohm Report, op cit
2. Social Work (Scotland) Act 1968, HMSO, 1968
3. *People and Planning,* Report of the Committee on Public Participation in Planning, (Skeffington Report), Ministry of

Housing and Local Government, HMSO, 1969
4. Seebohm Report, op cit

Chapter 15

1. B Wootton, *Social Science and Social Pathology*, Allen & Unwin, 1959
2. P Laurie, *Dear Kindly Social Worker*, Sunday Times Magazine, 17th May 1970
3. P & A Ehrlich, *Population, Resources, Environment: Issues in Human Ecology*, Freeman, 1970
4. Community Development Project, *Inter Project Report, 1973*, CDP Information & Intelligence Unit, 1974
5. J & E Cummings, *Ego and Milieu*, Tavistock, 1964
6. E Burns, *Social Security and Public Policy*, McGraw-Hill, 1956
   E Burns, 'The Financing of Social Welfare', in C Kasious, (ed) *New Directions in Social Work*, Harper, 1954

Chapter 17

1. B. Davies, *Social Needs and Resources in Local Services*, Michael Joseph, 1968
   Social Trends, Central Statistical Office, HMSO, 1970–73
2. E Grey and V Carver, op cit
3. E Grey and V Carver, op cit
4. B Davies, op cit
5. *American Journal of Public Health*, 58, 1968
6. The experiments referred to have been run by the author with various decision-making groups in Local Authority Social Services departments and voluntary agencies, but have a long history in industrial decision-making supported by operational research methods. For further exploration see — C Morris, *Management Science*, Prentice-Hall, 1969
7. B Davies, op cit
8. H Marriage, 'Report in the Symposium of British Association for Advancement of Science', Durham University, 1970
9. Private communication from H Marriage on the Psychology Division of Prison Welfare section of Home Office, 1974
10. R Finkle & W S Jones, *Assessing Corporate Talent: a Key to Managerial Manpower Planning*, NY, Wiley Inter-Science Group, 1970
11. J Algie, Unpublished NISW Case Study, 1973

Chapter 18

1. W Hocking, *Philosophy of Law and Rights,* Yale University Press, 1926
   W Hocking, *Self, its Body and Freedom,* Yale University Press, 1928
2. G Radbruch, *Grundzugeder Rechts Philosophie,* Leipzig, 1925
3. R MacIver & C Page, *Society,* Macmillan, 1955
   R MacIver, *Society, its Structure and Changes,* Long and Smith, 1931
4. Y Dror, *Ventures in Policy Sciences,* Elsevier, 1971
5. D Braybrooke & C Lindblom, *A Strategy for Decision,* NY Free Press, 1970
6. P Drucker, *Managing for Results,* Pan Books, 1964
7. K E Weick, *The Social Psychology of Organizing,* Addison-Wesley, 1969
8. A Etzioni, *The Active Society,* NY Free Press, 1968
9. V Pareto, *Sociological Writings,* Pall Mall, 1966
10. S Alinsky, op cit

Conclusion

1. Y Dror, *Ventures in Policy Sciences,* Elsevier, 1971
2. H Lasswell, *A Preview of Policy Sciences,* Elsevier, 1971
3. A Etzioni, *The Active Society,* Collier-Macmillan, 1968

Appendix 3

1. Papworth Village Settlement, Papworth Hall, Cambridge
   Enham El Alamein Village Centre, Andover, Hants
2. M North, *Personality Assessment through Movement,* Macdonald & Evans, 1972
3. V E Frankl, *The Will to Meaning,* World Publishing Co, 1969
4. F Perls, *Excitement and Growth in the Human Personality,* Penguin, 1973
5. M Frostig, 'An Approach to the Treatment of Children with Learning Difficulties', in J Hellmuth (ed), *Learning Disorders,* Vol 1, Special Child Publications, Seattle, 1965
6. W Glasser, *Reality Therapy,* Harper & Row, 1965
7. J Bradt & C. Moynihan (eds), *Systems Therapy,* Groome Child Guidance Center, Washington DC, 1971
8. J & E Cummings, *Ego and Milieu: Theory and Practice of Environmental Therapy,* Tavistock, 1964
9. C R Rogers, *Encounter Groups,* Penguin, 1970
10. S S Tomkins, & S Messick (eds), *Computer Simulation of Personality,* Wiley, 1963

Bibliography

Philosophy of Values

F Adler, 'Value Concepts in Sociology', in *American Journal of Sociology*, 62, 1956

E Albert, 'Classification of Values' in *American Anthropologist*, 58 1956

E Albert & C Kluckhorn, *Selected Bibliography on Values, Ethics and Esthetics*, Glencoe Free Press, Illinois, 1959

A Anderson & O Moore, 'The Formal Analysis of Normative Concepts' in *American Sociological Review*, 22, 1957

A Anderson, 'The Logic of Norms' in *Logique et Analyse*, 1, 1958

R Anshen, *Moral Principles of Action*, Harper, New York, 1952

A Brogan, 'Philosophy and Problems of Value, in *Philosophical Review*, 42, 1933

J Findlay, *Axiology*, Prentice-Hall, Englewood Cliffs, NJ, 1970

P Halmos, *Towards a Measure of Man*, Routledge & Kegan Paul, London, 1957

R Lepley, *The Language of Value*, Greenwood, NY, 1957

R Perry, *General Theory of Values*, Longmans, NY, 1926

P Rice, 'Towards a Syntax of Evaluation', in *Journal of Philosophy*, 71, 1944

P Taylor, *Normative Discourse*, Prentice-Hall, Englewood Cliffs, NJ, 1961

W Urban, *Valuation: its Nature and Laws*, New York, 1909

O Von Mering, *A Grammar of Human Values*, University of Pittsburgh Press, 1961

G Von Wright, *The Varieties of Goodness*, Routledge & Kegan Paul, London, 1963

Research into Values

G Allport, P Vernon & G Lindsey, *A Study of Values*, Beacon Press,

Boston, 1951

D Barrett, *Values in America*, University of Indiana, Notre Dame Press, 1961

C Belshaw, 'Identification of Values in Anthropology', in *American Journal of Sociology*, 64, 1959

R Brickner, 'Man and His Values Considered Neurologically' in *Journal of Philosophy*, 41, 1944

H Brogden, 'Primary Personal Values Measured by Allport-Vernon Test in *Psychological Monographs*, 66, 1952

R Carter, 'Experiment in Value Measurement' in *American Sociological Review*, 21, 1956

N Dalkey & O Helmer, 'An Experimental Application of the Delphi Method' in *Management Science*, 9, 1963

J Feiblemann, 'Towards an Analysis of the Basic Value System' in *American Anthropologist*, 56, 1954

E Kelly, 'Interest-values Inventory' in O Buros (ed) *The Third Mental Measurements Yearbook*, Rutgers University Press, New Brunswick, NJ, 1949

N Smith, 'A Calculus for Ethics: a Theory of the Structure of Value' in *Behavioural Sciences*, 1, 1956

L Thurstone, 'The Measurement of Values' in *Psychological Review*, 61, 1954

Objectives Orientation in Management

I Ansoff, *Corporate Strategy*, McGraw-Hill, NY, 1965

W Baker, 'Management by Objectives: a Philosophy and Style of Management for the Public Sector' in *Canadian Public Administration*, 12, 1969

J Barrett, *Individual Goals and Organizational Objectives*, Michigan University, 1970

R Boguslaw, *New Utopians: a Study of System Design and Social Change*, Prentice-Hall, Englewood Cliffs, NJ, 1965

P Drucker, *Managing for Results*, Heinemann, London, 1964

A Etzioni, *The Active Society*, Collier Macmillan, New York and London, 1971

C Granger, 'The Hierarchy of Objectives', in *Harvard Business Review*, 42, 1964

J Humble, *Improving Business Results*, McGraw-Hill, New York, 1968

A Kahn, *Studies in Social Planning*, Russell Sage Foundation, New York, 1968

C Kluckhohn, 'Values and Value Orientations in the Theory of Action' in T Parsons & E Shils (eds), *Towards a General Theory of Action*, Harvard University Press, Cambridge, Mass, 1959

P Le Breton & D Henning, *Planning Theory*, Prentice-Hall, Englewood Cliffs, NJ, 1961

J Mendelson, *Managerial Goal Setting: an Exploration into Meaning and Measurement*, Michigan State University, East Lansing, 1968

D Novik, *Program Budgeting*, Harvard University Press, Cambridge, Mass, 1967

W Reddin, *Effective MBO*, McGraw-Hill, NY, 1971

S Thompson, *Management Creeds and Philosophies*, Research Study, No 32, American Management Association, NY, 1958

F Wickert & D McFarland, *Measuring Executive Effectiveness*, Appleton-Century-Crofts,NY, 1967

Values and Social Services

J Auerbach, 'Value Changes in Therapy', *Personality*, 1, 1950

A Barton, 'Measuring Values of Individuals: Review of Research Bearing on Character Formation', *Religious Education*, (Research Supplement), 1962

W Boehm, 'Role of Values in Social Work', *Jewish Social Service Quarterly*, 26, 1950

T Dembo, *Investigation of Concrete Psychological Value Systems*, Report, US Public Health Service, Institute for Mental Health, Washington, DC, 1953

W Gottleib & J Stanley, 'Mutual Goals and Goal-setting in Casework' in *Social Casework*, 48, 1967

S Hellenorand, 'Client Value Orientations: implications for diagnosis and treatment', in *Social Casework*, 42, 1961

A Katz, 'Application of Self-help Concepts in Current Social Welfare' in *Social Work*, 10, 1965

M McCormick, 'The Role of Values in the Helping Process', in *Social Casework*, 42, 1961

D McLeod & H Meyer, 'A Study of Values of Social Workers', in E Thomas (ed) *Behavioural Science for Social Workers*, Collier-Macmillan, 1967

J Paull, 'Recipients Aroused: the Welfare Rights Movement', in *Social Work* 12, 1967

W Reid & A Shyne, *Brief and Extended Casework*, Columbia University Press, NY, 1969

S Rose, *A Statement on Goals*, School of Social Work, University of Michigan, Ann Arbor, Michigan, 1966

M Smith, *Social Psychology and Human Values*, Aldine, Chicago, 1969

C Towle, *Common Human Needs*, National Association of Social Workers, NY, 1953

F Turner, *Differential Diagnosis and Treatment in Social Work*, Free Press, Glencoe, Illinois, 1968

R Warren, *Truth, Love and Social Change*, Rand McNally, Chicago, 1971

E Younghusband (ed), *Social Work and Social Values*, Allen & Unwin, London, 1967

Specific Values Enunciated

E Albert, 'Conflict and Change in American Values', *Ethics*, 74, 1963

G Allport, *Nature of Prejudice*, Addison-Wesley, Reading, Mass, 1954

American Law Institute, Committee on Essential Human Rights, 'Statement of Essential Human Rights', in *The Annals*, 243, January 1946

S Bernstein, 'Self-determination: King or Citizen in the Realm of Values?' in *Social Work*, 5, 1960

E Bott, *Family and Social Network*, Tavistock, London 1956

A Brecht., *Political Theory*, Princeton University Press, Princeton, NJ, 1967

E Budd, (ed) *Inequality and Poverty*, W W Norton, NY, 1967

T Carver, *Essays in Social Justice*, Harvard University Press, Cambridge, Mass, 1925

J De Jongh, 'Self-help in Modern Society', Proceedings of 7th International Conference of Social Work, *Self-help in Social Welfare*, Bombay, 1954

L Festinger, *A Theory of Cognitive Dissonance*, Row & Peterson, NY, 1957

T Geiger, 'Valuation Nihilism', in *Acta Sociologica*, 1, 1955

E Ginzberg, *Occupational Choice*, Columbia University Press, NY, 1966

A Gouldner, 'The Norm of Reciprocity: a Preliminary Statement' in *American Sociological Review*, 25, 1960

E Guthrie, *The Psychology of Learning*, Harper, NY, 1952

P Halmos, *Solitude and Privacy*, Routledge & Kegan Paul, London, 1957

H Hartmann, *Ego Psychology and the Problem of Adaptation*, International University Press, NY, 1959

T Leary, 'Politics of Consciousness Expansion', in *Harvard Review*, 1963

E McDill & J Ridley, 'Status, Anomia, Alienation and Participation' in *American Journal of Sociology*, 67, 1962

J Martin, *Tolerance*, Wayne State University Press, Detroit, Mich., 1964

D Meier & W Bell, Anomia and Differential Access to the Achievement of Life Goals, *American Sociological Review*, 24, 1959

J Pieper, *Leisure*, Random (Pantheon Books), NY, 1962.

E Raab & H Folk, *The Pattern of Dependent Poverty in California*, California Social Welfare Study Commission, 1963

D Reisman, *Individualism Reconsidered*, Free Press, Glencoe, Illinois, 1954

R Sears, J Whiting & H Nowlis, Antecedents of Aggression and Dependency, in *Genetic Psychology Monographs*, 47, 1953

M Seeman, 'On the Meaning of Alienation', in *American Social Review*, 24, 1959

R Sennett, *The Uses of Disorder*, Penguin, Harmondsworth, Middx, 1970

R Titmuss, *The Gift Relationship*, Allen & Unwin, London, 1970

M Wallis, *Expression and Psychic Life*, Wiley, NY, 1959

R Warren, *The Community in America*, Rand McNally, Chicago, 1963

Subject Index

Access 172
Action *passim*, 9, 11, 13-15, 16, 17,
  217, 227-228, 229-232, 237, 264,
  265-270, 284, 290, 292, 305, 321,
  327-329, 348-349, 444-446, 447-
  455
Action Programmes
  (see Programmes) 265-270
Activities (see Action)
Activity network (see Network
  Analysis)
Adaptation 79
Addiction 78, 296, 394-395
Administrative Function 62, 243,
  261, 273, 281-282, 346
Adolescents (see Young People)
Adoption 54, 360
Advocacy 12, 56, 58, 60, 279, 406,
  426, 433
Agency, types of: (see also
  Organization)
  Administration 281-282
  Advocacy 149, 279
  Diagnostic 277
  Family Substitution 279
  Multipurpose 277
  Preventive 279
  Service-oriented 62
  Social Casuality 278-279
  Social Control 278
  Social Integration 281
  Social Planning 280
  Treatment 277-278
Aims (see Objectives)
Alcoholism (see Addiction)
Alienation 22, 31, 37, 69, 151-155,
  183, 189, 194, 201, 238, 248, 299,
  316, 432-434, 480, 481
Altruism 167-169

Amelioration 12, 26, 33, 218, 237,
  245, 274
Amenities 80, 81, 286, 403
Anomie 79-103, 182, 185, 201, 202,
  412-413, 480
Anxiety 87, 109, 111, 118-119, 120,
  160, 203-212, 221-222
Apathy 100, 148-149
Assessment (see Evaluation)
Awareness 72, 74, 78, 96-99, 179,
  181, 186, 188, 189, 216, 480
Axiology 9-10, 67, 70, 469, 470, 477

Balance of Objectives 13, 177-212
Banner Goals 12, 21, 23, 59, 345
Behaviour disorder 111, 144-145
Behavioural Therapy 76, 97, 105-107,
  109-110, 112-113, 120, 126, 145-
  146, 159-160, 238, 255, 296, 342,
  360, 403-437, 473
Benefits 28, 284-285
Blood donors 168, 286
Boarding-Out 217, 311
Boredom 161-164
Breakdown 22, 78, 123-126, 312,
  345, 421-422
Broker Function 275-276
Budgetting 13, 235-236, 243, 246

Case targets 12, 53-54, 221-226, 246-
  249, 266, 269, 314
Casework 19, 49, 51-52, 70, 71, 77,
  81, 86-87, 92-94, 97-99, 101-102,
  104, 105-107, 109-110, 112-113,
  119-120, 125-126, 128-129, 132-
  133, 138-139, 141-142, 145-146,
  154-155, 159-161, 163-167, 172,
  221-225, 236, 240, 260, 267, 287,
  360, 362, 370, 403-437, 439, 469,

470, 474, 479
Casual relations 178-191, 203-212
Central Government 12, 51, 257, 297
Change 14, 22, 49, 60-61, 166-167, 469, 474
Charity 135-139
Child Guidance 78
Child Poverty Action Group 95, 279
Children (and child care) 90, 91, 104, 111, 113, 120, 145, 217, 224-225, 247-249, 251, 268, 276, 290, 322, 360-361, 365-369, 381-384, 386-387, 471-472
Choice 14, 316-319, 335, 338-339, 351
Claimants' Union 38, 95, 280
Classification 15, 69-71, 72, 237, 240-241, 244-246, 290, 321
Clients 13, 52-53, 239, 244-249, 272, 282, 299, 305, 342, 471, 472
Client Problem Dictionary 31, 37, 245-246, 311-312, 321, 326, 338-339, 385-402
Collectivism 91-95
Community 53, 116, 140
Community care 60, 359, 362
Community development 12, 29, 67, 70, 114-115, 344-345, 413, 428, 475
Community organization 12, 56-57, 105
Community plan 213-214
Community settlement 21, 60, 281
Community work 26, 27, 28, 29, 77, 81-82, 87-88, 102-103, 105, 110, 115-116, 119, 122-123, 123-124, 125, 128, 133-134, 136-138, 140-141, 153-154, 158-159, 160-161, 163, 166-167, 170-171, 217, 221, 227-228, 254, 279, 280, 290, 319-321, 360, 363, 370-371, 439, 471
Comparison 299-301
Competence (see Social competence)
Conflict 9, 13, 19, 22, 24, 25, 30, 67, 93-94, 165, 191-192, 192-194, 201, 227, 288-289, 301, 336-337, 480
Conformity (see Social integration)
Consciousness (see Awareness) 67
Consensus 22, 23, 61, 177
Consequences (see Outcomes)
Constraints 284-285, 343
Constructive results 291
Containment 218
Control 192-193, 193-203, 214, 278
Coping behaviour 79-81, 143, 223-

224, 346
Corporate planning (and management) 17, 55, 69, 133, 236, 280, 352
Correctional system 50
Cost 309
Cost benefit analysis 171, 311, 321
Crisis 78, 124-126
Crisis therapy 360, 422
Criteria 13, 197-198, 292-295, 298, 305-306, 329-332
Critical path analysis (see Network analysis)
Curative functions 274-275
Custodial care 107
Cybernetics 17, 67, 171, 467, 473, 475
Cycles (of events) 203-212, 250-251

Day care 54, 141, 217, 236, 240, 279, 362, 363, 374-376
Day centres 32, 38, 78, 163, 362, 363, 426
Debilitative environment 78, 126-130, 222, 422-424
Debt 203-212
Delinquency 40, 154, 157-158, 228-232, 323-324, 388-389
Demand 27, 32, 241, 343
Dependency 72, 77, 103-107, 164, 224, 413-415, 480, 481
Depersonalization 78, 91-95, 316, 351, 409-411
Deprivation (see Poverty) 15, 139-142, 173, 211, 426-428
Development strategy 12, 64, 346
Development 110-116, 169-171, 183, 253-254, 471-472
Developmental services 252
Deviance 67, 155-161, 182, 200, 216, 238, 248, 278, 434-436
Diagnosis 34, 236, 268, 438
Diagnostic role 277
Domiciliary care 53, 54, 217, 236, 240, 246, 374-376

Economic objectives 218, 258-263
Economic security (see Security)
Education 50, 54, 70, 111, 146, 221, 222, 225, 278, 281, 407, 412
Effectiveness 25, 38-40, 65, 164-167, 171-176, 241-243, 253-254, 262, 290-334, 337, 347-349, 471, 472
Effects (see Outcomes)
Efficiency 171-176, 183, 184-185, 260-261, 307, 309, 310, 346

Elderly 31, 40, 78, 184, 217, 239, 251, 268, 276, 299, 315-319, 379-380, 391-392, 474
Emergency strategy 12, 54-55, 58, 62-63, 125-126, 345
Emotion 15, 85, 165
Emotional disturbance 188, 396-398
Emotional fulfilment 72, 78, 85-91
Emotional stability 78, 85-91, 182, 185, 187, 216, 222, 223
Emotional stress 67, 78, 85-91, 385-386, 408-409
Employment 38, 50, 57, 78, 123, 147-151, 221-224, 240, 253, 311, 361, 401-402
Encounter Groups 416, 433, 476
Ends (see Objectives)
Ennui 161-164, 436-437
Equality 21, 28, 67, 130-135, 179, 182, 185, 187, 188, 189, 197, 480
Ethics 67, 68, 99, 473
Evaluation 12, 14, 16, 33, 55, 168-169, 188, 236, 237, 247, 249, 290-334, 352, 441, 467, 468, 472
Extraceptive feelings 85, 165

Facilitation-inhibition mechanism 192-193, 196-203
Family 78, 79-80, 88-91, 118, 123, 158-159, 163-164, 221-222, 237, 238, 247-249, 269-271, 276, 314, 385-386, 447-455, 480
Family substitution role 279
Family therapy 217, 238, 360, 409, 419, 422
Feasibility 342
Field of action 236
Fieldwork services 246, 370-374
Financial problems 401-402
Fiscal system 50
Fostering 54, 311, 360, 365-366, 381, 408
Friendship 151-154
Frustration 69, 86, 182, 188, 194, 268, 473
Functions 14, 240, 272-276, 335, 345, 346
Futuristic services 251

Gestalt therapy 252, 408, 412
Gift relationship 167-168
Goal (see Objective)
G.P. 81, 89, 173, 221, 404, 406

Gratification 79, 80, 161-164, 180
Groupwork 37, 39, 54, 154, 217, 236, 260, 360, 370, 404, 407, 411, 413, 420, 425, 428, 429, 432, 435, 439
Growth 29, 78, 110, 116-117, 179, 185, 189

Happiness 21, 24, 67
Health 25, 50, 56, 70, 72, 169
Heterogeneous clientele 237, 280
Heterogeneous environment 22, 139-142, 180, 186, 201
Home helps 36, 38, 41, 141, 251, 287, 359, 376, 405, 419
Homeless 26, 38-39, 55, 57, 78, 159, 239, 252, 253, 276, 288, 289, 314, 380, 400-401, 437-445
Homogeneous clientele 280
Homogeneous environment 139-141, 185, 203, 280
Hospital 54, 78, 132, 171
Housing 26, 56, 57, 153, 252, 260, 278, 472

Identity 22, 92-95, 111, 471
Implementation 10, 235-243, 348-349
Inarticulateness 78, 107-110, 415-416
Income 26, 50, 107, 121, 138, 203-212
Incrementalism 335, 476
Independence 51, 67, 103-107, 224, 316-319, 319-321
Indicator 31, 60, 166, 290, 294-295, 304, 305-306, 321-334
Individualism 15, 67, 198, 480
Individualization 15, 72, 78, 91-95, 179, 183, 184, 186-187, 196, 201, 351
Industrial social work 149
Inequality 130-135, 189, 230, 424-426
Information 40-42, 64, 241, 298-299, 323, 470
Inhibition 334
Input 292-293, 300, 310
Insecurity 78, 117-121, 188, 203-212, 417-419
Insentience 96-99, 411-412
Insight learning 97-98
Integrated Managing, Planning and Action System (IMPACTS) 16, 350-355
Integration (see Social integration)

Intelligence 12, 84
Intelligence system 55-56
Intention (see Objectives)
Interaction 22, 26-37, 74, 155-161
Interests 26, 242
Intervention (see Method of
    Intervention)
Intraceptive feelings 85, 165
Inventory of Social Services Operations
    438-441
Irrationality 82-85
Isolation (see Alienation)

Justice 21, 67, 130-135, 480

Key results 265-270, 272
Kinesiology 44, 172, 238, 255, 406,
    468, 476

Learning 22, 60, 70, 110-116, 471-
    472, 476, 480
Legal offenders 399-400
Legislation 14, 79, 228, 273-276, 278,
    281, 297
Leisure 139, 161-164, 472, 480
Life support mechanisms 286
Local Authority 12, 235, 257
Logo therapy 408, 413, 476

Maintenance services 218
Malfunctioning (see Social
    malfunctioning)
Management 9, 10, 11, 12, 19-20, 45,
    48, 49, 258
M.B.O. (Management by Objectives)
    9, 19, 171, 350, 473, 478-479
Manpower planning 258, 351, 475
Marital relations 39, 71, 88-89, 203-
    212, 221-226, 269-271, 389-390
Market 28, 79, 167-169, 286
Meals-on-wheels 15, 32, 41, 81, 122,
    141, 237, 242, 287, 359, 405, 407,
    418
Means 10, 74, 259
Measurement 298-305
Mental instability 78, 82-85, 179,
    406-408
Mental wellbeing 25, 48, 187
Mentally handicapped 70, 78, 113,
    239, 276, 362, 380, 398-399
Mentally ill 78, 159, 239, 268, 276,
    310, 362, 380, 396-398
Mental stability 78, 82-85
Merger 217-218, 258, 260, 337
Method of intervention 254-255, 300,

343, 440
Milieu therapy 360, 414, 424, 426,
    427, 428, 430, 434, 436, 437, 475,
    476
Missions 12, 48-58, 59, 345
Mobility 44
Mobilization (see Occupational
    mobilization)
Model 13, 15, 42-45
Multi-problem families 71, 210-212

Needs 12, 24, 26, 27, 32, 34, 51, 61,
    76, 79, 85, 195, 237, 241-242, 250-
    251, 438, 468, 479
Network analysis 44, 289, 447-455,
    468
Nurture 316-319, 319-321
Nutrition 15, 31, 81, 237, 404

Objectives *passim*, 9, 10-11, 11-13, 263,
    (see also Targets) 478-479, 480
    Change-oriented 60-62
    Conflicting 72-75, 191-192, 263
    Definition 23, 30
    Integration 60-62
    Multiple 213-214
    Negative pole 12, 75-76
    Network of 17, 177-178
    Operational 17, 215, 265, 371,
        442
    Political 12, 59-64
    Positive pole 12, 75-76
    Positional 12, 283, 442-446
    Primary 339-340
    Service oriented 62
    Strategic 12-13, 65-176, 213, 235-
        236, 237, 238, 246, 268-269, 345,
        346
    Tactical 12, 13, 213-230, 236
    Trajectory 215
Occupational ineffectuality 147-151,
    430-432
Occupational mobilization 50, 183,
    184, 216, 286, 480
Occupational therapist 359
Operational research 17, 67, 171
Operationalizing objectives 13-14, 45-
    46, 65-66, 213-214, 215-217, 235-
    238, 265-272, 284-289, 295
Operations 14, 268, 284-289, 335
Organization 14, 236, 257, 279, 336-
    337, 350
Organization structure 34-36, 171,
    468
Outcomes 14, 16, 19, 70, 72, 172,

237, 264, 273, 288, 290-334, 347-349, 354, 450
Output (see Outcomes)

Participation 13, 22, 29, 56, 57, 79, 112, 114-115, 151-155, 170, 182-185, 189, 196, 201, 216, 248, 281, 288, 290, 331-332, 430, 480
Permutative results 290
Personality 164-166, 468, 470, 476
Personnel objectives 283, 341
Personnel section 442-446
Phobia 86
Physical malfunctioning 78, 80-82, 403-406
Physical wellbeing 25, 50, 73, 78, 80-82, 182, 187, 238, 316
Physically handicapped 56, 70, 78, 80-82, 106, 107, 123, 132, 135, 173-174, 179, 217, 239, 240, 276, 287, 312, 361, 392-394, 467, 468
Physically ill 78, 80-82, 96, 120, 179, 316, 361, 380, 392-394, 467
Planning (including social planning) 9, 13, 17, 26, 28, 35, 49, 50, 51, 55-56, 59, 63, 68, 72, 93-94, 119, 133, 138, 141, 174, 218, 225, 228-232, 235, 252, 257, 263-264, 266-269, 272, 275-276, 279, 280-281, 291, 302, 309, 345, 350-355, 467, 468, 469, 474, 478-479
Planning, Programming, Budgetting Systems (P.P.B.S.) 9, 19, 171, 263-264, 350, 473, 479
Police 50, 228-232, 257
Policy 10, 14, 19, 23, 71-72, 174, 243, 246, 266-269, 309, 315, 350, 468, 476
Policy sciences 67, 70
Poverty 28, 70, 78, 116, 121-124, 174-175, 184, 248, 345, 419-421, 480
Practical Assistance 221, 254, 346, 359
Prevention 237, 259, 260, 272, 279, 450-451
Preventive strategy 12, 63-64, 275, 279, 291, 343, 346, 374
Priority 12, 14, 37-38, 172, 225, 230-231, 237, 254, 257-264, 280, 315, 316-319, 335-349, 351-352, 373, 469
Priority scaling 27, 37, 38, 171, 350
Primary services 251
Prison 50, 323-324

Privacy 196, 480
Probation 50, 56, 111, 257, 326
Problems Dictionary (see Client Problem Dictionary)
Profession (and professionals) 71, 72, 218, 258, 281, 295-297, 315
Programme structure 238-243, 359-371
Programmes 235-238, 241-243, 250-253, 265-266, 335
Protection 273-274
Psychology 49, 68

Ranking 321, 324-329
Rational behaviour 72, 78, 82-85
Rationality 67, 78, 195, 200, 223
Reality therapy 385, 412, 413, 417, 476
Recreation system 171
Recreational fulfilment 161-163, 216
Recruitment 285, 336, 443
Refinement Programmes 242
Reformative function 59, 274-275
Regression 70, 110-116, 416-417
Rehabilitation 274, 277, 361, 374, 377
Remedial programmes 242
Replicative programmes 242
Representative programmes 242
Research 10, 64, 68, 98, 178-179, 190, 196, 279, 295, 298
Residential care 31, 54, 81, 107, 217, 236, 239-240, 244, 246, 249, 252, 253, 278, 279, 319-321, 360, 361, 362, 473
Residential home 78, 95, 101, 107, 196, 278, 286, 313, 329-332, 363, 375-384, 406, 415, 424, 436
Resources 13, 235, 236, 237, 241-243, 244-245, 246, 249, 256-264, 272, 284, 285, 335, 342, 348, 352, 354
   Allocation 258, 259, 260, 264, 337
   Disinvestment 262
   Increases 258-259
   Negative 263-264
   Positive 256-257
   Substitute 260
   Utilization 241-243
Responsibility 22, 100-103, 222
Responsive programmes 241
Results (see Outcome)
Retardation 110-116, 416-417
Rights 12, 27, 67, 96, 97, 132-133, 173-174, 182, 222, 279, 284-285

Roles 14, 67, 240, 277-283, 335, 345, 346, 469

Safety needs 73, 78, 111, 117-121, 183, 187, 216
Scaling 265, 293-294, 298, 302, 305, 316, 325, 326-327, 344
Scarcity 257-258
Scenario 12, 29-46
Schizophrenia 97, 111, 154, 183
Security 78, 121-124, 183, 187-188, 190, 201, 202, 287, 345
Selective service role 280
Self-actualization 67, 92-95
Self-awareness 96-99
Self-determination 15, 67, 74, 103-107, 179, 180, 183, 186, 187, 188, 195, 196, 199, 200, 236, 244, 345, 480
Self-evaluation 92-95
Self-expression 78, 79, 107-110, 185, 188, 189, 195, 200, 481
Self-fulfilment 25, 238
Self-help 103-107, 286, 480
Self-respect 22, 51, 92-95, 238
Sensitivity 96-99
Sentinel system 81, 291, 422
Services 13, 32-34, 240, 250-255, 264, 285, 286, 403-437
Service Activity Inventory 13, 32, 255, 287, 312, 321, 403-437
Simulation 31, 40-45, 214, 352, 408, 409, 467, 468, 469, 473, 476
Skills 13, 35, 64, 256, 267, 279, 292, 342, 343, 406, 408, 430, 432
Sleeper services 253
Social action 12, 57, 167, 276, 279-280, 345, 351, 426
Social casualty role 22, 37, 237, 278-279, 343
Social competence 67, 144-147, 181, 186, 187, 188-189, 216
Social environment 12, 22, 30-32, 42-44, 51-53, 73-80, 116-117, 126-130, 142-144, 221, 227-228, 261, 353-354, 422-424
Social indicator (see Indicator)
Social integration 31, 48, 74, 76-77, 155-161, 180, 188-189, 195, 197, 199, 200, 201, 295, 316-319, 319-321, 329-331
Social malfunctioning 26, 144-147, 428-430, 473
Social problems 31, 37, 238, 245-246, 266, 299, 311-312, 321, 326, 338-

339, 385-402
Social planning (see Planning)
Social planning function 275-276
Social planning role 280-281
Social Policy (see Policy)
Social Security 41, 50, 95, 123, 137, 241, 257, 475
Social Services *passim*
Social Services Act 19, 352, 467
Social Services Dept 23, 24, 50, 51, 217-218, 277-282, 300, 346
Social structure 42-45
Socialization (see Social integration)
Socially handicapped 359-360
Sociology 49, 68
Speciality services 253
Standards (see Criteria) 292-298, 337, 344
  Changing 298
  Manifest 297-298
  Nominal 297-298
  Personal 297
  Professional 295-297
  Qualitative 297
  Quantitative 297
Statistics 321, 322
Stigmatization 135-139, 186, 248, 426-427, 381, 426
Strategic objectives (see Objectives)
Strategy 12, 62-64, 240, 346-348
  Long range 346
  Maximax 347
  Maximin 347
  Maximizing benefits 346-347
  Minimax 347
  Mix 347
  Short-range 346
Stress 79, 86, 87, 111, 334
Stultification 110-116, 416-417
Supportive environment 78, 126-130, 179, 180, 189, 190, 202, 248
Surrogate 321, 323-324
Systems approach (including systems technology) 23, 31-42, 42-45, 51, 82

Tactical objectives (see Objectives)
Target 14, 265-271, 272, 287, 371-374, 442-443
Task 19-20, 265-269, 285-286, 293
Technology 24, 82, 217, 288
Tenants Association 221
Threshold 13, 194-203, 281, 294, 301, 315
Tolerance 135-139, 182-183, 187,

188, 189, 248
Training 10, 258
Treatment role 277-278
Treatments 208-212, 439-440

Universalist service role 280
Universalization 23, 24, 77
Unsupported parents 137, 247, 390-391
Urban development 49, 257

Valuation 67, 78, 99-103, 179, 182, 188, 216, 480
Values *passim*, 9-10, 24, 25, 67, 68, 77, 99-103, 190, 196, 268, 278, 315-319, 324-325, 335, 337, 338-339, 354, 467, 469, 470, 471, 473, 474, 477-478, 479-481
Voluntary organizations 57, 63, 259, 277, 344, 366

Welfare 21, 23, 25, 50, 278
Widows 291, 391-392
Work processes 11, 14, 284-289, 335
Workload 32, 42, 262, 307-308, 442, 474
Work centres 249, 291, 375

Young people 78, 225, 306, 388-389

Name Index

Algie, J 467, 468, 473, 475
Alinsky, S 62, 105, 114, 167, 345, 468, 471, 472, 476
Allport, G W 67, 469, 477, 480
Ames, L B 471
Amos, F C 473
Ando, A 191, 473
Aptekar, H H 104, 471

Baier, K 67, 70, 467, 469, 473
Bales, R 471
Ballard, R 119, 472
Baldwin, J 93
Bannister, D 467
Bateman, W 137, 472
Blum, G 67, 469
Boissevain, J 467
Bradt, J 476
Braybrooke, D 191, 335, 473, 476
Brecht, A 67, 70, 469, 480
Brentano, F 67, 469
Briar, S 104, 471
Buber, M 155, 472
Burckhardt, J 72, 469
Burns, E 281, 475

Cannan, C 473
Caplan, G 124, 166, 472
Carver, V 474, 475
Colby, K M 67, 469
Coleman, J 468
Croft, M 72, 471
Cummings, J & E 281, 475, 476

Dahrendorf, R 106
Dalkey, N 467, 478
Davies, B 310, 322, 475
Deacon, B 473

Dollard, J 182, 473
Doob, L 182, 473
Downie, R S 67, 469
Dror, Y 335, 350, 476
Drucker, P 335, 476, 478
Dumazedier, J 161, 472
Durkheim, E 185, 473

Ehrlich, R & A 280, 475
Eicker, W 468
Epstein, L 67, 70, 219, 469, 474
Erikson, E H 111, 138, 471, 472
Etzioni, A 166, 335, 350, 472, 476, 478
Evans, J 467

Findlay, J 67, 70, 469, 477
Finkle, R 329, 475
Forrester, J 468
Forster, E M 155
Fox, R 104, 471
Frankl, V E 476
Freud, S 162, 180, 198
Friedman, J 67, 70, 469
Fromm, E 186, 473
Frostig, M 111, 412, 417, 472, 476

Galbraith, K 171, 472
Gesell, A 111, 471
Gilbert, N 67, 70, 469
Gill, D 66, 468
Glasser, W 476
Goldberg, E M 219, 474
Goldson, R 178, 473
Goldstein, H 70, 469
Gouldner, A 85, 163, 173, 471, 472, 473, 480
Grey, E 474, 475

489

Griswold, B 104
Gullahorn, J E & J T 67, 469

Harris, A 40
Hartmann, G 67, 70, 469
Hazard, L 68, 70, 238, 469, 474
Hearne, D 472
Hellmuth, J 472
Helmer, O 31, 467, 478
Hilliard, R M 174
Hocking, W 335, 475
Hovland, C I 67, 469
Howard, D S 471, 473
Howlis, H 473, 480
Hunt, E B 67, 469
Hyman, H 67, 469

Ilg, F L 111, 471

Jehu, D 178, 219, 473, 474
Johanson, S 473
Johnson, L B 22
Jones, W S 328, 475
Joshi, M 468

Kahn, A 474, 478
Kasious, C 475
Kazantzakis, N 9, 13, 235
Kennedy, J F 22
Kluckhohn, C M 67, 469, 477, 478
Kushlick, A 150, 472

Lasswell, H D 67, 70, 350, 469, 476
Laurie, P 278, 475
Leibnitz, G 104, 471
Lessler, K 104, 471
Lewis, W 91
Lindblom, C 335, 476
Lindsay, G 67, 477
Lipkin, S M 104, 471
Lipsett, S 67
Lockyer, K G 468
Loehlin, J C 67, 469

McDonaghy, D 472
MacIver, R 335, 475
Maier, J 467, 472
Mallen, G 468
Mannheim, K 473
Marcuse, H 181, 199, 213, 473
Marmor, T 74, 471
Marriage, H 323, 475
Maruhyama, M 473
Marx, K 184
Maslow, A H 468

Mayer, J E 66, 468, 471
Meinong, A 67, 469
Messick, S 476
Miller, D 104, 471
Miller, N 104, 473
Morris, A 34, 56
Morris, C 467, 475
Morris, R 474
Mowrer, O 182, 473
Moynihan, C 476
Mudd, E 119, 472
Murray, H A 468, 469

North, M 476
Novick, D 472, 479

Page, C 475
Parad, H 124
Pareto, V 338, 476
Pavenstedtd, E 472
Perlman, H H 70, 469
Perls, F 476
Piaget, J 111, 471
Podell, L 115, 472
Pomeroy, R 115, 472
Powelson, J P 70, 469

Radbruch, G 335, 475
Reddin, W J 472
Redl, F 126, 472
Reid, W 67, 70, 219, 469, 474, 479
Reisman, D 161, 472, 480
Rescher, N 67, 70, 179, 467, 469, 473
Roberts, R 104, 471
Rogers, C R 476
Rosenberg, M 178, 473
Rosenblatt, A 67, 469

Schroeder, W 185, 473
Sears, L ⎱ 182, 473, 480
Sears, R ⎰
Seebohm, F 19, 22, 56, 63, 172, 217, 258, 260, 276, 467, 472, 474
Shyne, A 219, 474, 499
Silberman, C 201, 473
Silverman, P 119, 472
Simon, H 191, 473
Snow, C P 48
Specht, H 70, 469
Speigel, J 469
Spencer, H 67, 469
Spinoza, I 96, 177
Spranger, E 67, 469
Stein, H 70, 469

Strupp, H   104, 471
Suchman, E   473
Sullivan, H S   111, 178, 471

Tillich, P   284
Timms, N   104, 119, 471, 472
Titmuss, R N   167-169, 472, 481
Tomkins, S S   476
Townsend, P   474
Toynbee, A   21

Uhlig, R   469
Uhr, L   67, 469

Vernon, P E   67, 477
Von Mering, O   67, 70, 469, 477
Vossler, C   67, 469

Walker, D   469
Warren, R   66, 469, 479, 481
Watt, A   67
Weber, M   9
Weick, K E   335, 476
Whitman, W   80
Whiting, J   473, 480
Williams, W   467
Wiltse, K   104
Wohl, B   21
Woolfe, W   213, 474
Wootton, B   278, 475
Wulff, J   468

Yahr, H   119, 472